Wait for Me!

Wait for Me!

{ MEMOIRS }

DEBORAH MITFORD,
DUCHESS OF DEVONSHIRE

FARRAR, STRAUS AND GIROUX
NEW YORK

Farrar, Straus and Giroux
18 West 18th Street, New York 10011

Distributed in Canada by D&M Publishers, Inc.
Printed in the United States of America
Originally published in 2010 by John Murray (Publishers), Great Britain
Published in the United States by Farrar, Straus and Giroux
First American edition, 2010

Some passages in Chapter 14 have appeared in an earlier form in *Chatsworth: The House* by Deborah Devonshire, published in 2002 by Frances Lincoln Publishers, Great Britain.

Grateful acknowledgment is made to the following for permission to reprint copyrighted material: The John F. Kennedy Library Foundation for John F. Kennedy's letter; Maxwell Taylor Kennedy for Robert F. Kennedy's letters; Constancia Romilly Weber for Jessica Mitford's letter; and Brian Masters for his letter about Pamela Jackson.

Library of Congress Cataloging-in-Publication Data
Devonshire, Deborah Vivien Freeman-Mitford Cavendish, Duchess of, 1920–
    Wait for me! : memoirs / Deborah Mitford — 1st American ed.
        p.   cm.
    Includes bibliographical references and index.
    ISBN 978-0-374-20768-7 (alk. paper)
    1. Devonshire, Deborah Vivien Freeman-Mitford Cavendish, Duchess of,
1920–   2. Aristocracy (Social class)—Great Britain—Biography.   3. Nobility—
Great Britain—Biography.   4. Great Britain—Social life and customs—20th
century.   1. Title.

CT788.D524A3 2010
941.082092—dc22
[B]

                                                                    2010028794

Designed by Jonathan D. Lippincott

www.fsgbooks.com

1   3   5   7   9   10   8   6   4   2

To
Charlotte Mosley, my editor,
Helen Marchant, my secretary,
and my old friends Richard Garnett and Tristram Holland,
who gave me the confidence to keep trying

CONTENTS

NOTE ON FAMILY NAMES

My family used nicknames usually as terms of affection, but sometimes the opposite. To spare the reader the irritation of ever-changing names, I have generally used those we were given at our christening. This seems strange to me because I never did so in real life but I hope it will make things plainer for my readers.

For the record, my parents were *Muv* and *Farve* – obvious enough. Muv had a string of other names including *Aunt Sydney*, because that is what our cousins called her, and *Lady Redesdale*, which strangers called her. Farve was *Morgan* to Jessica and Unity, for no particular reason. Nanny was *Blor* or *m'Hinket*; she did not like either but did not try to stop us. Because of her black hair, Muv and Farve called Nancy *Koko* after the Lord High Executioner in *The Mikado*. Pam and Diana called her *Naunce* and to me she was the *Ancient Dame of France*, the *French Lady Writer* or just *Lady*. Pam was *Woman* to us all, with variations thereof. Tom was *Tuddemy* to Unity and Jessica ('Tom' in Boudledidge, their private language) and this was taken up by the rest of us. Diana was *Dayna* to Muv and Farve, *Deerling* to Nancy, and *Honks* to me. I still have to think who I am talking about when she is 'Diana'. Unity was *Bobo*, but *Birdie* or *Bird* to me. Jessica called her *Boud* ('Bobo' in Boudledidge). Jessica was *Little D* to Muv, *Stea-ake* to Pam and *Hen* or *Henderson* to me, but she was *Decca* universally – and remains so in this book. I have always been *Debo* to most, but *Hen* to Jessica, *Swiny* to Unity, and *Nine*, *Miss* and lots more to Nancy. I was *Stubby* to Muv and Farve, after my short fat legs which could not keep up (hence the title of this book). Our names changed with the wind but the ones none of us ever spoke were Nancy, Pamela, Thomas, Diana, Unity, Jessica and Deborah.

I always had nicknames for my husband, Andrew, which changed over time. For many years it was *Claud*, because when he was Lord Hartington he got letters addressed to 'Claud Hartington'. My mother-in-law was *Moucher* to one and all (after the character in *David Copperfield*) – I never heard anyone call her Mary. My elder daughter, Emma, is *Marlborough* or *Marl* because of her Girl Guide uniform, which was smothered in badges like the much-decorated Mary, Duchess of Marlborough. My younger daughter, Sophy, is *Moffa* – goodness knows why. The only one of my children's nicknames I have used throughout the book is *Stoker*, which for some reason he has never managed to throw off. He now signs himself 'Stoker Devonshire'. I call him *Sto*.

Hereditary titles in England are a maze of complications. It must be impossible for the uninitiated to grasp who is called what and why. My paternal grandfather, Bertram Mitford, writer, diplomat and Member of Parliament, was created 1st Baron Redesdale in 1902 in recognition of his diplomatic work in Japan and China. Until 1997 (when hereditary peers lost their age-old right to sit in the House of Lords), a Member of Parliament who was elevated to the peerage could no longer hold a seat in the House of Commons, but Grandfather continued to play an important legislative role in the House of Lords. On Grandfather's death, my father, David Mitford, as his eldest surviving son, inherited the title and became the 2nd Baron Redesdale. Had my brother Tom outlived him, the title would have passed to him. As it was, it went to my father's younger brothers and down the line to one of his nephews. The tradition of primogeniture in this country meant that the eldest son inherited not just the title but the bulk of any estate and fortune that went with it. This system kept estates together, unlike in France, for example, where under the Code Napoléon each generation claims an equal share (hence the chateaux on the Loire being empty of furniture).

After my marriage, my name changed three times. English peers (above the rank of Baron) have in addition to their principal title subsidiary ones, usually those that have been conferred on their ancestors. In my husband's case, the family name is 'Cavendish', the principal title is 'The Duke of Devonshire' and the Duke's eldest son has the 'courtesy' title of 'The Marquis of Hartington'. When I first married, I was 'Lady Andrew Cavendish', which is what I expected to remain as I had married the Duke's second son. When Andrew's elder brother was killed in the war, I became 'The Marchioness of Hartington'. After my father-in-law's death, Andrew inherited the dukedom and the vast estates that went with it and I became 'The Duchess of Devonshire.' Now I am 'The Dowager Duchess' as my son has succeeded to the title and his wife, Amanda, is the Duchess.

Wait for Me!

1

WE ARE SEVEN

Blank. There is no entry in my mother's engagement book for 31 March 1920, the day I was born. The next few days are also blank. The first entry in April, in large letters, is 'KITCHEN CHIMNEY SWEPT'. My parents' dearest wish was for a big family of boys; a sixth girl was not worth recording. 'Nancy, Pam, Tom, Diana, Bobo, Decca, *me*', intoned in a peculiar voice, was my answer to anyone who asked where I came in the family.

The sisters were at home and Tom was at boarding school for this deeply disappointing event, more like a funeral than a birth. Years later Mabel, our parlourmaid, told me, 'I knew what it was by your father's face.' When the telegram arrived Nancy announced to the others, 'We Are Seven', and wrote to Muv at our London house, 49 Victoria Road, Kensington, where she was lying-in, 'How disgusting of the poor darling to go and be a girl.' Life went on as though nothing had happened and all agreed that no one, except Nanny, looked at me till I was three months old and then were not especially pleased by what they saw.

Grandfather Redesdale's huge house and estate in Gloucestershire, Batsford Park near Moreton-in-Marsh, was inherited by my father in 1916. It was too expensive to keep up and was sold in 1919. My father looked for somewhere more modest near Swinbrook, a small village where he owned land, fifteen miles from Batsford. There was no house there suitable for a family of six children and a seventh on the way, so he bought Asthall Manor in the neighbouring village. I was born soon after the move and my earliest recollections are of the ancient house and its immediate surroundings. Asthall is a typical Cotswold manor, hard by the church, with a garden that descends to the River Windrush. It was loved by my sisters and Tom, and the seven years spent there were probably the happiest for parents and children, the proceeds of the sale of Batsford giving the family a feeling of security that was never repeated.

There was, and is, something profoundly satisfying in the scale of Asthall village. It was a perfect entity where every element was in proportion to the rest: the manor, the vicarage, the school and pub; the farmhouses with their conveniently placed cowsheds and barns; the cottages, whose occupants supplied the labour for the centuries-old jobs that still existed when we were children; and the pigsties, chicken runs and gardens that belonged to the cottages. Before cars and commuters, you lived close to where you worked and the shops came to you in horse-drawn vans. This was the calm background of a self-contained agricultural parish, regulated by the seasons, in an exceptionally beautiful part of England.

My father planted woods to hold game, as well as a short beech avenue leading up to the house, and his dark purple lilacs outside the garden wall are still growing there after nearly a hundred years. The house itself needed much restoration. My mother's flair for decoration and her talent for home-making ensured that the French furniture and pictures from Batsford were shown at their best. My father installed water-powered electric light – just the sort of contraption he adored; drawing heavily on his umpteenth cigarette, he would lean over the engineer, itching to do the job better himself. He made sure he had a child-proof door to his study by putting the handle high up out of reach. Sometimes we heard the voice of Galli-Curci singing Farve's favourite aria, coming loudly from the outsize horn of his gramophone – a twin of the one in advertisements for His Master's Voice. In another mood he might put on 'The Diver' ('He is now on the surface, he's gasping for breath, so pale that he wants but the stillness of death'), sung by Signor Foli in a terrifying and unnaturally low bass voice.

With foresight, or perhaps by luck, Farve converted the barn a few yards from the house into one large room with four bedrooms above and added a covered passage, 'the cloisters', to connect the two buildings. Tom and the older sisters lived in the barn, untroubled by grown-ups or babies, and made the most of their freedom. My father, who was famous for having read only one book, *White Fang*, which he enjoyed so much he vowed never to read another, entrusted Tom, aged ten, with the task of choosing which books to keep from the Batsford library. Nancy and Diana later said that if they had any education, it was due to the unrestricted access they had had to Grandfather's books at Asthall. Later, a grand piano arrived for Tom who showed great musical promise. Music and reading were his passions.

The First World War was not long over and life for the survivors was limping back to normal. There was little to record in our family in the first few years of my life. Nancy went to Hatherop Castle, a finishing school nearby, and was taken to Paris with a group of friends, where she first saw the architecture and works of art that inspired in her a lifelong love of that city. She wrote enthusiastic letters to our mother about the shops, the food and the days spent at the Louvre. Pam busied herself with her ponies, pigs and dogs. Tom was at Lockers Park prep school in Hemel Hempstead. His orderly mind was already preparing for a career in the Law and he paid Nancy to argue with him all day during the holidays. Diana was an unwilling Girl Guide and played the organ in church, putting into practice her theory that 'Tea for Two', if played slowly enough, did very well as a voluntary.

The years at Asthall passed in a haze of contentment from my point of view. I was aware of The Others but they were so old and seemed to Decca (Jessica, my daily companion) and me to be of another world. It was not until later that I got to know them. Unity, next up in age from Decca and not yet in the schoolroom, made her huge presence felt but, although always kind to me, she was not an intimate. Our life in the nursery consisted of the daily round, the common task, secure and regular as clockwork.

At the age of five we started lessons with Muv, who followed the admirable Parents' National Education Union (PNEU) system with its emphasis on learning through direct contact with nature and good books, and its disapproval of marks, prizes, rewards and exams. She taught us reading, writing and sums, and read us tales from the famous children's history book, *Our Island Story*. She was a natural teacher and never made anything seem too difficult. At the age of eight, I moved on to the schoolroom and a governess (trained at the PNEU's Ambleside College) and never enjoyed lessons again.

Our nursery windows overlooked the churchyard with its graves of wool merchants long since dead, the beautiful tombs topped with fleeces carved in stone. We were fascinated by funerals, which we were not meant to watch but of course we did. Decca and I once fell into a newly dug grave, to the delight of Nancy who pronounced fearful bad luck on us for ever. At that age, I was sure Farve would be buried by the path leading to our garden and even today I expect to see his big toe sticking up through the turf, which is what he warned me would happen if I misbehaved.

Beyond the churchyard to the left were stables, kennels and a garage. Early on at Asthall my father had a horrible accident in the stable yard: he was getting on to a young horse when it reared and fell backwards on to him, breaking his pelvis. The injury did not heal properly and, unable to throw his leg over a saddle, he never rode again. To the right of the churchyard was the vicarage. We adored the vicar's wife and long after we had left Asthall, Pam and I used to ride over and trot briskly up the drive, shouting for ginger biscuits. Across the road was the kitchen garden with its glasshouses and glorious white peaches, reserved strictly for grown-ups. Unity and our cousin Chris Bailey committed the heinous crime of sneaking into the greenhouse and stealing some peaches. There was a stony silence throughout the house while they were reprimanded by my father, which made a big effect on the younger ones. Farve has gone down in history as a violent man, mainly because of Nancy's portrayal of him as the irascible Uncle Matthew in her novels. While he could indeed get angry, he was never physically violent and his bark was far worse than his bite. We would tease him, goad him as far as we dared, until he turned and roared at us.

As soon as I could walk I shadowed Farve, struggling to keep up. He used to pick me up, throw me on to his shoulder and carry me over winter ditches and summer stinging nettles; the comforting feel of his velveteen waistcoat is inseparable from my memories of him. I must have been a great nuisance, but we saw eye to eye about everything. He took me fishing in the magic moment of the year when the mayfly were hatching and let me carry his net. As time went by, he showed me how to slide it under the hooked trout – no talking, no jerking – and land it on the bank. The sound of a reel when a line is cast on a trout rod equals early summer to me and the smell of newly cut grass, cow parsley, thrushes and 'All the birds of Oxfordshire and Gloucestershire' (Edward Thomas's Adlestrop is not far from Asthall) take me back to our stretch of the Windrush. No health, no safety, no handrail on the single planks that were our bridges as we crossed and recrossed over the river. It was paradise and I knew it. The river water had its own smell that rose from the easily stirred-up mud, and many years later when swimming among the weeds and mud in a pond high above Chatsworth, in the company of moorhens and mallard, nostalgia for the river at Asthall was almost too much and I was six again.

My father loved the river, described in the estate agent's brochure when Asthall was sold as 'of the most attractive character to a fisherman, including rapids, gentle swims and pool', but he was plagued by the idea of the coarse fish that competed with the trout. Like Uncle Matthew, he called on the services of a chubb fuddler who came and scattered magic seed on the water till hundreds of chubb rose to the surface, 'flapping, swooning, fainting, choking, thoroughly and undoubtedly fuddled'. Nancy's account of this annual event is one of the funniest passages in any of her books.

Farve made a pool in the river, even adding a diving board for the brave, where we learned to swim, held up by water-wings and wearing rubber bathing caps that cruelly pulled our hair. His own bathing costume was made of thin, harsh, dark-blue serge bound with braid. For the sake of modesty it had a skirt – 'my crrinoleeene' he called it in an exaggerated French accent. Unexpectedly, Farve and his brothers spoke perfect French, thanks to their tutor Monsieur Cuvelier, who lived at Batsford and taught them when they were boys. The old tutor came to stay at Asthall during the holidays and his presence always put Farve in the sunniest of moods; according to Diana, 'He and our uncles became boys again before our astonished eyes.' Walking back to the house after bathing, Farve used to pick up sticks and stones with his toes to amuse us. 'Look what my prehensile extremities can do,' he said, but however hard we tried our toes could not be as clever or useful.

In the name of culture, my sisters started the Outing Club. Farve's brother, Uncle Tommy, drove the older children in his car, an envied open-tourer that had a roof like the hood of a pram – with as many finger-pinching hinges – and windows of yellowing celluloid that cracked easily and were striped with sticking plaster. Unity, Decca and I went in Farve's car. I was the Club Bore as we had to keep stopping for me to get out and be sick; all I remember of these outings is the grass by the roadside. We visited Kenilworth Castle and Stratford-upon-Avon in pursuit of history and literature. Another uncle, my mother's brother George Bowles, accompanied us in the role of visiting professor and told us about the past glories of which Farve and Uncle Tommy were blissfully ignorant. I was too young to go on the outing to Stratford that passed into family lore, when Farve, pressed by Muv, took the older children to see *Romeo and Juliet*. Uncle Matthew's reaction in *The Pursuit of Love* is unmistakably that of Farve: 'He cried copiously and went into a furious rage because it ended badly. "All the fault of that damned padre," he kept saying on the way home, still wiping his eyes. "That blasted fella, what's 'is name, Romeo, might have known a blasted papist would mess up the whole thing. Silly old fool of a nurse too, I bet she was an R.C., dismal old bitch."'

When I was four, my parents, Decca and I drove to Scotland in stages to stay with a friend of my father. An obvious stopping place on the way was Redesdale Cottage in Northumberland where Farve's mother lived. Grandmother Redesdale was fat, pink-cheeked and smiling, with wispy white hair tucked into a small black cap. She was always dressed in black, unlike widows of today, and was a wonderful storyteller. She kept a Berkshire pig instead of a dog, the double of Beatrix Potter's Pig-Wig, which she took to church on a lead. No one thought it a bit odd – affection for animals was taken for granted – and she had a similar affection for my father whom she called 'Poor Dowdie', with an indulgent smile.

Christmas parties at Asthall were homemade and on Christmas Night we wore fancy dress – nothing grand, we picked up whatever was to hand. My father's only concession was to put on a red wig, but he never appears in the photographs as he was always behind the camera. Pam dressed as Lady Rowena from *Ivanhoe* and wore the same outfit every year: a long, floppy, low-necked gown, embellished with a row of orange-red beads. The beads are on my dressing table now and remind me of her every time I see them. Nancy was a dab hand at disguise and her costume was always the best. She loved making a bit of trouble and went missing one year when the family photograph was about to be taken.

We shouted and looked for her everywhere. Eventually there was a knock at the back door and a filthy, cold, wet tramp appeared. It was Nancy. When Asthall was for sale, it was the sister of Mrs Hardcastle, wife of the prospective buyer, who became Nancy's inspiration. Mrs Hardcastle's sister was no beauty: she had a thick black moustache and wore a cloche hat and mothy fur slung around her neck. Nancy used to appear quite often in this dreary disguise and once took in Mabel, who showed her into the drawing room.

My mother gave a Christmas tea party every year for the village school-children between the ages of five and fourteen. Lists of names and ages were kept from one year to the next and each child was given a toy and a garment by Father Christmas, who was played by the vicar. He arrived to an atmosphere of tremendous excitement: the big drawing room was darkened except for a few candles, handbells were rung and in he came through the window carrying his sack on his back. 'I come from the land of ice and snow,' he intoned in a deep voice to the dumbstruck children. The magic never failed. After an enormous tea, the children trooped out clutching their parcels and an orange, a treat in itself in those days.

My father did not wish for a social life. Muv would have enjoyed one but seldom suggested anything he would not want – she was aware of the hazards. Lunch guests were rare, but a memorable exception was the Duchess of Marlborough, the American Gladys Marie Deacon, sec-ond wife of the Ninth Duke, who came over from Blenheim Palace, the Marlboroughs' family seat. She produced a paper handkerchief, the first any of us had seen, blew her nose and stuck it into a yew hedge. My father was outraged. At lunch she asked him if he had read Elinor Glyn's *Three Weeks* (everyone was talking about the writer and her work at the time). Farve glared at her. 'I haven't read a book for *three years*,' he barked. That was the end of that subject and of the Duchess of Marl-borough. Years later, when Nancy invited some undergraduate friends from Oxford to lunch, my father waited for a pause in the conversation and said loudly to my mother at the other end of the table, 'Have these people no homes of their own?'

But Muv was amused by Nancy's friends. She once asked Henry Weymouth (later the Marquess of Bath, who opened a safari park at his Wiltshire family seat, Longleat) what his favourite way of spending the day was. 'Ratting,' he replied with conviction. There were even a few weekend parties where strangers were well diluted with aunts, uncles and cousins – relations were always first on the list. When Nancy was eighteen, Farve conceded that a dance must be given for her. Muv was unable to gather enough young men for the event and, according to Nancy, my father trawled the House of Lords and netted a few middle-aged fellows; they must have been surprised to be invited to a debutante dance. As the day drew near, Farve asked my mother what time the 'on-rushing *convives*' were expected. The poor fellow had to endure a repeat of this torture five more times as each daughter grew up.

My parents seldom had friends to stay. One exception was Violet Hammersley, who came on prolonged visits. 'Mrs Ham' was a near contemporary of Muv but seemed much older. She was born and had spent the first years of her life in Paris, where her father, Mr Freeman-Williams, was a diplomat. When he died, Mrs Freeman-Williams took her young family to live in London, where Muv remembered her as a friend of her own father. Mrs Ham was an unexpected friend of my mother: her circle was intellectual and artistic – from Somerset Maugham to Bloomsbury and beyond – while Muv was taken up with children and domestic affairs. According to Nancy she looked like El Greco's mistress and, with her dark hair and sallow complexion, would certainly have made an ideal model for the painter. She always wore black and was draped in shawls from head to foot. We called her 'the Widow' or 'Wid', not to her face, but when it occasionally slipped out she put on the expression of resignation usually reserved for Nancy's teases.

By the time I knew Mrs Ham, her late husband's bank, Cox & Co., had failed and her means were much reduced. Gone was the house on the river at Bourne End and with it the Venetian gondola and gondolier. She had retired to a small Regency house in Totland Bay on the Isle of Wight, where her garden shed, known as 'The Mansion', had been converted into two guest bedrooms. It was dreadfully damp but because it was Mrs Ham's we loved it. We never tired of asking her how she had lost her money. Her face would take on a tragic look and, with exaggerated pronunciation of every syllable, she said, 'and thien the biank fiailed', which was met with howls of laughter from us all. She was a strict pessimist: according to her the past was black, the future blacker. It was a triumph when my sisters persuaded her to dance her version of the cancan to the tune of 'Ta-ra-ra-boom-di-ay'. She lifted her layers of skirt, pointed her toe and was off. But just the once.

Mrs Ham was famously mean. One day, when told that some friends were coming to call on her, she asked me in a sepulchral voice, 'Does that involve sherry?' When she came to lunch with us in London, my father would stand waiting on the steps with half a crown in his hand to pay the taxi; he knew she would fumble in her purse and say she had no change. Her arrival in our house was marked by the strong antiseptic smell of TCP that filled the bathroom and the passage. Farve teased Mrs Ham mercilessly. She thrived on the attention but was never quite sure when he was joking – that was his way with many people and the pair of them were a regular turn.

In spite of the difference in generations, Mrs Ham became an intimate friend of my sisters and mine because of her deep interest in our doings. My mother kept a distance from our passions; she looked on them with amusement but did not get involved. Mrs Ham, on the other hand, seemed fascinated by whatever we told her, however exaggerated and dotty – chiefly about love and romance, of course – and we confided in her as in an agony aunt. To sit on the sofa next to her, her face close to mine, to have her listening with intense concentration to me and me alone, was something I had never experienced and found irresistible. It was thrilling when she said, '*Child*, are you in love?' Naturally we always were and told her about it in lengthy detail. The idea of any grown-up being in the least bit interested amazed us; no wonder she was a welcome guest. I wrote hundreds of letters to her, as did we all, and we got lovely ones back, usually beginning, 'Horror Child', and admonishing us for not writing more frequently.

Many years after we left Asthall, I went back to see the house and found to my joy the old telephone, thin as a parasol handle, still on its cradle, the same plate rack above the sink in the pantry and the same lino still on the nursery floor. The feel of it underfoot and all that went with that room made me long for Nanny Blor, for the comfort of her lap, her hymn-singing and prayers at bedtime. Nanny's real name was Laura Dicks. Her father was a blacksmith and she came from Egham in Surrey. How she got the nicknames 'Blor' or 'm'Hinket' I do not remember. In 1910, when my mother interviewed her, she was thirty-nine and not robust, and it seemed doubtful whether she could push the pram up the hill from Victoria Road to the park, laden with heavy toddlers in the shape of Pam, aged three, Tom, nearly two, and four-month-old Diana. My parents wavered, and then Nanny saw Diana. 'Oh, what a lovely baby!' and that was it. She arrived to stay for more than forty years.

Like my mother, Nanny was always there, unchanging, steady, dependable – the ideal background for a child – and, like my mother, she was always scrupulously fair. If Nanny did have a favourite it was Decca, an irresistibly attractive child, curly-haired, affectionate and funny. But I was unaware of this and loved her with all my heart, as we all did. She was the antidote to Nancy and a very present help in time of trouble, 'the still small voice of calm'. She was neither tall nor short and you would not have picked her out in a crowd. Her clothes were those of her profession: grey coat and skirt, black hat and shoes and, in the summer, a quiet cotton dress with a white collar. On car drives, when I always felt sick, I used to cling to her gloved hand. The gloves were made of something called 'fabric', which must have covered a lot of possibilities. I never saw her lose her temper or even be really cross though she muttered at us sometimes. She must have been more sorely tried than any other Nanny, but we were always forgiven and treated to a bedtime hymn. Her favourites were 'The Ninety and Nine' ('There were ninety and nine that safely lay/In the shelter of the fold,' Nanny sang, 'But one was out on the hills far away/Far off from the gates of gold'), 'Shall We Gather at the River?', 'Loving Shepherd of Thy Sheep' and 'Now the Day is Over'. She was deeply religious and must have suffered from not being able to attend her own Congregational church when we were at Asthall, or later Swinbrook, but she never said so.

She did not criticize us much, neither did she praise. 'No, darling, I shouldn't do that if I were you,' or 'Very nice, darling,' was as far as it went, her eyes on her needle or the iron, the regular tools of the nursery. Signs of arrogance, conceit or vanity she called 'parading about' and discouraged them with a little sniff and cough. 'It's all right, darling, no one's going to look at you,' became her standard saying when we complained that our dresses were not smart enough for a party. She carried this dictum a bit far when Diana, eighteen years old and staggeringly beautiful in her wedding dress, said, 'Oh Nanny, this hook and eye doesn't work. It looks awful.' 'It's all right, darling,' Nanny soothed, 'who's going to look at you?'

I read now about the necessity of self-esteem in children. We would have become impossibly pleased with ourselves had we been indulged with such a thing. As it was, our ups and downs were high and low enough, and Nanny sat on any ups. Her own childhood had been strict no doubt, but she never imposed her parents' rules on us. She accepted our governesses and their different ways without a murmur, as she did my mother's unusual, not to say eccentric, rules about food and medicine. When the time came for us to leave the nursery for the schoolroom, she never questioned the authority of the governesses, though I am sure she must have suffered at losing the little ones and sometimes suspected, rightly, that the governesses were not all they should be. As soon as we could after lessons, we rushed back to talk to her. She was the one we loved.

We seldom went shopping or had new clothes. When I was eight, Diana married and her sister-in-law, Grania Guinness, was the same age as me but taller. She had the most wonderful dresses from Wendy, the ultimate in children's clothes for style and beauty, and when a parcel arrived with a dress she had outgrown, my excitement was intense. Otherwise, Fair Isle jerseys and a 'smart' coat for church were about it. Skating was an exception and I was allowed one of those lovely short full skirts that make whatever you do on the ice look better.

Our underclothes were woollen vests and knickers and an extraordinary, but apparently necessary, concoction called a liberty bodice, which had no freedom about it so how it got its name I cannot imagine. It was tight and made of some harsh stuff, with here and there straps and buttons that did nothing. The nursery fireguard with an extra brass rail was Nanny's drying place; it answered perfectly and the faint smell of damp wool was part of childhood. Nanny did her best to make us self-reliant and tidy and to instil in us the other qualities she thought necessary. It was an uphill task. When I threw my underclothes into a heap on the floor, she said, 'Put them the right way, they're all inside out.' 'Well, m'Hinket,' I replied, 'tomorrow they won't be inside out.' 'Now, darling,' she said, 'what if you had an accident and were taken to hospital? Think what a shock the nurses would have if they saw your vest inside out.' Even when very young I thought nurses might have seen worse things, but I have not forgotten what she said.

One of the rare holidays we had as young children was going with Nanny to stay with her twin sister, whose husband kept a hardware shop in the main street of Hastings. They lived above the shop and we lodged with them. The smell of paraffin and polish, the brushes, brooms and besoms that hung from the ceiling, the freezing-cold grey sea with a ginger biscuit reward for going in – all were lovely in their way but as we could not take our ponies, goats, rats, mice, guinea pigs and dogs it seemed a waste of a fortnight to me. Nanny's own holiday was the worst moment of the year. Diana told me that, aged three, I refused to eat, in spite of our Churchill cousins' nanny coming to take Blor's place for those fourteen ghastly days. It was Diana herself who persuaded me to swallow the shovelled-in food.

We never considered Blor's own life. Like Mabel and Annie, the head housemaid, she was so much part of the family that she was not consulted about moves or anything else that might affect her. She just came with us. Long after her role in the nursery was over, she remained a vital part of the household, washing, ironing, sewing and darning; just her being there meant the world to me and my sisters. She accompanied Decca and me on our rare shopping trips to Oxford. We stopped for tea at the Cadena Café or, if we were feeling rich, at Fuller's which meant walnut cake with a perfect icing, the acme of a good tea.

Being the youngest of a family had its advantages. Rules were stretched a bit and I was my father's favourite – whether that was because I was the last or because I shared his interests I do not know. The disadvantage was being an object of The Others' derision, 'So *stupid*, you can't keep up, you're such a BORE.' They made a circle round me, pointing and chanting, 'Who's the least important person in this room? YOU.' But this was outweighed by the fun of being with the older ones, even though I could not keep up. We fought, of course, as well as baited and teased each other, but after tears came the laughter and I look back on my childhood as a happy time. I thought our upbringing was exactly like everyone else's. Perhaps it was not.

2

FARVE AND MUV

Nancy wrote about our childhood in her novels, which to her amazement, and ours, became best-sellers. People still ask me, 'Was your father really like Uncle Matthew?' In many ways he was. Nancy made him sound terrifying but there was nearly, though not always, a comic undercurrent not apparent to outsiders. I adored him. He was an original, with a total disregard of the banal or boring. He had a turn of phrase he made his own, delivered with a deadpan face and perfect timing. Strangers stared at him nonplussed but we knew just what he meant. 'That feller whacked merry hell out of the piano,' described an admired musician's performance. Ordinary words were memorable when they came from him and two favourites were 'mournful' and 'degraded': 'Take your degraded elbows off the table,' he ordered Diana, aged fourteen. He was easily irritated by a non-favourite and encouraged them to 'go to hell judging your own time'. An unloved was dismissed as 'some mournful woman' and whatever this anonymous female did was wrong. She (and other people's babies) might also be 'a meaningless piece of meat' and that was that. A 'putrid sort of feller' could never aspire to anything better. In our family Farve was all-powerful: we appealed to him when we thought something was unfair and he could overturn any order given by a governess or anyone else in authority over us. Even my mother did not question his word.

Like others of his kind, David Mitford did not care a hang what people thought of him, take him or leave him, and it never occurred to him to toe the line or trim. He was honest and looked honest: tall and upstanding, blue-eyed and extraordinarily handsome, he had thick white hair and moustache by the time I remember him. He was unmistakably an English countryman. His prized possessions were his rod and gun, locked away and untouched by anyone except himself, and his car. After the financial crash of 1929, the Daimler and beloved chauffeur had to go and were replaced with a Morris that Farve drove himself. He had been friends with William Morris, later Lord Nuffield, since the motor magnate's Oxford bicycle-shop days and we were brought up on the legend that Farve had been asked to invest in Morris's business but decided against it – one of several unlucky financial decisions on his part. The car was treated as if it were alive, safely put away in the garage at night and never expected to go long distances without a rest. Propping up the bonnet, Farve would check the oil, wiping the dipstick on a clean rag to ensure accuracy, and top up the radiator water religiously. The petrol tank was replenished from cans, except when we went to Oxford and an adored attendant at the Clarendon Yard Garage, another William, was given the job of filling up while he talked to my father about engines. Farve was a good driver and enjoyed driving, but the sight of a female in charge of a vehicle was sometimes too much for him. If a car came too close or made the smallest mistake with the rules of the road he shouted, 'Blasted woman driver', to which my mother was often able to say, with truth, 'Funny thing, she's dressed as a man.'

'My good clothes' were cosseted like his car and gun. Mabel the parlourmaid was in charge and he was always well dressed. In the country, his appearance was indistinguishable from that of a gamekeeper, an occupation that would have suited him down to the ground. He wore a brown velveteen waistcoat, alternating with moleskin; a gunmetal watch – no silver chain but a leather bootlace; gaiters with huge chunks of shoes that were made for him; and he carried a stout thumbstick, a walking stick with a forked top, that completed the illusion. As years went by, the gaiters gave way to trousers fashioned from an impenetrable material called Mount Everest cloth – 'thorn proof, dear child'. In London he was conventionally dressed but for one garment: a black cloak inherited from his father (Farve would never have bought such a thing himself), which he wore when forced to go out in the evenings. In his mid-thirties he went to a dentist and asked him to take out all his teeth. The dentist refused, saying it was dangerous. 'All right then,' said Farve impatiently, 'I'll go to someone who will.' An hour or so later there was not a tooth left in his head. Thereafter 'my good dentures' chewed up Muv's excellent food.

Farve shopped only where he was known. His regular ports of call were the best, and certainly the most expensive: Solomon's, a fruit shop in Piccadilly opposite the Ritz; Fortnum and Mason, where he was friends with the tail-coated assistants; Berry Bros, where he bought wine for our occasional guests (he drank only water); and Locke's the hatter. All these were within a stone's throw of each other and on the way to his club, the Marlborough in Pall Mall. His favourite shop, however, was the Army and Navy Stores, which stocked all the stuff of Empire: folding chairs with canvas seats and backs, enamel bowls with buttoned waterproof lids, a chronometer for his desk (so he could see if anyone was a quarter of a minute late), string and labels of lasting quality, the latest in camp beds, rust-proof filing cabinets, gritty Lifebuoy soap that smelt strongly of carbolic (his idea of complete cleanliness), thick woollen underclothes (stocked no doubt for Arctic explorers) and the precious Primus stove for his early-morning tea.

He walked to this holy of holies in Victoria Street with a lurcher and Labrador at heel – no leads. He put the dogs to sit in the entrance and waited with them for the doors to open at 9 a.m. My mother asked him why he had to be there so early. 'If I am any later I am impeded by inconveniently shaped women,' was the reply. He often brought back a little present for us, always beautifully packed, which gave it an air of importance. My mother was not sure of his taste in anything decorative and he told me that when buying something for her, he always said to the shop assistant, 'A lady will be in to change these next week.' And so she was.

Punctuality was drilled into us. If one of us dawdled before an outing Farve went without the laggard. Pam, daydreaming, was once left behind on a longed-for afternoon at the zoo – a lesson learned the hard way and cited again and again as a purple warning. Nancy's portrayal of Uncle Matthew standing at the front door, watch in hand at 11.55 a.m., awaiting someone expected at midday, muttering to himself, 'In six minutes the damn feller will be late,' is Farve exactly. He also had a horror of anything sticky. I once asked him what his idea of hell was. 'Honey on my bowler hat,' was the answer. His all-seeing eyes spotted a spill anywhere down the long dining-room table. Honey, jam and marmalade were all high-risk, but the sight of Golden Syrup in its wonderful green and gold tin made him particularly nervous, and he insisted on it being ladled on to the suet pudding by a grown-up. This was a regular occurrence because suet pudding was a favourite with us all. Farve got up and hovered as Mabel went round the table and we were relieved when the last person had been served with no spillage. What a mercy that no modernizer at Tate & Lyle has tampered with the design of the Golden Syrup tin, with its picture of bees buzzing round a dead lion and the line from the Bible, 'Out of the strong came forth sweetness'. I have always been fascinated by it and only wondered much later how it came to be associated with a pudding made of beef fat.

Two things annoyed Farve in my mother's otherwise impeccably run house. If a housemaid was rash enough to remove the deepest ashes from the grate where a wood fire burned, she was in trouble. Farve was right: it is the ashes that hold the heat and ensure a quick start in the morning. He found a way of avoiding the second annoyance. After break-fast he refilled his coffee cup and took it to his study. He let it get cold and drank what he called his 'suckments' at intervals during the morning. A tidy, new-to-the-job maid took the cup back to the pantry, emptied and washed it. This enraged my father: 'Some monkey's orphan has taken my suckments.' Thereafter he locked the cup in his safe.

Farve was impatient, intolerant, impulsive, loyal, courageous, loving, fastidious, unread and possessed of great charm, all underwritten with courtly good manners – to most. Every now and then his short fuse made him lash out. He was profoundly irritated by some of the young men Nancy invited to the house and more than once lost his temper with her friend James Lees-Milne, the future author and diarist. On one occasion Jim leant down to pick something up and a comb fell out of his pocket: 'A man carrying a comb – well!' On another famous occasion, Jim advocated friendship with Germany and Farve turned him out of the house. Poor Jim went to his motorbike but it was raining hard and it would not start. In despair he found the back door and was rescued by Mabel who hustled him upstairs. As he was creeping out of the house the next morning he met Farve. 'Good morning,' said Farve. He had forgotten the whole episode and offered Jim our usual generous breakfast.

Farve either liked you or he did not, there was no middle way. My mother sometimes tried to reason with him, but reason was not part of his makeup and, unlike her, he had favourites. This was unfair but he never tried to hide or moderate his feelings, it was part of his honesty. There was often a 'Rat Week' when he would pick on one of us for some-times imaginary offences. Decca, who was able to twist him round her little finger and take liberties with him that none of the rest of us would have dared, fell out of favour for a while for no apparent reason. Unity became more silent and unresponsive in her teens because Farve was always watching her for some trifling misdemeanour.

It had been the same with his own brothers and sisters. He never liked his younger sister Joan but was fond of the man she married, Denis Farrer. 'The very desiccated Old Dean', he called him affectionately. Denis was not a dean, it was just a play on his name, but it was a spot-on description of that thin, sharp-featured fellow in middle age. Farve was once talking to an acquaintance about the Farrers and said, 'The only trouble with the Old Dean is that he married a ghastly woman.' 'Oh?' said the acquaintance. 'I thought she was your sister?' 'Yes, she is. A poi-sonous creature.' It was no wonder that people were surprised by him. Aunt Dorothy, wife of his adored brother, Uncle Tommy, was a non-favourite. She was said to be 'frightfully rich' but we never saw any sign of this alleged wealth and she was 'careful', to put it mildly. My parents went to lunch with Uncle Tommy and Aunt Dorothy in their house at Westwell, near Burford. The fare was sheep's hearts. 'Still beating on the plate,' my father told us afterwards. He did not go again.

Farve was the second son in a family of nine – five boys and four girls, none of whom inherited Grandfather Redesdale's love of art and archi-tecture or his passion for the Far East. The eldest son, Clement, was killed in action on the Western Front in 1915. Clem was a heroic figure to his siblings, and my father and his other brothers were brought up in his shadow. He was better at everything than any of them, an example to be emulated, and was his parents' great hope for the future. Clem acted as guardian to his first cousins, the six Ogilvy children, after their father, the Sixth Earl of Airlie, was killed leading a cavalry charge against the Boers at the Battle of Diamond Hill in 1900. Their mother, Mabell, wid-owed at thirty-four, devoted the rest of her life to her children, the Cor-tachy estate in Angus and Queen Mary, whose close confidante she was and whom she served for forty-three years as Lady of the Bedchamber (a role that required her to attend the Queen on ceremonial occasions).

Clem married one of his wards, Helen Ogilvy, in 1909. Helen had startling blue eyes and black hair, a rare combination, but she went completely white at the age of twenty-three. Their first daughter, Rosemary, was born in 1911 and their second, Clementine, shortly after Clem's death. As Clem had no son, my father was next in line to inherit the Batsford and Swinbrook estates. Farve was very much a second son and his childhood had been blighted by unhappiness at school. He hated every moment of it and longed to be home, free from lessons and out of doors at all hours with the keepers. As a boy he had a terrible temper, which worried his parents and anyone in authority over him. Clem had gone to Eton but Grandfather decided that Farve should be sent to Radley. I believe Grandfather was afraid that one of Farve's outbursts of temper would have damaging repercussions for Clem's school career.

It was towards the end of his time at Radley that Farve first set eyes on Sydney Bowles. Grandfather Redesdale (before his peerage) was newly elected to Parliament and invited a fellow MP, Tommy Bowles, to speak at a meeting. As was his wont, Bowles brought his children with him. Sydney described her first sight of David as he stood with his back to the fire at Batsford, wearing an old brown velveteen coat: 'A wonderful figure of a young man . . . He looked splendid to me, and he was indeed very handsome. So when I was fourteen and he was seventeen, I fell in love with him.' No doubt Muv kept the picture of this beautiful young man in her mind but, as happens with teenage girls, it was superseded by other fancies.

After leaving Radley, Farve's dearest wish was to join the Army but he could manage only 19 marks out of 2,000 for Latin, or so he told us, and he failed the entrance exam. Whether or not this unlikely score was the reason, history does not relate, but fail he certainly did and he often used to say to us, 'What good would Latin have been to me in the Army?' Grandfather Redesdale had a friend with tea estates in Ceylon and Farve was sent out there to work as a planter. When he arrived he was shocked by the hard drinking of his colleagues and decided then and there to be a teetotaller, a decision he kept for the rest of his life. 'Sewer' was Farve's word for the worst of the bad, usually prefaced by 'damned', and it became part of the language of our family. In truth it was *suar*, Hindi for pig, 'the accursed one', picked up while he was in Ceylon;

but it sounded better in English, especially when you pictured what he meant.

My father's escape from Ceylon was the Boer War. His first home leave in four years coincided with the outbreak of hostilities and he seized the chance of joining the Army at last. Clement was already serving in the 10th Hussars and in January 1900 my father enlisted as a private in the Oxfordshire Yeomanry, and later transferred to the Northumberland Fusiliers. He was in his element, popular with men and officers alike, and was immediately given a commission. In 1902 he fought at the Battle of Tweebosch under Lieutenant General Lord Methuen and was lucky to survive a chest wound that destroyed one lung. (This did not stop him from being a chain-smoker. 'Have a gasper,' he would say when greeting any man he met, opening his neatly packed gunmetal cigarette case. A woman smoker was, of course, taboo, his daughters included. Only Decca broke the rule when she grew up.) After being wounded, Farve lay for three days, near death, on an ox cart, trundling over rutted roads to the field hospital at Bloemfontein. He was invalided home for a long convalescence. His strong constitution pulled him through, but it was a close-run thing.

My parents met again some ten years after they had first set eyes on each other, and this time it was David who fell for Sydney. Whatever and whoever had come between them since their last meeting, there must have been an immediate rapport. Farve went to Tommy Bowles to ask permission to marry his daughter. 'How do you plan to support her?' asked Bowles. 'I've got £400 a year and *these*,' said Farve, holding up his hands. The engagement was announced and they were married on 6 February 1904. Their honeymoon was spent on board Bowles's schooner and nine months later Nancy was born. Farve wrote to his mother just before the birth, 'I am sure I only wish that everyone could be so happy, there would be little left in life to complain of. I don't deserve it, but I am grateful.' Grandfather Bowles gave my father a job in the office of *The Lady*, the magazine he had founded in 1885 specifically for women and which is still famous today for its classified columns advertising for domestic and other help. A more unsuitable occupation for the country-loving would-be gamekeeper is hard to imagine.

When they were first married, my mother was shocked to realize that my father had read only one book. She persuaded him to listen to her reading aloud some classics, starting with Thomas Hardy. She chose

Tess of the d'Urbervilles with its descriptions of farm and heath land, which she thought he would enjoy. When she got to the sad part, my father started crying. 'Oh, darling, don't cry, it's only a story.' 'WHAT,' said my father, his sorrow turning to rage, 'do you mean to say the damn feller made it up?' I was born after the days of *White Fang* and never saw my father open a book.

Farve stuck at the office of *The Lady* for ten years until the outbreak of the First World War. As a result of his one lung, he was regarded as permanently unfit for active service but this did not deter him, aged thirty-seven, from joining his old regiment. He was sent to France in September 1914 as an officer reinforcement to the 1st Battalion of the Northumberland Fusiliers. Soon afterwards, his health broke down and he was invalided home. Determined to return to the front, he again succeeded in getting passed fit and rejoined his regiment's 2nd Battalion in April 1915. He was appointed transports officer, in the belief that it would be less strenuous than the front line, but his arrival coincided with the opening of the Second Battle of Ypres. As Brigadier H. R. Sandilands wrote in Farve's obituary:

> Night after night (and sometimes twice nightly) he had to take up supplies to the battalion through the town of Ypres, which was under constant heavy bombardment. His method was to quicken the pace on approaching the town, and then to lead his wagons at full gallop through Ypres until clear of the Menin Gate. The men worked in two shifts, but David Mitford declined the offer of any relief, and accompanied every convoy. Thanks to his leadership, the battalion, throughout the Battle of St Julien, was never without its supplies: and, miraculously, he succeeded in delivering these without the loss of a man.

The strain of these days proved too much and Farve was once more invalided to England, where for the remainder of the war he trained the Special Reserve.

Grandfather Redesdale died in 1916, a year after his beloved Clem was killed. His finances had been hard hit by the enormous cost of rebuilding and maintaining Batsford. The place had been run on the extravagant lines of Edwardian England, with palatial stables for carriage horses, riding horses and Grandfather's famous stud of Shires. My grandmother's little book that records menus of many courses opposite the names of her guests (to ensure no repetition from one visit to the next) was usual in such a household, but my grandfather was also a gardener and I have never seen, except in this little book, a description of the flowers on the dinner table.

When my father inherited Batsford, it was obvious to him that his old home would have to be sold. Soon after the end of the war, a buyer was found in Gilbert Wills, later Lord Dulverton, chairman of the to-bacco company W. D. & H. O. Wills, makers of the Virginian cigarettes Farve always smoked. Gilbert and my father became lifelong friends. Farve seldom stayed in other people's houses but made an exception for Gilbert and joined him in Scotland to shoot grouse on a moor rented from Lord Cawdor. (After the Second World War, Nancy was asked by the film director Alexander Korda to work on a script. She was proud of this coup and told my father about it. 'What?' he said, incredulous. 'I never knew old Jack Cawdor was interested in films.') Farve did not care for Gilbert's wife, Victoria, and, to irritate her, took his own apples and Keiller's Dundee marmalade – 'my anti-scorbutics' – whenever he went to stay. When we asked him why he did it, he said he did not want to get scurvy and could not 'rely on her housekeeping'.

Our own household added up to too many women; a wife, six daughters and a governess at every meal must have made Farve long for male company. This he found at the Marlborough Club and in the House of Lords. I am glad for his sake (and for theirs) that peeresses in their own right did not arrive in the House until after Farve died. Although he was a firm believer in the hereditary system, the idea of women making a nuisance of themselves in those hallowed surroundings would have 'fair turned him up', to put it in his own language. As for life peeresses, I can imagine his reaction to that 'army of unkempt females', all 'lower than the belly of a snake'. As it was he enjoyed his work, representing the needs of country people. He was thorough and served on several committees, chairing the one to do with drains. I expect it had a grander name but drains was its job. He brought a world of common sense, unknown to politicians today, to these deliberations. He came back from London with rich tales of his fellow peers, all told in his deadpan way, with the ancient titles of Black Rod and Sergeant-at-Arms trotted out as though they were next-door neighbours. According to him, Lord Someone-or-Other had 'passed a motion on the floor of the House . . . (long pause) . . . and left it on the paper for weeks'. To us, used to cleaning up dogs' messes on the floor of our house, this was screamingly funny.

In May 1934 Farve moved rejection of Lord Salisbury's Private Member's Bill to reform the House of Lords. Reform had been discussed for years and was to be mooted for another six decades before it was eventually passed. In his speech my father said, prophetically, that those who wished for reform did so because they were afraid that if a Socialist government came to power, it would want to abolish the House of Lords. If it found a reformed Upper Chamber, however, it might tolerate it. 'But would they?' asked my father. 'Let their lordships make no mistake, they would not. Such a government would tolerate precisely nothing that interfered in any way with their plans and arrangements, and they would abolish anything that did. They would find no greater difficulty in abolishing a Constitution made in 1934 than one of greater antiquity.' (All but ninety-two hereditary peers were turned out of the House of Lords in 1999 by Prime Minister Blair, who had no plan with which to replace them; a stranger to common sense, he preferred the grand gesture and the big spin.)

In the same speech – he was known as 'the peer of but a single speech' – Farve reiterated his faith in the hereditary principle. He believed that a man who had spent all his life in politics or public affairs was more likely to have a son capable of following in his footsteps than a man who had never paid attention to either, 'especially when that son had been brought up in the atmosphere of public work and in the knowledge that the day would come when he would have to bear his part in that work'. The idea of public service is so out of fashion now that to mention it is to court criticism, even ridicule. Jack Kennedy's words, 'Ask not what your country can do for you, ask what you can do for your country', have been turned on their head. Yet you only have to think for a moment to realize that there is much sense in what Farve believed.

When it came to business my father was easily tempted by romantic ideas of making a quick fortune. In 1912 he joined the gold rush to Canada but, unlucky as always, the ground he staked out was the only bit for miles around where there was no gold. He believed everyone to be as honest as he was and gullibility made him an easy target for charlatans. On a legendary occasion, one Andia (Marquis of) persuaded him to invest in a business that made tasteful cabinets for hiding wirelesses, which in those days were huge and hideous. It all ended in court with the 'Marquis' suing for slander. The case was dismissed and Andia unmasked. Randolph Churchill went to the court hearing with his sister Diana (their mother was Farve's first cousin). 'It's so unfair,' said Diana, 'Cousin David was *bound* to win because he looks like God the Father.'

I never knew my mother in her full beauty. She was forty when I was born, sixteen years after Nancy. Like my father, she had blonde hair and blue eyes, and her fine, regular features were a softer version of his. Totally without vanity, she did not seem to care what she looked like in everyday life, but when dressed up for an occasion she outshone her contemporaries. She loved clothes but possessed few and must have worn the same ones for years. I remember individual coats, skirts and dresses and an occasional evening dress; they were always original and exactly right for her. She was selfless to a rare degree and lived for her husband, her children and a small circle of friends, many of them family. High on the list of people she minded about were those who worked for her. She belonged to a generation of women who were brought up to accept their husbands' decisions and to make the best of their circumstances. 'For better, for worse, for richer, for poorer,' were the widely accepted conditions of marriage then.

Muv has been written about in books and newspapers, not because she sought recognition but because of her daughters. She is usually portrayed as vague, undemonstrative and cold, but I do not recognize her from this description. Vague she may have seemed to strangers, but she noticed and always understood our worries, real or imagined, and carried out her role as mother, wife and housekeeper in a way that a vague woman could never have done. In the 1920s and 30s she was responsible for what now seems an enormous indoor staff, as well as her family. She must have been sorely tried by us and there was seldom a day when a meal went smoothly. She presided above the noise, pretending not to notice the quick exit, banged door and tears, or the uncontrolled laughter sparked off by the silliest remark. She would sometimes go into a kind of reverie, abstracting herself from the ceaseless banter but remaining still present, a much-needed influence for calm. Telling Muv something thrilling or frightening seldom evoked more than, 'Orrnnhh, Stubby, fancy'; or 'Did you really? I do hope not.' She had heard it all before, of course, from each sister in turn. She rarely gave advice and when she did it was to underline what Nanny said, 'Don't draw attention to your-self.' Muv tried to prevent what she called 'announcements' such as 'I'm just going to wash my hands,' 'I'm going upstairs,' or, a shade more wor-thy, 'Help, I've forgotten to feed the guinea pigs.' She said, oh-so-truly, 'All that is not of interest to anyone.' What none of us realized at the time was just how much she taught us by her own example – and I can-not imagine a better one. By the time we were old enough to be aware of this, it was too late to tell her.

I have never known anyone as fair as Muv. She had neither favour-ites nor victims. That alone must have been almost impossible with such a disparate lot of girls, with diverse personalities and interests. Whether her disappointment every time another girl was born had an effect on us, perhaps a psychiatrist could say; certainly I was never aware of it. Tom, being the only boy, was always the exception. Her insight into the char-acters of each of her daughters gave her an uncanny knowledge of what we were doing; she did not have to be told by a busybody friend, she knew by instinct. We (or certainly Unity, Decca and me – I was too young to know about the older ones) were aware of this and our feeling of guilt when overstepping the mark was a steadying influence. Long after it was all over Muv told me that each daughter had had two or three years of adolescent rebelliousness or just bad temper, which had made life diffi-cult for everyone in the house. As there were six of us, she went through twelve years of this kind of tension and it is not surprising that she re-treated into her own thoughts from time to time. Her deafness in old age increased the impression she gave of being miles away. Two naughty grandsons fighting each other almost to the death said with glee, 'Granny Muv doesn't mind, she's so lovely and deaf.'

My sisters complained that she was strict. Perhaps after trying to make five girls stick to the rules she got tired of saying no and I was al-lowed a little more rope – but only a little as the tramlines of approved behaviour were still in force. It was not till the 1939 war that circumstances swept these away. One surprising indulgence was that I was allowed to go out hunting alone from the age of twelve. Our old groom, Hooper, accompanied me to the meet and left me with the other hunt members, and we met again for the ride home. A friend of mine, an only child who longed to do the same, told her mother about this. 'Oh, it's all right for Lady Redesdale,' said the mother, 'she's got five more girls so it doesn't matter if anything happens to Debo.' As ever, my mother's reasoning was wise: out hunting someone is always around to look after you, but my friend was still forbidden. When I was nineteen I lost my nerve out hunting. A new horse turned out to be one of the clumsy few more likely to fall at an obstacle than clear it. Two days on this crasher was enough, and to my lasting sorrow I never went out hunting on a horse again.

My mother liked figures. She remembered our London telephone number, Kensington 6476, by saying 'six for seven-and-six is one-and-three each'. Her household account books recorded every penny she spent: 'Utensils 15s 9d, Cleaning Materials 1s 2d, Vegetables 2s 10d'. In 1933 the under parlourmaid was paid £18 a year, Nanny £74 (up from £45 when she first arrived) and Mr and Mrs Stobie, the cook and gardener, £116. We all knew that if Muv had been in charge of our family finances everything might have been different. As it was, she had to juggle with what she was given and somehow remain solvent; intuition took her in the right direction and she never overspent. She was the one who put down roots and became part of the place where she lived, and it was she who bore the brunt of my father's extravagances and unlucky investments. It must have been hard for her each time we moved but I never heard her say so. I wonder now how much Farve told her when another crisis was building up. As children, none of us was privy to such discussions – if indeed they took place. Money was not spoken about as it is now, when it is often the sole subject of conversation, with a bit of illness thrown in.

Muv told me that had she had to earn her living she would have been happy as the woman at the *caisse* in a Paris restaurant, usually a formidable female dressed in black who sat enclosed in a raised glass cage above the tables and collected the cash from the diners' bills. The nearest Muv got to her ambition was to be County Treasurer of the Oxfordshire Federation of Women's Institutes. When she was totting up at the end of the year, a few pence out caused her major anxiety and we knew to keep out of her way. She was determined that we should all be as good managers as she was, and she started us off with a few pence a week pocket money. We graduated at the age of twelve to what was grandly called 'an allowance', eleven shillings a month, out of which we had to buy stockings, gloves, sweets, presents and any other extras we wanted. The amount was increased annually, bringing more responsibility, until we were seventeen and £100 a year had to cover most of our travelling as well as a complete wardrobe. When you compare our allowance with the wages of my parents' indoor staff, the Great Unfairness of Life is brought home.

When I was about ten, Muv got us all together to test our future housekeeping skills for an as yet unknown husband. Under the headings 'rent, rates, wages, heating, cleaning materials, food, clothes, travelling, and other necessities', she instructed us to account for an income of £500 a year. We pored over our sheet of paper, trying our best to apportion the money. Nancy finished almost before the rest of us had started. We read out our proposals and when it came to her turn, she waved her paper and said, 'Flowers: £499. Everything else: £1.' Muv gave up.

Muv's own childhood was unconventional, to say the least. Her mother, Jessica Bowles, née Evans-Gordon, died in 1887 when expecting her fifth child. Sydney was just seven years old. The family consisted of two brothers, George and Geoffrey, and Sydney and her younger sister Dorothy, known as Weenie all her life. A governess, Miss Henrietta Shell (Tello), joined them soon after their mother's death.

Sydney's father, Thomas Gibson Bowles, was illegitimate – a fact of no consequence now but in the second half of the nineteenth century the sins of the father were visited on the children and his origins carried a slur. His was an unusual case in that he was brought up by his father, Thomas Milner Gibson, a Radical MP, and little is known about his mother, a Miss Susan Bowles. When he was three years old Tommy Bowles was taken to live at his father's house in Suffolk (Mrs Milner Gibson must have been a generous woman to include him in her own brood). No public school would accept an illegitimate boy, so from the age of twelve he was educated in France. After a brief stint as a junior clerk in the Succession Duty office at Somerset House, he became a freelance journalist and magazine publisher, and was elected to Parliament in 1892.

Tommy Bowles' brains, forceful character and originality of thought made him a man to be reckoned with and he was a strong influence on his children. The sea was his passion. He held a master mariner's certificate and spent as much time as possible on board ship. After the death of his wife, he sold Cleeve Lodge, the house near the Royal Albert Hall in Kensington where he and Jessica had lived since their marriage, and moved his family to the country. But he could not settle to life in England and in August 1888 set off in his schooner, the *Nereid*, to Egypt and the Holy Land, taking with him Miss Shell, his four children and a dog. My mother was eight and Weenie only three. The eight-month voyage made a deep impression on the children. A habit learned at sea stayed with Muv all her life: the fear of running out of fresh drinking-water meant she never filled a glass, even of tap water, more than one-third full.

The *Nereid* was nearly wrecked in a hurricane off the coast of Syria, Grandfather having left Alexandria against the advice of the port authorities. Muv's account of the storm and their eventual safe landing enthralled us as children. Many years later she told me that they set sail in such dangerous conditions because Grandfather had discovered that while he was away exploring Upper Egypt, Tello was having an affair with a young naval officer. Muv remembered the man coming on board the *Nereid* and singing, 'You Are the Queen of My Heart Tonight'. Grandfather, who was enamoured of Tello himself, was so angry he insisted on leaving immediately.

Tello went out of the children's lives for some years after they returned to England. Then one day my mother was walking down Sloane Street when she saw, to her joy, Tello accompanied by four little boys in sailor suits. It transpired that the eldest was the son of the naval officer in Alexandria, but the next three were sired by Grandfather and were my mother's half-brothers. He had forgiven Tello her peccadillo, set her up in a house in London and made her editor of *The Lady*, a position she held for many years (including those when Farve was managing director of the magazine). My mother always wondered why he had not married her but guessed it would have been because of the eldest boy. Tello and Muv took up their friendship where they had left off and after her marriage Muv often invited her old governess to stay at Asthall. Tello was an inspired storyteller and we delighted in her company.

Back from the voyage, Grandfather took his family to Wilbury House, in Wiltshire, belonging to Sir Henry Malet. Sir Henry was hard up and had welcomed Grandfather's offer to share the household expenses. My mother was not fond of the daughter of the house, Vera, with whom she had to do lessons, but the beautiful Palladian house made a lasting impression on her at an age when sensitive children notice the details of their surroundings. Muv never again lived in a fine eighteenth-century house like Wilbury, her ideal, but her ability to make her succession of houses attractive and original on little money was one of her outstanding talents. She did not bow to fashion, mixing furniture and objects from different periods which many people would have thought unsuitable for their surroundings. She used what was available, and her instinct for colour has lived with me through the years. Whether it was a manor house or a tiny cottage, her stamp was unmistakable and the results, I thought, perfection. Junk shops drew her like a magnet and in the streets behind Marylebone Station she found bargains in furniture, china and anything that took her fancy. She never employed a decorator or sought advice; she knew what she wanted and got it done. When she was first married and living in a small house in Graham Street, Pimlico, she was amazed when a fashionable older woman asked her, 'Is your drawing room green and white or white and green?' To her chagrin Muv had to admit that it was indeed white and green. This must have been the nearest she ever came to following a trend.

Grandfather was MP for King's Lynn from 1892 to 1906 and when the House was sitting the family lived at No. 25 Lowndes Square. When Muv was fourteen, her father gave her the job of running his household, which she performed to his entire satisfaction. Not only did he have a beautiful daughter but a dependable housekeeper too. Grandfather had other lady friends besides Tello, including Lady Sykes, whom my mother particularly disliked and whose visits she dreaded. She described her as 'drinking and painting her face too much' – both were habits Muv abhorred.

The widowed father did not wish to cope with dressing his two daughters so he decided they should wear thick serge sailor suits, day and evening, winter and summer, at home or away. Not till Muv was eighteen did a woman friend of Grandfather's tell him that it was time for her to be dressed more conventionally. One evening he was the guest of honour at a dinner given in Hammersmith Town Hall by the mayor. He was ready to leave, dressed in tails and a white waistcoat, but could not find Sydney who was to accompany him. So he called Weenie, who was in the garden with the dogs. Still in her grubbiest sailor suit, with no time to wash or tidy, she grabbed her cap and was whisked off. The elegant ladies in gloves, gowns and jewels must have been surprised to see her being led into dinner on the arm of the mayor and placed on his right at the top table. Muv and Weenie were used to their father's eccentric behaviour. He never gave them birthday or Christmas presents and when they complained that their friends all got something, he rounded on them saying that he housed, fed, watered, clothed and educated them and that was enough.

When they were in London, Sydney rode every day with her father in Rotten Row. She rode side-saddle, as did all women at the time, and for a few weeks every year when she was a child, the pommel of her saddle was fixed on the off (right) side, to ensure that her left hip grew in alignment with her right. The daily ride in Rotten Row provided not only exercise but also the opportunity to meet friends, part of the social life that Muv enjoyed. But the real fun for the two sisters was skating at the Prince's Club, the ice rink in Montpelier Square. Muv fell for the skating instructor, Henning Grenander, a Swedish champion figure-skater, who was the equivalent of today's ski-guides, so adored by their clients. Waltzing with him seemed to Muv the height of romance.

In August, Grandfather sometimes took his family – along with some of his unusual habits – to a rented house on Deeside in the Scottish Highlands. He believed in Turkish baths and set one up in an empty dog kennel which was heated to the desired temperature with hot bricks. He sweated in the kennel and emerged sometime later to be drenched with buckets of cold water thrown from the roof by the butler. Muv's abiding love of Scotland dated from these visits. She had holiday romances there, including one with a young suitor called Eustace Heaven. My sisters and I thought this the most wonderful name when she told us about him, half-laughing, years later.

When Sydney was a debutante the first dance she went to, curiously enough, was given by the Duke and Duchess of Devonshire at their London house in Piccadilly. She was chaperoned by her father and they were early arrivals. I remember her telling me of Louise Duchess's painted face and fixed smile, and how the Duke stood behind her, half asleep as usual. What Sydney did not know was that the Duke woke up the next morning and saw thick fog outside. He turned over in bed, muttering that there was no point getting up – not realizing that the window was covered by the tent left over from the night before.

When Weenie was eighteen, Grandfather unwillingly agreed that a dance must be given for her. The guest list became too large for Lowndes Square, so Weenie brought in builders to break through the wall into the next house, whose owners were conveniently away. After Sydney married, Weenie, aged eighteen and equally as capable as Sydney, took over her tasks and faced the same difficulties with the drunken menservants in the household. There was a troublesome chef who was given notice several times but refused to leave. In order to get rid of him, Grandfather decided to shut the house and go to China, taking Weenie with him. On the day of departure the trunks were packed and stowed in the 'growler' that was to take them to the station to catch the boat train. Grandfather came down the steps and said, 'It's raining, my dear Piggy. We won't go.'

Weenie soon became engaged to Percy Bailey but knew nothing of what was in store. Grandfather was told that someone must explain the facts of life to her before she married. When these were disclosed, she exclaimed, 'Surely no *gentleman* would ever do a thing like that!' On her wedding day, she arrived at the church with Grandfather and his last words to her before walking up the aisle were, 'Piggy, I shall never know what I owe the Aylesbury Dairy now.' He had no more daughters to look after his household bills.

Grandfather died in 1922 so I never knew him but he was a strong influence on Muv in many ways, including diet. He had noticed that among the children living in London the Jewish ones were the healthiest, and decided to bring up his own family according to the dietary laws of the Old Testament. Muv adopted these rules and we were fed accordingly. The language in which the Lord spoke to Moses is as threatening as a thunderstorm. We did not feel deprived of 'eagle, ossifrage and osprey', which are an 'abomination' and therefore banned from the table, but swine being 'cloven-footed' but not chewers of the cud meant no bacon, and the rule against eating anything without fins and scales but that lived in the water meant no shellfish. I did not taste lobster until I was eighteen.

In spite of her unusual views, Muv's cooks always produced good food. She was influenced by Grandfather's foreign chefs and her table combined the best of French and English styles. She was no cook herself and when she and my father lived in a shack in Canada while prospecting for gold, she told us that she had bought a chicken, put it in the oven and was horrified on carving it to discover the crop and gizzard still full of corn which floated into the gravy. She was unexpectedly indulgent about our own food fancies, which many parents would have forbidden. Unity was addicted to mashed potatoes in her early teens and ate them to the exclusion of almost everything else. Bread sauce was my favourite, eaten with a spoon. My other craving was for Bovril, which Muv believed to be full of hated preservatives. She refused to buy it, but let me have it and charged it against my pocket money.

Muv flirted with Christian Science but could not take its founder, Mrs Baker Eddy. Her simpler creed was that, if left alone, the Good Body would cure itself without Mrs Eddy's help. She mistrusted the medical profession and used to say, 'Doctors are so nice but if only they could get away from their training.' Perhaps as children we were lucky that ninety per cent of the time, the Good Body did the job. When there was a crisis, Muv did get in a doctor but she preferred more unorthodox treatment. I once had a fierce attack of indigestion and a masseur, a follower of the Swedish osteopath Dr Kellgren, was called in. He gave me a rough pummelling all over and after a while I turned bright yellow. 'That's good,' he said, 'that's the bile coming out,' and I felt better. Muv was criticized by other parents who were sceptical of massage and disapproved of the infrequency of the doctor's visits, but their children envied us because, like sausages, Syrup of Figs and castor oil were banned. Muv paid no attention to whether or not we went to the lavatory; she knew that the Good Body would see to it in the end.

In 1931 tuberculin testing for cows became mandatory. Three of Muv's herd of Guernseys reacted positive to the test. This annoyed her and she refused to get rid of them, telling the cowman, 'What? Get rid of those beautiful animals. Certainly not! The children can have the milk', and have it we did. She believed that wholegrain, stone-ground wheat – nothing added and nothing taken away – was 'the bread of life'. She was critical of Lord Rank, 'the wicked miller', and regarded his ghost-white loaves (the cheapest kind of bread bought by the greatest number of people) and pale brown Hovis a confidence trick because the germ of the wheat had been removed, thereby lowering the bread's nutritional value. All such processed food was described as 'murdered food' by Muv's brother, Uncle Geoffrey, whose maxim was 'Don't keep it, eat it'. (He lived on bread, chocolate and the occasional herring.) All tinned food was considered close to poison; sardines were the exception and my father also bought something called 'glass tongue', which was visible through the jar. When refrigerators came into fashion, Muv said in a far-away voice, 'I don't really like refrigerators; they make the food so cold.'

3

SISTERS AND TOM

Until she married in 1933, my favourite sister after Decca was Nancy. She called me Linda, sometimes adding 'May' when it suited for a rhyme ('Linda May drives the clouds away/What would life be without Linda May? Grey'). She made me laugh and cry about equally but what I remember now is the laughter. She was so funny, lively and imaginative that, in spite of the tears, I could not resist her company. The sixteen years between us made her almost another generation, but whenever she was at home I spent hours sitting on the end of her bed listening to gossip and secrets about the people she had met while staying with friends. The confidences were safe with me as I had no one to repeat them to: Muv and Nanny would not have listened and Decca was not interested. They were a window on a glamorous life, embellished no doubt, and they made me long to meet the butterfly people she described, a world away from the nursery and schoolroom.

Nancy was a conundrum if ever there was one. She was everything and its opposite: loyal–disloyal, generous–mean, kind–unkind, steadfast–treacherous, hardworking–lazy, tolerant–intolerant. No wonder her biographers have found it difficult to steer through this maze of contradictions to arrive at the person she was. In life she exaggerated until the truth was hard to dig out but she often hit the nail on the head in her books. Sophia, a character in her novel, *Pigeon Pie*, who had a talent for 'embroidering on her own experiences', and who rushed from hyperbole to hyperbole, ending on a wild climax of improbability with the words 'it's absolutely true,' could be a portrait of Nancy. The one constant, however, was the pure pleasure Nancy's company gave; the way she lifted spirits when she came into a room, her talent for turning serious into ridiculous and for seeing people and situations as no one else did. She sparkled, not only her eyes but all of her, and was the star of any gathering. Her elegance was inborn, her figure unchanging, never too fat or too thin, and long before she had money to spend on herself, her clothes were always just right. Her swinging walk took her for miles in town and country and few could keep up with her.

She was not happy in youth, being well and truly unemployed for those years, with nothing to live on except the small allowance from our parents. Marriage was the career that we all aspired to – we were not trained to do a paid job. We learned how to keep house by example, but even that was with a future husband and family in mind. No work equalled no money. Any unskilled job, working in a hat shop, for instance, was frowned upon as 'taking money from someone who really needed it'. Nancy did not marry until she was nearly thirty and until then led an aimless existence, staying with friends for long periods but coming home in between to wherever we were living at the time. 'Sat about' are words which recur in my own diary as I grew up, and I well remember what we called 'aching voids of boredom'. It was a teenage disease, like being rude to our parents – especially to Muv who came in for criticism from all of us. It was not surprising that there was discontent on all sides. In *The Pursuit of Love* Nancy describes the agonizingly slow passing of the hours and days: 'What's the time?' asks Linda. 'Guess,' says Fanny. '"A quarter to six?" "Better than that." "Six?" "Not quite so good." "Five to?" "Yes."'

Nancy's fertile mind found an outlet in teasing – not difficult in my case as the slightest hint of pathos was guaranteed to bring tears, but none of us was spared; being laughed at was part of the rough and tumble of life in a large family. One day there was a headline in the paper: 'SLOWLY CRUSHED TO DEATH IN A LIFT. MAN'S LONG AGONY IN THE LIFT SHAFT'. Nancy only had to say SLOWLY and Decca and I dissolved into tears. It became too much for the grown-ups and was banned, so Nancy tapped it out with her hand or foot, watching our faces to see the effect. When my bedtime was at seven, she started looking hopefully at the clock at a quarter to. When the blessed moment came at last and it was time for me to go, she shooed me out saying, 'As soon as you've gone I shall do the Joy Dance.' Sure enough, when I got upstairs I heard loud stomping and clapping of hands coming from down below.

'No one will want to marry *you*,' she used to say. 'WHY?' I wailed. To be told by a grown-up sister that there was no chance of happiness as a wife and mother, when marriage was the only prospect, was a crushing blow. 'Why? Well, not only have you got a deformed thumb, there is the *gland* . . .' Perhaps because we drank milk from the cows that had reacted to the tuberculin test, I did indeed have a lump in my neck, which is still there. Nancy explained that it hubbled and bubbled when I was asleep and that no man could stand it. She sang:

> *The hounds and the horses*
> *Galloping over the land*
> *All stopped to hear*
> *The hubbling, bubbling of the gland.*

And added a second verse:

> *The lords and the ladies*
> *Dancing to the band*
> *All stopped to hear*
> *The hubbling, bubbling of the gland.*

I was convinced there was no hope for my future.

When Muv was expecting Nancy, Farve's letters make it clear how certain she was that her first child was to be a boy. She referred to the unborn as 'him', named him Paul and knitted and sewed blue garments. After a punishing fourteen hours in labour, the nine-and-a-half-pound baby was not blue-eyed, fair-haired Paul but dark-haired, green-eyed Nancy. The birth was far from the fairytale experience that Muv had looked forward to and was followed by weeks of extremely painful breast-feeding. We were all born at home. The doctors' rule in those days was that after giving birth, a mother should stay in bed for three weeks, flat on her back for the first two; the 'patient' was then allowed up for a few hours each day, extended as time went by until a normal daily routine was restored. Muv found this regime frustrating but kept to it. The pendulum has now swung too far in the opposite direction and she would have deplored the way mothers and their newborn infants are turned out of hospital after a few hours.

My father's sister Frances, Aunt Pussy, was five years older than my mother. She was the most beautiful of my father's sisters and was full of memorable sayings, such as 'I love this coat. It looks so cheap and was so expensive.' Aunt Pussy had no children of her own when Nancy was born and no experience of what is now called 'childcare'. But she had theories on how children should be brought up: they must never be crossed, corrected or criticized and must be allowed to develop in an atmosphere of heavenly peace. Muv was impressed by Aunt Pussy's notions about bringing up children and put them into practice with Nancy – at least until Pam was born. When Aunt Pussy eventually married and was expecting a baby, she spent hours in museums gazing at portraits of children by Greuze, hoping her baby would resemble them. Alas, her only child, Clementine (Pussette), was the opposite of one of Greuze's exquisite children and was mentally retarded.

Nancy always told me that she was perfectly happy till she was three when Pam arrived, although how she remembered is open to question. The birth of a new baby and the attention it receives can be hard on an older sibling and this was perhaps the origin of Nancy's jealousy, which later focused on Diana whose beauty and brains were unsettling to her eldest sister. The jealousy was hidden but to those of us who knew her it was very much there.

Pamela was as different from Nancy as you could imagine. She was called Woman, with a few variations, by all of us for the simple reason that she was so womanly. She had huge cornflower-blue eyes and naturally stripy blonde hair of the kind envied by many girls and achieved with difficulty by expensive hairdressers. She was slightly lame, after an attack of polio at the age of three left her right leg weaker and shorter than her left. She was nursed at home and made an almost complete recovery. Later on she adored riding, but because her grip on the saddle was too weak to manage jumps she was never able to go hunting.

Pam had much in common with Muv, her interests fixed firmly on the kitchen and garden rather than some fanciful library or the political leaders chosen by her siblings. There was no risk of extreme views or controversial talk; she was just herself, a comforting, sensible presence with no sharp edges. She was not quick-witted and could not keep pace with words and nuances, which made her a sitting target for Nancy whose teasing verged on bullying. But Pam's good nature saw her through a persecuted childhood and she laughed about it later on. She was never out of favour with Farve and because she never deviated from the steady path of a country person she was the favourite of our aunts and uncles.

Dogs played an important part in Pam's life; she invested them with human characteristics and organized her existence around their needs, to an extent unusual even in an Englishwoman. Food was of paramount importance and she was a stickler for well-chosen menus. A friend of my mother once turned up unexpectedly for lunch. As bad luck would have it, Muv must have taken her eye off the ball early that morning when meals for the day were being planned. To Pam's dismay, rice appeared twice: savoury in a risotto and creamy in a rice pudding. 'Stublow,' she told me, wide-eyed with horror, 'it was ghoul, *two* rices at *one* meal' – a kitchen gaffe remembered for the rest of our lives. Any disaster thereafter was called 'two rices', in Pam's voice – the most exaggerated 1930s voice of any of us, which, to make the best effect, rose and fell according to the story she was telling. At a smart dinner party in Paris she once surprised the guests by explaining a cut of pork to her neighbour, emphasizing her point by standing up, slapping her thigh and saying, 'Il faut le couper *là*' – you have to cut it *there*.

During the General Strike of 1926 Pam came into her own. A canteen for volunteer lorry drivers was set up in a big barn by the main road to Oxford, always called the Top Road (it is a smart restaurant now but it is still the canteen to me). So off went the sisters with heaps of sandwiches and an oil stove to brew the tea. Pam did the early shift. She had got everything ready, but no one came. Disappointed, she lay on the road pressing her ear to the tarmac, hoping to hear the sound of rumbling wheels. Silence. After a while a dirty old tramp wandered in and demanded tea. Pam, half afraid, brought him a cup. He sidled up to her and said with a leer, 'Give us a kiss, Miss.' Pam was terrified, and tripped and twisted her ankle as she fled. Once again, the tramp was Nancy.

I hardly knew Tom. He was eleven when I was born and already more than halfway through prep school. He was a serious, thoughtful child, adored by parents and sisters and, although aware of his unique position in the family as the only boy in a troop of girls, he somehow remained unspoilt. He had a carved head of regular features and, like my father, the steady, confident gaze of an honest man. It is not enough to say that he was good-looking – which is how all his contemporaries described him; he had the kind of personality that drew attention and made you look at him even when he was silent. Unlike Nancy, whose face changed with every passing thought, Tom's expression was impassive. He did not join in our silliness but was amused by it and when he laughed, sometimes unwillingly, at our idiotic jokes, a one-sided smile, which we called 'blithering', appeared. To make him blither was a small triumph and worth the try. He once suffered that curious complaint called Bell's palsy and the muscles on one side of his face froze and for a while the smile did too. A sister took a photograph and it records his bizarre, lop-sided smile.

Tom had the gift of making one want to please him, which was perhaps the secret of his success with women, and he left a trail of disappointed lovers who did not quite come up to his standards. His bugbear was depression, an affliction from which my sisters and I did not suffer. He sometimes came home from London unexpectedly and hardly spoke for days but sat, at times reading, at times not, oblivious to his surroundings and to Decca and me jabbering away in Honnish, our private language. The depression lifted as mysteriously as it came and off he went to whatever he was supposed to be doing. He was the peacemaker of the family and managed to remain friends with everyone throughout all the political upheavals. He was the most steadfast and attractive person in the background of our lives and we all deferred to him, including Muv and Farve.

Tom's letters to Muv from prep school chiefly concerned food. The hungry last years of the 1914–18 war must have been hard on growing boys and 'sossages' and fried bacon are often mentioned, perhaps as a tease because they were outlawed at home. Tom made lifelong friends at school with Basil Blackwood, later the Marquess of Dufferin and Ava, and Jim Lees-Milne. Nanny told me of my introduction to Jim. At three months old I was taken with parents and sisters to a school cricket match in which Tom and Jim were playing. Jim lobbed a ball into my pram, which got him a brisk telling off from Nanny – the closeness of the near-fatal blow no doubt exaggerated. (I do not suppose Muv noticed.)

From prep school Tom won a scholarship to Eton and could have gone there for nothing, as a 'Tug' in Eton language, but because Farve could afford the fees it was decided that he should go as an 'Oppidan Scholar', leaving the place for a needier boy. Tom thrived at Eton, where his friends Jim and Basil were also pupils. His musical talent flourished and his tutor allowed him to have a piano in his room – an unusual concession, but he realized it was a part of Tom's being.

Diana left home to get married when I was nine. I saw little of her until after the war and did not really get to know and love her till then. Her beauty was the first thing that struck you; she was beautiful when she was born in 1910 and remained beautiful until her death. Without make-up or artifice, and often in clothes that she wore till they were thread-bare, she was always the best-looking woman at any gathering. She was a great reader with a huge appetite for literature and was the intellec-tual equal of Tom, to whom she was closest in age and interests. Like Decca and Unity, once Diana had decided on a course of action there was no deviating or turning back and, like them, she was drawn to ex-treme politics. It was more surprising in her case as almost everything else about her was open-minded and tolerant.

Her immediate understanding of human frailty and her extraordi-nary sensitivity made Diana doubly attractive, and later on it was inter-esting to see how people who were prejudiced against her because of her politics melted on meeting her. Her rigid views on race were partly influenced by Grandfather Redesdale, an advocate of Teutonic suprem-acy, and were hardened by the experience of war and her unyielding nature. I do not share her views but my love for her overcame this side of her character, the greater part of which was pure and selfless. She was always the one to volunteer for some boring family chore and went out of her way to be kind to anyone in difficulty. As she grew old, she became almost saint-like in her goodness.

Unity was always the odd one out. She arrived in this world in August 1914 to the sound of troops marching to war and departed it thirty-four years later in tragic circumstances. Larger than life in every way, she could have been the model for a ship's figurehead or Boadicea, with her huge navy-blue eyes, perfectly straight nose and fair hair worn in two long plaits. Perhaps because of her teenage diet of mashed potatoes, her teeth were her only bad feature. (In those days cosmetic dentistry was in its infancy and you took what nature gave you.) As a child she was a dreamer, obstinate, fearless of authority, disobedient, affectionate and easily hurt, with a precocious talent for drawing and design. When she was about eight, she drew an unforgettable picture of a man walking in a field wearing a turban and little else. He had a bag hanging around his middle and was broadcasting seed as though it were peas and beans. The title of the drawing was 'Abraham and his Seed Forever'.

Unity was devoted to Decca, a closeness that withstood their political differences. They communicated in Boudledidge, a private language invented by Decca. No one in the family understood it except me, but I would never have dared speak it – it was their language, not mine, and I would have been pulled up sharply had I tried. I was satisfied with Honnish, which had a background of the local Gloucestershire accent, elongated and shortened according to the importance of the words. If someone upset Unity at meals, she slid slowly and noiselessly to the floor and remained under the table while the chat went on above, surfacing only when she thought the episode was forgotten. My parents never drew attention to it. She understood the power of silence and carried it to such a degree that it was sometimes what the Army describes so well as 'dumb insolence'. One of the lessons in the PNEU programme was 'narration', when pupils had to recount a passage that the teacher had read out. Muv asked Unity to do this simple task but for some reason she dug in her heels and refused. 'Come on, darling, you must remember something,' said Muv. Unity shook her head. 'Not one word?' Muv insisted. 'Very well then,' said Unity, staring furiously ahead, '*the*'.

Decca was my boon companion all through childhood. She was bold, original, imaginative, generous, vulnerable, lazy, clumsy and comical in the extreme. We shared everything and life without her was unimaginable. We talked all day in Honnish, and when we slept in the same room we chatted for half the night as well – what about, heaven knows, but no secrets were hid. We had each other when the grown-ups and older sisters were difficult or when the Great Unfairness of Life seemed too much to bear.

Having opposite interests, we did not compete: Decca was a reader, an observer rather than a doer, and clever, with a talent for words that eventually made her famous. She was not interested in sports or games of any kind, she disliked the out-of-doors and was oblivious to the seasons. (When loyally accompanying her second husband, Robert Treuhaft, on a hiking holiday in an American national park, she intoned, 'Nature, nature, how I hate yer,' as she stumbled along a rocky path.) A feeling for interior decoration – so strong in my mother and inherited to the last degree of perfection by Nancy and Diana – was left out of her. Nor did she seem to care about her appearance: clothes were merely coverings to keep her warm; colours and shapes were thrown together hugger-mugger and made you wonder at her choice. Her mind and energies were engaged elsewhere, mainly with people and politics. Her unswerving loyalty to those she loved and biting criticism of the many she did not were shades of my father – perhaps the only trait they had in common. When you were with her, all else faded in the face of her strong personality and you forgot everything except her company.

Decca had two pet animals and a bird, adored and transformed by her into human characters and, like Pam with her dogs, they were invested with considerable importance. The bird was a ring dove, complete with a beautiful wicker cage, which she had bought with long-saved pocket money. The dove became tame and flew above her head as she bicycled down the long hill to Swinbrook village, looking like the picture of the Holy Ghost in our children's illustrated Bible. It was an object of envy to me, who had neither bird nor bicycle. Her black spaniel, Tray, was a later shadow and was named after the dog that gained the upper hand over Cruel Frederick in *Struwwelpeter*, Heinrich Hoffmann's cautionary tales. Their terrifying pictures were a constant reminder of what could happen if we overstepped the mark. The Great Agrippa, so tall he almost reached the sky, was my father to the life in his dressing gown when he had just got out of 'my good clothes'. Little Suck-a-Thumb, blood pouring from the boy's amputated thumbs, and the smoking remains of Harriet, the result of her disobedience with matches, all hit the targeted conscience.

Decca's other creature was Miranda, an orphan ewe lamb she had brought up on the bottle. Miranda soon grew into a clumsier, pushier version of Tray and went everywhere with her loving owner, shoving people and furniture out of the way with a butt from her bony forehead. After the annual shearing, her fleece was sent to the Witney Blanket Company where the wool was transformed into a blanket with 'Miranda' woven in red into the border. The sheep and the annual blanket were an important part of nursery life. Miranda became the symbol of all the virtues, backed up by no less an authority than the Bible, which regularly harps on the necessity of separating the sheep from the goats (sheep being the superior of the two). Whenever a passage referring to this ancient state of affairs was quoted in church, Decca got excited and made the face and sounds she kept for Miranda, a kind of grimace where one side of her mouth went down, which made a sucking-in noise when she breathed. This was lost on the air because we were at the back of the church and no one except the parson could see what she was doing. If he noticed, he must have wondered what had possessed one of the younger members of his congregation.

I sometimes wondered what it would be like to be an only child, but the stimulation of being one of a crowd, all older than me, was an education in itself. I could never keep up but I learned to hold my own.

4

SWINBROOK HOUSE

Asthall Manor was host to a poltergeist, one of those nuisances that accompany teenage girls. It crashed and banged in the attics and, according to legend, pulled off the cook's bedclothes. My sisters thought it was one of the reasons why Farve decided to sell the house in 1926. He loved building and having a project on the go and set about enlarging a farmhouse above Swinbrook village. I have never seen a photograph of the original house and do not know if Muv was consulted before Farve got to work on it. Judging by what emerged, I imagine not.

While the house was being finished we went to Paris and stayed in a cheap hotel. Farve took his car. He got into trouble with a policeman, who stood blowing his whistle and waving his windmill arms at this driver on the wrong side of the road. Farve wound down his window and shouted, *'Sorry, no Frrrench,'* in an exaggerated French accent (to make it easier for the policeman to understand). There was a bidet in our hotel bathroom and Nanny, Decca and I, who had never seen such a thing, hurried out to buy goldfish assuming that was what it was for.

After a few months we came home to Swinbrook for the first time. Farve was delighted with his new house. My mother had done her best to make the interior as attractive as possible, given the newness of the shell. Neither of my parents were gardeners, surprisingly in the case of my mother as people who are good at decorating are often good at gardening. She particularly disliked white flowers, saying they were like bits of paper blowing about. My father's favourite flower was scarlet *Anemone fulgens*, a specialist's bloom not often seen in a garden. He treasured the two or three bulbs that succeeded out of the many he planted, and it was the end of the world if a rampaging dog or child were to step on one of these objects of untold value.

I loved the house from the start. The others did not. They had lost the Asthall barn and their freedom and had only the long drawing room to sit in, which they had to share with Muv. They were of an age to complain to whoever would listen and the cry, 'It *is* unfair', was often heard. Lesser complaints ruled the day: 'The knives and forks are so cold we can't eat with them' or 'Unity's got a rat and I've only got hens.' Our bedrooms and Nanny's were on the top floor and were painted white, each with a border of a different colour. Mine was green. The interior doors of the house were made of elm which, as every schoolboy knows, is prone to warping. Farve insisted that it was 'damn good wood', but Nancy said that even when it was locked, you could put your head round the visitors' bathroom door and see what was happening inside. The dining-room table was made of two long pieces of oak, sixteenth-century style (perhaps it was sixteenth-century; it is not the sort of thing children notice). The boards did not quite meet, making a little valley down the middle which we sowed with seeds and watered. It was the usual game of Tom Tiddler's Ground and, greatly daring, we would taunt Farve with this until he shouted at us to stop.

My mother stretched at meals. From her outspread arms her hands made circles in the air, first one way then the other, which she said was good for the digestion. She also yawned. I expect the governesses were surprised by this but they were surprised by many of her foibles. Farve drank water out of Grandfather Redesdale's magnificent goblet made from the melted-down gold medals won by his Shire horses. Farve did the carving. Mabel noticed short commons for the unloved and used to push the plate against his arm till he topped up the helping. She kept the remains of breakfast – forbidden sausages and ham – that came out of the dining room on shooting days, and we were into the pantry like lightning.

Mabel's domain was a refuge for us children. Like Nanny, she was usually unflustered but even she set about us when she had work to do and we annoyed her too much. 'GET OUT OF MY PANTRY,' was always followed by a kiss, her aquiline nose coming first, followed by kindly eyes. She and the under parlourmaid wore the same uniform: a dress of blue-and-white toile de Jouy in a traditional bird pattern, smart and clean-looking (my mother's idea, of course) with a white linen apron and white organdie cap threaded with black velvet ribbon.

Farve and Mabel understood each other perfectly. In most such households her position would have been held by a man, a butler, but because of my mother's bad experiences with drunken men in her father's pantry, she preferred a woman. After twelve years with us Mabel accepted a proposal of marriage from Mr Woolven, a regular visitor who was in charge of preparing the inventory of whichever of our houses was, for reasons of economy, being let. He was probably the only eligible man Mabel ever met. When she told my father the glad news he was furious. 'I would never have engaged you if I'd known you would leave at once,' he stormed. Yet they remained friends and Mabel always came back in an emergency. I thought her home address the most romantic imaginable: 'Mabel Windsor, Peacock Cottage, Queen Camel'.

Swinbrook village and its inhabitants seemed eternal. Winnie Crook, whose initials gave us children such pleasure, ran the post office. She served tuppence-worth of acid drops in a twist of paper, weighed on the same brass scales as the letters. Our other delights were Fry's peppermint cream, which broke off into conveniently sized bits, and good old Cadbury's tuppenny bars. I do not know if she sold anything more expensive but these were what we could afford. There was the village idiot who chased Nancy and no one thought anything of it, Mrs Price, who lived up a bank and was nearly a hundred years old, and at the Mill Cottage, Mrs Phelps, whom Farve mistook for a heifer calf when she was bent over weeding her garden.

The formidable Mrs Bunce was in charge of the Swan Inn and kept strict order; anyone out of step had to beware of the consequences and we never heard of any late-night fracas, even on a Saturday. She wore a black dress fastened at the neck with a cameo brooch and a sacking apron over her substantial front to keep off the meal that she mixed and fed to her turkey poults. The turkeys lived in a paddock opposite the pub and Mrs Bunce's stately figure could be seen slowly crossing the road – a car was a rare sight in those days and there was no need to hurry. There was sawdust on the stone floor of the pub and a charming curved settle in the parlour. The box tree that grows by the door had already reached its full height and I would love to know when it and the ancient wisteria next to it were planted.

The blacksmith, a huge man and a Methodist preacher, was a great figure in the village. His forge was as good as Vulcan's own to me (with Venus nowhere to be seen) and he let me pump the giant bellows. He was one of those men with whom animals are calm and the horses stood peacefully to be shod, resting their foot on his leather apron. I loved the hiss and smell of the smoke billowing from the smouldering hoof when the red-hot shoe was fitted. It left a mark where the hoof had to be trimmed and out would come an enormous file and the ragged edges fell away. What a skill it was and taken for granted by us.

There was also my father's gamekeeper with his broody hens and pheasant chicks, and his gruesome larder of magpies, jays, stoats and weasels, nailed to the branch of a tree. The Gibbet Oak (where men, not birds, were hanged) still stands by Widley, the wood where I found my first butterfly orchid. Farve put a stoutly built railway van in the main ride of Hensgrove Wood to serve as a shelter in the worst weather and for the keeper to store his multifarious kit. I was taken to see it the other day and it still stands, nearly a hundred years later, just as I remembered it.

We went to church of course, at St Mary's, Swinbrook. Muv and Farve sat on the short pew at the back and we directly in front of them. The effigies of the Fettiplace family on the north wall near the altar fascinated us: six life-sized stone men lying on their sides, heads supported by their hands, elbows resting on stone pillows. John Piper described them in the *Shell Guide to Oxfordshire* as 'intelligent, wicked-looking former lords of the village, lying on slabs like proud sturgeon'. This powerful family's claim to fame is that they disappeared some two hundred years ago, as did their house, although traces of the garden terraces are still visible in a field. We all believed this story but many years later a mention of the family in one of my books sparked a letter from a Fettiplace, to whom I wrote to apologize for saying she did not exist.

My parents made several contributions to the church, replacing the Victorian tiled floor with stone flags and installing oak pews. Farve had promised to give the pews should he ever have an unexpected windfall. This unlikely event came about in 1924 when he placed an ante-post bet at huge odds on Master Robert in the Grand National and the horse won. It belonged to our cousin Joe Airlie and there was a great celebration. My father had originally wanted a horse's head carved on the end of each pew to record how the munificent gift had been paid for, but the Bishop refused. Farve thought this hypocritical of the Prince of the Church as he knew perfectly well where the money had come from. Muv gave four brass chandeliers including a small pair with double-headed eagles at the apex that stand out to good effect against so much stone.

The weekly repeated prayers were not crystal-clear to a seven-year-old. What did 'dissembleth', 'cloke,' 'unfeignedly' and 'abhor' mean? And what on earth was the Virgin's womb? 'His servant David' was Farve – though it was difficult to imagine him as anyone's servant unless it was Lieutenant General Lord Methuen's; 'We have erred and strayed from thy ways like lost sheep' brought on Decca's grimaces reserved for Miranda; 'And thou, child,' was Mrs Ham speaking. It was a language that seeped into my subconscious and I cannot bear to hear the new version. Prayers seemed interminable and held up the longed-for freedom when I could be out of doors again. Fidgeting about, I licked the pew beneath my face (the taste of the polish is with me now). I thought everybody did this, but apparently not. Years later I buttonholed a few friends and they vehemently denied such a disgusting habit. I then asked my old friend, the writer Patrick Leigh Fermor, 'Did you lick the pews?' 'Yes, of course,' he said without hesitation, his understanding and memory of childhood undimmed.

Farve took the collection and tortured us by stopping twice in front of Aunt Iris, his penniless sister, nudging her the second time round. She used to frown and slap his hand which started us on the peculiar agony of church giggles. Decorating the church for Easter was our job. I never got further than primroses regimented along the window sills in potted-meat jars. If Easter was late, I included a few cowslips (picking these offerings for Our Maker is illegal now). None of us was much good at decorating but at least we tried. We regularly signed the visitors' book 'Greta Garbo' and 'Maurice Chevalier'. We must have been an almighty nuisance to those in charge.

The poultry farm at Swinbrook was Muv's one chance of running a profitable business. The man who looked after it was called, unbelievably, Mr Lay. The hen's food smelt delicious: warm mash in the mornings made of sharps, middlings and household scraps; wheat and maize in the afternoons. I too kept hens for commercial reasons and sold the eggs to Muv to bolster my pocket money. In Honnish, 'hon' meant 'hen' and had nothing to do with 'Honourable', as some ignoramuses later thought. (As the children of a baron 'The Hon.' was affixed to our names.) The Honnish Hons were Decca and me; the Horrible Counter Hons were Nancy, Tom and Diana. The Hons' meeting place was the linen cupboard, private and warm. We spent hours sitting on the slatted shelves writing our rules, enlarging Honnish vocabulary and eating Cadbury's cooking chocolate from its blue wrapper, wheedled out of Mrs Stobie in the kitchen. Mrs Stobie was a wonderful cook but, like so many of her profession, prone to moods. We knew by the loudness of the banging of pots and pans how she was feeling and kept out of her way when the decibels rose.

Decca and I were by then in the schoolroom where more serious lessons had succeeded my mother's grounding in reading, writing and sums. I am sorry to say there was not just one governess but a succession of them, and my sisters had already been through a fair few by the time we came on the scene. We were perfectly foul to them and made their lives intolerable, so naturally they left. But awful as we were, some of them were pretty peculiar too and I do not know how they thought they could teach. The usual subjects were a dead loss but one of the governesses, Miss Dell, encouraged us in the difficult art of shoplifting – stealing really. My mother found out (the shopkeepers did not, thank goodness) and Miss Dell disappeared.

Decca and I spent a lot of time answering advertisements and sending off for free samples, anything from shampoo and deodorant to milk powder for babies. Decca let her imagination rip when describing the maladies that affected her non-existent babies and the hopes she held out for the various patented foods and remedies. This made the arrival of the postman, Mr Beckinsale, the highlight of an otherwise dull day. Mr Beck, his waterproof canvas bag slung over one arm, pushed his heavy bicycle up the hill to Swinbrook House. He went straight to the pantry to drink tea and talk to Mabel, while Decca and I hovered until Mabel sorted the post and a little parcel addressed to 'Mrs Jessica Mitford' appeared (the idea of an unmarried mother was unthinkable). This meant milk powder.

Decca also wrote to the agony aunts of women's magazines with wildly improbable tales, or asking for advice on imagined predicaments. To her delight these were sometimes published. 'Dear Mag, I have a little plum-coloured silk dress which has gone under the arms, the rest of this garment is fine and I am reluctant to throw it away. Please advise. Worried, Swinbrook House, Burford, Oxon.' I often wondered if the recipients of these requests ever guessed that they were from an under-employed eleven-year-old, practising the style which was one day to make her fortune.

The first big change in our everyday lives came in September 1929 when Unity went to boarding school. It had been her dream to join our Mitford and Farrer cousins at St Margaret's, Bushey, a church school in Hertfordshire. As she was so naughty with the governesses (she used to pick up poor Miss Dell, who was rather small, and put her on the sideboard) my parents gave in. She loved the school but her difficult characteristics came to the fore and she was what Nanny would have called 'her own worst enemy', longing to be part of school life but incapable of accepting its rules. To Unity's surprise and sorrow, she was sacked after just over a year. The reason, so she said, was that when reciting 'A garden is a lovesome thing, God wot' she added the word 'rot', but I imagine she also caused general unrest in her class and that the other girls looked on her rebelliousness with some awe. Decca and I were thrilled at the idea of her being expelled but my mother always said, 'No, children, she was asked to leave', as though it was quite different.

Unity going away to school brought rumblings of discontent from Decca, who was just twelve and longed to go to boarding school herself. She became moody and critical, no longer the comical, charming little girl she had been. She kicked against anything conventional and eventually took up the politics of malcontents. Although I had her to myself in term time, I was no good as a confidante as I could not understand, nor had I sympathy for, her longing to escape from home. I was pleased with life and the idea of boarding school was anathema. She opened a 'Running Away' bank account with her pocket money and the Christmas envelopes from aunts and uncles. It was treated as a joke by the rest of us, but to her it was deadly serious.

My older sisters never stopped saying how much they disliked
Swinbrook – Nancy called it 'Swinebrook' or 'The Buildings' – and this
must have been depressing for Farve. Perhaps because I was completely
happy there, he was especially indulgent to me when a new entertainment to enliven Sunday afternoons opened in Oxford: the grand ice-
skating rink in the Botley Road. Farve and his younger brother, Uncle
Jack, were keen on the Austrian instructresses, known as the Ice Maidens, and they were part of the attraction.

Muv and Farve were already proficient skaters; waltzing and elemen-
tary figure skating came easily to them, as they did to me. The afternoons on the ice were sheer joy. I had learnt to skate on a family holiday
in Pontresina in 1930. We went over to the Suvretta House Hotel in
St Moritz and I found an unlikely partner in the middle-aged Conservative statesman Sir Samuel Hoare. We skated together and even gave a
little show one afternoon. Back at the Oxford rink, I improved quickly
and 'they' (I suppose the 1930s versions of talent spotters) asked Muv if
I could be trained for the national junior team. She refused, realizing no
doubt that it would be a full-time job. I did not know of this till much
later and was sorry not to have had the chance of excelling at something
at last.

Our groom Hooper was my best friend during the Swinbrook years
and for a long time afterwards. He had worked for Grandfather Redesdale at Batsford before the war and came back to the family immediately
after the Armistice. Farve was aware that he suffered from shellshock
after his terrible experiences in the trenches, and that his temper could
explode without warning. When Unity's lack of interest in her horse irritated Hooper or when she made some clumsy gesture that frightened
it, he would shout, 'I'll take yer in that wood and do for yer!' But he never
did. In spite of these outbursts, Muv and Farve trusted him. Ponies and
hunting were my passions and it was thanks to Hooper that I was able to
enjoy them. As soon as I could escape from lessons I was in the stables
watching and learning the daily routine. Hooper was the first of several
professionals, whose lives were devoted to country and sport, with whom
I felt entirely at home and whose companionship I valued.

One of Hooper's jobs was to drive our horse-drawn float laden with
egg boxes twice a week from my mother's chicken farm to the station at
Shipton-under-Wychwood to catch the London train. I went with him

and was sometimes allowed to drive. The eggs were packed in wooden boxes that held several trays lined with woolly brown felt, which was all very well until an egg broke. The boxes were padlocked and were treated with respect by the porters, who would have the empties ready for us to take home on the return journey. They had huge labels attached, one addressed to 'Lady Jean Bertie' and the other to 'The Marlborough Club'. I never met Lady Jean Bertie and, of course, never went to the Marlborough Club, but those names are engraved on my memory.

One of these journeys took place on 11 November 1927, nine years after the end of the First World War when memories of that terrible conflict were still vivid. Everyone observed the two-minute silence on Armistice Day. Hooper took out his watch and exactly at 11 a.m. brought the cart to a halt, removed his cap and got down to hold the horse's head. No sooner had he done so than the old mare swayed and fell dead. I suppose she had a heart attack. She had been brought out of the Army at the end of the war, having seen service in France. Her death during the silence made a terrific impression on all us children and Hooper wept for her.

Sunday afternoons meant skating and Saturdays meant hunting. Nothing in this world can touch the latter for excitement: the huntsman's horn, the shiver of the horse that presages something thrilling, the whimper of the first hound to find a fox and the crashing noise when the whole pack joins in – it has been described *ad infinitum*, but nothing comes up to the real thing. My father refused to pay more than £35 for a pony but I was lucky to get one of the best for that. Doughnut was everything to me. We had no horse box so I rode to meets, anything up to eight miles away. Coming home on the Stow–Burford road in horizontal sleet (there was nowhere to shelter) I was sometimes joined by Tony Hardcastle, son of the man who had bought Asthall from my father. When the weather was at its worst and we were soaked through and freezing, he would say that he would come back and haunt the road when he was dead. Driving to Swinbrook now, I look for him as we pass the Merrymouth Inn, but he eludes me.

I was always in love with one or other of the followers of the Heythrop. When I was nine Dermot Daley, who wore a swallow-tailed pink coat out hunting, was the particular attraction and I came home full of tales about him. Nancy tortured me by saying that she had heard that he was head over heels in love with M., a dreary girl who lived near Swin-brook. Nancy was too clever for words and knew exactly how to pick on what I would mind most.

It was at about this time that Nancy fell in love for the first time. Her affair with Hamish St Clair Erskine was never going to lead to marriage but it simmered on – half-heartedly on his side, wholeheartedly on hers – for several years. My parents could not bear him, especially Farve who realized that he was homosexual. Hamish was also a Roman Catholic, had no proper job and was soon banned from the house. Nancy's friends included many who were decidedly effeminate and they were usually disliked by Farve. Among them was Mark Ogilvie Grant. Teetering down to breakfast one morning at the dreaded hour of 8 a.m., he was greeted by my father who made a grand gesture of taking the lid off a sizzling dish, 'Brains for breakfast, Mark, PIG'S THINKERS.' (Familiarity eventually made Farve quite fond of Mark.)

There were several other young men, however, whom Farve could not help liking in spite of his prejudice, and he excused their lack of interest in field sports with, 'Well, I suppose he is a *literary cove*.' Peter Watson, a gentle, innocuous fellow, was one of these. The only telephone at Swinbrook was in Farve's business room and it was his property, not to be used lightly for a chat with a friend and certainly not without Farve's formal consent. If he thought a daughter was taking too long over some arrangement, he cut her short with, 'Put the telephone down, you're paralysing the line.' Peter Watson rang up one day and asked to speak to Nancy. Farve answered the telephone and, without moving the mouthpiece, shouted into the hall, 'Nancy, that hog Watson wants to speak to you.' Poor Peter was Hog from then on.

On another occasion Nancy's friend Mary Milnes-Gaskell came to lunch with her nails painted a dashing blood-red (the first time I had seen newly fashionable nail varnish). My father looked at her. 'I am so sorry,' he said, deadly serious. 'Why?' she asked. 'I am so sorry to see you have been in a bus accident.' As I got older and we moved to smaller houses, I was quite pleased that we did not have room for guests because you never knew what my father would say to make them feel uncomfortable.

By the time she was sixteen Diana longed to be grown up and leave home. She was sent to learn French in Paris where she met the painter

Paul César Helleu, a friend of Grandfather Bowles, who had made several portraits of my mother and became an immediate admirer of Diana, the first of many to sit at her feet. Two years later, in 1929, Diana married Bryan Guinness, heir to a brewing fortune, who was training to be a barrister and whom she had met when she was a debutante. Muv was against the marriage to begin with: she thought Bryan too rich and Diana, at eighteen, too young, but she gave in eventually. Decca and I missed being bridesmaids because we had whooping cough, but after their marriage we often went to stay with them at beautiful Biddesden, their house near Andover, which had been built in the early eighteenth century by General Webb, one of Marlborough's generals. Diana immediately made friends with her neighbours: Robert Byron, a contemporary of Bryan at Oxford, came over from Savernake Forest, Lytton Strachey and Dora Carrington at Ham Spray adored her, as did John Betjeman, Henry and Pansy Lamb, Augustus John's daughter Poppet and her younger sister, Vivian, whom I admired as a rider. All these writers, painters and poets were figures of fascination to Decca and me. One of them, Harold Acton, did something that horrified me. He took a log out into the snow, pretended it was a baby and murdered it. So realistic was his performance that the scene haunted me for years.

The enigmatic Carrington fascinated all who knew her and I too fell under her spell. She gave me some fan-tail pigeons which I treasured. I was interested in botany at the time, with the help of Bentham and Hooker's books on plant classification. One of the volumes described wild flowers in scientific language far beyond my ken, but a thinner one had four line-drawings to a page with every known native variety of flower, tree, grass, fern and sedge in the British Isles. I coloured these in as and when I found them, recording the date and place. Carrington was quite taken with this and I looked on it as a bond between us. She wrote to Lytton saying I had won her by my 'high spirits and charm'. It was certainly mutual and I was sad when, unable to face life after Lytton died, she borrowed a gun from Bryan, ostensibly to hunt rabbits in the garden at Ham Spray, and shot herself. Her death was a terrible loss for Diana who had become very fond of her.

Tom left Eton in 1927 and decided to study music and see something of Europe rather than go to an English university. My parents understood this wish. He was the next best thing to a concert pianist and music meant a great deal to him, and they were keen for him to pursue it. They also thought seeing something of Europe before he started studying for the Bar would be part of his education. He travelled to Italy and Spain, and to Austria, where a series of lucky chances took him to Schloss Bernstein in the Burgenland. The castle had been in Hungary until the end of the First World War when it became part of Austria. It was owned by a Hungarian, János Almásy, who became a friend of Tom and had him to stay for several months as a paying guest.

On his return to England in 1929, Tom settled in London to read for the Bar. His friends included the future politicians Nigel Birch, Jack Donaldson and Viscount Hinchingbrooke, Garrett Moore, who, as Lord Drogheda, became chairman of the Royal Opera House, Robert Byron, the writer, and the film producer John Sutro, as well as Jim Lees-Milne and Basil Dufferin – an urbane and talented collection of contemporaries whom Muv called 'the Fat Fairs', as good a description of them as any (with the exception of Garrett Moore who was neither fat nor fair). They started the Worst Play Club and when the actors saw Tom and his friends sitting in the front row of the stalls, they knew how the young and clever rated their production. Alfred Beit, who was the son of the financier and art collector Sir Otto Beit and who later married our cousin Clementine Mitford, sometimes joined the group. The Club went to Bayreuth and Vienna for opera and concerts (to enjoy, not denigrate) and were amused by Alfred's meanness over small sums of money – 'Will you buy the newspaper? I don't want to break into another sixpence' – as he was far better off than most of them.

In summer 1929 Tom took part in an art hoax at Diana and Bryan's London house in Buckingham Street. Two hundred people were invited to meet the self-taught 'artist', Bruno Hat, who came from somewhere in Germany. Brian Howard, the poet, and the artist John Banting produced a series of works on cork bathmats framed with rope – pictures of extraordinary ugliness, forerunners of the kind of thing we are asked to admire today. Evelyn Waugh wrote an introduction to the catalogue, 'An Approach to Hat', and the party was a great success. Guests inspected the paintings, murmuring their appreciation of the avant-garde. Lytton Strachey bought a picture to please Diana. Bruno Hat was in poor health but managed to make an appearance. Pushed in a wheelchair and muffled in scarves, he wore a black moustache and tinted glasses. After uttering a few words of an unknown dialect in guttural growls he was unmasked as Tom, who stepped out of the chair, threw off his coat, moustache and specs, delighted with the success of the joke. (In 2009 one of Bruno Hat's pictures was sold at auction for £18,000 – I wish we had kept an outhouse full of them.)

One of Tom's friends was the MP and art collector Philip Sassoon, a highly civilized charmer and host, who in August 1930 asked Tom to stay with him at Port Lympne, his house in Kent. Philip provided an unusual entertainment for his guests: seven small aircraft, one piloted by Philip himself, the rest by professional pilots. Tom recorded the outing in a letter to Muv:

> The party consists of Cousin Clementine and Winston, Sir Samuel Hoare & wife, Cousin Venetia [Montagu] and Aircraftsman Shaw [T. E. Lawrence].
>
> I am a little disappointed with Shaw. He looks just like any other private in the air-force, is very short and has in his five years of service become quite hardened. He is not a bit like the Sargent portrait of him in his book. Last night I sat next him at dinner and he had Winston on the other side. Winston admires him enormously. He said at one moment 'If the people make me Prime Minister, I will make you Viceroy of India.' Lawrence politely refused and said he was quite happy in the air-force. When asked what he would do when in five years time he has to leave, he said simply 'Go on the dole I suppose.'
>
> It is curious that he should enjoy such a life, with no responsibilities, after being almost king in Arabia. Some say it is inverted vanity: he would have accepted a kingship, but as he didn't get it, he preferred to bury himself and hide away.
>
> This morning we flew over to see Colonel Guinness at Clymping, about 80 miles away. We had 7 machines and flew in perfect formation over Brighton and other resorts – very low to frighten the crowd. Lawrence was thrilled at flying: he said the air ministry had stopped him flying a year ago. Winston drove his machine a little way. I hadn't realized that he had done a lot of piloting before the war.

We flew in arrow-head formation

<pre>
                         Philip
           Winston   Sam Hoare
      Me   Lawrence
           Venetia   Bryan Thynne
</pre>

(Each with a pilot)

and landed in the field next door to Diana's cottage . . . It took
about an hour getting there, and ¾ hour back, as we didn't return in formation.

It was amusing flying *very* low on the edge of the sea and
jumping the piers at Brighton and Littlehampton – to the astonishment of the people there.

Tom's fellow guests and their aerial expedition sound like something out of a Hollywood production. Few other letters from Tom to my
parents have survived and none about politics, which is a pity as I would
have loved to have known his thoughts.

Pam never lacked admirers and in 1928 became engaged to Oliver
'Togo' Watney, a neighbour at Swinbrook. My father detested Togo's
mother whom he called 'the Witch of Cornbury' (the Watneys' marvellous house near Charlbury). A London wedding was planned. The dining room was filled with presents – in those days the merest acquaintance
sent something – and an oyster-coloured silk trousseau had been ordered. But as the day grew closer it became obvious that Togo would not
go through with it. To Pam's disappointment, he broke off the engagement and the piles of presents had to be packed up and returned. My
mother, who realized that Togo would not have made Pam happy, was
relieved – better to make the break before than after the marriage.

In order to give Pam a complete change of scene, my parents, who
were planning to sail for Canada on one of their gold-prospecting trips,
decided to take her with them. It was long before ocean liners provided
gyms and swimming pools for exercise, and Pam and my parents marched
round and round the deck of the big ship, greeting their fellow passengers. 'I would like to introduce you to my cook,' my father said, indicating Pam. They walked on and in due course bumped into the same
people. 'I would like to introduce you to my housemaid,' and so on,

down the domestic hierarchy each time they met, to the bemusement of their fellow passengers. Pam blossomed at The Shack, the wooden cabin built by my father on land he had staked out. With no domestic help and my parents all to herself for the first time, Pam's innate talents, which were just waiting to be appreciated, came to the fore. On practical matters she always knew best (which was sometimes irritating, especially to Decca and me when we were still of an age to be bossed about).

When they returned, Diana realized that Pam would be at a loose end at Swinbrook and suggested to Bryan that she take charge of the farm at Biddesden. It was a time of agricultural depression and no farms were profitable, but Bryan could afford to run his as a hobby rather than a business. Although she had no formal training, Pam understood intuitively the work involved and did her best to keep expenditure down. She bought replacement stock for the herd of Guernsey dairy cows at local markets. Once in a while she made a bad purchase. We were all treated to her description of how thrilled she had been with a well-bred bargain and her dismay when she got her home and discovered 'the brute was bagless' – her exaggerated voice rising to a scream. It became a family saying for any failure, and, like many family sayings, found its way into one of Nancy's novels, this time *Wigs on the Green*.

Pam lived in a farm cottage at Biddesden and was independent for the first time. Her car was as important to her as her dogs. She dug deep and bought a rare Italian breed called an OM ('For comfort, Stublow, she's a Rolls') and set off to explore Europe with friends. Her memory for food was remarkable. 'In Austria we had a most wonderful first course. It wasn't a soufflé and it wasn't an omelette, in a dish about that high,' she said, indicating two or three inches with her fingers, 'Oh Stublow, it was SO delicious.' While farming at Biddesden she met John Betjeman, one of Diana's legion of friends. He fell for her and wrote a poem, 'The Mitford Girls', which ended, 'Gentle Pamela/Most rural of them all'. Pam thought John comical in the grubby trousers he bought at a WI jumble sale for a shilling but, although fond of him, she had no thoughts of marriage.

5

RUTLAND GATE AND
OLD MILL COTTAGE

When Asthall was sold, Farve bought the lease on a house in London. He considered attending the House of Lords his first duty, and we stayed in London when the House was sitting and during the Season, from May to July. No. 26 Rutland Gate, Knightsbridge, was a big house for a big family. It stood alone, with the graveyard of the Russian Orthodox church on one side and the entrance to No. 4 Rutland Gate Mews, which also belonged to my father, on the other. Opposite was Eresby House, belonging to Lord Ancaster, and from our nursery window I could see the Willoughby girls playing tennis on the two courts in their garden. Our house had nine indoor staff, who came with us from Swinbrook, a ballroom as well as a drawing room and enough bedrooms for all of us (though Decca and I shared). There was a wonderfully unhygienic communication system between each floor. You blew down a mouthpiece with an almighty puff that made the connecting device on another floor fly out with a whistle. With your ear pressed to this dual-purpose mouthpiece, you could hear the caller talking from the floor above or below.

The dining room, the scene of lunches and dinner parties for whichever of us was a debutante at the time, was decorated in the newly fashionable stippled paint finish – one of the rare occasions when my mother followed fashion. The drawing room, which had large, south-facing windows, was one of Muv's great successes. Pale grey and gilded, it was furnished with pieces of Grandfather Redesdale's French furniture that had survived the Batsford sale and these gave it an air of importance. Muv sat bolt upright at her *secrétaire à abattant* (a marvellous, plain and perfectly proportioned bit of furniture made by Charles Saunier) from

8.30 a.m. until she had finished her housekeeping chores and accounts. She was very fond of chocolate and in one of the drawers there were always boxes of Terry's langues de chat and chocolate pastilles in their round boxes.

Muv ordered food over the telephone from 'Wicked Old Harrod' (her name for expensive but reliable Harrods), which was delivered a couple of hours later in a silent, electrically driven van. More often she walked to the Brompton Road where she could find Mac Fisheries on a raised pavement with fish of all colours, shapes and sizes displayed in picturesque fashion on miniature icebergs. Muv was always on the look-out for herrings and used to say, 'It's not the price that makes the dish, the herring is the king of fish,' though I suspect the price did make her rather like herring.

Mrs Munro's was well established in Montpelier Street, near the auction house Bonhams, where rolls of good-taste chintz and trimmings were sold. Owles and Beaumont (Owls and Bowels to us, of course) was a decent draper a few doors from Harrods. Muv always started there because it was 'reasonable' but when she could not find what she wanted, she sighed and went back to 'Wicked Old'. Long after the war was over, my sisters and I used Harrods Bank as a meeting place. Conveniently situated on the ground floor (which is now all marble and make-up), the Bank had green leather chairs and sofas. Our dogs joined the Kensington ladies' Pekes and Poms in the Harrods underground kennels, while we sat above them, chatting and watching the world go by. Sometimes Muv and Aunt Weenie met us there and the real customers stared when we made too much noise. The Bank hosted a carol service every Christmas, where God, Aunt Weenie, Muv and mammon met. I cannot imagine such a performance in Cosmetics now, where supercilious girls sell ultra-packaged face creams.

Tattersalls, the horse auctioneers behind Knightsbridge, was still just going when I was a child. The atmosphere of the place was cleverly evoked by the artist Robert Bevan, whose paintings bring back the clatter of hooves and the horse copers of his time. I wish I had a roomful of Bevans. A pony drew the Express Dairies' milk cart and knew at which houses to stop. It gave Pam's arm a sharp bite one day when she had some sugar for it. When a huge bruise appeared on the night of a dance she tied a satin bow round her arm. Coal and coke were delivered on a long wagon drawn by a Shire horse that wore a canvas nose bag containing oats and chaff – his 'bite'. There was plenty of time for the horse to eat while the men, dressed like Stanley Holloway in *My Fair Lady*, shovelled the fuel down the coal hole. There was a water trough in nearby Knightsbridge so all the Shire's needs were catered for.

The basement of Rutland Gate was the domain of the odd man, Mr Dyer, guardian of the boiler, who received and stacked the fuel to his (and Farve's) satisfaction. Mr Dyer slept by his boiler. I never saw him upstairs nor heard him complain of his subterranean existence. The basement was connected by a door to the garage in the Mews, which was for the cars and chauffeurs that had succeeded carriages, coachmen and grooms. Tom referred to it simply as 'the garage', as though that was all it was, but it had in fact several small, low rooms on the upper floor. My mother made the most of things, as she always did, and the little rooms were transformed by her colours, curtains and covers. The main house was often let during the Season, when many country dwellers took a London house and paid an attractive rent, and we would retreat to the Mews. Coming home from parties we had to pick our way in long evening dresses between the cars and pools of oil to reach the narrow stairs.

Decca was fascinated by the white slave trade which she had read about in some book. She saw white slavers everywhere and so, of course, did I – half-thrilled and half-repelled at the idea. She was certain that a perfectly innocent fellow living in Rutland Gate was a slaver. 'Why?' asked Muv. 'Well, when Debo and I are taking the dogs out in the morning he looks at us and says "Good morning". He's just waiting his chance to bundle us into a taxi and we'll wake up in South America.' The 'slaver', who carried a rolled umbrella and doffed his black homburg to us on his way to work, turned out to be Anthony Sewell, who later married a daughter of the architect Edwin Lutyens. He was a friend of Nancy, who no doubt told him what Decca thought.

The financial crash of 1929 changed our lives drastically. Farve was badly hit and was lucky to find tenants for his houses during those disastrous years. Swinbrook was let to Sir Charles Hambro and Rutland Gate to Mrs Warren Pearl, an American who annoyed my mother by painting everything, including the floors, green. We retreated to the Mews and to Old Mill Cottage in High Wycombe, about thirty miles from London. The cottage had been in the background of our lives ever since I can remember. Grandfather Bowles leased it for my parents and their growing family in 1911 and when he died in 1922 Muv was able to buy it for £1,250. It proved a good investment, a place to go back to whenever money was short, and we came and went according to the state of Farve's finances.

A small, cheerful, rambling house, it was made up of two cottages, joined at right angles around an open yard; the third side was formed by Marsh Green Mill, which was let to Mr Mason, the miller. With its stables, outhouses and big mill pond, it formed a busy, harmonious whole. Our dining room looked out on to the yard where the lorries arrived with sacks of wheat and left with bags of flour. When we overstepped the mark at lunch – and we often did – Muv tried to change the subject by pretending to see the miller out of the window and saying in a languid voice, 'Mr Mason, there you are!' It never worked, but became part of our language.

In the dining room, once a kitchen, Decca and I found a new place for the Hons' meetings: the old brick bread-oven. The cottage had no walk-in linen cupboard like the one at Swinbrook, only useless shelves, so this oven hiding-place was ideal. There Decca and I and the third Hon, Margo Durman, my friend who lived across the road, sat in the dark, giggling and pondering our futures, totally happy away from the grown-ups. No one stopped Margo and me from playing in the loft or on the ladder-like stairs of the mill, whose banisters were as smooth as satin from the thin layer of flour that lay on every surface. No one bothered about the unprotected machinery whirring away and the hundred-weight sacks ready to fall on us.

The mill pond was a world of frogs, dragonflies and myriad other summer insects. Across the road were beds of watercress, dark green and deliciously peppery, which grew on gravel in crystal-clear water that flowed from an artesian well. My mother gave the mill pond to the town of High Wycombe. It was what is now described as a 'feature' and she thought the town would like to have it as an adjunct to the Rye, a big open space that had been bequeathed by the Carrington family. She would be dismayed to know that the City Fathers of High Wycombe have thought fit to fill it in.

A large garden, with an orchard and fields beyond, completed the property. The famous Chiltern beeches covered the protecting hill, which was laced with public footpaths and bridleways. It was so different from

Swinbrook, where the woods belonged to my father and we never met a soul. Here we often saw what we thought were sinister-looking men walking alone; we called them 'singletons', fully expecting to be murdered by them. A little way along the road was a sewage farm and a sawmill. We imagined that the loud sigh from the saws as they cut up the tree trunks came from the sewage farm – though how those light-weight rotating arms dripping water could have made such a giant sigh, we did not know.

Farve escaped his children and their animals by turning the garden shed into his study. Decca said that it was where his 'old eyes would close for ever', so it became the Closing Room. He thought it perfect – quiet, isolated and full of the ugly furniture that my mother had banned from her domain. The ponies came with us to High Wycombe and my father bought Hooper a house for £480 on a new housing estate just above our field. Hooper used to knock on the window of the Closing Room, push his 'book' under my father's nose, saying, 'Is your Lordship vacant?' My father settled the carefully itemized accounts – linseed hoof oil and the like. Soon after tea he would disappear into the only bathroom, which was in our part of the house, change into his Great Agrippa dressing gown and set off to the Closing Room to luxuriate with the weather forecast and the six o'clock news. At this hallowed moment of the day no one dared disturb him.

Farve had taught himself to crack a stock whip after seeing the American Rodeo at Wembley in 1924 and he practised his skill on the lawn at High Wycombe. The whip had a short, stout stock and a long, plaited cowhide thong which required great strength in the wrist to get it going. Farve stood winding it round and round above his head until it had gathered enough momentum and flew out at full length, making an almighty crack like a rifle shot. To be accurate took skill – it was like fly fishing with a very heavy line. Farve could slice a chosen twig off an apple tree from a distance and told us that experts could knock a cigarette out of the mouth of a brave volunteer.

Our governess at the time was Miss Pratt. She was not interested in education but loved playing cards, especially Racing Demon. We played from 9 a.m. till 11 a.m., had half an hour's break, then more Demon until lunchtime. We became expert at this testing game, which depends on speedy co-operation of hand and eye. My mother discovered what we were doing and Miss Pratt left. There was no time to engage another governess, so Decca and I (aged eleven and nine) were packed off to a day school in Beaconsfield. Every morning at assembly we sang the same hymn: 'For Those in Peril on the Sea'. I asked why. Answer: 'The Head's brother is in the Navy.' I could not imagine why it was so perilous to be in the Navy in peacetime.

Decca liked the school. She was clever and appealing; I was dense and cross, and hated every moment of the crowded world of lessons. I did not understand what the teachers wanted or why. It was made worse by the horrible lunch, to which we said 'No thank you'. My mother was informed and was sympathetic. She persuaded my father to see the headmistress and tell her that we would bring a banana instead. We could rely on Farve when it came to the crunch, and that lunch *was* the crunch. I wish I had been a fly on the wall at the interview between those two people who were both accustomed to getting their own way. My father won and it was bananas from then on.

Decca had acute appendicitis while we were at the Old Mill Cottage and the operation was performed on the nursery table. I was jealous of all the attention paid her and when the stitches came out, she put them up for sale and I bought one for sixpence. (In her memoirs, *Hons and Rebels*, she says she sold her appendix to me for £1, which was impossible as I did not have £1.) Another difficult time was when Muv, aged fifty-seven and not used to being unwell, got measles. She was dangerously ill but the only evidence was a sheet dipped in disinfectant every few hours and hung over her bedroom door. In spite of these precautions, I caught the disease (the only one in the house who did) and although not as ill as my mother, I remember having to spend Christmas in bed.

BACK TO SWINBROOK

By April 1931, Farve's finances had improved enough for us to return to Swinbrook. For me this meant freedom to go riding again without meeting anyone, to fish on the Windrush and follow Farve on his rounds of the woods and farms. In the schoolroom, Decca and I had Miss Hussey, another product of the PNEU system and by far the best teacher we ever had. Each term we had to learn a hymn, a psalm and a poem, and at the end of term we recited our choices to Muv – and anyone else who would listen. It was normally easy to bamboozle a new governess; we simply turned the pages of the relevant book till we came up with the pieces we had learned the previous term (the hymn book fell open readily at 'Now the Day Is Over') and off we went. My mother never noticed the repetition but when Miss Hussey arrived there was no fooling her and, to our annoyance, she made us learn new pieces. My poem was 'The Lament of the Irish Emigrant' by Selina Dufferin. The first lines, 'I'm sittin' on the stile, Mary/Where we sat side by side/On a bright May mornin' long ago/When first you were my bride', made me cry, but I learnt to look on it as a game and was able to go on – just. Decca chose Edgar Allan Poe's 'Annabel Lee', which she spouted at a tremendous rate, running all the words into one. There were so-called exams at the end of the summer term but I often managed to have flu at the appointed time. Luckily Muv was not interested in exams.

In 1932 our ordered life received a shock when after four years of marriage Diana left Bryan for Sir Oswald Mosley. Sir O had been a political figure since the age of twenty-one, first as a Conservative and then as a Labour MP. He had resigned in 1930 because of his disillusionment with Ramsay MacDonald's failure to deal with unemployment. Supremely confident that he himself had the answers to Britain's economic problems, he was about to launch the British Union of Fascists when he and Diana met.

Muv and Farve did not talk about Diana in front of us younger children; it was not the way then – any disagreeable subject was discussed privately. I was conscious of some pall of sorrow and anger affecting my parents, but was barely aware of the reason. Sir O was married with three young children and had no intention of leaving his wife. My parents were dismayed when Diana openly became his mistress and were shocked that Bryan was named the guilty party in her divorce. Bryan went through the motions of spending a night with a prostitute in a Brighton hotel, which in those days was how many divorces were arranged, but Muv and Farve considered it dishonest. Bryan was miserable about the separation – nothing could have been further from his wishes – but Diana was a forceful character and had decided on her future. My parents continued to see her and her two Guinness sons, Jonathan and Desmond, and she often came to Swinbrook, spending Christmas with us there in 1934. But Decca and I were not allowed to visit her at her house in Eaton Square because she was 'living in sin' (now so ordinary – you 'take a partner' as though going into business). It never occurred to us to question Muv and Farve's wishes and it is why I did not get to know Diana until after the war.

In April 1932 Tom qualified as a barrister and was called to the Bar. He began the slow process of getting briefs and making a name for himself in the chambers of Norman Birkett KC. He had many girlfriends. The first, Penelope (Pempie) Dudley Ward, was the prettiest, most lively and charming girl imaginable. They were both too young to think of marriage but remained friends until Tom's death. He moved on to more sophisticated women, most of whom were married and did not threaten his independence. They never came to Swinbrook, for obvious reasons, and Tom was discreet about his private life. Diana knew of his various friendships but she was not one to betray confidences.

Nancy was leading her unsettled life, staying away with willing hosts but still dependent on my parents for a home. She began writing, at first short articles on London Society for *The Lady*, which had been handed on by Grandfather Bowles to Uncle George. Her usual fee was £2 and sometimes £3, which caused much rejoicing. Articles for *Vogue* and *Harper's Bazaar* followed but they did not provide a regular income. Things were made more difficult by Farve's passionate dislike of any reference to us in the papers, so Nancy had to hide these whenever she had anything published. In 1931 her first novel, *Highland Fling*, a comedy set in a Scottish houseparty, was well received by the reading public and brought in a little more money. Decca and I were excited to see the finished book and thought the portrait of Farve as General Murgatroyd highly comical. There was a pile of the book at W. H. Smith in High Wycombe with a big notice announcing 'Local Authoress', which we also thought funny.

Nancy's rocky affair with Hamish Erskine dragged on, but after four years he grew tired of what was for him a charade and he broke it off by telling Nancy he was engaged to someone else. Nancy may have half expected it, but it was nevertheless a cruel blow. Diana understood her miserable existence and gave her a room at Eaton Square. Almost at once Nancy met Peter Rodd. It was a classic case of the rebound, but she believed herself to be truly in love. I wrote in my diary on 14 July 1933 that Nancy had sent me the most extraordinary letter, and that I could hardly believe it. In it she said that she was 'perhaps' going to be married to 'a very choice' person and wanted me to be the first to know. 'I love him a most terrific lot,' she wrote. 'If we can get some money we shall marry, and if we can't we shan't and that's why it's an important secret because if we don't it's a bore if everyone knows.' I am afraid I told Miss Hussey and Decca, but swore them to secrecy so that when Nancy announced the news they would pretend they knew nothing.

I liked Peter. He talked to me as he would to a grown-up, which was unusual – at thirteen you were still considered very much a child. The wedding was an excitement for Decca and me, particularly after missing Diana's. I thought carefully about what to wear and decided on a midnight-blue velvet dress. The stuff, as always, came from John Lewis, and Gladys, my mother's retired maid who ran up our clothes, did her best. The dress was to have a fur collar made from an unknown creature with jaws that snapped on to its tail to fasten it. It had been given to me by an aunt and I thought it most glamorous. I proudly showed it to Nancy a few days before the wedding. 'Oh,' she said, 'I see you've got a mouse's skin at last.' Down went self-esteem once more and furs were 'mouse's skins' thereafter.

Nancy and Peter went to live at Rose Cottage, Strand-on-the-Green, near Chiswick. It seemed an idyllic start but it was not long before the marriage began to falter. Nancy did her best to keep up appearances but Prod, as she called Peter, was no good at marriage – he lived from hand to mouth, never held down a job and disappeared for long periods. After the outbreak of war things got worse. He started bringing drunken pick-ups back from the pub who were prone to steal any money left around. Nancy was miserable.

After leaving St Margaret's, Unity briefly attended Queen's College in London. She enjoyed it but, once again, was asked to leave. Years later I met one of her school friends and asked why. 'Because she plucked her eyebrows,' was the reply. It is more likely that Unity's huge personality was too much for the staff. She 'came out' in 1932 and Decca described her in this her first year of grown-up life as 'a rather alarming debutante'. The round of dances took place and Unity went as was expected. Legend has it that she sometimes took her rat, but legends cannot be relied upon.

Her great new friend was Mary Ormsby Gore and they used to meet under the clock at Selfridges to go to the cinema. Unity was always punctual, Mary always late. Unity said she got flat feet from waiting but that it was worth it. She adored the cinema and often went to the Empire in Leicester Square as soon as it opened in the morning, and sometimes stayed to watch the whole programme through two or three times. She invited friends to spend the weekend at Swinbrook who were called the 'Saturday afternooners' by my mother, because by that time Unity was bored with them and poor Muv had to entertain them as best she could for the rest of their stay. One or two remained friends, among them the writer Micky Burn, a stalwart defender of the alarming debutante.

Unity first went to Germany in 1933 with Diana, who had been invited by Hitler's press chief, Putzi Hanfstaengl (whom she had met through Beatrice Guinness, who was married to a distant relation of Bryan's), with the promise that he would introduce her to the newly appointed Chancellor. Both Diana and Unity were enthralled by the wave of enthusiasm that was gripping Germany, but for Unity National Socialism came as a call. In adolescence her difficult character had been waiting for just such an outlet and now that she had found one, she threw herself into it with religious fervour. She saw in Hitler the saviour of a country that had been humiliated by defeat, whose economy was in ruins and whose people were demoralized. Germany took up her whole being. With her blonde hair and blue eyes, Unity even embodied the Nazi ideal of womanhood and her classic face, till now always serious in photographs, was suddenly lit from within. Having discovered that Hitler often lunched or dined at the Osteria Bavaria, a small restaurant in Munich, she went there day after day in the hopes of seeing him. (She would be arrested as a stalker today.) In February 1935, Hitler eventually noticed her and sent someone across the room to invite her to his table. It sealed her fate.

Unity's life has been gone over by journalists and biographers, but they often miss the fact that she was not the only English girl to fall for National Socialism. Her uncompromising nature took her to further extremes than most but there were many other girls who, like her, were sent to Germany as part of their education and were swept up by the movement. Away from home for the first time and hungry for new experiences, they were almost without exception fascinated by what they saw and thrilled by the excitement that surrounded Hitler. At their impressionable age, the music and glamour were infectious. Among these girls was our cousin Clementine Mitford who struck up a close friendship with an SS officer (an episode in her life that was conveniently forgotten after her marriage to Alfred Beit).

Decca left home when she was sixteen to learn French in Paris with her best friend and cousin, Ann Farrer. I imagine Muv and Farve debated as to what to do with me now that I was the only one left in the schoolroom. Money was becoming a worry once again and it was less expensive for me to go as a weekly boarder to a school in Oxford than to have a governess. One of my great friends, Lilah McCalmont, was already at the school, which would have made everything easier. Unluckily she was ill at the start of the autumn term, so off I went alone. The school was in the Banbury Road where it occupied two gaunt Victorian houses – a couple of rabbit warrens with no escape. It was crowded with pupils who greeted each other in an exaggerated fashion, like a Joyce Grenfell reunion, ignoring the new girl who had no idea of what to do or where to go. At the age of fourteen, I felt at home with animals but was nervous of people, and this building crammed with strangers was the worst kind of misery.

The house smelt strongly of lino, girls and fish. The smell flowed up the stairs and lodged under the ceiling of the attic room that I shared with Lilah's empty bed. I was miserable – no dog, no pony, no Nanny. Supper the first night was cod, encased in a thick blanket of black skin – horrible to look at and revolting to taste. The second night it was hot blackberries. Even now, over three-quarters of a century later, I can still smell those hateful suppers. I arrived at the school on a Wednesday and went home for the weekend on Friday. By that time I had fainted in geometry, failed to understand the point of netball and been sick several times. Muv kept me at home for a few days and I begged her not to send me back to that hell-hole. We came to a compromise: I would go back for the rest of the term (it was already paid for and it was too late to make other arrangements) but as a day girl.

So it was me instead of the eggs that arrived at Shipton Station every morning for the stopping train to Oxford, and came back at teatime – both journeys in the dark. I have never ceased to be thankful to Muv for allowing it. My aunts and most of her friends said it would be the ruin of me, 'So *spoilt*, that girl will be impossible.' But Muv stuck to the plan and I survived. At the end of that awful term, she understood that another experiment at another school would end in more tears, so Miss Frost, a nice, steady governess, came to teach me. Celia Hay, the daughter of friends of Muv, joined me and we did lessons together.

In 1935 Farve's money worries came to a head. Swinbrook House and its estate were extravagances he could not afford, and in April the house was let to Duncan and Pamela Mackinnon. Three years later it was sold to them, together with all the land. I minded more than I can say. I have seen it happen elsewhere: when children are uprooted from the place they love just when they are at their most vulnerable, when all their antennae are out and they have become almost physically attached to a house and its surroundings, the loss of all that is familiar is a kind of amputation. As one who becomes hopelessly addicted to sticks and stones, gateways with their ruts and puddles, anthills, thrushes, freshwater springs, kingcups, dog roses and may (soon to be hips and haws), wood anemones under oaks, silent woods in August, milk-white walnuts in autumn, the smell of new creosote on chicken houses, saddle soap and horse manure – having to abandon all these made leaving Swin-brook, 'the land of lost content', hard to bear.

The prospect of the upheaval no doubt occupied my parents for months beforehand. This time there could be no compromise: it was hard cash – or the lack of it – which decided the sale. Unhappy myself, it never occurred to me how much Farve must have minded the finality of losing the last link with his father's Oxfordshire legacy. Unity under-stood and wrote to him in May 1935, 'Poor old Forge, I AM sorry you have had to leave Swinbrook . . . I'm sorry for myself too because al-though I didn't like living there, it was lovely to come back to. But I do think it's dreadful for you.'

After leaving Swinbrook, we moved between London and High Wycombe. I went to the Monkey Club, a 'finishing school' off Sloane Street, for a few months. It was not a domestic-science kind of place: we attended lectures on politics, history, art and the other subjects thought necessary to be tucked away in our bird brains for future refer-ence. I met Georgina (Gina) Wernher, who became a friend for life through shared interests, including a passion for hunting; and the beautiful Aye-sha of Cooch Behar, who later married the Maharaja of Jaipur and pur-sued a political career in her own country, surviving a spell in prison in the 1970s. I planned to marry all the Maharajas in India and, failing that, the President of Turkey with the irresistible name of Mustafa Kemal Atatürk.

Lessons over at last, I lived for pleasure. I refused to go to Paris to learn French, horrified at the idea of missing a season's hunting, and never did learn the language. The only time I minded this uncivilized gap was when I was invited to a grand dinner in Paris years later and sat next to Georges Pompidou. He could not (or would not) speak English. We smiled at each other and crumbled bread for what seemed an end-less evening. Our host, Nancy's friend Gaston Palewski, sat opposite and was highly amused – I think he may have done it as a joke.

I spent the winter of 1936–7 with Aunt Weenie and Uncle Percy Bailey in their tiny cottage at Maugersbury by Stow-on-the-Wold, and hunted twice a week with the Heythrop. Hooper and my horse lodged in Stow. He rode down in the morning, stopped outside my bedroom window – which was the same height as he was on the horse – and we discussed plans, where the hounds were meeting and whether it was within the eight-mile limit we had set ourselves for me to ride to a meet. The health of my horse was paramount: I had only the one and all depended on her. It was out hunting that I first met Derek Jackson and became fascinated by this strange being who rode unruly thorough-breds with short leathers, like the jockey he aspired to be. The older, steadier followers of the hounds were deeply suspicious of him. Derek owned some steeplechasers, trained by Bay Powell, which he often rode himself and I persuaded Pam to take me to Windsor races where I knew Derek would be riding. They fell in love and were married in December 1936. I was mortified, having decided that in a few years I would marry Derek myself.

While Pam and Derek were on honeymoon his identical twin, Vivian, was killed in a sleigh accident in St Moritz. Derek never recovered from this tragedy. Not only did the brothers look alike and talk alike, they both loved riding, had a total disregard of what others thought of them and followed the same scientific speciality – spectroscopy. I only once saw them together. 'I agree with Derek,' 'I agree with Vivian,' I heard them repeat, with a quack and a grunt for emphasis, in hoarse and breath-less voices that seemed to emerge – all passages to the nose closed – from deeper throats than anyone else's.

Pam's marriage brought happiness to begin with, though being mar-ried to Derek was never an easy proposition. He was vital, generous, cou-rageous, bisexual, unfaithful, unpredictable, rich – and therefore able to indulge every whim – and he was also rude and loved to shock. He must have been an embarrassing companion at times and Pam was witness to many scenes. They were at Paddington Station one day to catch a train to Oxford and found all the doors into the first-class carriages locked – the kind of incompetence that drove Derek into a rage. They had to walk along the platform and through a third-class carriage to find their seats. Derek waited till the train had got up steam then pulled the com-munication cord. The brakes went on and the express train ground to a halt. The guard entered their carriage but before he had time to speak, Derek held up his right hand, his pale suede glove blackened by the dirty chain. He told the guard that it was a disgrace to the GWR and that the glove must be taken and cleaned immediately. On another oc-casion he was riding in a race at Sandown Park and, not unusually for him, committed an infringement of some rule. He was had up before the stewards who fined him £20. Derek handed the chief steward a £100 note and told him to keep the change.

Derek worked at the Clarendon Laboratory in Oxford under Professor Lindemann and lectured at Oxford University. He and Pam lived at Rignell, an undistinguished twentieth-century house built of the almost orange stone that is quarried on the borders of Oxfordshire and Warwickshire. The furniture came from Heal's and Derek's fine collection of Impressionist paintings decorated the walls. Pam added her own touches and persuaded him to buy a hauntingly romantic picture by Corot of a pool in a wood, the shimmering green of the trees reflecting mysteriously in the water. She also reigned in the garden and on the farm. Her naturally calm nature could alter in a flash if anyone was thoughtless with the animals. In the great frost of 1940, when the farmhands had been called up, a couple of lads were left in charge of the cattle and horses. Pam found the tank that supplied water to the heifers frozen solid. 'Oh,' shrugged the boy looking after the cattle, 'they're all right, they'll lick the ice.' 'How do *you* know?' Pam exploded, '*you've* never been an in-calf heifer.'

I will never be sure whether Pam's professed dislike of children sprang from her unhappiness at being childless. We never spoke of it, but it was obvious that Derek did not want children. When she became pregnant, he took her to the north of Norway and drove for miles over bumpy roads with the inevitable result of a miscarriage. Her dogs, which Derek also adored, took the place of children. Trudy, the first of her long-haired dachshunds, was a special favourite and Pam's highest praise for anything, human or animal, was, 'just like the little dog herself'.

In April 1936 Muv took Unity, Decca and me on a Hellenic cruise aboard the SS *Letitia*. The purpose was Education. An impressive list of lecturers was advertised, including Sir Mortimer Wheeler, director of the London Museum at the time, and all was set for an uplifting fortnight round Greece with stops in Turkey and Asia Minor. We thought a cruise was for fun and romance and we treated it accordingly. On the first night Muv called us to her cabin. 'Now, children,' she said, 'we must all stick together.' What a hope. Decca fastened on to an unsuspecting fellow called Lord Rathcreedan, half-hero, half-butt. I expect he was suitably embarrassed by her attentions but equally intrigued. Unity discovered a political adversary in the Duchess of Atholl, a small dark woman known as the Red Duchess because of her support for the Spanish Republicans. She looked as if she had never enjoyed herself or laughed in her life. Towards the end of the fortnight, for the entertainment of the passengers, she and Unity had a political set-to on the platform used by the lecturers.

There was one man we took against. He had a beard, wavy fair hair and wore a hairnet on trips ashore. 'He looks like a chicken,' Decca said, and so the Chicken Man he was.

> *Heaven, I'm in heaven*
> *And my heart beats so that I can hardly speak*
> *And I seem to find the happiness I seek*
> *When I'm out with the Chicken Man*
> *Dancing beak to cheek*

Decca sang, looking straight at him, getting as close as she dared. We named one of the distinguished academics who we wished were not on board 'the Lecherous Lecturer', for no reason other than we liked the alliteration. (In *Love in a Cold Climate* Nancy turned him into Boy Dougdale, who did have a taste for young girls.) We were always playing with words. 'In a way', was 'in an Appian way' to me and Decca. It did not mean anything, it just seemed to suit.

I found a handsome man on board called Adrian Stokes, 'incredibly old, over thirty', I wrote in my diary. He looked like a blond eagle and I fell for him. He was a painter, art critic and ballet-lover, and when I got back to London he took me to Covent Garden to see the Ballets Russes. We saw Léonide Massine and the three 'baby ballerinas', Tamara Toumanova, Irina Baronova and Tatiana Riabouchinska, and Alexandra Danilova in *Symphonie Fantastique*, *Shéhérazade* and *L'Après-midi d'un Faune* and, my favourite of all, *La Boutique Fantasque*. At sixteen, I was not allowed to go out alone with a man so Nanny Blor came as chaperone. Goodness knows what Adrian (or Nanny) made of this, but it was the rule, take it or leave it, and luckily for me Adrian took it. Fixed in my memory is the 10 p.m. delivery of letters at Rutland Gate. I was always hoping for one from Adrian and used to sit in the hall ten minutes before the post was due. When, absolutely to time, a loving letter fell on the mat, squashed between Hansard and various circulars addressed to my parents, it was unbelievably exciting.

One of the *Letitia's* last ports of call was Constantinople, to see the Blue Mosque and other necessities. The highlight was a visit to Topkapi Palace where two pathetic eunuchs were on show to the tourists. The idea was to get them to talk in their squeaky voices. When we got back to the ship, Muv summoned us to her cabin. 'Now, children,' she said very slowly, 'you are NOT to mention those eunuchs at dinner.' We dined every night at the Purser's table and the poor fellow must have had enough of us.

My father had taught me to drive a car when I was nine. We went into the big, flat field at Swinbrook called the Prairie and I was put through the paces of gears, accelerator, brake and clutch. The movement called 'double declutching' was easily mastered when there was no traffic and only endless grass to drive over. My father was extraordinarily patient (he was not, however, entrusted with teaching my mother to drive – one of my sisters had to do that) and the result of his tutorials was that I passed my test on my seventeenth birthday. The examiner seemed to be on my side. We drove down a lane and he asked, 'What does that sign mean?' 'Sorry,' I said, 'I don't know.' 'Do you think it's a humpback bridge?' 'Oh, *yes*,' I said, 'a humpback bridge,' which indeed it was. I have a feeling examiners would not be so helpful now.

High on the list of places I loved going to was Cliveden, Waldorf and Nancy Astor's palace overlooking the River Thames. The house was a social whirl of important entertaining, as well as a family home for the Astors' five children. The visitors' book read like a *Who's Who* of the period: writer and playwright George Bernard Shaw made the first of many visits in 1926, Winston Churchill was an occasional guest, as were King George and Queen Mary, Charlie Chaplin, Joseph Kennedy and the aviator Amy Johnson. The younger sons of the house, Michael and Jakie, were two of the funniest, most attractive fellows I knew. I whizzed over from High Wycombe in the new freedom of my third-hand Austin Seven, a ramshackle object that looked a bit odd parked next to the Royces in the forecourt at Cliveden. But it got me there and that is surely the point of a car. The huge house, the very height of luxury, was arranged for the comfort and pleasure of its guests: flowers such as I had

never seen – young apples trees covered in blossom, and jardinières full
of pelargoniums arranged in blocks of colour; a vast red velvet sofa in
front of the hall fire, big enough for several people to sleep in; the white-
and gold-panelled dining room, imported lock, stock and barrel from
Madame de Pompadour's dining room at the Château d'Asnières. Adding to the continual excitement was the uncertainty of who I might sit
next to and what on earth I would talk to them about. Mr Lee was the
king of butlers and the superb food was handed round at speed. At a
crowded Sunday lunch, Lord Astor's valet, Mr Bushell, helped at table.
He was unable to resist a grumble and when handing the soufflé to
Jakie, I heard him say in a loud whisper, 'Life's a bugger, Mr Jakie.'

Nancy Astor was the star. Small, upright and sharp as a needle, she
was a born entertainer – often at someone else's expense. She would fix
her ice-blue eyes on her victim and stop them dead in their tracks. A
dreary educationalist from the Midwest was droning on and on until
she cut him off with, 'That's very interestin'' – a Virginian, she dropped
her g's – 'but I'm not interested.' When her husband inherited the title
of second Viscount Astor and moved to the House of Lords, Nancy decided to fight his vacant constituency and in 1919 became the first
woman to take her seat in the House of Commons. She was politically
inexperienced but her effrontery and sharp wit made her an opponent to
be reckoned with. She was heckled one day by another Member. 'Why
don't you think before you speak?' he jeered. 'How do I know what I
think till I've heard what I've said?' came her quick reply.

She was always kind to me, perhaps because she saw me as no threat
to any of her four sons. They had many serious girlfriends to whom she
could be unfriendly, but I was never one of them and I loved her.
Michael and Jakie pricked any pompous bubble coming from the mouths
of the motley crew of politicians, writers, clergy and royal people who
gathered at Cliveden. They both became MPs after the war, if rather
unwilling ones. Michael had a safe seat in Surrey which he treated
in cavalier fashion, disappearing for months at a time. His Chairman
needed him on urgent business one day, but no one knew where he
was. Eventually he turned up and got a ticking-off, to which he retorted,
'You must take me as you find me – if you can find me.' I was lucky to
have been an extra in the theatrical performance that was Cliveden in
those days.

The rules of the game of staying in other people's houses were incomprehensible to those who had not experienced them. They were brought home to me when I spent a glorious winter week with Gina Wernher at Thorpe Lubenham in Leicestershire. Her mother, Lady Zia, was a great-granddaughter of Tsar Nicholas I and her father, Sir Harold Wernher, was Master of the Fernie Hounds. I was lent two superb horses, a revelation of what tip-top hunters could be. To lend a horse is always risky and I was flattered to be trusted with these two beauties. The niceties of behaviour meant that you simply proffered grateful thanks for this generosity, but should you need a stamp (cost 1½d) you must pay for it. You may not use the telephone or send a telegram, unless you had broken your neck or some other disaster (in which case you must pay for the call). You may not leave your car right by the front door, nor should you lock it or take the key as this would be a slur on the honesty of the household. As a female, the downstairs lavatory was strictly out of bounds.

Nearly all my contemporaries smoked, which was not only acceptable, it was usual. I did not as Farve forbade it. Food fads did not exist or were certainly not discussed. The idea of answering a dinner invitation with a note of what you could or could not eat would have been preposterous and did not happen. Punctuality was essential and you must not keep the grown-ups waiting. You must try to talk to your dinner neighbours and not sit hunched, silent and hidden under a canopy of long hair (like the girls of the next generation). The status of an unmarried girl was low but as soon as she married, even if only eighteen, she qualified as a chaperone. All very odd, but that is how it was in 1937.

At Castle Howard there were no grown-ups. The parents of Christian, Mark, George, Christopher and Katie Howard had died by the time I first went there. (My mother told me that their father, Geoffrey Howard, had a glass eye and used to surprise people by tapping it with a fork at meals.) The freedom of being able to say and do what you liked was rare in those days of convention. At Castle Howard the rules were there for breaking and we had riotous fun in that glorious house with no one to tell us to stop. Mark, two years older than me and my great friend in the family, was handsome in spite of a broken nose, clever, and with an infectious enthusiasm that made him popular wherever he went. His rambunctious family was full of wild Stanley blood, and Liberal politics and religion were subjects of fierce argument under Vanbrugh's roof. There were Bonham-Carters and Toynbees galore, intellectuals and politicians in the making, all arguing, with Christian, aged twenty, the eldest of the group, shouting to be heard above the din, and spitting in her hurry to get out her words. She became a Lay Canon and was active in bringing about the ordination of women – no doubt she would have been the first female Archbishop had she lived fifty years later.

Decca did the Season in 1935. She said she had 'rather guiltily' enjoyed it, but it was obvious that she was longing to get away from home and begin a life of her own with people who shared her strengthening left-wing convictions. Perhaps she was jealous of Unity, who by this time had made friends with the German leaders, and her success may have driven Decca further into the opposite camp. Muv saw it all and understood Decca's unhappiness. She cast around for something to engage her attention and decided to take us both on a world cruise. It was an example of her concern for each of us when we most needed it – I am sure she did not want to go for herself but thought it would fill a gap for Decca. To make it even more fun, she suggested that Decca bring a friend, so Virginia Brett, a fellow debutante, was invited to come too.

In January 1937 Decca went to stay for a weekend with a cousin, Dorothy Allhusen, where she met another cousin, eighteen-year-old Esmond Romilly. He had run away from Wellington College and had already seen action fighting for the International Brigade in the Spanish Civil War, and was planning to return. For Decca it was love at first sight; romance and ideals rolled into one. It was the perfect match at the perfect time – except that the world cruise was now nearly upon us. How could she go to Spain with Esmond and escape into her dream? Esmond devised a cunning plan. They forged a letter purporting to come from Mamaine Paget, a debutante friend of Decca, in which they pretended that Decca had been invited on a motoring tour of northern France with Mamaine and her twin sister. This tempting invitation was for two weeks, so Muv would be reassured that she would be back in good time for the cruise. Muv was completely taken in and, even though it was cutting it fine, she wanted Decca to enjoy herself. Perhaps we also looked forward to two weeks without her discontented presence in the house.

On 7 February Muv and Farve saw Decca off at Victoria Station to catch the boat train to Dieppe, where she was to join the Pagets. Or so they thought. After waving goodbye to her, my father never saw her again. The plan was for Decca to meet Esmond on the train, and for them to make their way together to Paris to obtain a Spanish visa for Decca. When they arrived, however, they were told they would have to apply in London. In Dieppe, while waiting for the ferry to take them back to England, they discovered that the fictitious address that Decca had given Muv actually existed. There were letters waiting for them and Decca was able to answer a letter from Muv, sending her news of the imaginary sights she had seen in France.

While she was in London, Decca composed another letter to Muv telling her that she had run away with Esmond and asked Peter Nevile, a friend of Esmond, to deliver it to Rutland Gate when instructed. By this time Esmond had fallen in love with Decca and they decided to head for Spain, visa or no visa, and get married. In mid-February Decca wrote to Muv from Bayonne (hundreds of miles from where she was supposed to be) saying that she was staying with the twins longer than expected, but would be back by 20 February at the latest. Muv had a premonition that all was not as it should be. She rang a Paget aunt in London and learned that the twins were in Austria. Decca had vanished. My parents had no idea where she had been for the last fortnight or how to begin to find her. They were desperate.

Rutland Gate was like a morgue. No gramophone. No one laughed. We talked quietly when we did talk, going over the same old ground again and again. Where had she gone? And why? Was she alive? Someone sat permanently by the telephone. Farve contacted Scotland Yard and the Foreign Office. Decca was a missing person. On 23 February, after what seemed an eternity, Peter Nevile arrived at Rutland Gate with Decca's letter. 'Worse than I thought,' said Farve when he read it. 'Married to Esmond Romilly.' Peter Nevile tried to persuade Farve to give him a story to sell to the newspapers (Decca and Esmond were short of money) but Farve was disgusted by the idea and sent Peter packing.

Muv wrote immediately to Decca at her last known address in Bayonne, begging her to come home. The web of deceit was as much a blow to my parents as her actual disappearance. In the hopes that it might help find her, Farve gave an interview to the *Daily Express* and a full-

Aged three, with my eldest sister, Nancy

My mother and father (Muv and Farve)   With Decca (*right*) at Hastings

By the River Windrush at Asthall

Asthall Manor

Muv and Farve with (*back row*) Nancy, Tom; (*middle row*) Diana, Pamela; (*front row*) Unity, Decca, DD. Asthall, 1926

LEFT: Skating at the Suvretta
House Hotel, St Moritz, 1930

RIGHT: At Swinbrook with
Nanny Blor

BELOW: Driving my donkey,
Tonks, with Cecilia Hay (*left*),
1934

Adrian Stokes, DD, Decca, Muv, Unity. Athens, 1936

DD (*left*) with Myra and Gina Wernher. Thorpe   DD, 1938
Lubenham, 1937

Debutante, 1938

RIGHT: Muv's account book showing the cost of my coming-out party

130 people came to dance

		Band	18. 18.
Relations & married	20	Food	14 1
		Drink	17 17
Men	60	Hire	4 8
Girls	50	Extra helpers	5 15
		Extras	1. 10
Total came	130	£ 62. 2.
Asked			
Relations & married	34	Dinner for 18	
Men	104	Food	4. 0. 0
Girls	64	Champagne &c	3 0 0
Total invited	202	Helpers &c	2 0 0
			9. 0. 0

BELOW: Muv at 26 Rutland Gate, London

RIGHT: At the races with
Andrew, September 1938

BELOW LEFT: With Unity
(*left*) at Mill Cottage,
Swinbrook, 1940

BELOW RIGHT: My brother,
Tom. Munich, 1935

Greeted by Sergeant Major Brittain after our wedding, 19 April 1941

Getting about in a show wagon during petrol rationing. Churchdale Hall, 1943

With Andrew's grandmother, Evelyn Devonshire (*centre*), and Kathleen Hartington (Kennedy) (*right*), 1944

Canvassing with Andrew during the 1945 General Election

At Edensor House, 1948: (*left to right*) DD, Stoker, Evelyn Devonshire, Prince Philip, Andrew, Princess Elizabeth, Eddy Devonshire, Emma, Mary Devonshire. (*By kind permission of Ron Duggins*)

With Sophy and Evelyn Waugh. Edensor House, 1957

Wearing the hat bought in Paris by Evelyn Waugh

Kitty Mersey, 1953

DD, 1950. (*Courtesy of the Cecil Beaton Studio Archive at Sotheby's*)

Nancy (*left*) and Decca at Rue Monsieur, Paris

Pamela with her dachshunds. Zürs, 1964

Diana and Oswald Mosley. Venice, 1955

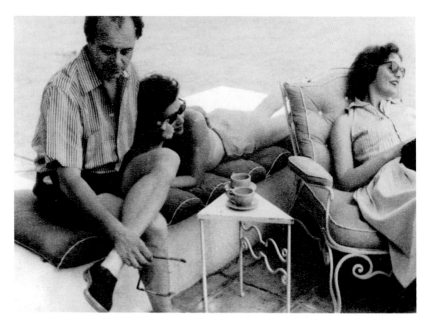

Aly Khan, Teresa de Sousa Campos (*centre*) and DD. Rio de Janeiro, 1955

DD (*left*) and Nancy on the Lido, Venice. (*By kind permission of Marina Cicogna*)

page article appeared headed, 'PEER'S DAUGHTER OF 17 ELOPES. SPAIN SEARCH'. It carried a picture of me instead of Decca. Tom advised us to have the paper up for libel, which we did, and the case was settled out of court. I was awarded damages of £1,000 on the grounds that the article had put me out of the marriage market for the rest of my life, but even this unexpected windfall meant little to me. I had lost my old Hen. I adapted Harry Roy's song 'Somebody Stole My Gal' to 'Somebody stole my Hen/Somebody stole my Hen/Somebody came and took her away/She didn't even say that she was leavin'.' Too true.

Decca and Esmond were traced to Bilbao. Peter Rodd came up with the idea of making Decca a ward in chancery so that she could be extradited legally and placed under court supervision, which indeed happened. Nancy and Peter went to France to try to persuade her to come home but without success. Soon after this, Muv made the journey to Bayonne where Esmond and Decca were now living. Decca told her that she was pregnant and when Muv got home she persuaded Farve and the judge that the marriage should go ahead.

I did not go to her wedding. There was a long-standing plan for me to visit Florence after the now-abandoned cruise, with Margaret Ogilvy, my much-loved cousin, to learn some Italian and see the sights. My parents said I should stick to the arrangement. Perhaps they were sparing me an emotional meeting with Decca after the nightmare of her elopement, perhaps they were afraid that the press might fasten on to me for a story. Her disappearance was devastating and severed the deep ties of childhood for ever. Although fears for her safety were now in the past, a mixture of misery and anger was still very much with me. Looking back, I realize that Decca could not have told me about Esmond and her plans as it would have put me in an impossible position, but at the time I could not see it. So I went to Florence. My diary tells of the famous galleries, museums and buildings, and of our visits to San Gimignano, Padua and Siena. If we had seen the Palio, the horse race round the cobbled Piazza del Campo in Siena, I might have taken some notice, but the memories I have of this slice of my education are of delicious bread and coffee and little else.

Decca and Esmond were married in Bayonne on 18 May 1937. Esmond's mother, Nellie Romilly, and Muv were present. Muv wrote to me that afternoon:

My Darling Stubby,

There has not been a minute to write till now . . . this morning Decca came early & we had a great rush to get her ready in time for the wedding at 12 o'clock. I took a silk dress from Harrods for her to be married in and we bought a hat and brown coat and brown shoes and gloves in about half-an-hour. She looked very nice in all her new clothes and Nellie had brought a suit for Esmond and he looked quite smart too & a red carnation in his buttonhole. There was quite a small crowd outside and of course the frightful newspaper men with cameras. The *Daily Express* man of course surpassed himself and said to me could he ask me when our consent was given to the wedding. I said yes he could ask but that I should not answer.

The one thing that really delighted little D[ecca] was the gramophone. She talked of it the whole time, how wonderful it would be to have it to play. It is a very nice one, it is supposed to be a 'club' from you and Bobo. It cost about £7 or a little less and there is a nice case for the records. I think they are leaving here tomorrow & going to Dieppe for a week or a fortnight. It will be very nice for them to have a change. They are evidently very happy together and I feel much happier about them . . .

All love darling,

Muv

The letter illustrates Muv's selflessness and the effort she made to give her blessing to 'Little D' and Esmond. She travelled to Bayonne (third class no doubt) laden not just with a dress for Decca, but with Unity's and my present of a gramophone and heavy records as well.

After the wedding Muv joined Margaret and me in Florence, and we went on from there to Venice. After a few days Margaret had to go back to Florence to finish the term. I was sad to see her go. Had she been allowed to stay with us, she would have had some unforgettable experiences instead of stumping round picture galleries with a well-meaning but dull Italian hostess who had done it thousands of times before.

Muv and I set off through Austria, taking the train to the Burgenland to stay at Kohfidisch with Countesses Jimmy (confusingly, a woman –

Joanna) and Baby (Francesca) Erdödy. Tom had fallen under Baby's spell when he was living in Austria and they had been fond of each other for some time. The sisters collected us at the station in the local version of a shooting brake drawn by a pair of horses, and we drove along the tracks through endless woods to their house. It gave us a taste of the size of some of the great Central European estates – those that had managed to survive the fall of Austria-Hungary and the First World War. Jimmy said something surprising, but in such a matter-of-fact voice that it sounded as if it happened all over the place, 'My father was also the father of a number of the people who work here.' I suppose the *droit de seigneur* lasted in those parts of Europe longer than elsewhere and she took it absolutely for granted. I looked at the farm workers and stable staff with renewed interest.

After two nights with the Erdödys we went on to Schloss Bernstein, where Tom had spent contented months with the Almásys. I had never seen such beautiful country: from the terrace of the ancient castle we had a view across half of Europe and I understood why Tom was so enchanted by the place. The morning of our arrival, our host, János Almásy, was arrested for being a suspected Nazi sympathizer. He did not return until 10.30 p.m. that night and was told to report to the police the next morning, so I barely saw him.

From Bernstein, our lightning tour took us to Vienna for a night and on to Salzburg, where Unity met us in her little car and drove us to Munich. On the way we stopped at Königssee, where Unity telephoned to see if Hitler was in his house at Berchtesgaden. The answer came back that he was in Munich, which we reached the following day. I described our arrival in my diary:

7 June 1937
We went straight to Hitler's flat to see if he was there & as there were two soldiers outside we knew that he was, so we rushed to the Osteria Bavaria where they said that he had left 5 minutes before, so we rushed back to his flat & saw his cars all being prepared for him to go to Berchtesgaden. We left our car down a side street & Bobo & I rushed across the square to his house. One of the guards said 'Wait in the hall' so we went in & after a bit someone came down & said 'Hitler would like you to come

up' so Bobo & I went up & she was shaking all over & the door of his room was opened & there he was standing there. He seemed very pleased to see Bobo & she introduced me & we all three went & sat on some chairs by the window. He isn't very like his photos, not nearly so hard looking. Soon Muv came up & tea was brought in & we all went to wash in his bathroom & he had some brushes there with 'AH' on them. The flat was all in brown and white, really rather ugly & quite plain. He talked quite a lot about the Spanish war & the bombing of the *Deutsch-land*. He said we must all go to the Parteitag. We sat there for about 2 hours & then he got up & we all said goodbye & he shook hands twice with each of us. When we got down stairs there was quite a crowd waiting to see him go.

Neither Muv nor I could speak German, so Unity interpreted. There was no formality. Noticing that we were grubby and travel-stained when we arrived, Hitler showed us to the bathroom himself. He and Unity were at ease with each other and the tea party went on as it would have done with anyone anywhere in the world. Our host rang the bell on the tea table. No one came. He rang again, shook his head and gave up. No one else was present at tea and that a small domestic nuisance like a broken bell could happen even to a head of state made us feel at home. I wrote to Decca: 'We have had quite a nice time here & we've had tea with Hitler & seen all the other sights.' Looking back, what is surprising is that he postponed his departure for two hours so as to be able to sit and chat to Unity and, through her, to us.

7

DEBUTANTE

In March 1938 I was eighteen, the age to 'come out', which meant being a debutante. Those who took part in this curious and artificial way of life considered it as normal as the summer sporting calendar on which the London Season hung: the racing at Royal Ascot and the Epsom Derby, the cricket at Lords and the rowing at Henley. Dance bands, dressmakers, milliners, hairdressers, caterers, hotels, restaurants, florists, hire car firms and photographers all benefited from the trade whipped up by the frenzy of the Season.

It was a vintage year for beautiful girls. Two Sylvias (Lloyd Thomas and Muir); Ursula (Jane) Kenyon-Slaney, tall, blonde and willowy; June Capel, unbeatable for looks and charm; Gina Wernher, of unmistakable Russian descent, with high cheekbones and slanting eyes; Pat Douglas, striking, with veritable violet eyes; Sally Norton, whose perfect figure in Victor Stiebel, the South African–born British couturier, was made for jealousy; Clarissa Churchill, with more than a whiff of Garbo in a dress by Maggy Rouff of Paris. Pamela Digby – whose famous career was to culminate in the American ambassadorship to Paris – was rather fat, fast and the butt of many teases; and there was Kathleen (Kick) Kennedy, sister of John F. Kennedy, not strictly a beauty but by far the most popular of all.

Joseph P. Kennedy had arrived as US Ambassador to the Court of St. James at the beginning of March and nothing like the Kennedy family had been seen before in the rarefied atmosphere of London diplomatic circles. For the next seventeen months they enlivened the scene. Vital, intelligent and outgoing, Kick was able to talk to anyone with ease and her shining niceness somehow ruled out any jealousy. Suitors appeared instantly but I noticed from the start that none of the other girls was annoyed by her success and I never heard a catty remark made behind her back. She was five weeks older than me and we soon made friends.

My other great friends were my cousins, Jean and Margaret Ogilvy, whose father, Joe Airlie, we all loved, though we were not so fond of their mother, Bridget. She was narrowly conventional to a ridiculous degree and her daughters had to be dressed just so before they were allowed out: shoes, stockings, gloves, hats, all had to be approved. When we were young Decca and I feared that if our parents were killed in an accident we might be left to Bridget in their wills, and what misery that would be (misery for Bridget too now I come to think of it).

The Ogilvy girls, Gina Wernher, Kick and I met for lunch at each other's houses time and again in the heady atmosphere of that summer. Gina lived at Someries House, which stood in its own big garden in Regent's Park. (It was demolished after the war and is now the site of the Royal College of Physicians, an unimaginable change in the landscape of pre-war London.) Our afternoon diversions included the Pathé newsreel cinema in Piccadilly, 'the eyes and ears of the world', a one-hour programme that included news, a Walt Disney film and an inferior imitation. If there was talk of war to come we did not believe it and continued to live for the present.

Royal Ascot in mid-June was the social highlight of the Season. I had first been in 1936 when I persuaded Muv to take me to see the Gold Cup. We went on to the Heath where you could go 'for nothing' and get close to the winning post. No reason to dress up, you just joined the crowd. Muv would have been far happier staying at home but did it to please me, which was typical of her. The race turned out to be the epic struggle between Lord Derby's mare Quashed and the American Triple Crown winner Omaha, belonging to the New York banker William Woodward, and Muv and I saw the final strides of this British triumph close to. It fired my interest in flat racing (I already followed National Hunt steeplechasing because of being so keen on Derek) and I still follow it with interest today. In 1937, Muv took me to Aintree by train for the day and we saw Royal Mail win the Grand National. It was a long day and I cannot believe she enjoyed it, but she knew I passionately wanted to go so booked some seats and off we went.

I went to Ascot again as a debutante, this time to the Royal Enclosure with friends. You wear a badge with your name pinned on your coat (I have often wished this happened at other social events when I am stumped as to who is who) and dress up in your best. I persuaded Madame Rita – who displayed her hats on sticks with padded tops in her cheerful showroom on the first floor of a house in Berkeley Square – to make a copy in spotted muslin of a 'fore and aft', the traditional tweed cap worn by deer stalkers, the ear flaps tied with a white satin ribbon on top of my head. It was ridiculous, but lots of Ascot hats are ridiculous. It was the racing I loved more than the social side, but both were all they were cracked up to be. We rattled down from London in one of the many special trains that took you to the racecourse. The sight of a crowd of overdressed women and top-hatted, tail-coated men assembled on one of our dirty old stations is somehow incongruous, like women in evening dress and men in black tie leaving for Glyndebourne in the middle of the afternoon.

I was as fascinated by the carriage horses in the King and Queen's procession – the famous Windsor Greys and Cleveland Bays – as I was by the thoroughbreds. There was something moving about the King and Queen's carriage appearing on the racecourse as a tiny dot a mile away and getting slowly bigger as it drew nearer; it was thrilling to see the skill of the postillions as they swung the carriage round to enter the paddock, judging to perfection the width of the entrance, and to hear the cheer of the crowd and the band playing the National Anthem. When the King had a winner, it was hats off all round and it was wonderful to see the tumultuous reception given to the horse and its owner. The feel of the crowd was much the same on the smart side of the course as it was on the Heath, an interest in horses bringing them together.

My allowance of £100 a year had to pay for the clothes I needed for the Season. My two or three evening dresses were run up by Gladys at £1 a time and the stuff came, as usual, from John Lewis. I never remember a failure and although I envied girls with dresses by Victor Stiebel, mine were always unique. A coat and skirt from Mr Nissen, tailor of Conduit Street – a major item but one that lasted – cost 8½ guineas. We were never without Madame Rita's hats. Our hairdresser, Phyllis Earle in Dover Street (reached by a number 9 bus, getting off at the Ritz), charged 3/6 for a wash and set. My shoes, which came from Dol-

cis in Oxford Street, were cheap and decent to look at but painful after
a few nights of round and round the dance floor. Muv gave me some of
her elbow-length evening gloves made of doeskin, so gleaming white
and smart they set off the dullest dress. They had to be cleaned each
time they were worn and were posted to a firm in Scotland, so famous
that 'Pullars of Perth' on the printed labels was enough of an address.
The gloves were returned, pristine, in no time. I also had some white
cotton pairs (which were looked down on) as reserves.

The shops in Brompton Road were reached through the Hole in the
Wall at the bottom of Rutland Gate. Dangerously tempting were the two
furriers who sold skins from the whole gamut of the animal kingdom, from
rabbit to sable, including now-banned species such as baby seal, ocelot
and leopard. Red fox was frowned upon by hunting people. Silver, blue
and white Arctic fox were all right, but priced miles out of reach. Wool
shops selling a kaleidoscope of coloured skeins from Sirdar and Paton &
Baldwin were a feature of every London street; there were patterns and
wool for rug-making and darning, and for knitting everything under the
sun, including dogs' coats, which I knitted for my whippet Studley.

There were balls on Mondays, Tuesdays, Wednesdays and Thurs-
days, and often two on the same night. From time to time there was a
Friday dance in the country (but not on a Saturday as it was not thought
seemly to dance into Sunday morning). The hostess asked friends to
give dinner parties before the ball and sent a list of prospective guests.
At dinner, which was given in a private house or hotel restaurant, a debutante was seated between two young men who were expected to dance
the first two dances with her on arrival at the ball since she might not
know anyone early in the Season. Some obeyed this rule, but others often spied a more attractive friend and abandoned their dinner partners.
Popular girls were booked up at once but the ladies' cloakroom was a
refuge for those who had no partners. 'Can I borrow your powder?'
'Yes, but no crevice work please.' Chat about last night's dance, who was
doing what, and the rest of the talk common to girls of our age in ladies' cloakrooms all over the world (seemingly idiotic now but very real
then), filled the gap till the next dance when, with luck, a partner was
booked. The dances were numbered so you somehow found who you
were supposed to meet and took to the floor, stepping on each other's
feet and exchanging banalities.

With no partners to seek them out, some of the debutantes hated every minute of this nightly routine, yet it was an admission of failure to go home before 1 a.m. At dances in the country you were given a programme with a tiny pencil attached by a silk thread, and a space to write the name of your partner next to the number of the dance. Men would say, 'May I see your programme?' All very well, but what if it was blank? I learned to put 'John', 'George', 'William', 'James' – none of whom existed but it looked better. Sometimes you got caught by an unwanted fellow, sometimes the one you wanted did his best to get away. It was a kind of game and a lesson in how to struggle through as best you can.

Meanwhile the unlucky chaperone – in my case Muv, who had already been through this charade five times with my sisters – changed into evening dress and, eyeing her turned-down bed with longing, telephoned for a taxi to take her to the ball. Mothers, aunts, or anyone who fitted the chaperone bill, sat on the caterers' gold chairs that surrounded the dance floor and waited until their charge had had enough. Occasionally Farve gave Muv a night off. He refused to take part in the festivities and never penetrated as far as the ballroom, but sat on one of those rickety hall chairs common to all big London houses, still in his evening cloak. One distraught hostess approached him and asked, 'Lord Redesdale, would you take the French Ambassadress into supper?' (a sumptuous meal that appeared between dinner and breakfast for the greedy or for those who had not yet dined). 'NO,' he said furiously, 'I'm waiting for Stubby.' The poor woman had no idea who Stubby was but wisely retreated and left him alone.

The sprinkling of older men who might take one of the patient mothers to supper were mostly unknown to Muv, so she often spent the late-night hours chatting to her neighbours. She watched the dancing and enjoyed seeing the wild gyrations of the Big Apple and the more staid Lambeth Walk. The bands – Joe Loss, Carroll Gibbons, Roy Fox, Nat Gonella, Ambrose and sometimes even the great Harry Roy – were indefatigable. Tunes and lyrics by Cole Porter, Noël Coward and Irving Berlin, which have never been bettered, went through our heads night after night. Robert Cecil and Hugh Fraser were the two most energetic dancers: coats off, pouring with sweat, stumping and thumping with no real steps, just enjoying themselves madly. Muv said, 'If young men all go on like this there will be a war.'

At a ball given by Lady Louis Mountbatten for Sally Norton I danced with Jack Kennedy. 'Rather boring but nice,' I wrote in my diary. We danced again the next evening: 'I don't think he was enjoying the party much,' I put in my diary the next day. Muv who, like everyone else, was intrigued by the Kennedys and full of admiration for Mrs Kennedy (who had easily outdone her in the childbearing line) observed the goings-on at one of these dances from her usual place with the other chaperones. She noticed Jack and, after watching him for a while, turned and said to a friend of mine (who later repeated it to me): 'Mark my words, I would not be surprised if that young man becomes President of the United States.' I do not know what made her say it, but she sometimes had that sort of premonition. I had none whatsoever and did not get to know Jack well until after he became President.

Gina Wernher was six months older than me and came out in 1937. Because we were friends I was allowed to go to her dance, even though it was a year before my official coming out. Her mother, Lady Zia, was related to many of the royal houses of Europe and these were represented in strength at the party. Our own recently crowned King and Queen were also there which lent glamour to the assembly. I dined with the Wernhers at Someries House, terrified of all the unknown bejewelled ladies, and found myself next to a girl who was obviously put out by the absence of the man who should have been sitting between us. She was Ann de Trafford, later the wife of a great friend, Derek Parker Bowles. We got through dinner somehow. Luckily Tom was at the dance and, realizing how nervous I was, rescued me when I needed him.

A change from dancing was the night when, among a crowd of other girls, I was presented at Court. This was the formal confirmation of having arrived – grown up at last. Before the days of television, the queue of hired cars lining up in the Mall to drop their passengers at Buckingham Palace was a free show for Londoners – like watching film stars arriving at a Leicester Square première. The cars could be stationary for some time, so the occupants were sitting ducks for any critical onlookers and their outspoken opinions. Gossip columnists sharpened their pencils, but for nothing worse than a description of the debutantes' clothes. The girls all wore white, with three white ostrich feathers in their hair and no jewellery. Their mothers, or whoever was presenting them (it was rumoured that two peeresses were paid to bring out debutantes by the mothers of girls who would not otherwise have been eligible as they and their mothers were unknown to Buckingham Palace), wore diamonds and every brooch they could lay their hands on.

I was presented in May. Muv and I waited in a room in the Palace for an hour and a half before making our entrée, while in the background 'The Donkey's Serenade' (So I'll sing to a mule/If you're sure she won't think that I am just a fool/Serenading a mule) played through amplifiers. When it came to our turn, I followed Muv, careful not to step on her train, and curtseyed first to the King and then to the Queen. I was not nervous because I knew exactly what I had to do and everything was so precisely organized, as it always is at Court. We made a quick getaway afterwards to have our photographs taken by Lenare.

One of my first big dances in 1938 was at Chandos House, given by Lady Kemsley for her daughter Ghislaine Dresselhuys. The men armed the girls into dinner – already an old-fashioned custom then – and I was allotted to Lord Howland. The poor fellow was as shy as I was and we felt silly walking down the long passage, clamped unhappily together and with nothing to say. At that age Ian Howland (later the supremely comic Duke of Bedford who brought thousands to Woburn Abbey with his showmanship and vociferous welcome to all and sundry) was what we described as 'wet'. 'If all the dances are going to be like this,' I said to Muv, 'I'm not going.'

My own dance was held at Rutland Gate on 22 March, early in the Season; the bigger, smarter parties took place from May onwards. Three hundred guests were invited, including the familiar sprinkling of elderly uncles and aunts. Basics ran along the usual lines: gold chairs and a butler were hired for the evening, helpers were brought in to greet the guests and serve at table, and a bedroom near a bathroom became a ladies' cloakroom. (Nanny presided over the Ladies – goodness knows who looked after the Gents.) But the food at supper was not the usual Hunca Munca beef that disappointed the two bad mice in Beatrix Potter's story, or the cold ham and chicken-à-la-king that we saw every night. Muv had a talent for making the commonplace original. Kedgeree (a mixture of rice, hard-boiled eggs and flaked salmon, mildly spiced, lashed with cream and served hot) was the best dish imaginable and the guests fell on ours with delight. Instead of ice cream, rich mousses and pastries, she gave us black cherries and Devonshire cream. We ate off eighteenth-century Berlin porcelain decorated with European birds, butterflies and moths; even the steel knives and silver forks had painted china handles. The service had belonged to Warren Hastings and was bought by a Mitford ancestor at the sale to raise funds to pay for Hastings' trial. Heaven knows how much of this priceless china was smashed in the hurried washing-up after midnight. It is now wrapped in cotton wool at Chatsworth.

Two weeks after my party, I was invited to a dinner given by Lady Blanche Cobbold for her daughter Pamela before Lavinia Pearson's dance. I sat next to Andrew Cavendish. We were both just eighteen. Ignoring our neighbours, we never stopped talking throughout dinner. That was it for me – the rest of the Season passed in a haze of would-he-wouldn't-he be there; nothing and nobody else mattered. Meeting him was the beginning and end of everything I had dreamed of. A month later he left for Lyons 'to learn French' for a term (I never saw, or rather heard, any evidence of this in later life but it did not seem to matter). I missed him during his absence, but it was all the more exciting when he came back, and we managed to meet at parties time and again.

Three dances stand out in my memory that year. Mrs Kennedy gave a dinner-dance for Kick and her eldest sister Rosemary at the American Embassy in Prince's Gate on 2 June. My cousin Jean Ogilvy, who came out the year before we did, had taken on the pleasurable task of introducing Kick to her English contemporaries and to the unwritten rules and nuances of social life in this country. It was Jean who helped Kick arrange the seating at table and that was perhaps why I was lucky enough to find myself at Kick's table with Jean, Elisabeth Moncrieffe, Prince Frederick of Prussia, and, according to my diary, a 'very dull', nameless American. The three other men at the table – John Stanley, Robert Cecil and Eric Duncannon – were of a similar age, all heirs to large estates. Ambrose's famous band played and the cabaret was Harry Richman, brought over from America for the night. But it was the Kennedys themselves who lit up the evening.

Three weeks later the Speaker of the House of Commons, Edward FitzRoy, gave a dance for his granddaughters Anne and Mary at the Speaker's House, his official residence in the Palace of Westminster. (No one made anything of it at the time but what a fuss there would be now if that historic house were used for such a frivolous purpose, and presumably free to Mr Speaker – a permissible perk that went unquestioned in those days.) The sun was well up over the Houses of Parliament when Muv and I left at 5 a.m. She had had a long wait that night. I remember the taxi-ride home because she was so angry with me. Dancing more than two dances with the same partner was strictly against the unwritten rules, but I was missing Andrew and had danced all night with Mark Howard. I expect Muv had had enough anyway without my bad behaviour. My diary for the next day says, 'Very dull day', and 'Duller still' the following. Perhaps this was a result of Muv's anger; it was rare for her to give us a ticking-off and it made a strong impression.

On 1 July I went to a ball at Bowood House in Wiltshire, for the coming of age of Charlie Lansdowne who, with his younger brother Ned Fitzmaurice, had become my great friends. After Andrew, I loved them best. The main house at Bowood, a large square Adam block, was still standing (it was pulled down after the war) and there was ample room for hundreds of guests. The garden with its eye-catching lake and cottage are set in the sort of idyllic eighteenth-century landscape that makes you gasp at the sheer beauty and Englishness of it. It was the most enjoyable evening I remember of all the glorious evenings we had that year. Andrew was back from Lyons and he and Tom Egerton stayed at the Swan Inn in Swinbrook. A girlfriend and I stayed next door at the Mill Cottage, which Farve rented after selling the Swinbrook estate. Tom and Andrew had met, aged thirteen, on their first day at Eton and remained lifelong friends. I too had grown to love Tom, and Andrew and I seldom planned anything that did not include him. Like Andrew, he was in the Coldstream Guards during the war and became famous in the regiment for rescuing the marmalade from the Officers' Mess at the Siege of Tobruk.

At the end of July, Andrew and I went to stay at Compton Place, his parents' house in Eastbourne, for Goodwood races. Also staying were Tom Egerton, Robert Cecil, my friends Irene (Rene) Haig, Zara Mainwaring and Jakie Astor. Andrew's brother, Billy Hartington, had invited Kick. Rene must have been irritated by Kick joining the party because until then she had been Billy's favourite. In September we all went to Cortachy Castle, Jean Ogilvy's home in the north-east of Scotland. Cortachy was the usual mixture of ancient and Victorian, surrounded by

farmland and grouse moors, and was made homely by the family of six
children. But after the riotous fun at Compton Place, we had to be on our
guard under the critical eye of Jean's mother, Bridget Airlie. Hugh Fraser and Andrew got into trouble for running on to the Perth racecourse
in front of the crowds and jumping the water jump.

Kick had by now become part of the scene and was as much with
Billy as I was with Andrew. The rest of the Kennedy family were in the
South of France that summer but Kick had struck out and was determined to spend those few days with Billy. Rose Kennedy, a forceful
character of whom all her children were in awe, was not pleased and I
wondered what reception Kick would get when she eventually joined
her family. As far as Mrs Kennedy, a staunch Catholic, was concerned,
it was out of the question for Kick to marry Billy because he was a practising Protestant. Kick went back to America when war was declared,
but her heart was in England and in 1943 she returned, ostensibly to
work for the American Red Cross, but really to join Billy; and despite
the opposition from both families, they were soon engaged.

In August I got a stiff letter from Muv, who was in Germany with
Unity, criticizing me for going to Castle Howard without telling her and
spelling out what was expected of me when I stayed with Andrew. 'I
hope if you went to Derbyshire that the Duchess invited you to visit and
not only Andrew, as I *do not* wish you to visit about at the invitation of
this boy or that.' By this time Andrew and I considered ourselves unof-
ficially engaged but there were some hiccups. He became fond of Di-
nah Brand, a niece of Nancy Astor, and more or less deserted me for
her. I minded terribly and had gone to Castle Howard to dry my eyes.
He also liked the look of Maxine Birley, daughter of the painter Oswald
Birley – a real beauty of whom I was deeply jealous. For a while Andrew
and I did not meet, but then all obstacles seemed to dissolve and we
took up as though we had never left off.

Like Farve, Andrew was very much a second son. His parents, Eddy
and Mary (always known as 'Moucher') Devonshire, adored their elder
son, Billy, the epitome of all that was good, clever and handsome. When
they were in London, the Devonshires leased No. 2 Carlton Gardens
from the Crown Estate (Devonshire House had been sold in the 1920s).
These big London houses were built for entertaining, not for family life,
and the grander the house, the less the younger members of the family

and the household staff were considered. Andrew had no bedroom at Carlton Gardens and slept on a camp bed in his mother's sitting room. Edward, the butler, slept in a cupboard on the stairs.

In the autumn term of 1938 Andrew went up to Trinity College, Cambridge, where he enjoyed himself to the full. Unlike me and my girlfriends, he and his friends were conscious of the looming danger of a war and this added to their frenetic search for pleasure. They got into scrapes and baited the Proctors to within an inch of being sent down. They drank too much, danced all night and rode hopeless hirelings in point-to-points. There was a rule that undergraduates had to be back in College by 6 a.m. and there were many early morning accidents as they raced back from London to be in on time. Andrew had a lucky escape when the car he was sharing with two friends overturned, landed on top of him and damaged one of his kidneys beyond repair. He was in hospital for a month and told me that his time there conveniently coincided with end of first year exams, so he did not have to take them. He was greatly relieved as he was sure he would have failed. After one escapade, Bernard van Cutsem, later Andrew's racehorse trainer, was described on a newspaper hoarding of the *Cambridge News* as 'MILLIONAIRE JESUS PLAYBOY'. Anyone not conversant with the names of the Cambridge Colleges might have wondered at this headline.

Newmarket was near by and more time was spent at the races than at lectures. I do not think Andrew or any of his friends went in much for learning – it came a long way down their scale of priorities. There were exceptions, of course, and there was a sharp drawing-in of breath when George Jellicoe, one of the principal party-goers, got a First in modern history. Andrew planned to visit me at the Mill Cottage. As he did not drive, he came by rail, cross-country from Cambridge to Oxford, but missed three trains running. I drove the nineteen miles to Oxford Station and back to meet him off each one. Muv grew exasperated and said, 'I should give up seeing him if I were you, he's unreliable.' I went to see him at Cambridge just once and even I, philistine that I am, was stunned by the beauty of the place.

The spring and summer of 1939 brought more freedom for me, now an ex-debutante. I was invited to a few dances and was allowed to see

Andrew unchaperoned. Our meeting place was often Keith Prowse in
Bond Street, where we spent hours listening to 78 r.p.m. records in enclosed, so-called soundproof, booths. We lunched at Luigi's in Jermyn
Street, the embodiment of new-found freedom, where a minute steak
and all that went with it, including a bottle of wine, cost a guinea. (When
war broke out Luigi was bundled off to Canada as an Enemy Alien –
anyone less of an enemy I cannot imagine.) The place for evening entertainment was the Café de Paris. It was expensive and a rare treat. We
were sometimes invited by friends, but often it was Andrew who paid.
The cabaret never failed to be the best: Beatrice Lillie and Douglas Byng
were the funniest; Frances Day, who sang 'It's De Lovely', the most glamorous; and the black band leader, Ken 'Snakehips' Johnson, was fascinating to look at. The last tune, signalling that it was time to go home,
was always 'Goodnight Sweetheart'.

After war was declared, the Café de Paris went on as if nothing had
happened – best dresses for women, uniforms for the men who had joined
up and black tie for the others. In March 1941 when the bombing was
at its height, the Café de Paris received a direct hit and many people
were killed, including Snakehips, aged only twenty-six. An acquaintance
of mine who passed by on foot later that night (the raid was so bad that
even the taxis had gone home) said that he would not have believed the
corpses and the mixture of blood and jewels had he not seen it with his
own eyes.

The nightclub we loved best was the 400 in Leicester Square. Drink
laws at the time were peculiar: members could buy a bottle of spirits,
write their name and the date on it, and on their next visit the unfinished bottle would be waiting for them. Sometimes overseas service
meant a long absence for a member, but the bottle was always there. A
hazard at the 400 was that it was also a favourite of Andrew's father, who
was apt to sit at a table near the narrow entrance with his friend Lady
Dufferin. We had to pass close by, which was embarrassing for Andrew
and Billy. In an attempt at anonymity, my future father-in-law labelled
his bottles with the name of a fish beginning with 'H' (for his courtesy
title 'Hartington'). Billy and Andrew discovered this and would ask Mr
Rossi, the maître d'hôtel, 'Have you got a bottle belonging to Mr Hake
or Herring or Halibut?'

This way of life cost Andrew far more than his allowance and he
owed money to his tailor and bookmaker. After a day's racing at Brighton,

he was chased by a Ladbroke's man the length of the train at Victoria Station. His long, nineteen-year-old legs enabled him to escape into the crowd, but the bills kept coming. One extravagance he did not fall for was a car of his own. He never liked the idea of driving and only did so under duress – and to the terror of his passengers. When he was in Italy during the war, he sometimes had to take the wheel but never afterwards. I became the driver when we married, except when he was on some official engagement and then the chauffeur drove.

On 6 July 1939 the last grand ball before the war was given at Holland House by Hon. Mrs Cubitt for her daughter Rosalind Cubitt. The King and Queen were there and it was full of friends – so many that it was difficult to circulate in the succession of small rooms of the old Elizabethan house. It rained so hard that arriving guests had to queue for an hour and a quarter because only one car at a time could drop its passengers under the covered porch. The awful weather was somehow a portent of things to come; most of us realized that it was the last time we would see anything like it and in spite of being one of the best parties of the Season, it was also a kind of farewell.

$$\mathcal{8}$$

WAR

I n 1938, soon after the sale of Swinbrook, my father saw an advertisement for Inch Kenneth, a small island in the Inner Hebrides off the west coast of Mull. He went to look at it, fell under its spell and bought it. Perhaps the fact that it was so far away, with nothing but the Atlantic Ocean between it and Newfoundland, made the island all the more attractive. Muv went to see it for herself and her love of Scotland and the sea made her pleased with it. The single house on the island had a modern exterior – the latest addition was built in 1934 – and fitted surprisingly well into the landscape. Sheltered to the north by a hill and fearsome cliffs, it faced south on to white sands and small coves. The ruins of the ancient chapel of St Kenneth, a follower of St Columbus, were close by and there was a farmstead and walled kitchen garden, but the house and its attendant cottage were the only human habitation. When the main house was empty, only John McFadyen – the cowman, shepherd, boatman and handyman all rolled into one – and his wife lived there. I veered between wanting to live on the island for the rest of my life and hating it. The weather was more important than in any place I have ever known: sublime when it was fine and the distant islands seemed to hover above the sea, infinitely depressing when the weather closed in and there was no escape until it was calm again.

I was on Inch Kenneth with Muv, Farve and Nancy on 3 September 1939, the day war was declared. John McFadyen, was called up immediately. He came to the house in his uniform of the Argyll and Sutherland Highlanders to say goodbye and we were all in the kitchen in floods, including him. (He came back safely, I am happy to say.) I was

left with three cows to milk. Two were of uncertain lineage but with a
distinctly Shorthorn look, the third was a lovely little Jersey heifer, a first
calver – on the skittish side. The cows' routine was sacrosanct: morning
milking at about 7.30 a.m., then they were turned out to graze till 5 p.m.
when the evening milking was due.

I do not know how many of my dear readers have milked a cow –
not just tried their hand at it but been in total charge of this wonderful
animal, who would be in considerable pain if left unmilked. The best
part is burying your head into the warm and comforting flank; the worst
is the flick of a tail over your eyes or hair, with a thin wet film of muck.
Each cow is different. The older Shorthorns were relatively easy – their
big floppy teats yielding the milk with a satisfying sizzle and spurt, hit-
ting the bucket held tight between my knees. The little Jersey was my
trouble. Her teats were short and embedded in her udder. The double
squeeze which brings the milk was hard on my hands, using unaccustomed muscles. Had I been a pianist, the muscles might have been
ready and waiting, but no such luck, and the sharp ache in my fingers
and across the back of my hands became acute. I cut my nails as short
as I dared to spare the flesh on the lower part of my palms, but even the
satisfaction of an endless supply of fresh milk and enough cream to
please the greediest seemed a high price to pay for the pain. The poor
little Jersey was restless and I was in despair when a cow kick (a hind
leg flashed forward – the opposite of a horse's kick) turned me and the
bucket over. The three-legged milking stool was upside down with the
rest. Being told not to cry over spilt milk is ridiculous; of course you cry
when all that effort goes to waste.

As soon as war was declared, we feared for Unity. She had always
said that in the event of war between England and Germany, her life
would be over. True to her word she went to a public park in Munich,
took out the small mother-of-pearl pistol she had bought for the purpose (she used to show it to us, telling us what she would do with it)
and fired a bullet into her right temple. My parents were well aware of
her threat and when they heard nothing from her they suffered the
same awful anxiety as they had when Decca disappeared – not knowing
whether she was alive or dead. Communications with Germany during
the Phoney War were uncertain but eventually they heard from Teddy
Almásy, János's brother, who wrote from neutral Hungary to say that

Unity was ill in hospital but was being well looked after. The letter arrived on 2 October. There was no further news for many weeks. We were
at Rutland Gate on Christmas Eve when the telephone rang. It was
János, who was with Unity. He had taken her on an ambulance train
from Munich to Berne, arranged by Hitler who kept in touch with her
progress. 'When are you coming to fetch me?' Unity asked. To Muv she
sounded her old self.

I was the only sister available to go with Muv on the long and possibly hazardous train journey through France to Switzerland. Although
there had been little fighting so far, no one knew when a German attack
might come. We set off together immediately after Christmas. The journey seemed as dark during the short days as it was during the long
winter nights. Arriving in brilliantly lit Berne after blacked-out England
and France lifted our spirits, as did the thought of seeing Unity again. It
was a false dawn. Our first sight of her was a shock: her face was the
same greyish-brown as her hair, which was matted and almost solid with
dried blood – she had not been able to bear anyone touching her head
since the day the bullet had smashed into her skull, nearly killing her.
Even her huge eyes looked different: one glance showed that the light
had gone out. She smiled and was pleased to see us but she was another
person. Muv and I looked at the sad, thin creature that was left and tried
to not let her see how horrified we were.

Unity had been unconscious for two months after shooting herself
but had slowly regained the use of her limbs. The clinic pronounced her
fit to travel and on New Year's Eve, accompanied by a nurse, we started
back to Calais in an ambulance carriage attached to the train. Long halts
at dark stations were followed by a few miles of jerky progress, accompanied by bangs and squeals of metal on metal. The whole process then
began again. The jolts every time we stopped and started were painful
and unsettling for the patient. The journey took so long that we missed
the boat to Folkestone and had to endure two interminable nights in a
hotel in Calais, where we were besieged by a hostile press.

Finally, on 3 January, Unity's stretcher was lifted on to the boat and
off again at Folkestone, where Farve was waiting for us; then into an
ambulance and at last we were on our way to the Old Mill Cottage in
High Wycombe. But not for long. The engine started making strange
noises and we drew to a halt. There was a long wait until another am-

bulance arrived to take us back to Folkestone. After all these alarms, it was too late to make the long drive to High Wycombe and we spent the night in a Folkestone hotel. Meanwhile the photographers, who had not been able to get close to us on the dock because it was a prohibited area, were snapping away and the reporters got their pictures and story when Unity was transferred from one ambulance to another. Farve was certain the breakdown had been fixed by the press. It was not till the following afternoon that we arrived home, after a journey that had taken four days instead of one.

Three weeks later, Unity was examined by Sir Hugh Cairns, Nuffield Professor of Surgery at the Radcliffe Infirmary in Oxford, who confirmed that the doctors in Germany were right not to have tried to remove the bullet which was lodged in her brain. Muv devoted herself to looking after Unity from the day we brought her home from Switzerland and it gradually became clear to us all that she would never be the same again. Muv wanted to take her to Inch Kenneth but the island was a protected area and as Unity was regarded as a dangerous individual by the authorities, permission was refused. Little did they realize her condition. The press was still plaguing us, so Muv and Farve decided that the Mill Cottage in Swinbrook would be less accessible than High Wycombe, where the yard could not be closed off and the miller's lorries came and went.

We were at close quarters at Swinbrook. My bedroom measured seven by eight feet (against the law now but it seemed perfectly all right to me). Unity slept in the next room and there was just a flimsy door between us. Since her suicide attempt she had taken against me, as she had done with others. 'It's awful,' I wrote to Diana in October 1940, 'she *so* hates me that life here has become almost impossible. The sitting room is so small and two enormous tables in it belong exclusively to her and if one so much as puts some knitting down on one for a moment chaos reigns because she hies up & shrieks "bloody fool" very loud.'

She was unable to concentrate and jumped from one subject to another, using the wrong words and getting angry when we could not understand her. She sometimes spoke of the Führer, but as from a great distance; her grasp on reality was that of a child. To add to the misery, she was incontinent. Muv washed her sheets every day in the small kitchen sink and when they were hung out to dry they dominated the little gar-

den. Mrs Stobie (now married to Philip Timms, my father's old foreman) came in to help. I overheard my mother interviewing an applicant
for the job once when Mrs Stobie was ill. 'I do the rough,' I heard Muv
say. That meant sawing the logs with what became known as a 'Queen
Mary' (so called because the widowed queen spent the war at Badminton House where she delighted in cutting down the Duke of Beaufort's
trees), chopping the wood for kindling, cleaning the grates in the morning and sweeping out the ashes.

The doctor advised Muv to encourage Unity to be independent and
after a few months she was able to take the bus to Oxford on her own,
sometimes asking her fellow passengers for money on the way. The highlight of her day was lunch at the British Restaurant, a kind of soup
kitchen where the doubtful stew and potatoes cost one shilling. She
sometimes queued up a second time, which you were not meant to do,
but the good-natured customers and staff never reported her.

She would attach herself to various people for a time and then take
up with someone else. Two people stand out for their patience: Mrs
Wells, the parson's wife ('*Blissful* Mrs Wells', Unity called her), and
Miss Bannerman who had an antique shop in Burford. These two good,
unprejudiced women often kept her company. Unity still needed a
cause, something to replace her love of Germany, and she turned to
religion. Over the years she joined – or tried to join – the Roman Catholic Church, the Christian Scientists and everything in between. This
led to terrible muddles with the local organizers of these different faiths
and Muv had to sort them out. Had Eastern religions been as popular
as they are today, I am sure Unity would have worked her way through
those as well. I was entirely selfish and thought of nothing except being
with Andrew and did precious little for either mother or sister.

Nearly all her contemporaries are dead so there are very few people
who remember Unity as she was before she tried to kill herself. (One
who does and who has fond memories of her is her old friend Micky
Burn, now aged ninety-eight.) Those who are interested in her life can
read thousands of words about her, written with the benefit of hindsight.
All are hostile because of her friendship with Hitler. She has become a
symbol of evil, her name synonymous with anti-Semitism. So why did
we all love her? I have searched for the answer, tried to find a word to
describe what it was about her, but cannot. Decca could not explain it

either: the strongest possible political division separated her from Unity but nothing could extinguish their love for each other. We knew the bad side, we knew she had condoned Nazi cruelty and that she had taken a flat from a Jewish couple who had been evicted; yet in spite of her racist views, vehemently expressed, and her admiration for the most extreme of Hitler's lieutenants, there was something innocent about Unity, a guileless, childlike simplicity that made her vulnerable and in need of protection. Nancy and Pam in their own ways, Tom, undoubtedly, Diana to a much greater degree, Decca, amazingly, and I, certainly, could not help loving her. Our parents, of course, and cousins felt the same way. It was not that those who loved her forgave her her beliefs, they went on loving her in spite of them. None of this will impress her enemies but it goes some way to account for the feelings of those who knew her. Perhaps it is too easy to say that she was inexplicable, but it is a fact.

Decca and Esmond returned to England three months before their baby daughter, Julia, was born on 20 December 1937. They lived in a house in Rotherhithe Street in south-east London, which I visited two or three times. Esmond made no secret of his dislike of our family and Decca and I usually met on neutral ground. Esmond was not there when I went to see the baby, who was suspended in a cradle out of a window that overlooked the River Thames – a bit of Nanny's lore to do with fresh air, no doubt. Decca was guardedly welcoming. Unsurprisingly, the old intimacy had gone but we had a good chat.

Then came their tragedy: Julia caught measles, which turned into pneumonia, and she died, aged five months. Decca wrote an agonizing account of her baby's illness and death in her memoirs, but never spoke of her misery to me or any of the family; she buried her sorrow deep. To my shame, I was entirely taken up at the time with dances and friends – following 'the devices and desires' of my own heart. Decca resisted any attempt at sympathy on my part and, understandably, cut herself off from me and the frivolous life I was leading. The day after Julia's funeral, at which none of the family were welcome, the Romillys went to Corsica where they remained out of communication for three months.

Tom acted as a bridge between Decca and our parents and was the only member of the family to make friends with Esmond. A great arguer, he was fascinated by the theory of politics rather than their practical application and was able, unlike my sisters, to discuss politics dispassionately. He was present at Mosley's infamous Olympia meeting in 1934, where he was photographed giving the Fascist salute, but he also spent hours talking to Esmond. He was as interested to meet Hitler with Diana and Unity as he was to debate communism with Decca and Esmond's friends. As a result, he was claimed by both sides as 'one of us' and remained on good terms with everyone throughout all the political upheavals.

In early 1939 the Romillys left for America to start a new life. Esmond joined the Royal Canadian Air Force in July 1940 and this brought about the greatest sorrow of Decca's life. On 30 November 1941 Esmond's disabled plane came down in the North Sea and he was posted missing. The word 'missing' is particularly cruel, leaving as it does a ray of hope that the person will turn up safe and well, even in the most doomed circumstances. As days go by, it becomes increasingly unlikely and yet, and yet . . .

It was in Decca's nature to be optimistic and she clutched at every straw, hoping against hope that Esmond was a prisoner of war. In December, Winston Churchill (whose wife, Clementine, was Farve's first cousin) went to America to confer with President Roosevelt and asked Decca, who was living in Washington, to meet him at the White House. Churchill told her that he had looked carefully into the matter of the plane's disappearance and that there was no chance of Esmond being alive. Even then Decca could not believe it. As she left the White House, Winston gave her an envelope containing $500. She was enraged at this display of charity – as if she could not look after herself. She was certainly not going to accept money from Churchill and she gave it away to friends.

After Esmond's death, Muv wrote to Decca telling her how delighted we would all be to have her back and pleaded with her to come home. Decca's Air Force pension was derisory, but a prouder woman you could not find; she decided to stay in America, take a secretarial job and manage somehow. Esmond's death must have nearly destroyed her. I do not doubt that their marriage would have lasted: they were so exactly right for each other. Her saviour was Constancia, 'Dinky', her ten-month-old daughter – all that she had left of Esmond and the dizzy few years they had spent together.

•

Diana and Sir Oswald married in 1936, after the sudden death of his
first wife, Cimmie, following an appendicitis operation that went wrong.
In May 1940 Sir O was arrested under Defence Regulation 18B, a wartime ruling that empowered the government to detain anyone considered a threat to the country, and he was sent to Brixton Prison. He was
not charged with any offence and so was not tried in a court of law. A
month later Diana was also arrested under 18B and taken to Holloway,
the women's prison. Max, her fourth son (and second by Mosley), was
eleven weeks old and she was still breastfeeding him. She was given the
chance to take the baby with her, but the bombing of London was expected at any moment and she decided to leave him with his brother,
eighteen-month-old Alexander, in the capable hands of Nanny Higgs.

What happened to Diana and my brother-in-law is well documented.
What is less well known is that the day after Diana was arrested Glad-
wyn Jebb, private secretary to Sir Alexander Cadogan at the Foreign
Office and an acquaintance of Nancy, summoned Nancy to his office.
He wanted to know whether she thought Diana's friendship with Hitler
and other high-ranking members of the Nazi party made her a threat to
the country, and asked her if she knew the purpose of Diana's visits to
Germany. Nancy told Gladwyn that she thought Diana 'an extremely
dangerous person'. What she based this statement on I do not know –
Diana never spoke politics to Nancy – and why she agreed to be questioned about a subject of which she admitted she knew nothing I shall
never understand. Diana had always been generous to Nancy and they
loved each other's company, which makes Nancy's denunciation all the
more inexplicable. But I do know that her underlying jealousy of Diana,
which went back to childhood, was still very present. It had been exacerbated by Diana producing four healthy boys and Nancy being unable
to have children following an ectopic pregnancy. Diana did not learn of
Nancy's action until 1985, twelve years after Nancy's death. It must
have been a fearful shock, however well she thought she knew Nancy,
such duplicity being entirely foreign to her own nature.

Diana described her experiences in Holloway in her memoirs, *A Life
of Contrasts*, and there is little I can add. I visited her several times and
saw enough to realize what an ordeal her imprisonment was. She was
allowed one visitor for half an hour every fortnight. The precious thirty

minutes was usually used by my mother, with or without Diana's children. There was always a wardress present at these meetings, one of whom became Diana's friend. The prison was overcrowded and there were many women to each lavatory. One of these had a red 'V' painted on the door and was usually empty, so Diana decided to use it. 'I shouldn't if I were you,' her friend the wardress warned her, 'it's for people with venereal disease.' Muv was so shocked by the filth of the visitors' lavatory that, in an uncharacteristic gesture, she wrote on the wall: 'This lavatory is a disgrace to HM Prisons'. Sir O also wrote an account of his imprisonment, but one detail he failed to mention is that the Lascar seamen who were held in the cells on the floor above him used to urinate out of the window, and the wind blew the results down into his cell below.

Tom, who was with the 11th Battalion King's Royal Rifle Corps (surprising his old friends by the eagerness with which he embraced army life), visited Diana whenever he was on leave. One day in autumn 1941 he went to see both Sir O in Brixton and Diana in Holloway. He told Diana that he was dining that night with Churchill and asked if there was anything she would like him to say to the Prime Minister. 'Only the same as always,' she answered, 'that if we have to stay in prison couldn't we at least be together?' After dining at 10 Downing Street, Tom wrote to Churchill on Diana's behalf, repeating her request. In December 1941, after eighteen long months apart, Diana and Sir O were reunited in Holloway, as were other husbands and wives held under Regulation 18B. Diana said that, unlikely as it may seem, one of the happiest days of her life was in prison: the day she and her husband were together again. The press made a great deal of this and it was picked up by the bus conductor on the north London route, who used to announce at the top of his voice, 'Holloway Jail. Lady Mosley's suite. All change here.' My mother gave him a stern look as she got off the bus to go through the huge prison gates.

Two years later, Sir O fell ill with phlebitis. The authorities were frightened that he might die in prison and in November 1943, after much discussion, the Home Secretary, Herbert Morrison, unwillingly agreed that the Mosleys should be released under house arrest. When this was announced, Nancy again performed her 'patriotic duty' and went to MI5 to volunteer that in her opinion Diana sincerely desired 'the downfall of England and democracy generally' and should not be released. This time

Nancy's fantasy had gone too far; she had no evidence whatsoever for her claim and luckily the government took no notice. Diana was never to know of this second betrayal since the relevant government papers were not made public until four months after her death. To me, Nancy's behaviour is so incredible that I would not have believed it had I not read it in black and white in an official document.

Derek Jackson worked at Professor Lindemann's Oxford laboratory until the Fall of France. He then joined the RAF as a wireless operator/air gunner, making over sixty sorties with 604 Squadron. At thirty-four, he was older than most of his comrades and Lindemann did not want to let him go, but by force of character Derek succeeded in joining up. Pam followed him around the country and was there to look after him in rented houses whenever possible. From 1943 until the end of the war he played a vital role in helping to develop ways of interfering with enemy radar.

Derek behaved in the air force much as he had done on the racecourse, astonishing his pilot on one occasion by giving instructions in German. When the Mosleys were released from Holloway and had nowhere to live Derek invited them to Rignell, but after a few days the Home Office woke up to the fact that Derek was doing top secret scientific work and the Mosleys were told they had to leave. Derek was incensed and when aroused could be a formidable opponent. He grabbed the telephone and rang the Home Office, demanding to speak to Herbert Morrison, who, as Derek knew, had been a conscientious objector in the First World War. To everyone's surprise Derek was put through and – as he enjoyed recalling later – he went into the attack: 'When *you* have got the DFC, the AFC and the OBE for valour, you can tell me what to do.' In spite of Derek's protestations, the Mosleys had to leave Rignell and went to a nearby inn, The Shaven Crown, where they spent Christmas 1943.

By 1940 the Free French had their headquarters in London and it was there that Nancy met Gaston Palewski, General de Gaulle's chief of staff. He was the lover she had been waiting for all her life and she fell for him hook, line and sinker. Gaston, always called 'Colonel' by Nancy, was in some ways an English person's idea of a typical Frenchman: not only did he adore women, he showed it (which does not often happen in

England). He was not handsome, but the speed of his clever talk soon made you forget his appearance. He had studied at Oxford and somehow knew reams of English poetry, nursery rhymes and quintessentially English jokes. He was as good a tease as Nancy and used to go on at her until she said, 'Oh Colonel, do shut up.' I got to know him in Paris after the war when staying with Nancy and became fond of him. He was one of those people you instantly felt you had known all your life.

Nancy spent much of the war working at Heywood Hill's bookshop in Mayfair. Heywood and his wife, Anne, had been her friends for years and he made a wise choice when he invited her to join the staff. No sooner did she appear in the Curzon Street shop than all her friends and acquaintances followed. In the bookshop, she was pinned down, available for chat anytime during business hours. Sometimes the laughter grew a bit much for serious book buyers and one customer said pointedly, 'May I be allowed to buy this volume please?' But the business Nancy brought was worth more than the odd lost sale. Household names from the writing fraternity, who also happened to be her friends, gathered at the shop and customers could see at close quarters what are now called 'celebrities'.

The wages were meagre, £3 10s a week, and Nancy was so short of money that she usually walked the two miles home to Blomfield Road to save the bus fare. On one flush day she was waiting in the queue at the bus stop in Park Lane after dark when a huge black American soldier came up and hugged her. 'Go away,' she screamed, 'I'm FORTY.' At one point she became a firewatcher and was asked to give lectures on firefighting. These soon came to an end. When she enquired why, she was told, 'Well, you see, it's your voice. We've had several complaints, someone even wrote in and said they wanted to put you on the fire.'

Enough has been written about the war for people who did not live through it to know that it brought tragedies and upheavals to everyone's lives. For each inhabitant of the British Isles there was a tale to tell. In our family, an unexpected sadness was my parents' decision to separate. The events leading up to the war – Decca's elopement and estrangement, Unity's attachment to Nazism, Diana's relationship with Sir O – had all poisoned life at home. Added to this was Muv and Farve's fundamental disagreement over Germany. At first, Farve had been impressed by Hitler but, as a born patriot, from the day war was declared he publicly renounced his former opinion and stood firmly behind the government. Muv refused to consider Hitler a threat and believed that it was a mistake to go to war. Neither of these strong characters would budge from their positions and it was painful in the extreme to see their unhappiness. Farve was permanently cross and for the first time I saw my mother truly angry.

Unity's suicide attempt was the last straw. Farve could not bear to see the day-in day-out hopelessness of her condition, which seemed to embody all the suffering brought on by the war. It became clear that he and Muv would be better apart so that the wireless news and propaganda would not provide daily fuel for their arguments. Muv never talked to me about the situation but I was, of course, acutely aware of it. Farve retreated to Inch Kenneth with Margaret Wright, who had been parlourmaid and later housekeeper at the Mews when 26 Rutland Gate was sold. Margaret was handsome and competent at her job but she was not used to the rough and tumble of family life. I felt her to be critical of my sisters and me – the opposite of Mabel – and she gave all her attention to Farve. She was one of those highly conventional women whose answer, in a prissy voice, you could guess before you had asked the question. She was such a boring companion that I often wondered how Farve could stand it, but he found her restful and undemanding. There was never any danger of a political argument and after a while she became indispensable to him.

These must have been terrible months for my poor mother. Added to her feelings about the war were the unhappiness of her marriage going awry, the ongoing worry of Unity's condition, Diana's imprisonment and Decca losing her soulmate in harrowing and uncertain circumstances. My own life was humdrum and almost carefree in comparison. According to Nancy, I was 'having a wild time with young cannon fodders at the Ritz', which was only partly true. Soon after the outbreak of war I worked in a canteen for servicemen at St Pancras Station and after Unity came home I did the same in Edinburgh to be with my Ogilvy cousins.

When war was declared, Andrew wanted to join the Coldstream Guards, in which his brother Billy was already serving as an officer, but there was a rush to join up and Andrew was told that he had to wait until there was a place for him. Frustrated, he returned to Cambridge. In December 1939, while he was marking time, he met Lady Digby (mother of my fellow debutante Pamela). 'What, Andrew? Still not in uniform?' she exclaimed. Andrew was incensed by this insult and never spoke to her again. I do not suppose she noticed, but she could not have said anything more wounding to a young man impatiently awaiting his call-up. This eventually came in June 1940.

When Andrew and I were in London we continued to drive around in my flimsy Austin Seven and when one nightclub got too hot with incendiary bombs falling close by, we moved to another. We took no notice of the bombing – it never occurred to us that we might be hit. In late 1940, on a visit to Andrew's parents' house in Derbyshire, we became officially engaged. My future mother-in-law said to Andrew, 'You have either got to marry that girl or stop asking her here.' So that is how it happened.

9

MARRIAGE

Churchdale Hall, where Andrew's parents had lived since 1923, sits like a broody hen spreading itself over the top of a hill above the village of Ashford-in-the-Water. It was a home if ever there was one, made so by the presence of Moucher, Andrew's mother, who in her self-effacing way was quite unconscious of the effect her goodness, beauty and ready understanding had on all around her. Andrew's sisters, Elizabeth and Anne Cavendish, respectively six and seven years younger than me and still in the schoolroom, soon became, and have remained, my great friends.

If my own father was thought eccentric, Eddy Devonshire ran him close. He wore paper collars, did not possess an overcoat and would stand, oblivious of the weather, in the freezing wind on Chesterfield Station in a threadbare London suit. He was a heavy smoker of ready-rolled Turkish cigarettes called Pasquale that he lit with a tinder cord, a curious bit of orange rope that looked like a dressing-gown cord. It smouldered away merrily even in a gale and was a useful lighter on outdoor occasions. It also smouldered away merrily in Eddy's coat pocket and made some decent holes, blackened around the edges; these became part of the suit, which he would never have dreamed of replacing. His ancient clothes sometimes let him down: he got both legs stuck in the ragged lining of one of the trouser legs of an old dinner suit and we waited a long time for him that night.

An expert fly-tier, Eddy was keen eyed and neat fingered, and told me he would have practised dentistry had his life been different. He made an odd sight, a white apron over his well-worn, blue velvet smoking-jacket, leaning across a table covered with all the ingredients for fly-tying. The smell of the glue was to become very familiar. He begged plumes from the hats of his women friends and, picking one up, would sigh with nostalgia and say things like, 'Ettie Desborough, Ascot, 1921.' Once the flies were ready, he lay in the bath imagining he was a salmon while Edward, the butler, pretending to be a fishing rod, jerked them over his submerged head. The ones the Duke judged most attractive were used on his stretch of the Blackwater in County Cork at the start of the salmon fishing season.

Eddy was not much good at small talk and often remained silent. Coming from a family that never drew breath, I found this silence intimidating, but our mutual interest in British wild flowers helped to break the ice. His copy of Bentham and Hooker is as good as a diary, with its neatly coloured-in line drawings of flowers and annotations of where and when he had found them. He returned from the funeral of his brother-in-law Evan Baillie, at Ballindarroch in the north of Scotland, delighted because he had stumbled on a *Trientalis europæa* in that remote glen.

Eddy was MP for Derbyshire West for fifteen years, until 1938 when his father, Victor, the Ninth Duke, died and Eddy moved to the House of Lords. He kept score of the number of votes cast in his constituency, one of the largest in the country, by planting crocuses at Churchdale in the parties' colours, blue for Conservative and yellow for Liberal, but he had to make do with white for Labour, there being no red crocuses. In the early years, Eddy was driven to meetings by his chauffeur, Lewis James, in a brownish-yellow 1914 Humber known as the Yellow Peril. (It is still roadworthy today.) Outside a rowdy meeting in a quarrying village one day, a man shouted insults about Eddy in front of Lewis. 'So what did you do?' asked Eddy as they drove away. 'I gave him one with my spanner,' said Lewis.

Keenly interested in the animal kingdom, Eddy was president of the Zoological Society of London from 1948 until his death. Herbrand, the Eleventh Duke of Bedford (whose best friend was a spider), was a member of the Society. On one occasion when Eddy was being driven home by Lewis James from the London Zoo, he heard a strange grunting, gabbling noise coming from the boot. 'James,' said Eddy, 'that is not a mechanical noise.' 'Geese, Your Grace. A present from the Duke of Bedford.' They drove on in silence.

•

Soon after Andrew and I became engaged, he went to Rutland Gate to talk to my father. A lucky thing happened, an incident when they both behaved out of character: Farve put his jumbo teacup, full to the brim, on the edge of a card table that sloped a little. It started to slide. Quick as a flash, Andrew grabbed it with both hands just before the fatal moment when the strong milky tea would have made a hateful puddle on the carpet – the sort of occurrence Farve abhorred. Andrew handed him the cup and was immediately accepted as part of the family. We decided to be married in London, at St Bartholomew the Great in Smithfield. We loved the ancient church and, perhaps subconsciously, craved the feeling of permanence it gave in the upside-down world of war and bombs when everything we knew was changing.

Miraculously, the church survived the Blitz and we were married there on 19 April 1941. My parents-in-law were kindness itself, letting us have the furniture we needed for the tiny mews house off Regent's Park where we lived while Andrew was stationed in London, making us presents of a car and a huge double bed, and giving me a pair of beautiful diamond and aquamarine clips. A sign of the formality of those far-off times was that they never asked me to call them by their Christian name: she was Duchess to me and he was Duke. It was the same for Andrew: Lord and Lady Redesdale never turned into David and Sydney. But these old rules did not interfere with friendship.

I was staying at the Mews with Muv and Farve two nights before our wedding when there was one of London's heaviest air raids of the war. For the first time, I was frightened. Two houses at the bottom of the street were sliced in half by a direct hit, and a bed was left hanging precariously over the edge of a floor. All the buildings near by were damaged and every window in No. 26 was blown out. The ballroom, where the reception was to be held, was covered in broken glass and the curtains, which were torn to shreds, had to be put out with the rubbish. Muv bought rolls of grey and gold wallpaper, shaped them into pretend curtains and nailed them to the windows. Luckily the weather was mild as the house was open to the elements. The caterers brought a cake in a white cardboard casing (no icing because of sugar rationing) and when the time came to cut it, all they had to do was lift the cover. Muv somehow got hold of champagne. The wine merchant begged her not to take too much of his precious supply as no more could be had from France.

I was married from the Mews and a photograph shows the wedding group in front of the dustbins. We had no pages or bridesmaids (although Mrs Ham offered to be one, dressed in black, of course). Victor Stiebel made me a dream of a dress from eighty yards of white tulle. I never thought I should own such a thing, and had we been married six weeks later I could not have done: clothes rationing came in and my dress would have taken several years' worth of coupons. Farve gave me away in his Home Guard uniform. He had refused promotion from Private to Corporal because he did not want the responsibility, but his shoes were better polished than many of his comrades'. He was only sixty-three but looks old and sad in the photographs. After it was all over, Andrew and I drove to the government office where I had been summoned to register for war work, along with a crowd of other girls of my age.

We went to my parents-in-law's house, Compton Place, for our six precious days of honeymoon. It was a week of intensive air raids. All night long the German planes throbbed overhead on their way to London – a constant drone of engines bent on their mission to destroy. Eastbourne was a restricted area because of being on the coast and, with the enemy only a few miles away across the Channel, it may seem a strange place for Andrew's family to have gone in wartime, but we all loved it and I often stayed there when Andrew was away. It suited my father-in-law as the train from Eastbourne to London was quicker and surer for him than the long journey from St Pancras to Miller's Dale, the nearest station to Churchdale. Compton Place had an Elizabethan core, brought up to date in the early eighteenth century by Colen Campbell, no less, and its furniture and plasterwork were superb. The lawns and tennis court were left unmown during the war and masses of bee orchids, which had lain dormant since the First World War, came up through the chalky soil.

Our great friend John Wyndham, a contemporary of Andrew at Eton and Cambridge, lodged with us at our cottage off Regent's Park. His appalling eyesight ruled out military service and he was a civilian, working for Harold Macmillan who was then Parliamentary Secretary to the Ministry of Supply. Like Andrew, John owed money. The bailiffs soon discovered where he was living and two of them spent one day sitting on a wall by the entrance to our cottage. John arrived back from work and asked them what they were doing. They explained and with presence of mind John said, 'Yes, Mr Wyndham is very elusive. I am looking for him too,' and joined them on the wall.

Soon after our honeymoon Andrew was posted to the newly formed 5th Battalion Coldstream Guards, later part of the Guards Armoured Division. For two and a half years they were sent to different camps around the country and I joined Andrew whenever I could. It was a period of intense activity and intense boredom for him. He said that the training in England was tougher in some ways than actually facing the enemy. On one bitterly cold night his battalion had to cross a swollen river in the north of England where several men lost their lives. On another occasion they were sprayed with blood from the local slaughterhouse; when the exercise was over they returned to camp, hungry and exhausted, to be given almost raw liver to eat. Such was the toughening-up programme. When the battalion was posted to Wiltshire we took a cottage in the main street of Warminster. Andrew went to the training camp by bus and on the way home he always brought a handful of wild flowers (to be identified in our Bentham and Hooker), including tall thistles which brushed the bosoms of the stout women sitting opposite. The battalion camped in the park of Siegfried Sassoon's house, Heytesbury, and Andrew was intrigued to see the writer, whom he greatly admired, wandering around his garden. He longed to talk to him but did not dare.

There was terrific excitement one summer's day when the Queen visited the troops on Salisbury Plain. Our friend Anthony Mildmay was the officer in charge and the men lined up to see Her Majesty drive by. They duly cheered and were bucked by her visit. Following her, sitting bolt upright in another stately Daimler, was the Queen's lady-in-waiting, Lady Nunburnholme, a cool, classic and correct English beauty. As the car drove by, Anthony was delighted to hear a soldier say loudly to his neighbour, 'Oo's the tart?'

We spent many evenings at Sturford Mead, on the edge of the Longleat estate, with Daphne, the beautiful, lively wife of Nancy's old friend Henry Weymouth. Daphne's house was always full of a cross-section of the British Army, all of whom were in love with her. (Henry Weymouth was in the Royal Wiltshire Yeomanry and spent the entire war in the Middle East, without home leave.) It was at Daphne's that we first met Evelyn Waugh. The phenomenal amount of drink that the writer downed made him tricky company and, as I was still shocked by drunkenness, I kept my distance. One night he poured a bottle of Green Chartreuse over his head and, rubbing it into his hair, intoned, 'My hair is covered in gum, my hair is covered in gum,' as the sticky mess ran down his neck.

When sober, Evelyn's charm was winning, but you had to catch him early in the evening. He wanted to be friends and was full of compliments, but they turned to insults before you knew where you were. The cleverness came through but so did the criticisms; everything was wrong, including me. After the war he made up for his sharp remarks at Sturford by buying me a hat at Rose Bertin in Paris, which he tried on himself in the shop. It was made of white felt, with two white birds perched above its blue straw brim. A Paris hat was a thing of the past and was a welcome present if ever there was one. Good old Evie.

Another figure of Sturford days was Conrad Russell, a dairy farmer, cheese-maker and intimate of the ardent Roman Catholic gang that gathered around Katherine Asquith at Mells in Somerset. Blue eyed and silver haired, he was clever like all Russells. We made friends on the farming level – I could not compete with his brainy neighbours but he realized that I was interested in the land and when he died left me his copy of Primrose McConnell's *Agricultural Note-Book*, which ranks high among my unstealable books.

One night when staying with Daphne we were awakened by the smell of burning. The house was on fire. We ran round the bedrooms, shouting to the sleeping guests to leave the house. Daphne's own door was locked; too much had been drunk that evening and it took what seemed an age to wake her. To add to the misery of that night, I put my bare foot in a huge dog's mess in the passage before we all got out – just in time. Panic produces strange reactions. In that house full of what are now described as 'decorative arts', all we managed to grab as we left were a few gramophone records. Poor Daphne lost many precious belongings and, to add insult to injury, was reported for infringing the blackout regulations. We were at Sturford Mead the night Henry came home. He was the handsomest man you ever saw and all seemed happy between him and Daphne. But the separation had been too long and their twenty-five years of marriage ended soon after his return.

Andrew's battalion was later posted to Norfolk, where I stayed in a pub at Hunstanton. We went botanizing in country that was new to both of us and, sitting on a straw stack, I fiddled with my wedding ring and dropped it. A gold ring in a pile of wheat straw is a goner so the ring is in that wheatfield still. Its replacement is a 'utility' one, gold in colour but probably of some baser metal. The loss of the wedding ring was made up for, however, by finding a corncockle – a rare flower in those days.

When I could not be with Andrew, his parents were the kindest of hosts. My mother-in-law was universally loved. She was vague and always late, but she never interfered or criticized and I was well aware of what a wonderful woman she was. In 1940 an unwelcome guest arrived at Churchdale to disturb our routine: Sir Edward Marsh CVO, CB, CMG, scholar, translator and long-time private secretary to Winston Churchill. He had been knocked down in the blackout by a London taxi and was taken, badly shaken but with no bones broken, to nearby Pratt's Club (owned by my father-in-law) to be tidied up. The Duke took pity on him and invited him to Churchdale to recuperate. He arrived. Almost at once, Elizabeth, Anne and I were irritated by him and his boring tales of his old boss and the stage folk he knew. There he was at supper every night with only us for an audience – my parents-in-law were often in London. He insisted on listening to the nine o'clock news, which interrupted our records of Harry Roy and the like, but as soon as Alvar Liddell's soothing voice came over the wireless telling of the latest disaster, Eddie fell asleep. The little click when we turned off the wireless to go back to our favourite dance bands woke him with a start, and it was back to Alvar Liddell.

For exercise, Eddie tossed a pack of playing cards on the floor and picked them up one by one. I often wondered why he could not do something more useful – dig the garden for instance – but no, he was too special for that. After he had been with us for about a month, a van arrived at Churchdale with his cellar (many cases of Drambuie) and we realized that he was in for a long stay. He was so dug in, and I suppose thought himself part of the family, that whenever the Devonshires moved from Compton Place to Churchdale and back, Eddie Marsh went too. He was head over heels in love with Ivor Novello (whose name he maddeningly pronounced 'I-*vor*') and was in a state of high excitement the day Novello came to tea at Compton Place, as Eddie's guest. Novello looked at my whippet, Studley, and said, his head to one side, 'What an enchanting bit of beige.' Studley was a serious dog, the hero of many hare-coursing days, and was not to be dismissed as 'a bit of beige'. That was the end of the composer of *The Dancing Years* as far as I was concerned. After fourteen and a half months, Eddie finally left. He would have stayed longer but Edward, the butler, and my sisters-in-law formed up to his hosts and said enough was enough. He arrived in November 1940 and left in January 1942. Talk about the man who came to dinner . . .

On 26 March 1943 our daughter Emma was born, and at the end of the year Andrew embarked for Italy with his battalion. Emma was then eight months old, and with another baby on the way we needed a house of our own. I moved into the Rookery, a dark, damp house in Ashford-in-the-Water belonging to Chatsworth, the Devonshire's Derbyshire estate. There were pigsties, stables and a paddock where I kept my driving pony. In the kitchen, a huge coal range took up one wall and smuts penetrated everywhere. The stove gave off such fierce heat, rapidly followed by the depressing sight of cold grey ashes, that our wartime rations were often inedible. Rationing and coupons ruled our lives. When I was in London for Andrew's last few days of leave before he left for Italy, he entrusted me with three hundred of the clothing coupons issued to soldiers to buy all the special kit they needed for going abroad. I was meant to be the reliable one, but I left the precious coupons in a taxi. It was a disaster because they could not be replaced, but Andrew never reproached me.

I lived at the Rookery with Emma, her nanny Diddy, three dogs, a pony and trap, a pig, a cow, and Violet, an evacuee with two small sons. I was blessed with Diddy – Ellen Stephens – who had arrived two months earlier, sent by Divine Providence. She was fifty-four, the minimum age at which any job other than 'war work' could be taken up, and it was our luck that her age coincided with our need. Babies thrived under her care: put a screaming infant into her arms and it immediately calmed down. Her influence went much further than the nursery and her intelligence, common sense, knowledge of the natural world and devotion to the children in her care gave them the best possible start in life. Diddy looked after Emma while I pretended to sort things at the Red Cross county clearing house in Bakewell. I was not much use to them as, pregnant, I was sick over everything without warning.

I got about in an old milk float drawn by a splendid pedigree Hackney mare and sometimes drove up the steep hill past Sheldon to the limestone plateau of the Peak District. Along the broad grass verges, stretching for a mile or more, were piles of bombs, long and thin, short and fat, unguarded, waiting. They became part of the scenery and then disappeared one day as mysteriously as they had arrived. The mare trotted along the empty A6 to Bakewell in no time. I tied her to a post near Mr Thacker's butcher's shop, where he let me help him cut up the meat in the back room and get a few scraps for the dogs. Tongue was offal and therefore not rationed. 'Any chance of a tongue?' I would ask. 'You're thirty-sixth on the list,' was always the answer. I do not think I ever got to the top. (A woman next to me in the queue, listening to people talking about the end of rationing, said one day, 'Well, if they give it up, meat will be rationed by price and that would never do.' As the years have gone by I have often thought about what she said.) One day a wounded soldier repatriated from Italy brought home a lemon. Such a luxury had not been seen for a long time and it caused a minor sensation when he put it on the post office counter at Ashford-in-the-Water and charged tuppence a smell – proceeds to the Red Cross.

We paid rent to the Chatsworth estate to live at the Rookery. You might have thought that we could live rent-free, but the house belonged to the Chatsworth Estate Company and the law demanded that all its tenants, including the family, should pay rent. Our income was small at the time and I was appalled by the size of the estate bill for logs, our only form of heating apart from the ancient kitchen range. (My mother-in-law always said that the bill for logs was the land agent's way of trying to balance the forestry accounts.) In one of the snowy winters of the war, I fell ill while on a prolonged visit to Churchdale and Dr Sinclair Evans was called. His practice took him up rough tracks to remote farms and he always dressed in the same thick tweeds and gumboots for any bedside he was called to; with the sleeves of his woollen vest showing round his wrists, he was a reassuring sight in an emergency. Dr Evans was an excellent diagnostician and pronounced pneumonia, which in those days was treated with pills called M & B. In spite of the pills, I was delirious for a while and he told me afterwards that I shouted, 'I'm not in debt, I'm not in debt', obviously the result of the huge bills for firewood from Chatsworth Estates Co.

In January 1944, Henry Hunloke, MP for Derbyshire West, my father-in-law's old constituency, resigned his seat and a by-election was quickly called. Henry had been with his regiment in the Middle East since the outbreak of war and felt that he could no longer adequately represent the voters' interests. More significant, perhaps, he was married to Eddy Devonshire's sister Anne and was in the process of getting a divorce. Derbyshire West had been held almost exclusively by a member of the Cavendish family since the sixteenth century. Andrew's brother, Billy, yet another Cavendish nominee, was selected as the Conservative candidate and in February 1944 got leave from his regiment to fight the election. His selection turned out to be unwise as it made people feel the influence of Chatsworth was too strong: Conservatives were annoyed because the selection procedure had been so hasty and the opposition felt that they had not been given enough time to mount their campaign.

Billy and Andrew did not get on well and there was jealousy on both sides. As the second son, Andrew felt left out of things: Billy was not only his parents' favourite, he was also in line to inherit the family title, fortune and estates. Billy suffered because Andrew was more attractive – not better looking, but quick, funny and popular with girls. It did not help matters that when Andrew was commissioned in 1940 the brothers sometimes found themselves near-neighbours when training. They were wary of stepping on each other's territory and the result was that I saw little of Billy in pre-war days. It was only in the run-up to the by-election that I got to know him and grew fond of him. He used to drop in for a drink on his way home to Churchdale and unwind after the punishing round of political meetings in village halls scattered over the constituency. Billy's opponent was Charles Frederick White Jr, a Socialist who had been active in local government for over thirty years. The fight was personal and grubby, and the meetings rowdy and sometimes rough. White's supporters taught children to chant:

Charlie White's a gentleman
Hartington's a fool

Before he goes to politics
He ought to go to school.

The country as a whole was fed up with rationing, discipline and the worsening conditions at home; and there seemed to be no light at the end of the tunnel. Nationalization of the coal industry was on everyone's lips and although mining was minimal in Derbyshire West, the constituency was surrounded by coal mines and heavy industry and the electorate was longing for change. As heir to one of the largest land holdings, and perhaps the greatest private collection of works of art in England, as well as several huge houses, Billy was a target for the anti-establishment brigade. He was beaten by 4,561 votes, receiving 41.5 per cent of the vote to White's 57.7 per cent. Billy's speech at the declaration of the poll was as memorable as his appearance: tall and fit from five years of army service, he was as handsome as a film star. 'It has been a hard fight,' he told his audience, 'and that is the way it goes. I am going out now to fight for you at the front. After all, unless we win the war there can be no home front. Better luck next time.' There were loud cheers, some of the women were in tears – perhaps they had a premonition of what was to come. One old lady standing next to me said, 'It's a shame to let him go, a great tall man like he is, he's such a target.'

The result of the by-election was a personal blow for Churchill, foreshadowing the defeat of Conservatism and Labour's landslide victory the following year. Derbyshire West had decided it wanted out with the old and in with the new, but the 'old' in this case was young and full of promise, while the 'new' was a grey man, lacking in distinction or appeal, with a bitter twist to his speeches. C. F. White sank without trace in the House of Commons. He hung on to his seat by only 156 votes in the 1945 General Election and decided, wisely, not to stand again in 1950.

Billy rejoined his regiment, now preparing for the invasion of France. Sadly, I could not go to his wedding to Kick on 6 May 1944 as I was still in bed after the birth of our son, Stoker. That Billy and Kick managed to marry at all was a tribute to their love for each other. It is difficult to realize the depth of antagonism that still existed in the 1940s between Protestants and Catholics. Billy came from a deeply religious Protestant background and Kick's Irish-Catholic parents felt just as strongly about their creed. At the eleventh hour, after a series of discussions with the head of the Roman Catholic Church in England and the Archbishop of Canterbury, the seemingly insurmountable obstacles were overcome and it was agreed that any sons of the union should be brought up in the Church of England and any daughters as Roman Catholics. My father-in-law had been haunted by the possibility that if his beloved Billy married a Roman Catholic any eventual heirs would be brought up in that faith, and the outcome satisfied him. Both he and Moucher became devoted to Kick, who was welcomed into the family by all. Rose Kennedy never accepted the decision and her relationship with her daughter suffered accordingly.

Billy and Kick had ecstatically happy moments together, snatching days and nights while preparations for D-Day were gathering speed. Six weeks after their wedding Billy left with his battalion for France and was part of the Allied advance that pushed towards Belgium at a fearful cost of British lives. They reached the border at the beginning of September, where they met stiff enemy resistance. Unbelievably, officers were allowed to wear pale-coloured corduroy trousers, a beret and to carry a swagger stick – an obvious target for a sniper. And so it was. On 9 September 1944 Billy, now a Major, was walking ahead of his company to lead an assault on the village of Heppen, when he was shot through the heart by a single bullet and died where he fell. His men were enraged. 'We took no prisoners that day,' one of them wrote to my father-in-law. Billy was buried at Leopoldsburg, one of nearly 800 Commonwealth dead in that cemetery.

Eddy and Moucher were devastated. Their hopes for the future died with their son. Kick, a widow at twenty-four, was in America for a memorial service for her elder brother, Joe Jr., a pilot in the US Navy, who had been killed in action. She returned immediately to Compton Place, where Billy's parents, sisters and I tried to comfort each other. I wrote to Muv, 'As always when someone you know intimately has been killed, it seems quite impossible that you won't see him again. I am afraid of writing to Andrew. I don't know what to say or how to say it . . . They don't hold out any hope of getting Andrew home till after the war. I wish Winston was here as it's possible he might understand and send for him. I do so want to see him and he would make the whole difference to his mother and father.' To Diana I wrote that I was worried that Andrew might go right under for a time.

When the news of his brother's death reached him, Andrew was in the front line of some of the fiercest battles of the Italian campaign. The enemy were holding every inch of the ground and his company was in the thick of it. It was a miracle that he came out alive.

He wrote to me on 22 September:

My Own Darling,

In an odd sort of way I have always known that the happiness of our family life was too good to last and now the tragedy has happened. It seems odd that Billy, with everything to live for and so brilliantly capable of carrying out the life that he had to lead, should be taken just when that life was beginning, but I do not doubt for one moment that there is a reason. Wherever he has gone, he has gone in the good company of his and our friends.

My darling, you must be having a difficult and utterly miserable time. If only I could be there to be of some use – but it is the greatest comfort to me to know that you are there. I know what a difference it will make to Mummy and Daddy. The thought of their grief is terrible. That is the wicked part of death – the grief and sorrow it leaves behind.

Darling, it seems out of place among the misery of the moment and I only mention it on the chance it will give you all a bit of pleasure, I have been given an MC – most undeserved. It is nice to have it and I hope Mummy and Daddy will be pleased.

Darling, I suppose our life is going to be very different to what we had planned. But I know whatever life has in store, with you beside me life has no fears.

God bless you, my darling. Don't grieve for me.

It was so typical of Andrew just to throw in that he had received the Military Cross, as though it had been at a vicarage tea party. He was, in fact, decorated for 'the cheerfulness and leadership he displayed' when his Company had to dig in under heavy shelling near a village called Strada, south of Florence, and was trapped for thirty-six hours in scorching weather with nothing to eat and, worse, nothing to drink.

It is difficult for people to imagine what it was like in September 1944. For myself, I was forever expecting a telegram to say that Andrew had been killed in action: the future was as uncertain as it could be. Dealing with the hardships of day-to-day life also took up much energy and, with two small babies, there was neither time nor inclination to think of what might happen after the war, which had been going on for five years and could still have turned against us. Andrew's new situation meant nothing to me at the time, except for the great sorrow of Billy's death and the sympathy I felt for Andrew.

Andrew's time in Italy changed him. He saw many of his comrades dead or wounded and had a particularly horrifying experience when his mentor, Sergeant King, was killed. He had told the Sergeant to stay put while he went to look over a ridge to see if there was any sign of the enemy. When he got back the gallant Sergeant had been blown to bits by a mortar bomb. Andrew rarely spoke of this or any other of his experiences during the war, but they must, as they did for millions, have had a traumatic effect. The process of becoming an adult was concentrated into a few hard weeks.

After Billy's death, my parents-in-law continued their peregrinations between Churchdale and Eastbourne, but Eddy vowed never to set foot inside Chatsworth again. He had lost heart and could not bring himself to be interested in the future of a house which five years previously had been the scene of joyous celebrations for his adored son's twenty-first birthday.

For me 1944 was a momentous year. Two events of the greatest joy were the birth of Stoker and the news in October that Andrew was coming home. But the bad news came thick and fast. A few weeks before D-Day I was staying at Compton Place. Eastbourne was crowded with troops and my mother-in-law invited Ned Fitzmaurice, who was in the Irish Guards, Luke Lillingston, from the Leicestershire Yeomanry, and other young officers to tea. She told them to go to the kitchen garden and help themselves to strawberries. 'Awfully sorry,' said Luke, 'I've done that already.' He had scaled the high brick wall and gorged on a private feast. Two weeks later he was dead from wounds received in action. He left a lasting memory of a most attractive man with a reputation for being a fine horseman and an old-fashioned thruster out hunting.

That was the start. During the months of July and August my four greatest friends were killed. Mark Howard was the first to go, hit by shellfire on 2 July near a village called Marcelet, north-west of Caen. (Billy replaced him as Company commander.) Then Ned Fitzmaurice, aged just twenty-two, was killed on 11 August in a hail of machine-gun fire as he was leading his platoon. 'He was game to the last,' wrote a Lance Corporal in his regiment, 'no one could ever imagine him to possess the guts he had. I only wish a good many more could have had half of his, he is the gamest little lad I have ever seen. His first time in battle and Second-in-Command of the Company that morning.' Nine days later Ned's elder brother, Charlie, was blown up with his tank in Italy. He had been in the Middle East and Africa and away from his family and friends for years. He was posted as 'missing', giving false hope to his mother. His body was never found. On 12 August Dicky Cecil, aged twenty-two, a Sergeant Pilot in the RAF, died from injuries suffered in a motorbike accident in this country. The deaths of these four, so soon to be followed by Billy, left their family and friends numb.

Tom had gone through the North African campaign and thence to Italy, where in January 1944 he happened to meet Andrew. He found him sitting by the side of a road brewing tea with his Company. 'Tell Debo that he was very cheerful,' Tom wrote to Muv the next day. Tom gave Andrew some chocolate and a bottle of whisky, and they parted. Tom returned to England at the beginning of July 1944 and enrolled on a course at the Staff College in Camberley. His friendship with János and Teddy Almásy, and others in Germany, made him recoil at the idea of being part of the victorious army that would advance through Germany to finish the job. He asked to be transferred to the Devonshire Regiment, which was engaged against the Japanese in Burma. It must have been a wrench to leave his old comrades of the King's Royal Rifle Corps but it was his decision.

He arrived in Burma on 22 February 1945 and three weeks later was appointed Brigade Major. He knew not a soul in his new regiment, but the fact that they were face to face with the Japanese Army was good enough for him. Five weeks after his arrival he was hit by a burst of machine-gun fire from the enemy position. He was taken, still conscious, to the regimental aid post and operated on to remove a bullet that had penetrated his neck and lodged in his spine. He died six days later on 30 March and is buried near the Irrawaddy River, north-west of Mandalay.

Muv was at Inch Kenneth when the news came and Farve broke it to her in a telegram. 'I do not know how to tell you this,' he began. Tom's commanding officer sent a letter to my parents: 'It would be difficult to imagine a better regimental soldier,' he wrote.

> He had courage, an iron sense of duty, an immense capacity for work, perfect manners and an unfailing interest in all the details of soldiering which can be so tedious and are yet so important for the efficiency and happiness of the battalion. Tom was not the easiest of men to get on with. He held strong views which he defended with skill and wit and he did not suffer fools gladly: but those to whom he gave his confidence and affection will have to travel far before they find a better or more loyal friend.

At the end of the war, a memorial to Tom was installed above my parents' pew in Swinbrook Church, and I am glad it is there for all to see. It is my lasting regret that I did not know my brother better.

After D-Day, Muv and Unity were given permission to go to Inch Kenneth, where I joined them in August 1944. It was misery. Farve, who had spent much of the war on the island, sat stony-faced at table while Margaret's trite remarks about what she had heard on the news dampened any attempts at conversation. It was hard to believe that Farve was the same man who, whenever one of us children made a critical remark about Muv, used to get up from his dining-room chair at Swinbrook and rush round to tell her that her hair was molten gold and that she was more beautiful than the day. (It used to make us laugh – she was well past middle age and was indifferent to her appearance.) Now he seemed to hate her. Instead of joining us after supper, he washed up with Margaret. There were no more jokes. Muv's piano was silent. It was no longer her house.

Unity's odd behaviour added to the strained atmosphere. She summoned Muv and me to the island's ruined chapel one day, wound a sheet round her waist as a cassock and pretended to be a clergyman taking the service. She forgot the words to the 'Te Deum' and 'Jubilate' and stumped back to the house, angry with herself and us for witnessing these shortcomings. It was all unbearably sad and the feeling of wretch-edness was intensified by the isolation of the island; there was no one to talk to and nowhere to go – no cinema for Unity, no club for Farve, no antique shops for Muv. What should have been an idyllic place for a summer holiday was a kind of hell.

Recently a young journalist came to interview me about what I was doing the day war broke out. During the course of the interview, I re-counted the deaths of my only brother, Andrew's only brother, a brother-in-law and my four best friends. 'So,' she said, 'did the war affect you in any way?'

10

CHILDBIRTHS AND DEATHS

You might think having a baby is a natural function that happens when women wish it – and sometimes when they do not. But unforeseen hazards arise and things can change quickly from good to bad. When Andrew and I were first married, the false calm of the Phoney War was over and we did not know when he would be ordered abroad or whether either of us was likely to survive. We both wanted children and there was no question of postponement. We never imagined that everything might not go according to plan.

Almost immediately a baby was on the way and, like so many of our friends and contemporaries, we were happily anticipating the birth. Andrew's battalion was stationed in Hertfordshire at the time and we were living in a rented house at Shenley. I booked into Lady Carnarvon's nursing home, the Claridges of such places, which had been evacuated from London to Barnet, a few miles away. I went to a gynaecologist, Mr Gilliatt (later Sir William), generally accepted to be the leader in his profession, and all seemed to be going well. In November 1941, two and a half months before the baby was due, I fell ill with pain in my back and a high fever. (I was told later that E. coli was to blame.) Before the local doctor realized that something was wrong I went into labour and was hurried to the nursing home.

The baby was born after the well-named labour, which lasted several hours – an experience as every mother knows of extreme pain replaced by euphoria when the child is finally born; a new life starts and there is joy all round. But it was not like that. I heard the baby cry – animal instinct plays a big part during and after a birth and the cry of a newborn is the reward for the immense physical effort – and although I knew it was born too early, I had a wild hope that he (for it was a boy) would survive. The famous gynaecologist arrived when it was all over. He walked into the room, gave my stomach a rough push saying that was to get rid of the afterbirth, and added as he left, 'You don't expect the baby to live, do you?'

A few hours later, a nurse came to tell me that the baby had indeed died. I realized then what wonderful people nurses are; the worst jobs are always left to them, especially by grand doctors. Andrew arrived on compassionate leave and that was an immense comfort. It was a difficult time for him too as it had never occurred to him that such a thing could happen and that the outcome could be so sorrowful. The poor little baby was named Mark and buried in St Etheldreda, the parish church at Hatfield, just outside an entrance to the garden of Hatfield House where Andrew's Salisbury grandparents lived.

Despair slowly gives way to a sense of emptiness, grief for what might have been and feelings of self-reproach. Was it my fault? What did I do wrong? It was not easy to get back to day-to-day life. The loss of a premature baby was nothing in comparison to the sufferings caused by the war – the deprivations, the indiscriminate bombings and the daily deaths of young servicemen – but my own sense of failure, of being unable to achieve what most women can, remained. It was made worse when I heard of friends who had produced healthy babies with no difficulty. One of these friends, thinking to be kind, made me godmother to her child, not realizing how painful it would be.

Sixteen months later, on 26 March 1943, Emma was born, naturally and happily. Andrew's battalion was still in England and I spent the last six weeks before the birth with the Salisburys at Hatfield, to be near the nursing home in case of a second disaster. Their kindness has never been forgotten. Alice Salisbury, Andrew's grandmother, was a woman of irresistible charm – liberal, worldly-wise and funny. She used to stand in front of one of Hatfield's huge log fires and hitch up the back of her skirt to warm her behind. The house had become a hospital for wounded soldiers and the resident doctors often came to dinner. The fare was meagre by that stage of the war and was served on a Lazy Susan that revolved in the middle of the table. It whizzed so fast that you had to be quick to grab a bite to eat. I loved that visit and its successful ending.

Just over one year later, in April 1944, our son was born under rather different circumstances. Andrew had left for Italy, and I was staying at

Churchdale with the Devonshires. Dr Evans arranged for 27 April to be his day off so as not to be interrupted. I was in the kitchen garden looking for something green to eat when he arrived armed with an injection to set me off. In what seemed no time at all it was over, the easiest birth of all my babies, and off went a message to Andrew, by now advancing on Rome. On 4 May Andrew wrote saying that he had received the news and what huge pleasure it gave him.

Sister O'Gorman, the Irish monthly nurse who had seen me through good times and bad, was with me for the confinement. (I suppose she had a Christian name, but 'Sister' was what we all, with great respect, called her.) As smart as paint when on duty in Lady Carnarvon's pink uniform, impatient when a patient was not really ill, Sister O'Gorman was a brilliant nurse and nothing could detract from that. But I was surprised when I opened a drawer after she had left to find dirty stockings mixed up with broken biscuits – an unexpected legacy from this loved woman. She was an extraordinary support during my strange experiences, genial and funny as only the Irish can be. Rather shame-faced I told her that when I was pregnant my craving had been for coal. Derby Brights were my particular favourites and I ate a good deal of them, breaking off the shiny bits and blackening my teeth in the process. 'Oh,' she said, 'that's nothing. My last patient ate Vim' (a kind of scouring powder).

Before Andrew left for Italy, we had decided on names. If a boy, he wanted 'Peregrine', to which I added 'Andrew' and 'Morny' after Mornington Cannon, a jockey I admired. Our family is famous for nicknames and, inevitably, when he was about four, the name 'Peregrine' became rather a mouthful and was replaced by all sorts of nicknames. The ugliest, I suppose, was 'Stoker', but it stuck. When Andrew came home in March 1945, his contented, easy-going son was eleven months old.

The following autumn I was pregnant for the fourth time. That is to say, I was pregnant for a while. In December, for no apparent reason, I had a miscarriage – no illness, no shock, no accident – and I lost a lot of blood before the doctor could get to me. Being fairly early on, I was sad, but it was not advanced enough to compare with the loss of the baby in 1941. Life went on without too much disruption. A couple of months later I could not do up my skirt and felt the stirrings of another baby. Incredulous, I went to Dr Evans. 'Yes,' he said, 'you must have miscarried a twin,' and explained that it could sometimes happen.

By this time, Andrew and I had moved from the Rookery to Edensor House in the small village within the park at Chatsworth. I went into labour six weeks early, for no particular reason that I know of but far enough on for the baby to be all right. Dr Evans came and so did the district nurse, an old friend. I heard them talking through the haze, the pains grew to be almost unbearable and there was the baby. 'A lovely boy,' they reassured me, wrapping him up and putting him in his cot. Sister O'Gorman had not yet arrived from London and they left me, saying they would be back in a few hours. Dr Evans and Nurse Parry returned when the baby was seven hours old and apparently healthy, to hear him give a great sigh and die. The shock of the loss of this baby must have gone deep with Dr Evans. As he was leaving the house he fainted dead away and poor Andrew arrived from a distant engagement to face not just the misery of the dead baby but Dr Evans lying unconscious in the hall. We named the child Victor and he was buried in the family plot at St Peter's, Edensor.

For this last confinement, Dr Evans had borrowed a contraption called a gas and air machine, used as an analgesic in childbirth. As the pains get more severe you clamp a mask on to your face with both hands and gulp the blessed gas as hard as you can. As you lose consciousness, your hands drop and with them the mask; then back to normal till it is repeated all over again. It is such a clever idea: you cannot overdo the gas and it helps at the worst moments. The Baslow practice did not own such a machine, which I thought I could remedy and did. Dr Evans brought the new device with him on an ordinary visit and we tried it out sitting on my bed, flopping over backwards as we each blacked out in turn. (I suppose today we would be had up for charges under all sorts of new laws.)

There was a third unhappy ending in 1953. Again premature, she too was alive and crying before quietly fading away. We gave her the name Mary and she is buried at Edensor alongside her brother Victor. Andrew had the harrowing duty of arranging the funerals, each with its tiny coffin. I was spared this because in those days, where possible, the mother was kept in bed for two or three weeks after giving birth. No one suggested that I should go to the services and I remained completely removed from them.

The cumulative effect of these failures made me wonder how it was that we had two perfectly healthy children, who were progressing just as children should. People sympathized at the losses and with the kindest intentions would say, 'Look at those two. How wonderful to have them.' It was indeed wonderful, but people who have not been through the searing experience cannot understand that you mourn the lost ones and that nothing can replace them. Nevertheless, had Emma and Stoker not survived I think the tragedies would have overwhelmed me.

When Sophy was born on 18 March 1957 and all was well, there was much rejoicing. For the first four months of pregnancy I stayed in or near my bed, constantly fearful of what now seemed the inevitable disaster. The reward for this slight inconvenience was inestimable and went a long way in restoring a sense of achievement. Sophy was born in a London hospital, where the doctor brought his spaniels to cheer his country patients. I was so apprehensive that I did not buy any new clothes for the baby, and the washed-out woolly things and old-fashioned gowns surprised the nurses in the smart maternity wing. As soon as Sophy was born I remember shouting. 'Is the baby all right?' Then, louder, 'IS THE BABY ALL RIGHT?' I could hardly believe it when they said that she was perfect. The fourteen-year gap between Emma and Sophy sometimes caused people to ask, 'Who was your first husband?'

As time went on, I appreciated more and more the incredible good fortune of having Emma, Stoker and Sophy, and the sadness for the other three faded. But writing about them now made me wonder whether the three who did not survive had been christened. Bleak notices of the burials of Mark, Victor and Mary appear in the Records Offices in Hertfordshire and Derbyshire, giving their ages as five hours, seven hours and four hours respectively (their short lives contrasting pathetically with all the old people on the lists). The vicar at Hatfield kindly made some enquiries and found a note about Mark's burial, but no record of a christening. Nor were there any records of a christening at St Peter's, Edensor. It is only recently that I discovered from Mrs Symonds, widow of the Reverend Tom Symonds, Vicar of Edensor 1954–71 (who had been told by Francis Thompson, the long-serving librarian at Chatsworth), that my mother-in-law baptized all three children in an emergency ceremony, recognized by the Church of England (and the Roman Catholic Church). I cannot imagine a better person to do it. I am glad I know the recorded facts of these births and deaths so their sorry chapter can now be closed.

11

INHERITANCE

In October 1944, six weeks after Billy was killed, I received a letter from Andrew telling me that he was coming home. I could hardly believe it. 'Oh dear, I am nearly off my head,' I wrote to Muv, 'I don't know whether I'm coming or going.' Andrew wrote that he would be back about the middle of December as he had to stay at a Reinforcement Depot for about a month and would then get a boat and come home. 'Oh can you imagine how wonderful it will be for me and for his mother and father,' I told Muv, 'I am nearly dying.'

Andrew eventually arrived home in March 1945. He had been withdrawn from his battalion and sent to a training camp near Naples at the request, as he later discovered, of Harold Macmillan, who was Minister Resident with Cabinet status at Allied Force Headquarters in Algiers. Macmillan was married to Eddy Devonshire's sister Dorothy, and was known as 'Uncle Harold' in the family. In spite of the relief Andrew knew it must have brought his mother and father, he bitterly resented being taken away from the front. He never spoke to me about it, but I know that the order to go to the training camp was the hardest to obey in his five years of army service. In his memoirs, *Accidents of Fortune*, he wrote that when he rejoined his comrades who had fought on during three hard months, he was unable to look them in the eye.

With the horrors of the Italian campaign still fresh in his mind, it must have been difficult for Andrew to adjust to a calm life in the country where there was no petrol and the strictest food rationing yet. He had to decide his future. He was now heir to his father's estates but Eddy, aged fifty, was still in charge. Andrew's mind turned to politics, which had always been his overriding interest. He knew that he had no chance of being selected for a winnable seat so had to make a start with a safe Labour seat, which would serve as a good apprenticeship. He tried for two constituencies in the East End of London – Mile End and Shoreditch – but was turned down by both. The fact that he was the son of a duke and had been to Eton and Cambridge was enough to ensure he was not selected; his war record counted for nothing. He tried for North East Derbyshire but was again unsuccessful and was beginning to lose heart when Councillor Ernest Robinson, chairman of the few Conservatives in Chesterfield, persuaded the committee to hear Andrew put his case. To Andrew's joy, he was adopted and it was the beginning of our long association with that town and the many men and women of all political opinions with whom we made friends.

Andrew's father seldom gave him advice but when he did it was taken and used again and again. 'There is something you should ram home,' Eddy said to Andrew, 'and you cannot repeat it too often. No government has any money of its own, the only money it has to spend is what it gets from you and me in taxes.' You could see by the expression on the faces of some of Andrew's audience that they did not believe it (and some people probably still do not). I remember another piece of advice Eddy gave, delivered in his usual dry manner. 'Andy,' he said, 'mark my words, wherever there is trouble in the world there is a clergyman behind it.'

I have always voted Conservative and would never do otherwise. When we were young, Decca used to say in a sarcastic voice, 'There you go again. You're a Conservative policeman,' whenever I attempted to forestall a row with our parents. I was never tempted to follow any extreme cause, but I did get worked up in the 1945 General Election (and in subsequent elections), partly because of the personalities involved and partly because of my dislike of any Socialist government and their pretences. I was not interested in Communism or Fascism – I had had too much of them in my childhood.

Nationalization of the coal mines was the main topic in the run-up to the 1945 election, and feelings ran so high that the police were often present at meetings. We were spat at and our car was rolled till it nearly turned over. Audiences were rowdy and the heckling sometimes aggressive. On one occasion, a man at the back of the hall shouted to Andrew that he wanted to shake his hand. Andrew was so surprised at this friendly gesture that he jumped off the stage and ran down the aisle, where an accomplice shot out his leg and sent him crashing to the floor. He picked himself up, dismayed but unhurt, and returned to the platform with the audience laughing. I always thought that the way the Socialists pre-sented nationalization to the coal miners was grossly unfair. The miners were led to believe that their lives would be transformed from one day to the next when the National Coal Board took over. In the event they found themselves back underground, the old hierarchy still in place. The only change, it seemed to me, was that there were more managers, while the men who mattered came to the surface as grimy as ever.

The election was a landslide victory for Labour, following the trend set in Derbyshire West the previous year. Andrew was beaten by over 12,000 votes, but he had whipped up such enthusiasm among his sup-porters that we had almost persuaded ourselves he could win. He stayed with Chesterfield after 1945 and spent a great deal of time in the con-stituency where he became well known. In the 1950 General Election, the boundaries of the constituency were changed to include the indus-trial district of Staveley and some of the worst housing in the neigh-bourhood. Labour won again with an even larger majority.

In March 1946 we moved to Edensor House in the small village of Edensor. I never liked it: the house faces north and east, has no view and was impossible to warm during fuel rationing, but it is less than a mile from Chatsworth and my father-in-law thought Andrew should be nearer the big house and the estate office, and learn how things were run. Eddy had no intention of going to live at Chatsworth himself – Billy's death had seen to that. As far as I know, he kept his vow of never setting foot in the house again, with one exception: he gave away his daughter, Anne, at her wedding to Michael Tree in the chapel at Chatsworth in November 1949. But he did not sleep in the house and chose to stay with Andrew and me at Edensor, as he had always done since the end of the war whenever he came to Derbyshire on business.

Even before the tragedy of Billy's death, the house had never held happy memories for Eddy, and his childhood had been made miserable by continual criticisms from his mother, Granny Evie. He told me that every time he came home from boarding school his mother made him cry on the first day of the holidays. (Surprisingly, he later wrote affectionate letters to her, showing that his regard for his mother was ambivalent.) In 1925 his father, Victor Duke, had a stroke. He lived on for thirteen years but was very different to the benign person he had once been. He lost his temper with everyone and lay about him with his stick: station masters and footmen were his regular targets. When Victor became acutely ill, my old friend Dr Evans visited him daily and described the ordeal:

> Every morning the routine was the same. I must enter the sick room and sit down quietly in a chair at one side of the fire, His Grace would be sitting on the other side reading *The Times*. Whatever happened I must not make a sound until he lowered the newspaper and peered over the top. His temper was known to be uncertain. I was told that sometimes his valet had to crawl under the breakfast table to lace up his boots. In this position His Grace found it impossible to belabour him with his walking stick.

Victor went on shooting after his stroke and was extremely dangerous, swinging round with his gun with no regard for his neighbours. Billy and Andrew were placed either side of him, which naturally put Andrew off the sport as he was in mortal fear of his grandfather's gun. (Moucher even went so far as to buy the boys bullet-proof spectacles.) The only person at Chatsworth liked by the Duke was John Maclauchlan, the autocratic head keeper, who took him rabbit shooting, which Victor preferred to set-piece pheasant shoots. On one occasion, the Duke took a grandson, Peter Baillie, with him on this ploy. Peter, aged about six, created a legend in the family by turning a sackful of ferrets upside down on to the Duke's head and, surprisingly, did not get into trouble for this bold action.

No wonder Chatsworth was an unhappy place during those years. Granny Evie tried to carry on as if nothing had happened but the house and estate lacked a leader and it showed. Victor paid no attention to the head land agent, who ruled at the estate office and was responsible for everything beyond the garden at Chatsworth, including the estate villages, tenanted farms, woods, sporting activities, quarries and all the buildings on the aforementioned. Things gradually went downhill. Neither Eddy nor Moucher had the authority to run the many different departments, and it was a relief to everybody when, in May 1938, Victor's life came to an end. Eddy and Moucher delayed moving into Chatsworth while essential plumbing work was carried out and camped there the following Christmas before setting off in the New Year for a long tour of Australia and South Africa. Eddy was Parliamentary Under Secretary for Dominion Affairs, a post he held until 1940. As soon as war was declared, he and Moucher packed up Chatsworth and went back to Churchdale.

After the war Eddy spent more and more time in London and Compton Place. In 1947 Francis Thompson, the long-serving librarian and keeper of the collection at Chatsworth, wrote to him warning him in no uncertain terms of the dangers to the family's reputation and to Chatsworth itself if no action was taken to preserve the house and its collection. He advised the Duke that in his opinion Chatsworth should be opened to the public on a proper commercial footing. Eddy and Moucher had already started thinking about reopening the house on a small scale and Mr Thompson's letter must have given them a jolt.

During the war Chatsworth had been brought to life by the three hundred girls and staff from Penrhos College in North Wales. Sometime before the war, their school buildings had been requisitioned by the Ministry of Food and the school had had to find alternative premises. With his usual foresight, my father-in-law, knowing that schoolgirls would be more sympathetic tenants than soldiers, had made the arrangement before war was declared. In March 1946 the girls returned to their Welsh premises and Chatsworth was left empty. Andrew and I often walked along the footpath from Edensor and across the river to explore the cold, dank, echoing rooms. Basic maintenance was being carried out, and in the bitter winter of 1946–7 house carpenters were shovelling snow off the roof to forestall dry rot. Once a week the clocks were wound, so bang on the hour they struck and chimed in unison, but there was no one to hear them. The contents of the house had not been touched since September 1939, when they had been packed up to allow the Penrhos girls to start the autumn term in their new quarters. All manner of things, from the Memling Triptych to wastepaper baskets, were piled up in the library; Old Master drawings were stuffed into drawers and smaller objects had been stored in a walk-in safe.

My parents-in-law decided that the garden at Chatsworth should be kept up and the house 'maintained' and, for the first time, the money paid by visitors went to the upkeep of the house instead of to local hospitals.

When work on reopening the house began, the old generation of carpenters, electricians, masons and plumbers were all nearing retirement age but they knew every inch of the place and its contents, and their help was invaluable. The women's side of things was less straightforward. No English women would do domestic work in such a place; they had had enough before the war of 'going into service', the memory of the long hours and the old discipline was too much and they took other jobs.

Moucher turned for help to two Hungarian sisters, Ilona and Elisabeth Solymossy, who had worked for Kick at her London house. To Moucher's relief the Solymossys not only liked the idea of coming to Chatsworth, they also recruited a polyglot collection of nine other Eastern Europeans. To walk down the back passage when they were on their way to lunch was like going into the Tower of Babel, and the smell of goulash (or its first cousin) pervaded all. I often wondered how my family and I would have got on had we been in their shoes, turned out of our homes for ever and left to fend for ourselves in a foreign country. This wonderful team, dressed like Miss Moppet with cotton handkerchiefs tied round their heads, dusted, sorted, scrubbed, polished and sewed throughout the winter of 1948–9. The shabby, grubby rooms were slowly made presentable and were ready when the house reopened at Easter 1949.

Eddy was drinking too much and risking his health for all to see, which created a worrying atmosphere at home. He was obsessed with chopping wood and had learned from the woodmen how to fell a tree and use the iron wedges that enabled the saw to cut without 'binding'. At Compton Place he would disappear for hours on end to an outhouse where he worked away, sawing and stacking piles of logs. He came in for dinner but went back to the outhouse immediately afterwards and did not return until after midnight, his old velvet suit impregnated with sawdust.

The physical effort, coupled with too much alcohol, was to prove a fatal combination. On 26 November 1950, while engaged in his favourite occupation, Eddy suffered a massive heart attack and just managed to reach the hall of the house before collapsing. He was fifty-five. (The death certificate was signed by the infamous Dr John Bodkin Adams, our GP at Eastbourne, who the following year was accused of murdering one of his patients; it was then discovered that more than 160 others in his care had died in suspicious circumstances. This suspected serial murderer had seemed very affable to me when he looked after Stoker and Emma while they had whooping cough during the war.)

Andrew was in Australia when his father died. Eddy had asked him to look for suitable places for investment, as he had already done in Kenya and Tanganyika. I was staying with Aunt Weenie at her cottage near Stow-on-the-Wold. Moucher and Andrew's sisters were at Compton Place, where I joined them to await Andrew's return from the Antipodes. Even though Eddy had looked so ill lately, my mother-in-law was stunned and blamed herself for not doing more to stop him drinking.

The effect of Eddy's death was immediate and profound: he was missed not only by his family and friends, but also by his colleagues in politics and throughout the Commonwealth, where he had travelled extensively during his years as Under Secretary of State for the Colonies. My mother-in-law outlived him by thirty-eight years, during which time her house in London became a magnet for her family and friends, and for the politicians, writers and many others who loved her company. For Andrew, Eddy's death meant that he not only lost a father, friend and wise counsellor, he also inherited a monstrous debt. The financial consequences of Eddy's death were to take years to unravel and absorbed almost all Andrew's attention for two decades. In 1926 Victor Duke had formed the Chatsworth Estates Company and at the time of his death the majority of the shares belonged to Eddy, his son and heir. Eddy made a similar arrangement in 1946 and handed over the bulk of his fortune to the Chatsworth Settlement Trust for the benefit of his descendants. Five years had to elapse before this became free of death duties, which under Mr Attlee's Labour government had soared to a dizzying eighty per cent. Eddy died fourteen weeks before the five years were up and Andrew was faced with raising millions of pounds to satisfy the Treasury's demands. Four-fifths of the value of the land and investments, and of works of art that had been collected by the family for over four hundred years, had to be found. It seemed strange to me that the family of a man who had given a lifetime of public service should have to pay such a vast fine on his death.

There was much heart searching, but as I knew little about the works of art at Chatsworth or the value of individual objects in the collection, I had nothing to do with the decisions. It was not my business and I did not see any of the reports of Andrew's meetings with Currey & Co., the family lawyers who played such a big part in subsequent trans- actions. But, as was his habit, Andrew often left letters from Currey lying about, thrown down wherever they landed after breakfast; I regarded these as fair game and sometimes had a sideways squint at them to try to glean what was happening. It was the first time I had heard money spoken of so freely (like illness it was not discussed in my youth); now, suddenly, the value of everything was being tossed around. Andrew con- ferred with his mother but Moucher was not exactly the right person to talk to as she was unaware of the value of anything. I once asked her the price of some object she liked the look of: '£40,' she said. 'No, £4. No, £400,' it was all the same to her. As a storehouse of sympathy, however, she was unbeatable.

Andrew took the decision to sell 12,000 acres of agricultural land in Dumfriesshire, 42,000 acres in Derbyshire, town property and wood- lands in Sussex, and a house in London. Most of the glorious furniture and books from Compton Place were sold and the house was let to a language school. The kitchen garden (scene of the strawberry theft just before D-Day) was built on and a brutish 1950s edifice took the place of that beautiful, productive garden. Nine of Chatsworth's most important works of art went to the nation in lieu of duty and found their way to major institutions. The lion's share went to the British Museum in the form of Claude's *Liber Veritatis*, the Greek bronze head of Apollo, the Van Dyck Italian sketchbook (luckily Professor Michael Jaffé, who later worked on the catalogue of Dutch drawings at Chatsworth, found an- other at the back of a cupboard), the tenth-century Benedictional of St Aethelwold and over 140 early books, including fourteen works by Caxton's head printer, Wynkyn de Worde.

Holbein's life-size cartoon of Henry VII and Henry VIII went to the National Portrait Gallery; Rubens' *The Holy Family* to the Walker Gallery in Liverpool; the fifteenth-century Dutch hunting tapestries were allocated to the Victoria and Albert Museum; *The Donne Triptych* by Memling and *The Philosopher* by Rembrandt (which to Andrew's de- light was later relabelled by scholars a 'studio production') went to the National Gallery. There was a purple warning to the followers of fashion in art (and they are many): when the contents of the Sculpture Gallery, including several Antonio Canovas, were valued, the total lumped together (it was evidently not thought worthwhile to list them separately) came to under £1,000. These neoclassical masterpieces that Granny Evie dismissed as lumbering Victorian obstacles are now the stars of the parade of sculpture in their own gallery at Chatsworth and are, I believe, worth a great deal of money. An almost unbelievable about-turn in sixty years.

All this was still not enough to clear the debt. On 12 August 1954 Andrew was sitting in the train to London when he had the inspired idea to offer Hardwick Hall, the glorious sixteenth-century house built by Bess, the shrewd, charismatic progenitrix of the Cavendish family, to the Treasury in lieu of cash. Granny Evie, who was nearly ninety, was still living in Hardwick at the time. She loved the house – 'Hardwick Hall, more glass than wall', as the saying goes in Derbyshire – with its vast rooms and the Long Gallery where pictures hung over the tapestries, like jam on butter, each being of historic importance. But to her credit she accepted the plan. Before the agreement was signed, Moucher kept re-minding me of things I should take from the house. 'You must go and get the Minton dinner service which is in the cupboard behind the kitchen,' she said, and suggested a few other easily portable bits and pieces. I was pregnant with Sophy and could not trudge round the seemingly endless rooms to rescue some of the eighteenth- and nineteenth-century items of furniture that were not contemporary with the house. But I did save the pretty, blue-ribboned Minton dinner service and we used it at Chats-worth during all the years we lived there.

Protracted negotiations were finally completed and the house, to-gether with 3,000 acres of surrounding farmland, was accepted by the government and handed over to the National Trust in 1959. The Trust has looked after it as we never could have done, and the family are eternally grateful both to Andrew for arranging the transfer of owner-ship and to the Trust for its fine stewardship.

The final payment of death duties was made on 17 May 1967, but interest had been accruing since 1950 and the full debt was not cleared until 1974.

12

EDENSOR HOUSE

We spent thirteen years at Edensor House, from 1946 to 1959. Although I never liked the house, we settled in and the pleasure of being in the park and near Chatsworth outweighed the disadvantages. Emma and Stoker were three and two respectively when we moved in, and Sophy was born in 1957. While Andrew was busy sorting out the financial repercussions of my father-in-law's death, the day-to-day implications seeped more slowly into my life. Two occasions gave me a jolt and made me aware of what was to come. I was in the garden at Chatsworth one day and Bert Link, the head gardener, came up and asked me, 'What would you like us to do?' I realized then that the 105-acre garden was now part of my remit. And a few weeks after Eddy's death, Moucher handed me an old Elastoplast tin fastened with a rubber band. When I opened it I was amazed to see some family jewels, including row upon row of pearls. The pearls were such an inseparable part of my mother-in-law – I had seldom seen her without them, town or country, day or night – that I could not imagine wearing them and gave them straight back to her. But I kept the other pieces, including a star ruby brooch which I had made into a clasp for my own cultured pearls. This necklace, together with a high-collared shirt that appears in many portraits and photographs of me, became my uniform. After Andrew's death, I handed the family jewellery on to my daughter-in-law, Amanda. It was not mine, just as it had not been Moucher's: it belongs to Chatsworth, to be worn by the wife of the Duke of Devonshire.

I gradually began to take on more of the tasks of former duchesses of Devonshire, and found myself responsible for seven houses: Chatsworth, Hardwick Hall, Bolton Hall in Yorkshire, Lismore Castle in southern Ireland, Compton Place in East Sussex, a London house and Edensor. No wonder I put down 'Housewife' when filling in a form that demanded my occupation; I was wife to all of them. People sometimes ask what it is like being a duchess. The answer is that I honestly do not know because after it happened none of my intimates – either among the people who worked at Chatsworth or my friends far and wide – treated me any differently. I sometimes notice a change of gear, rather than attitude, when I am introduced to people but it does not last long – they soon see how unnecessary it is and behave normally.

Granny Evie had lived at Edensor House during the war and took to austerity with a will; the degree of cold she tolerated and her hateful food (nettles downward) were a lesson to us all, and she continued in the same vein when she moved to Hardwick. She indulged in various imaginary illnesses, finding something wrong with her womb caught from her dog, or catching tulip fire from the tulips. Dr Evans told me that she had a 'somewhat macabre' interest in medicine. 'To prevaricate was risky,' he said. On one of his visits, Granny told him that she was trying out a new cure for rheumatism and showed him a length of frayed electric light flex knotted around her waist. Dr Evans remained non-committal. 'I am not sure how I should wear it,' said Evie, untying the flex and putting it on the other way round. 'It does not matter, Your Grace,' said Dr Evans, dead-pan, 'it's an alternating current.'

Granny Evie was not altogether easy to get on with, being critical of the younger members of her family, but she was fond of Emma and Stoker and was kind to me, I think because of Diddy, a paragon among nannies. When the children were about six and seven, they often went over to see Granny at Hardwick. Gardening and painting were on the agenda for these visits. One wet day Granny looked at the tapestry that hung on the curve of the magical stairs between the first and second floor of the house and thought it rather gloomy. She got out some poster paints and encouraged the children to do their best to cheer it up, and I do believe that if the tapestry has not been moved they could still find signs of their unusual graffiti.

From the age of ten, Emma went daily to St Elphin's School, five miles away in Darley Dale. St Elphin's was founded in the early nineteenth century for the daughters of clergy and there were a number of such girls during Emma's years. When John Betjeman went to talk to the school on Speech Day, he was delighted by an item on the programme: 'Tug of War between Clergy and Laity'. I had been appointed a Visitor (I never knew what it meant but it sounded good) and sat next to John on the platform. I glanced at his notes and saw, 'Oh you do look nice, ALL of you.' I was much encouraged to see that this famous poet needed prompting on big occasions like the rest of us.

My memories of living at Edensor are full of laughter. Family and friends often came to stay, for no other reason than the fun of it. The house had only two spare rooms and when we had more people staying we used Moor View, a large cottage at the top of the village. Guests did not like having to turn out on cold winter nights and those chosen to go up the hill were known as the 'Suicide Squad'. But they kept coming back and many were to remain lifelong friends.

I inherited Jim Lees-Milne from Tom and Diana, and saw more of him as years went by. It is a pity that people reading about him now are told of his sexual proclivities and seem to overlook the work he did for the National Trust during and after the war. I loved Jim's company and I loved both him and his wife, Alvilde. His private life was his own. Randal, Eighth Earl of Antrim, was also a regular. I did not know him well when he first arrived and called him 'Lord Antrim'. This old-fashioned form of address stuck and became a nickname, confusing those who heard it and knew that he was a friend. In 1966 he realized his ambition when he was made chairman of the National Trust; he brought the best of amateurism to that organization and a light-hearted feel that it has never regained.

Another regular was Kitty Mersey, the sister of my friends Charlie and Ned, killed in the war. Their father, the Sixth Marquess of Lansdowne, was a brother of Granny Evie so Kitty was Andrew's cousin. She and her husband, Edward Bigham, stayed with us for a night in summer 1947 and we made friends immediately. Kitty had the same irresistible sense of humour that had made her brothers such wonderful companions and it was good to find them again through her. She had suffered terribly over their deaths; they were by far her favourite human beings, and it was a bond between us. How she got her nickname 'Wife' is convoluted. There was a famous Lothario whom neither of us knew but whose wife was called Kitty. To make sure that people knew he was referring to his wife and not to one of his many mistresses, he would say, 'Kitty-my-wife', almost as one syllable. We took to doing the same with Kitty Mersey. This was soon shortened to 'my wife' or 'the wife', and it became a habit, like ridiculous nicknames often do, and was applied to any best friend of either sex.

Evelyn Waugh was a difficult guest and when he drank too much he was impossible. Everything was wrong: the wine, his bedroom, the out-look and, judging by his behaviour, the other guests too. Try as I might to remedy housekeeping shortcomings, I failed. Kitty was staying at the same time as Evelyn on one of her visits and when we went up to bed she came to talk to me in my bedroom. In no time Evelyn was in with a complaint. 'The curtains don't meet and I won't be able to sleep,' he grumbled. 'So sorry,' I said, 'but there is nothing I can do about it now.' Off he stumped but was soon back. 'If you turn the hall light off, I won't see my way to the bathroom.' 'All right,' I said, 'I'll leave it on.' A while later, another knock on the door, louder and more insistent this time. 'What is it now?' I said. 'I thought you ought to know,' Evelyn announced with a look of triumph on his face, 'that the pot in my bedside table is full.' I shall never know if it was true but doubted it as he did not bring the evidence with him. The next day he was going to stay with the writer Osbert Sitwell at nearby Renishaw and I begged him not to tell of this appalling oversight. Two days later I received Evelyn's bread-and-butter letter, which ended, 'No one has shown any curiosity about the strange Trove of Edensor. They wot not of the pot.'

In spite of his uncertain ways, Evelyn remained a friend and a gen-erous one. He sent us the limited edition of *Brideshead Revisited* in its floppy dark blue cover, which is in the library at Chatsworth, and he sent me his other works as they were published, inscribed in friendly terms. In *Love Among the Ruins* he wrote, 'For Darling Debo, the Beard-less Duchess, with love from Evelyn' (the frontispiece depicts a goddess with a beard); he also sent me a copy of John Betjeman's *Continual Dew*, inscribed on the blue endpapers: 'A blue rose for Debo from Eve-lyn'. The best is his *Life of Ronald Knox*. I was sitting with Kitty Mersey when it arrived. As soon as I saw the unprepossessing beige cover and title, I put it down with the rest of the day's post, thinking, 'I'll have to write and thank for that but I certainly won't read it.' Kitty, being a reader, picked it up and flipped through the pages. The inscription read,

'To Darling Debo with love from Evelyn. You will not find a word in this
to offend your protestant sympathies.' There were no words – all the
pages were blank. The perfect present for a non-reader. When *Antiques
Roadshow* came to Chatsworth, I proudly took *Ronald Knox* with its
virgin white pages to the book expert, longing to know what price he
would put on it. He was amused but would not risk a valuation and
moved on to the next person in the queue.

Osbert Sitwell came to see me one day when I was ill in bed. Poor
Osbert, the wretched Parkinson's disease had taken hold and his hand
shook violently. He looked at it sadly and said, 'All this wasted energy, it
ought to be working a mill.' He invited Andrew and me to the annual
fête in the garden at Renishaw. Osbert was doing his duty by the stall-
holders, having a chat here and there, and he spotted a man in uniform.
Thinking it was the leader of the band, he said, 'Thank you, my man. Your
music was excellent.' He was talking to the local head of the St John
Ambulance Brigade, but that little mistake passed him by. His sister,
Dame Edith, did not come into the garden but swished about indoors
wearing her usual ground-length skirt and huge rings on long, white
fingers. On another occasion when we lunched at Renishaw, she wore
a feather hat and long fur coat that she never unbuttoned. She told me
that the chief things she remembered her mother saying were, 'We
must remember to order enough quails for the dance,' and 'If only I
could get your father put into a lunatic asylum.'

My sisters also came to stay at Edensor. Muv brought Unity for our first
Christmas there. Our other guest was Adele Astaire, sister of Fred and
the widow of Andrew's uncle Charles Cavendish. Farve said he could
not come because he had no clothes, which was nonsense – Margaret
was a more likely reason. Andrew insisted on having the Christmas-tree
party for the village children either before Unity arrived or after she left
because she embarrassed him so much with the vicar. I saw his point.
She used to ask any man of the cloth she met why he had chosen that
profession, whether he wished he had been made a bishop and if he
enjoyed sleeping with his wife.

Eighteen months later Unity was on Inch Kenneth with Muv when
she collapsed with a violent pain in her head and a high fever. They got

her as far as the hospital in Oban, but she had meningitis and there was nothing the doctors could do. She died on 28 May 1948 and was buried in Swinbrook churchyard. Muv had devoted her life to Unity since we had brought her home in January 1940, and I know how much she worried about what would happen to Unity should she outlive her. This haunting fear may have made the parting easier.

Pam, the only one of my sisters who went on telling me what to do when I was grown up, used to knock on our door in the morning and tell Andrew and me that it was time to get up. Once she had let her dachshund out no one could have gone on sleeping anyway – the din was loud enough to waken the dead. The dog had many nicknames, as did her litter of puppies. Walks with Pam and these loved ones were punctuated with stops while, holding a riding crop aloft as a threat (never carried out), she shouted, 'Come AT ONCE,' followed by a string of names and nicknames.

Nancy stayed with us when Stoker was about two and a half. 'Can you talk?' she asked him. 'Not yet,' he replied. She judged teenagers by their behaviour at bonfires: the slouching laggard who hardly picked up a stick to keep the blaze going was 'no good' (the sort my father would have dismissed as 'a meaningless piece of meat'). I have often thought this as good a way as any of assessing a sixteen-year-old, to be recommended to Human Resources. Trial by bonfire is now my rule.

Nancy wrote *The Pursuit of Love* in 1945 in the first flush of love for Gaston Palewski and it glows through the pages. The novel was an instant success and made her financially independent for the first time. We were all amused by it, including Farve, who laughed at the caricature of himself, although we knew that the entrenching tool, with which Uncle Matthew was supposed to have whacked to death eight Germans, really belonged to Sir Iain Colquhoun of Luss (it was one of Nancy's flights of fancy that it had been wielded by Farve). Nancy put her family life into the book, including expressions that were part of our intersister shorthand. As a child, I had shortened the Whyte Melville quote that headed the cover of *Horse & Hound* ('I freely admit the best of my fun I owe it to Horse & Hound') to 'You must freely admit', which was shortened to 'Do admit', and used when trying to get Nancy's attention. It appears again and again in the novel, where I suppose I am Linda. Much as we enjoyed it I do not remember any of us thinking *The Pur-

suit of Love would last, yet sixty-five years later it is still hugely popular and is considered a classic.

In 1946 Nancy moved to Paris to be near Gaston and remained in France, the country she adored, for the rest of her life. She had a theory that when you were travelling to the Continent the sun came out exactly halfway across the Channel and, going the other way, threatening clouds gathered as soon as you approached England. She found a ground-floor flat in a house on the Rue Monsieur in the Seventh Arrondissement, and often let me squeeze into the dressing room behind her bathroom for a few days' stay. She had a large drawing room with an iron stove around which everything revolved in the winter. It gave out terrific heat but took a lot of looking after, having to be fed regularly with logs – like a horse with oats. Nancy knew its ways and stood over it with yet more logs to satisfy its voracious appetite. She loved the flat, which was a mixture of England and France, just as she was. There was an exquisite Sheraton roll-top writing table in the drawing room, more for show than work, an Aubusson carpet under an English sofa and a French chaise longue. The dining-room chairs were a wedding present from Diana.

When she was working, Nancy pulled the telephone out by its roots, stayed in her room and wrote in bed. Her housekeeper Marie, a comfort-maker if ever there was one, looked after her. Marie came from Norman farming stock and was shaped like a cottage loaf. She wore black shoes and stockings and had a shuffling walk that one thought must end in disaster when she was carrying a tray, but it never did. She was a natural cook and could make any potato taste delicious; her only shortcoming was that she could hardly bear to make English puddings and they were what Gaston loved. Nancy and Marie had long talks on the subject and, although Marie disparaged them, her efforts pleased Monsieur Palewski. She shopped at the local market and came home one day with a live hen which was to be the main dish for a lunch party the following day. The hen was shut in the oven for the night and in the morning there was an egg. She was reprieved and lived in the garden, faithfully laying for several years.

English friends visiting Paris were delighted to find Nancy there. Cecil Beaton was one of them. He and Nancy were always ready for a skirmish, scoring hits and spurring each other on to near-lethal digs. It was an entertainment for their friends that never failed to amuse. The jokes got nearer and nearer the knuckle till there was an explosion, then silence for a while until neither could resist starting up again. Soon after the opening of *My Fair Lady* in New York, where his costumes had brought gasps of wonder from the audience, Cecil came back to Europe, tired out by the pressures but thrilled by the acclaim. The papers had been full of it and everyone knew that it was just as much Cecil's triumph as Julie Andrews' and the composers' Lerner and Loewe. Cecil lunched with Nancy in the Rue Monsieur. She knew all about the success of the musical and of how Cecil had lived and worked with it day and night for weeks on end. A pause in their chatter and Nancy asked casually, 'When you were in New York, did you see *My Fair Lady?*' 'Yyyesss,' replied Cecil in his sheep-like bleat.

I never saw Nancy in fussy or ugly clothes. She bought few, but of the best, her perfect figure showing them off as their creators would have wished. She took me to see the clothes at Dior, Lanvin, Jean Dessès, Madame Grès, Balmain and Schiaparelli. Compared to the shops in England, they were fairyland during those early post-war years. A walk down the Faubourg St Honoré, which we called Main Street, was made impossibly tempting by the window displays and we hungered for everything. Usually we looked and longed, but did not buy – like going to a gallery to admire the pictures. When we did fall for something there was huge excitement. I dug deep for a grand evening dress made of white organza covered with velvet appliquéd flowers, which went over a silk under-dress in Schiaparelli's famous shocking pink. Some years later Cecil asked to borrow it for an exhibition at the V&A. What he meant (but did not say) was that it would join the permanent collection, so it was goodbye to my best dress – which is still there.

Hubert de Givenchy had just started his own house and was a natural successor to the great Balenciaga, the acknowledged master of couture. When he opened a boutique on the ground floor of the house where he had his workshop, it became our first port of call. The *vendeuses'* interest in every detail of dress, coat or whatever it was they were selling made them so much more appealing than their English counterparts, who gazed out of the window thinking of men, hunting, or whatever English women think of – anything except the dresses they were trying to sell. Hubert's staff would make the necessary alterations so that the finished garment fitted exactly, then one of them would go upstairs to see if 'Monsieur' was available. Hubert himself would come down to talk to us, wearing a white coat like a doctor, and tweaked the shoulders and hem before casting an approving eye. It was the height of pleasurable shopping. I still wear some of Hubert's clothes, made forty years ago and as good as ever.

In the 1950s my mother-in-law did voluntary work in the East End of London. She was a friend of Bunny Mellon, wife of the Anglophile philanthropist Paul Mellon. Bunny was curious to know more about Moucher's charity. She heard of the poverty among the women and how cheered they would be by some new clothes, so on her return to America she arranged for what looked like cardboard coffins to be sent to Moucher at Eaton Square. Out came wondrous garments by Balenciaga: brocade evening dresses, a black winter coat lavishly trimmed with black mink, and piles of less showy but beautifully made coats, skirts and cocktail dresses. Moucher said that my sisters and I could take our pick, which we did, replacing the Balenciagas with decent, unworn clothes of our own that satisfied my mother-in-law's charitable purposes.

The master couturier's clothes had come to a good home: they were well out of our reach to buy first-hand, but no one could have appreciated them more and we wore them time and again. Diana looked dangerously beautiful in the black coat with black mink facings. We met for lunch one day in London, at the Aperitif Restaurant in Jermyn Street, she a vision in The Coat. We sat down and looked round. I spied Paul Mellon and said, 'Oh, I must go and say hello.' Diana gave a scream and tried to make herself look small (impossible), terrified that he would recognize his wife's coat and snatch it off her back. She and Nancy shared a white satin evening dress they called 'Robeling', which was kept for the grandest occasions. Nancy also had one of those simple linen dresses that are immediately recognizable (by those accustomed to such luxuries) as the very height of haute couture. She wore it in Venice where a friend remarked on it. 'Oh well,' said Nancy, 'I always think one should have ONE good dress.' It was so like her not to admit to its origin.

In 1951, the Mosleys bought the Temple de la Gloire at Orsay, twenty miles from the centre of Paris. Built in 1801 as a folly, it was a small, classical building of faultless proportions: the perfect background for Diana. A lofty drawing room on the first floor opened on to a balcony, which was supported by two generous flights of stone stairs that led to the garden. The balcony overlooked a pond (referred to as a 'lake', but not exactly Windermere). I first went to the Temple on a misty evening; a travelling circus was encamped outside the gates and a camel was tethered to the railings, which added to the surreal atmosphere.

When the Mosleys bought the house it was surrounded by strawberry fields, but as time went by villas grew up around it. Every new house seemed to have dogs that barked, yapped and bayed in unison at certain times of the day. It was an unholy din, not unlike a pack of foxhounds that has suddenly picked up the scent of a fox. As a young man Sir O loved hunting and had the best of it with the Quorn at Melton Mowbray. He knew reams of sporting verse by heart and when the dogs set up their racket, I would say to him. 'Listen! *They've found!*' This provoked a torrent of word-perfect recitations of 'The Dream of an Old Meltonian' and 'The Good Grey Mare', which made me cry every time I heard them. Diana's laughter at his recital alternated with my tears. I loved my visits to the Temple: not only did I often have Diana to myself, but the atmosphere she created wherever she lived was the perfect antidote to any worries.

I met all sorts of people while staying with the Mosleys (some of them could not speak English, which served me right for preferring hunting to learning French when I was sixteen). When the Duke and Duchess of Windsor moved to an old mill at Gif-sur-Yvette, they became the Mosleys' neighbours. Andrew and I had first met them years before in the South of France when staying with our friends Loel and Isabel Guinness in Cannes. The Windsors lived at nearby Château de la Croë and when they invited the Guinnesses to dinner, they included us in the invitation. The Duke was very attractive, with his shining blond hair and irresistible touch of pathos. He wore a kilt at dinner with all its extras, including laced-up pumps and a dirk in his stocking. A piper went round the dinner table playing his deafening music – more suited to the misty glens than the Côte d'Azur in the heat of July.

'Are you the Duchess of Devonsheer?' the Duke asked me. I said I was. 'Aw, I didn't like her. She used to tell on me and it got back to my mother.' (Granny Evie passed on information, probably got from her son Charlie Cavendish, to Queen Mary about the Duke's visits to nightclubs when he was a young man.) I asked him if Granny Evie had been nasty when he met her face to face. 'Nasty? Smarmy as be damned,' he said. We got over this poor start and dinner was extremely enjoyable, the Duke speaking with nostalgia of England and the English, whom he called 'the British'.

The Windsors had a pack of pugs that had superseded their Cairn Terriers. 'Aren't they beguiling?' said the Duchess, using an adjective I had never before heard attached to any member of the canine race, let alone a pug. I could not like her, she seemed so brittle, her face bony, angular and painted, her body so dangerously thin she might snap in half. It was difficult to understand why the Duke adored her, but he certainly did and was in love with her until the day he died. He never took his eyes off her during dinner and shouted down the table, 'Wallis, Wallis, did you hear that?' when there was something he thought she might have missed.

I saw the Windsors again in August 1963, on a visit to the Mosleys, and wrote to Mrs Ham:

> I'm in the plane going back from Paris to Manchester and the old homestead having had two days on the other side of the medal with the Mosleys. We dined with some Bismarcks and there were the Windsors. He was in a hilarious mood and made Diana and me laugh so hopelessly that we were nearly out of control. He said when Grandfather Redesdale used to go to Sandring-*ham* to advise on trees and gardens, 'us bunch of kids' used to get very excited as he always gave a pound to each. He told me he (the Duke) stopped quite often with Queen Mary at Marlborough House and that, although she was much more forthcoming when she was old, 'that woman was as hard as nails'.
>
> He got me and Diana and Sir O together and said 'Now we are us four Britishers'. He told of romances at Melton 1,000 years ago. Altogether the charm, the pathos and the Cockney American accent finished me. She (the Duchess) kept pointing at me and Diana, saying 'Look at those brilliant Mitford brains. I'm not going to let them go on talking to the Dook unless I can hear what they're saying.' So she came over to listen to the pearls.

Years later I discovered a curious quirk of the Duchess. Our Chatsworth housekeeper, Dorothy Dean, who had been housemaid to the

Windsors at Château de la Croë, was discreet and never gossiped about her old employers. But one day she did open up a little and told me that the Duchess would only employ blondes in the house: the footmen, the housemaids and even the people in the kitchen were all fair-haired. Why, I do not know. She herself was dark.

In February 1952 Decca invited me to stay in California. I had not set eyes on her for thirteen years, and then only briefly because of Esmond's hostility, but we had kept in touch by letter. In the intervening years she had married her second husband, Bob Treuhaft, and had had two sons, Nicky and Benjy. Dinky, her daughter with Esmond, was now eleven years old. I was nervous as to what I should find after so long. The flight to California was punctuated by many stops for refuelling and seemed endless, and when we eventually touched down at San Francisco, I felt weary and bemused. And there was Decca. A new person, trousered, American in appearance and accent – someone I did not recognize. It was the oddest sensation and filled me with a feeling of intense loneliness. What was I doing, thousands of miles from home, meeting a stranger who had once meant more to me than anyone in the world?

My engagement book for the week in California reads: 'Tuesday 12 February: dinner with Communists.' 'Wednesday 13 February: dinner with more Communists.' King George VI had died a week earlier and the left-wing extremists of California did not let this pass. The sarcasm that spewed from Decca's dinner guests was relentless and difficult to bear; none of them had ever been to England yet they launched into bitter criticism of everything I knew. Whatever I tried to say in defence of the King and our way of life was laughed out of court or greeted with a 'You would say that, wouldn't you' sort of look. One evening, the conversation turned to how to do away with the royal family. Manners were not their priority.

Decca and Bob were generous hosts and took me to Carmel, where we stayed in a hotel for a couple of nights. There I met 'brunch' for the first time and thought it perfect: all my favourite foods laid out. As we were leaving, I noticed that Decca had packed the towels. I asked her if she had done it by mistake. 'Oh, no,' she said, 'they are lovely and white and ours are horribly grey.' When I said, 'Hen, that's stealing', she replied, 'Oh, it's all right, hotels are insured for that sort of thing.' So my reputation for being the 'Conservative policeman' rose, as did my surprise at her thieving ways.

The visit was dispiriting. I knew Decca had tried hard to make me enjoy myself, introducing me to her friends and political colleagues, but it fell on stony ground because of their hostility and lack of understanding of any view but their own. I thought afterwards that she may also have felt nervous about seeing me after so long and had mustered her friends to bolster her confidence. If I had been alone with her for a week it would have been different. We did have some talks about the old days when glimmers of the Decca of the past came through. The bright spot was Dinky. She was – is – beautiful and practical, taking charge of Decca and looking after the boys far better than she herself had been looked after by Decca. It was no wonder that she chose nursing as her profession when she left home. Her patients were the lucky ones.

When Decca came to England in 1955, her first visit since the war, she must have been stunned by the changes she found. In California she had talked of her relations and English friends as if they were just as she had left them in 1939. In spite of the loss of her beloved Esmond it was impossible for her to understand what the vast upheaval of six years of war had meant to the people and places she had once known.

My next visit to the Americas was very different. In 1955 I went to Brazil for the Carnival in Rio de Janeiro as a guest of Aly Khan. I had first met him at a party in London and often saw him on the racecourse. We had become friends and he was the easiest of company. His wife, Rita Hayworth, was one of the four most beautiful women I have ever seen (the others were Elizabeth von Hofmannsthal, Madame Martinez de Hoz, wife of a South American diplomat, and my sister Diana). Her features were perfect, her mass of truly auburn hair sprang straight from her forehead and cascaded down to her shoulders, and she moved like the dancer she was.

When I arrived at the airport in Rio after the long flight via Dakar, I was held up at immigration; the trouble was the rigmarole on my passport: 'Her Grace Deborah Vivian Cavendish Duchess of Devonshire'. 'Yes, that's me,' I said. The official looked again. 'Where are all the others?' he asked. He took a bit of convincing that I was the one and only, but eventually allowed me to enter. While Aly travelled the country looking at thoroughbred stud farms, I stayed with polo-playing friends of his and went racing with them. In their drawing room where in England there would have been a fireplace with chairs and a sofa, there was a pool instead. But there was no writing table, no writing paper and no way of buying stamps. My hosts could not understand why I wanted these things – necessities for me that seemed positively eccentric to them. Muv began to panic when she heard nothing from me. I explained to her later that they would say things like, 'We'll go to São Paolo tomorrow and buy some', but tomorrow came and we never went.

When Carnival in Rio began we did go and it was everything it is cracked up to be: a stream of beating drums, music that stayed in the head long after it was over, wildly extravagant costumes, nearly naked dancing girls with fruit, flowers and feathers piled on their heads and the male equivalent dressed (or not dressed) in anything they fancied. This uninhibited crowd paraded the streets all night. It was good-natured and happy, with a few hours of semi-quiet after dawn while the revellers gathered strength for a repeat performance. The heat was as extreme as the enjoyment.

We were having dinner at a restaurant one evening when in stumbled a South American polo team dressed as English governesses. Wobbling on court shoes with heels they could not manage, these athletic and gloriously good-looking young men wore demure navy-blue crêpe de Chine dresses with elbow-length sleeves and white cuffs, flat straw hats plonked on their heads, a string of decorous beads, black lace gloves stretched over their huge hands and square, white handbags dangling from their hairy arms. They had all grown up with English governesses so knew exactly how to dress. The tallness and masculinity of these young men made their get-up supremely comical, the best fancy dress ever.

On my last day we flew to a remote stud farm where we rode on cowboy ponies over mountains and ravines where you would not dream of taking an English horse. There were bridges made of two planks, and paths so steep I had to cling to the horse's mane so as not to slide off. We rode for four hours, the last in the tropical dark that falls so suddenly, with fireflies, jungle noises and the delicious smells of flowering trees all around us. We galloped home behind our guide. I asked him afterwards why there had been such a hurry. 'Because of the vampires,' he said.

I also stayed at Aly's house in Neuilly, a mile or so from the centre of Paris. We went to marvellous nightclubs and restaurants, including Maxim's, and turned night into day, sometimes with friends of his, sometimes on our own. Aly took for granted the glamour of this round of pleasure and I was fascinated to see the Continental version of what I already knew in London. But he also had duties, which he took seriously, and there was a group of Ismailis sitting patiently in the hall of his house at all hours waiting for an audience.

You never knew who you were going to meet at Château de l'Horizon, Aly's house on the sea near Cannes, where fellow guests ranged from beautiful women friends to international racing people, with a sprinkling of showbiz thrown in. Ray Stark, the film producer, was there one year with his wife, Fran, a daughter of Fanny Brice, the original 'Funny Girl'. Ray and I were fellow sufferers in not being able to speak a word of French. He was trying hard to learn and was delighted with his progress. 'I know that *glace* is not "glass" and that *chocolat* is "chocolate". Today I discovered that *eau* isn't "oh!" it's water. But I can't imagine why the shops have notices saying *soldes* when a sale is going on. No point in going in if everything is sold.' He was to leave a book in my room. 'Which is your room? I know, the one with the star on the door.' I was stunned by such flattery and missed the Starks and the daily bulletin on his linguistic progress when they left.

One day Aly arranged for me to dine with his father, the old Aga Khan, and his stately Begum, who lived in the hills behind Cannes. As I drove to the house through what seemed to be acres of bedded-out begonias I wondered what I was going to find. I was lucky: the old Aga (whom Nancy referred to as 'Father Divine') made me feel as if I had known him all my life. As I left, he gave me a book and told me very definitely to read it. A far cry from the Ismaili tract I had expected, it was a novel called *In Love*. At 2 a.m. the telephone by my bed rang. It was the Aga: 'How are you getting on with that book?' he asked.

Another friend from that period was Ann Fleming – whose shining life was so sadly cut short by cancer. Many friendships were made in her sunny house on a corner of Victoria Square in Westminster. Ann could seat only eight in her small dining room (we did not know her in her palmy days when she was married to Lord Rothermere and lived at Warwick House, one of the few big private houses left in London), so there was no room for passengers. I sometimes heard her say, 'I would love to ask so-and-so, but I can't sink his boring wife at my table.' She was a dab hand at getting her chosen ones to talk, prodding them into an argument, or anyway a spirited discussion, on every subject under the sun. Andrew loved the arguments and stayed till the early hours.

Lunch or dinner with Ann never failed to be entertaining: politicians, writers, painters, poets, lawyers, Oxford dons and actors, a *Who's Who* of their professions, were all bundled together with no holds barred. More arrived after dinner and the talk got louder. The politicians were mostly Labour: Hugh Gaitskell (who was in love with our hostess), Richard Crossman, Anthony Crosland and Roy Jenkins were all regulars. I never shared Ann's admiration for Arnold Goodman, Harold Wilson's solicitor and adviser, who adored her and on whom she came to rely.

The historian Robert Kee and Lucian Freud were often at Victoria Square, and Francis Bacon too if you were lucky. He did not speak much but commanded attention just by being himself. His face, sad in repose, lit up when he gave his one-sided, wholly captivating smile. One person I often saw but never got to know was Ann's husband, Ian Fleming. He let himself into the house after dining elsewhere. We heard the front door shut and a second later he would put his head round the dining-room door and scan the table. Not liking what he saw, he shook his head and went upstairs to bed.

13

LISMORE

The first sight of Lismore Castle as you come over the Knock-mealdown Mountains in County Waterford makes your jaw drop. A place of mystery and romance, the huge grey castle – half giant, half fairy – rises from the rocks above the banks of the River Blackwater. 'Built by King John, lived in by Sir Walter Raleigh and plumbed by Adele Astaire, it looks like a castle out of *Le Morte d'Arthur,*' wrote Paddy Leigh Fermor, a frequent visitor. Steeped in history, it has been the colourful background to tragedies and rejoicing, from civil wars to fantastic festivities, for over eight hundred years.

Andrew's uncle, Charles Cavendish, was given Lismore Castle with its surrounding estate and superb salmon fishing in 1932 as a wedding present by his father, the Ninth Duke. (It had been the Devonshires' Irish home since 1753.) Charlie died in the castle twelve years later, aged thirty-eight, a hopeless alcoholic – the generally accepted reason for his early death. Charming, good-looking and shy, he was loved by all who knew him. After Cambridge, where too much drink and a succession of bad falls in point-to-point races weakened his health, his parents thought a spell in America would do him good and sent him to New York to work in a financial firm. His time there coincided with Prohibition and his health, far from improving, was made worse by the illegal hooch.

Charlie came back to England and fell in love with Adele Astaire, the dancer and entertainer who, partnered by her brother Fred, had taken London by storm in *Lady Be Good, The Band Wagon* and *Funny Face.* Adele retired from the stage at the height of her fame to marry Charlie and, as time went by, having once been the more famous of the two siblings, she referred to herself as Fred's sister. Charlie and Adele made their home at Lismore, travelling a great deal and leading a whizzing social life, but always in the shadow of his addiction.

Adele was a fascinating creature of irrepressible vitality but she was also capricious and used a torrent of bad language. 'Oh Dellie, oh Dellie, oh *Dellie*,' her mother, Ann Astaire, used gently to reprimand her from the other end of the dining-room table, but it did not stop Lady Charles Cavendish's all too vivid descriptions of friends and foes. By the time war broke out Charlie was unfit to join up and remained at Lismore, leading the half-life of an alcoholic, assisted by his wickedly complicit butler who gave him whisky camouflaged in a mug. Ann Astaire, a wonderful woman who is still fondly remembered at Lismore, stayed at the castle and did what she could for the ailing Charlie, while Adele went to London and delighted the GIs at the American Red Cross centre.

The castle and its estate had been an outright gift from the Ninth Duke to Charlie, and would have gone to one of Charlie's children in due course, but that was not to be. Adele and Charlie had a daughter in 1933 and twin sons in 1935, all three of whom were premature and died soon after birth. After Charlie's death, Lismore was left to Adele for her lifetime or until she remarried. In 1947, she married fellow American Kingman Douglass, and Lismore came to Andrew. Andrew nearly put his foot in it with Adele when we were married: she sent us a coffee service for a wedding present and as he had just been commissioned in the Coldstream Guards and had other things on his mind, he forgot to write the necessary thank-you letter. Adele was furious and told him she would get Charlie to leave the place to a cousin. The threat produced the required flowery note and all was well.

I first went to Lismore in the autumn of 1947; it seemed to me like a dream on that visit and remained so ever after. For nearly fifty years Andrew went for the opening of the salmon fishing season in February and we both spent every April there. In 1947 there was still a station at Lismore and the train from Rosslare stopped a few hundred yards from the castle. You could do the last bit of the journey from London on foot, walking up the short drive – or avenue as it is called in Ireland – between the walls of the upper and lower garden. This brought you to the ancient arch of the gatehouse, so low that I used to fear for the butcher boy's head when he stood up in the pony trap that delivered the meat to the castle.

The courtyard walls, which are at odd angles to each other, looked for all the world like an Oxbridge quad. The avenue of tall yews, whose branches met high overhead to form a dark tunnel, was, according to Miss Bolton (my sister-in-laws' governess), where Sir Walter Raleigh had walked and she saw his ghost whenever she went to that bit of the garden.

If by some magic I could be transported blindfold from where I am sitting now to the high-ceilinged hall of the castle, the first intake of breath would tell me I was at Lismore. The vague smell of peat and wood, just the general feel of that loved place, would bring nostalgia for the unchanging sights and sounds of half a century. In spite of its size, the castle was as welcoming as can be. Kathleen Nevin, the castle cook, is the world's best. Every morsel of her food had to travel from the kitchen, along a passage, up a flight of steps and across Pugin's extravagant banqueting hall with its star-covered ceiling and chandeliers copied from those in the House of Commons (or is it the other way round?), until it arrived, still perfect, in the dining room. The brass stair-rods were polished to brilliance. The water ran blue from the copper pipes, staining the baths the colour of a swimming pool. In one of the bathrooms, photographs of Fred Astaire dancing in his top hat, white tie and tails hung next to photos of King Edward VII arriving at the castle in a grand carriage in 1904. The hall with its huge fireplace led to a small sitting room perched high above the river with dreamlike views over woods and far-distant mountains. In the Irish climate the outlook was never the same two days running and the light could change by the minute.

The views from the adjoining drawing room were even more dramatic. King James II spent a night at Lismore in 1689 and is said to have approached the huge bay window then started back in surprise when he saw the sheer drop below. The other window looked east, downstream over the Fifth Duke of Devonshire's beautiful bridge, the arches of which span both the river and The Inches, the fields on the far side that are often flooded. From the window you had the strange experience of looking down on the backs of swans flying below. On the edge of the river, year after year, a heron stood like a sentinel in a little pebble-bottomed inlet watching his stretch of the water. I hardly ever saw him catch a fish but he must have thought it worth his while waiting there patiently on one leg, and I wondered if it was always the head heron that inherited that spot. Tony and Bindie Lambton came to stay for long visits and Tony, who was a renowned shot, used to aim an apple at the heron from the drawing-room window. He never hit it, but the bird would fly off slowly in the lumbering way of herons, to prove that it was untouched.

As if all this were not enough there was Lismore itself, its shops, Protestant and Catholic cathedrals and its people. There were few cars in the town and on Sundays and Fair Days the donkey carts and pony traps followed in single file across the bridge to double park along Main Street. Until the 1960s, horses, goats and donkeys were hobbled as they grazed the Long Acre, the grass on the roadside verges. Travellers and tinkers were plentiful (though how they existed I cannot tell). For us, coming from austerity England, the fact that meat and other food was not rationed added to the unreal atmosphere. There was heady excitement when we discovered on the counter of the Arcade, the draper's shop, rolls and rolls of the top-quality black cloth worn by priests, and we bought lots of it to take home to make coats and skirts.

Living near by in a house belonging to the castle dairy farm was Mrs Feeney, who cooked all her food in an iron pot that hung on a chain over an everlasting fire. Her daughter, Mary, who became a great friend of mine, told me that the taste was second to none, which I can well imagine as the goodness lay in all the ingredients being combined in one pot. Mary Feeney, who made many of the curtains at Lismore Castle, had been taught dressmaking by Ann Astaire and excelled at it. I wore her creations at both the grandest and humblest occasions and always felt happy in them. Norah Willoughby behind the counter of the newsagent's shop knew her customers well and gave them a tremendous welcome when they came in one by one to buy their paper. The town's ancient doctor came to visit me once when I was pregnant. Dressed in curious old-fashioned hunting clothes of green breeches and shiny black leather gaiters, he glanced at the letter sent by my English doctor, looked at me and said, 'The woman doesn't *always* die from this disease', and then left to join the hunt.

There was plenty of room at Lismore for friends. They arrived with children and dogs off the Fishguard–Rosslare boat. Our old friends Richard and Virginia Sykes came with their children. Tatton, the eldest, aged about five, was a bit namby-pamby and held up his spoon (kept in the usual damp cupboard), and whined to Diddy, 'My spoon's rusty.' 'Rusty?' said Diddy. 'That's iron. It will do you good.' Robert Kee was always a welcome guest. His interest in Ireland, which gave rise to his histories of 'that most distressful country', was inspired by his love for Oonagh Oranmore, one of the three blonde Guinness girls, daughters of Lord Iveagh. Robert is strikingly handsome, strikingly clever, articulate like no other, and as good a writer as he is a talker. *The Green Flag* is generally accepted as being the best of a long list of his works on Ireland. He slid into television naturally and the news magazine *Panorama* was lucky to have him as its presenter during that programme's most influential years. As an interviewer he was penetrating without being rude and he never interrupted or bullied his victims.

In 1958 Robert brought his friend Cyril Connolly to stay. I was intrigued to meet this famous writer and critic, who was admired by his peers and apparently loved by women. Cyril had put about the idea that he wanted to buy a house in Ireland, but I soon realized it was just an excuse to see inside some of the houses in the neighbourhood. This resulted in embarrassing telephone calls and visits to people who had no intention of selling. If the plasterwork and proportions were not up to Cyril's expectations, he got as far as the hall then lost interest, leaving me to look at the other rooms and thank the owners for the invasion and obligatory drink. Cyril was said to be a gardener and to understand plants. The climate at Lismore allows all sorts of wonders to be grown that would perish in Derbyshire. Andrew and I were able to plant mimosa and different kinds of magnolia, including the best *Magnolia sprengeri* 'Diva' I have ever seen. We also planted a *Magnolia delavayi*, whose growth was so rapid that, like the hedge in *The Sleeping Beauty*, it would have obliterated the door to the lower garden had it not been drastically cut back every year. When Cyril came to stay, the lower garden was planted for spring and the *Chaenomeles* along the wall was quite a feature. The pink form of the shrub is called 'Apple Blossom' – muddling, but anyone who knows about plants knows the confusing habit plant breeders have of calling a daffodil 'Buttercup' or a nectarine 'Pineapple'. Cyril duly admired it. 'Oh yes,' said Emma, conversant from an early age with such botanical traps, 'Apple Blossom.' 'No,' said Cyril sententiously, 'it's a *Chaenomeles*.' Emma gave him a pitying look and that was that as far as Cyril was concerned.

Paddy Leigh Fermor came to Lismore for the first time in April 1956. He described his visit in a letter to our mutual friend Daphne (ex Bath, then married to Xan Fielding).

The whole castle and the primeval forest round it were spellbound in a late spring or early summer trance; heavy rhododendron blossom everywhere and, under the Rapunzel tower I inhabited, a still, leafless magnolia tree shedding petals like giant snowflakes over the parallel stripes of an embattled new-mown lawn: silver fish flickered in the river, wood pigeons cooed and herons slowly wheeled through trees so overgrown with lichen they looked like green coral, drooping with ferns and lianas, almost like an equatorial jungle. One would hardly have been surprised to see a pterodactyl or an archaeopteryx sail through the twilight, or the neck of a dinosaur craning through the ferns and lapping up a few bushels out of the Blackwater, which curls away like the Limpopo, all set about with fever-trees . . .

Paddy provided all the entertainment anyone could wish for and has been the quickest and funniest companion for more than half a century. The classical scholar, famed writer and acclaimed war hero spent his time bang down to earth when he was at Lismore. He took up the idiotic songs that Decca and I had invented as children and whirled and twirled round the dining room singing this gibberish loudly. To one who had translated 'Widdecombe Fair' and 'John Peel' into Italian (and sings them at the drop of a hat), such nonsense verses came naturally and he entered into the spirit of things with gusto. Taking a cork from a wine bottle, he shut one eye, studied it close up with the other and said, 'What Irish newspaper am I?' The *Cork Examiner*, of course.

Andrew loved Paddy and they went on walks and climbing expeditions in the Pyrenees, Greece and Peru. When he was at Lismore Paddy and I went on long rides, seeing no one all day, up and around the mountains and through the woods to the Grand Lodges, neo-Gothic extravagances that were built as the entrance to a house that never was. Royal Tan was in the stables. A five-times runner in the Grand National (he came second in 1951, won in 1954 and was third in 1956), he had been given to me by Aly Khan, who bought him from Vincent O'Brien's stable when his owner, Joe Griffin, went bust. By the time the old fellow came to me, he had had enough of travelling and refused to enter a horse box. He also did things his way, stopping in the road for no apparent reason and no one could make him budge. Enticements, threats, a lead from another horse, nothing was any good. This exasperated Paddy but he had to concede defeat. 'The trouble with Royal Tan,' he said ruefully, 'is he doesn't like riding.'

When Mrs Hammersley came to Lismore, she brought a travelling companion to help during the journey. On one of her visits the novelist L. P. Hartley filled the role. I hoped he had enjoyed his stay and was disillusioned when in one of his books I read a description of his bedroom at Lismore, down to the smallest detail – and it was not flattering. The sting in the tale was 'a pair of soapstone bookends with no books between them'.

Another of Mrs Ham's carriers of shawls and bags was the Bloomsbury painter Duncan Grant, who was amused by her gloomy forecasts and used to egg her on to describe all the horrors she believed lay in store. (Some of which have come to pass, such as the degradation of art and the appalling misuse of the English language.) Irresistible to both men and women, and with a charm to floor the crustiest of human beings, Duncan became a good friend of Andrew's and mine. He was middle-aged by the time we knew him but still wickedly attractive, with turned-up eyes that disappeared when he laughed. He brought his paints when he came to stay and was the easiest of guests, working away wherever he happened to be. Modest as he was, Duncan would be amazed by the prices his paintings fetch at auction today and by the pleasure his and Vanessa Bell's decorations give to visitors to Charleston, their once very private Sussex home, now open to you and me.

Mrs Ham provided a wonderful subject for Duncan and his two portraits of her are among my treasured possessions. I wish I owned another portrait he made while staying with us. It is of Margaret Murphy, a little red-haired girl who was one of a big family living at the Grand Lodges. Heaven knows how her widowed mother managed with so many children to feed and no husband as breadwinner, but manage she did and was always cheerful and hospitable when I took visitors to call on her at the not-so-grand Grand Lodge, where there was no running water, or any other of the amenities judged necessary today. The Mrs Murphys of this world are the ones who ought to be given medals.

Harold Macmillan came to stay with his wife, Dorothy, who adored Lismore, having spent early springs there when she was a child. Uncle Harold had a lot of the actor in him and to entertain us one evening he played the punter to Porchy Carnarvon's bookmaker. Without rehearsal and dressed in whatever they could find in the hall, including loud-checked caps and binoculars, they gave us a sketch worthy of any theatre. Uncle Harold liked walking alone. One day we dropped him some miles from the castle and he made his way home, deep in thought, with no one to bother him. He had been trudging along a lonely lane for about an hour when he saw a donkey leaning its head over the roadside wall. Uncle Harold, who was getting weary, stopped and said, 'Ass, how far is it to Lismore?' The donkey took no notice but a man emerged from behind the wall, curious to see the daft fellow who had asked a question of a donkey. Little did he guess he was looking at a former Prime Minister of Great Britain and Northern Ireland.

Our weeks at Lismore were enlivened not only by a stream of visitors from abroad but also by neighbours, including a number of friends and relations who, disenchanted with England and its Socialist government, had decided to emigrate. Pam and Derek were among our first guests and they fell for Ireland. Derek was attracted by its lack of bureaucracy and bossiness, not to mention Attlee's penal taxation, and decided to buy Tullamaine Castle in County Tipperary, where he set up a racehorse training establishment. He and Pam entertained a great deal – too much for Pam to manage single-handed – and they employed a succession of cooks. None of them came up to Pam's high standards and she used to come over to see me and regale me with her kitchen woes. 'Stublow, ordering with Mrs B is a nightmare,' or 'Isn't game soup the richest and loveliest soup you ever laid hands on? Well, a milky affair came up.' This said in a dramatic voice that grew lower and more urgent until the last sentence might have been recounting a world-shaking disaster. To Pam it was. Between cooks she produced the meals herself. I telephoned one day to ask if she could come to lunch. 'No, of course I can't,' she said crossly, 'I'm much too busy making egg mousse for sixty.' (I had forgotten it was the day of the Tipperary point-to-point that was run over the Tullamaine farm.)

Derek was a human time-bomb ready to explode and was not cut out for an enduring marriage. As time went by and he had no success with the racing venture, he began to grow restless and miss his scientific work – a part of his life that was impossible to share with the Tipperary locals. Robert Kee, knowing of Derek's brilliance, once said to him, 'I'm afraid all I know about maths is that two plus two equals four.' Derek thought for a bit and said, 'I've often wondered.' In the 1945 General Election I asked him if he was going to vote Conservative. He exploded and, hardly able to get out the words, said, 'How can I vote for a man who speaks of the *third alternative*?' A rare grammatical error from Winston cost him Derek's vote.

Derek had always been unpredictable, darting off to left and right, and he now spent more and more time away from home, leaving Pam with the racehorses as well as a large house to look after. It became obvious that their years of marriage were at an end. As always when life seemed to conspire against her, Pam faced the separation with courage. After Derek left, she must have had an impossibly difficult time but carried on as best she could and never complained to her sisters, though Diana and I were aware how unhappy she was.

Tullamaine was sold in 1958 but Pam stayed on as a tenant until 1960. We all knew she was careful, but sometimes her watching of the pennies was so comical it has to be recorded. She told her new landlord that the house needed rewiring. He obeyed and sent round some workmen. Pam then said she must have a cow to provide milk for the workmen's tea. He sent round a cow that gave four gallons a day. The workmen only used a pint, so Pam bought four piglets and fed the milk to them. Even they could not get through it all so she sent the rest to the creamery. She was staying with friends when a cheque for £10 arrived from the creamery. Her host, who happened to be a land agent and versed in such matters, said, 'I suppose you're going to pass it on to the landlord.' 'OH NO!' cried Pam. 'After all, *my* gardener milks the cow. But for me his workmen would have to *buy* their milk.' So she kept the cheque, the cow, the pigs and the workmen.

Sophy's first stay at Lismore came when she was a year old. The older children's cot and all that went with it were long gone, but I knew that Pam would still have the cot that Diana's sons slept in when they lived with her during the war. I wrote to ask if I could borrow it. She answered at once to say yes but suggested I get it painted as it was obviously in a poor state. She had some perfectly good blankets, she said, with a few moth holes, and added, 'If Miss Feeney cut them into the right size leaving out the eaten parts she could put some pretty ribbon to bind them and this would save a lot.' She also offered linen sheets: 'Some large double bed sheets which are rather worn but here again Miss Feeney could find plenty left to make cot sheets.'

In the same letter, she reminded me that the sale of the contents of Tullamaine was about to take place. It is wonderful what a country house sale can produce. The glasses she had bought at Woolworths in Clonmel sold for four times their purchase price, even though the exact same ones were available in Woolworths down the road. She included a lot of eggs in the sale that had been stored in Ali Baba pots of brine since the spring flush of the year before. Diana and I teased her that they were all bad and would go off at intervals like pistol shots. But everything went for tiptop prices and several times I heard her announcing loudly, 'Nothing is to go out of this house till it's paid for.'

After she left Ireland, Pam went to live in Switzerland. She took her dogs with her and decided to stay there until they died, not just because of the quarantine regulations but, as she explained in an interview to a German magazine, because she thought they would prefer to spend their old age on the Continent. She made many friends in Switzerland. Diana said that she was the local star and when she walked down the street in Zurich she was greeted by gnomes of high degree with, 'PAMAILAH. How are you? How *vonderful* to see you!' She was loved and appreciated for her unique qualities, and her friends listened open-mouthed to her oft-told tales of childhood. She shared a house with her friend Giuditta Tommasi, an Italian riding teacher. Today any such relationship is immediately connected to sex, and two men or women who choose to live in the same house are said to be homosexual. In some cases no doubt they are, but in many others they are just friends who share a roof. In either case, it is of secondary interest. I find this guessing about the sex life of friends or relations tiresome in the extreme. It is the people who matter; their private lives should be their own.

In 1951 the Mosleys also bought a house in Ireland, the mid-seventeenth-century Bishop's Palace (a grand name for what Diana described as 'a pretty old house') in Clonfert, near Ballinasloe in County Galway. Diana and Sir O lived between France and Ireland until 1963, when they decided to settle permanently at the Temple de la Gloire. Sir

O kept an office in London and remained politically active, an ardent European, until the late 1970s but felt that while he remained in England he would be subject to the spite and obstruction of British officialdom. The Bishop's Palace needed re-roofing, heating, bathrooms and the rest of the necessities for modern comfort. In the unhurried way of Ireland, these additions took some time and it was three years before it was finished to Diana's high standards. On a cold December night in 1954 an ancient beam in a chimney that had been dried out by the new central heating caught fire and before help could arrive the house and most of its contents were well alight. The desperate whinnying of horses in the nearby stables woke the family and, miraculously, no one died in the conflagration. Diana described how all that was left of her four-poster bed, newly trimmed with pale blue silk, were a few red-hot springs. Portraits of her by John Banting and Helleu, drawings by Augustus John, Tchelitchew and others, were reduced to cinders. Diana, her husband and their two sons, Alexander and Max, were homeless.

Andrew immediately lent them Lismore Castle where they spent Christmas in mourning for Clonfert. When a house called Ileclash, 1½ miles from Fermoy and overlooking the Blackwater, came up for sale, although it was a poor substitute for Clonfert, they bought it. This was good news for me as it was only about twenty miles away. We were both busy, but not too busy to meet halfway in the village of Ballyduff (called Ballyduff Cooper by us, of course). The Ballyduff Cooper summits became a feature of life and we would sit enclosed in the privacy of the car, talking to our hearts' content. Diana used to walk from Ileclash to the shops in Fermoy. A necessary part of a visit to that busy town was to lean on the bridge that overlooked the broad Blackwater and watch the torrent below. Diana leant and watched. She was aware of a man next to her doing the same and they stood there together for some time. ''Tis all going to the sea,' he said at last. ''Tis,' she replied, after some thought.

Eddy Sackville-West moved to Ireland in 1956 mainly to escape the responsibility of Knole, his family home in Kent, and all that went with that vast and ancient house of many courtyards, which, with its endless rooms, was totally unsuitable for a bachelor. He did not want to live in such a place and, like many others, fell in love with Ireland. He bought Cooleville in the village of Clogheen, the other side of the Knockmealdown Mountains from Lismore, and made it his own creation. Nancy often stayed with Eddy, combining it with a visit to Lismore. (I think she preferred Cooleville.) Eddy was unmarried and what my father called a 'literary cove', a lover of music and books. Andrew enjoyed his company and he became a regular dinner guest at Lismore. He arrived one evening when no one had been in to tidy and everything was lying about. His first words, in a trembly voice, were, '*Secateurs* on the *mantelpiece, saws* on the *hall table.*'

At the time we had a craze for an after-dinner billiard-table game called Freda. It was not athletic and dangerous like Billiard Fives but it did involve running round the table at vital moments. For this, his only attempt at such sport, Eddy brought a little case with daytime trousers and shirt – to save his dinner jacket from possible damage. A convert to Roman Catholicism, he fitted well into the Irish landscape but his romantic view of the country sometimes caused him to invest his duller neighbours with imaginary qualities. When he laughed, which often happened when he was describing one of them, he drew his knees up to his chin. But even he was brought down to earth by the food they served when it was their turn to entertain him. 'There is no excuse,' he wailed with emphasis on each word, 'for coarsely mashed potatoes.'

Andrew's uncle, David Cecil, came to Lismore several times. He was a great friend of Elizabeth Bowen and asked me one day if she lived near by. I had heard of the novelist but knew nothing of Bowen's Court, the family house in County Cork that she inherited in 1930. I asked David if I should invite her to lunch. 'Yes, do,' he said. Elizabeth came and we all fell for her big-boned charm and hesitant speech that came out with such good stuff. She invited us back to Bowen's Court, the archetypal Irish house: dilapidated, beautifully proportioned and freezing cold, except for the sitting room where you could imagine happily spending days in her company. On the top floor of this big and almost empty house was a long broad gallery – unusual in a house of 1776 as it harped back to an Elizabethan plan. At either end of the gallery, which had floorboards as wide as an old oak would allow, there were tall windows and on the south window, engraved with a diamond, was: 'Baby Bowen 1899', commemorating Elizabeth's birth. The floor of the yard that led to the garden was made of the knuckle bones of sheep – something I have never seen before or since. Like everyone who had known the house, I was appalled when I read that Elizabeth had had to sell it and that a few months later the new owner knocked it down. Poor Elizabeth. When she returned to Ireland it cannot have been with pleasure.

We all loved Betty Farquhar, a fierce hunting lady who lived at Ard-sallagh, a small, well-proportioned house that stood on a rise near the town of Fethard. She was a product of the Shires and the world of the Quorn, Belvoir and Cottesmore hounds – those legendary packs that she had hunted with six days a week before the war. I once asked her what it was like. 'Ow, just like going to the office,' was the reply. She could dismay a stranger when introduced to him by turning and asking at the top of her voice, 'Who is this *ghastly* man?' Her house was a surprise, with its pieces of stained glass by Evie Hone and paintings by Irish art-ists of the 1930s and 40s that would fetch a king's ransom today. Her garden was immaculate, as was her appearance; unlike some ex-pats she never went to seed or lowered her standards.

Twice widowed, Betty had no children and fell in love with Ireland through Sylvia Masters, the friend who shared her life and who had grown up at nearby Woodruffe. A legend of courage and originality, Sivvy was Master and Huntsman of the Tipperary hounds long before any woman dreamed of such a thing. She won 101 point-to-points, riding against men who gave no quarter because of her sex. Sivvy was quiet but stood out in a crowd with her straight, daffodil-yellow hair and large eyes. Children adored her and she encouraged them in everything their parents forbade, slipping fags into their hand as soon as the grown-ups were out of sight. Her brother, the actor and playwright John Perry, was a great friend of Binkie Beaumont, the theatrical impresario who ruled the London stage for thirty years. Thus Sivvy and her brother covered a broad spectrum, from hunting hounds to *The Winslow Boy* and *The Little Hut*.

Clodagh Anson, the most loved of spinsters, was a distant cousin of Andrew (their grandmothers were sisters). She lived alone in a damp house across the river 'belonging to the castle'; an eye-catcher among the trees for our north-facing rooms, it carried evidence of the Troubles in the form of bullet holes here and there. Clodagh was the only person I knew of Anglo-Irish background who was accepted by the inhabitants of Lismore, and beyond, as one of them. Unworldly to the last degree, she was the antithesis of a snob and the best of company; it did not matter who was staying with us, she captivated the lot. Tall, ugly and with charm to beat the band, she had lived through the 'bad times' in Ireland and her throwaway tales of her experiences as a girl could have come straight from those inimitable Anglo-Irish writers, Edith Somerville and Martin Ross. When she was eighteen her mother, Lady Clodagh Anson, took her to London and made a half-hearted attempt to bring her out as a debutante. Lady Clodagh devoted herself to down-and-outs and their London house was a refuge for beggars. When returning from a grand ball, her daughter had to pick her way over sleeping tramps in the hall, all described in Lady Clodagh's two volumes of memoirs, *Book* and *Another Book*, which are among my unstealables.

At Lismore, Clodagh kept unusual hours and did not wake till lunchtime. From the castle kitchen I could see the blind of her bedroom window pulled firmly down till 12.45 p.m., even when she was lunching with us at 1 p.m. She loved her garden but it was often dark before she was ready to start work so she weeded and dug by the headlights of her ancient car and when the battery failed she wore a miner's lamp so as to be able to garden late into the night. She was a regular churchgoer to the magnificent Church of Ireland cathedral in Lismore. When the service started at 10.30 a.m. Clodagh was always half an hour late and came in with a clatter of banged doors and dropped books. It was decided to start the service at 11 a.m., to give her a chance. She made the same noisy entrance at 11.30. The service was not delayed further or the congregation would have had no lunch.

In 1987 Hubert de Givenchy and Philippe Venet came to stay. I asked Clodagh to lunch and told our unworldly neighbour a bit about them beforehand, how they were leading couturiers in Paris and therefore the world. Over lunch, I heard Clodagh tell Hubert that she was going to stay with her brother in Rome. 'I believe you are a dressmaker,' she said. 'Should I have the hems of my cotton frocks taken up or let down this summer?' With impeccable manners, Monsieur de Givenchy turned to her and said, 'Madame, I cannot advise you, but I would like to make you something to wear when you go to Italy.' We went to measure her. (Hubert and Philippe wore gumboots because they had heard her house was damp.) Clodagh was top-heavy and walked headfirst, her jutting nose hanging over clicking false teeth, and her big hands those of a gardener. She stooped and had a pronounced dowager's hump, which meant that the measurement between her shoulders was some inches longer than that of her long-forgotten bosom. Hubert and Philippe could not help smiling as they made a note of these measurements, but Clodagh was unaware of it. A few weeks later a couple of strong cardboard boxes, with the magic name of Givenchy attached, arrived at Clodagh's house. She had no idea how lucky she was but her friends were jealous of her windfall trousseau from the Avenue George V.

Wendy (nothing to do with Peter Pan but short for Wendell) Howell was a grand American gone native ('How yer *dawgs*?') whom I prized as a friend because she did not take to just anyone and made an exception for me. She liked whippets and whisky and had too many of both. Lots of husbands (including a Roosevelt) had come and gone and she eventually settled with a lady vet in one of those Irish cottages which were rare then and now only happen on postcards. It had an earth floor and stable doors and, in the sitting room, a vast opening for the fireplace where, if you bent down to look up the chimney, you could see a big patch of sky. At the entrance to the cottage was a sculpture of two whippets, old friends to me as they were an echo of a similar model by Gott at Chatsworth. Wendy held a pilot's licence but luckily never offered to take me for a spin.

Obbie, the Twelfth Duke of St Albans, lived at beautiful Newtown Anna, by Clonmel. He had converted his garden shed into a sitting room, 'the finest room in Europe,' he announced. It still had a lot of the garden shed about it and reminded me of my father's at High Wycombe. Like Farve, Obbie had fought in the Boer War, the First World War and joined the Home Guard in the Second. And, like Farve, he had refused promotion to Corporal saying he did not want the responsibility. Another trait they had in common was unpredictability. Obbie once telephoned my mother-in-law and, with no preliminaries, said, 'Moucher, you're not a has-been, but a has-been has-been,' and put down the receiver. During the Second World War, when food was rationed and it was strictly against the law to ask anyone in a neutral country to send any, Obbie delighted in sending postcards, open for all to read, from neutral Ireland to his niece Betty Salisbury, whose husband Bobbety held, at various times during the war, the posts of Paymaster General, Secretary of State for Dominion Affairs, Colonial Secretary, Lord Privy Seal and Leader of the House of Lords. The postcards read, 'I will send the *ham*, *butter, bacon* and *steak* you asked for tomorrow,' and arrived at intervals throughout the war.

Another reason for enjoying Lismore was the company of our land agent, John Silcock. When he was a young man and had just finished his training, he had a farewell chat with the Norfolk landowner on whose estate he had been working. 'I'll give you two pieces of advice,' said the landowner. 'Don't go to Ireland and don't marry your principal.' John did both and it was through Irish connections that he came to run Lismore, spending two days a week in the estate office. He was the best of company and got on well with the people who worked at Lismore, which made life smooth for all concerned. I spent hours with him, touring the farm and woods, listening to his tales of working in Ireland. I used to say to Andrew, 'You know, John is wonderful.' This was repeated so often that he became 'Wonderful John', later shortened to 'Wonderful'.

A surprise is always around the corner in Ireland. There was an elephant skull by a bend in the road to Cappoquin and at Ballynatray human bones were dug up in the little churchyard and scattered to allow a new coffin to be buried there. In our early years at Lismore, the beautiful house of Ballynatray belonged to Horace Holroyd-Smyth. The billiard table served as the dining table, with the remains of breakfast at one end, teacups at the other and lunch in the middle. I am not sure about dinner but I remember thinking what a good idea it was. The silver cups won by Mr Horace's point-to-pointers were shiningly clean and obviously prized far beyond anything else in the house. Mr Horace and his fiancée loved hunting so much that in the closed season they listened to a gramophone record of a hunting horn: 'Gone Away', 'The Find', and 'A Kill', all blown to perfection by an expert; and the response of the hounds was tantalizing to hear in the off-season. The hounds were fed on salmon, the cheapest food available because they were caught in a trap at the bottom of the garden as they swam up the Blackwater.

Social life dies hard in Ireland. During the war when there was no petrol for cars, Mr Horace went out to dinner on his tractor dressed in his dinner jacket. In the 1930s Ballynatray took paying guests and Penelope Betjeman and Joan Eyres Monsell (later to marry Paddy Leigh Fermor) slept there on a riding tour. One of the party discovered an unwelcome object far down in the bed: the mustard plaster worn by someone who had died of pneumonia. I cannot help wondering if this was true or whether John Betj invented it. It would have been typical of that house – and of John. The last time I went to Ballynatray, three pigs and a couple of hounds were asleep in the sun, guarding the front door.

Careysville, sixteen miles upstream from Lismore, had some of the best salmon fishing in Ireland. It had been rented by my father-in-law during the 1930s and when it came up for sale soon after the war, he bought it. Andrew took his fishing friends there for the first two weeks of February. They spent the day on the river and usually stayed at Lismore but sometimes at Careysville House which in my father-in-law's day was so cold that it was normal procedure to pick up the rug off the floor and put it over the thin eiderdown. The soil was good and snowdrops in the garden grew so thick and tall that the hounds drew them for a fox.

A green and white hut, more of a cricket pavilion than a fishing hut, stood on the flat ground by the riverbank and was where we had lunch. The food was carried in baskets down the steep steps by beautiful Irish maidens whose job it was to do just that. The fare was always exactly the same: cold meat, salad, hot baked potatoes, a rich Christmas pudding and cheese (usually the squashed-up kind in silver paper). Had there been any deviation from this menu there would have been a revolution among Andrew's guests. I never took to fishing – a terrible waste when I could have had the best – but there was always a queue of aficionados for the limited number of rods, so it was just as well.

Careysville produced its own unforgettable people. John O'Brien, the head ghillie, was Andrew's friend and was one of the reasons Andrew loved the place so much. The two men talked to each other all day long of much more than fishing and any rare moments of silence were without awkwardness. Sport produces a unique friendship and Andrew was deeply affected by O'Brien's death in 1964. He was crossing the river with two other ghillies when their boat overturned in turbulent water and all three non-swimmers were drowned. Andrew never felt the same about Careysville again.

Billy Flynn was another ghillie remembered by all. His charm and funniness and tales of the fishery were Ireland at its most beguiling. With his lifelong experience, he hardly needed scales to tell the weight of a fish and a 29½ pounder was brought up to the magic 30 lbs by Billy stuffing plum pudding into its mouth. One day the children and I had been talking about ghosts and I asked Billy if he had ever seen one. He thought for some time and said, 'Sure, I saw a sow where never a sow there was.' I went to visit him in hospital when he was dying of a horribly disfiguring cancer of the face; his grossly enlarged cheek and jaw were awful to see and he could only whisper. He wanted to tell me something. I bent down and could just hear, 'Will there be fishing in heaven?'

Our weeks in Ireland had their sombre side. The years of the Troubles in the north had their repercussions in the south. Alfred and Clementine Beit were attacked by thieves at Russborough, their house in County Wicklow, and locked in separate cellars while the gang made off with the best of Alfred's world-famous pictures. Lord and Lady Donoughmore were kidnapped, bundled into a car, driven for miles in the dark at speed and held hostage for four days. Andrew was not put off by these attacks, but after Bloody Sunday in 1972 the Irish government increased the number of Garda looking after him – up to fourteen at any one time – and a police car travelled in front and behind him wherever he went. Three different routes take you from Lismore to Careysville and on the orders of the Garda he had to decide at the last minute which he would take, and several men stayed with him all day on the riverbank. In 1974, after Lord Mountbatten and three members of his family were murdered, even I was given a policeman. He must have been bored walking to the shops, the farm and endless times round the garden. He pointed to a stone sundial one day and asked me what it was. 'A sundial,' I said. 'Oh, does it still work?' It does, but its hours on duty are not long in Ireland.

The time came when all the old friends had departed from our Irish life and Andrew himself was not well. He was no longer able to walk up and down the steep steps from Careysville House to the river, and his failing eyesight made it difficult to cast over the wide water. The death of John O'Brien, the spirit of Careysville, and the loss of other friends made the place too full of ghosts and he stopped going. The castle was made over to Stoker and we retreated from Ireland, where we had had such happy times.

14

MOVING TO CHATSWORTH

Soon after my father-in-law died, Andrew said to me, 'Chatsworth may not go on as a family home, but I don't want to be the one to let it go.' He was thinking not only of the house itself, the garden, the stables and everything else that goes with Chatsworth, but of what selling would mean to the people who belonged there. This was a major consideration in the struggle to keep it going.

The 1950s were grim for this country. Rationing did not end until 1954, nine long years after the end of the war, and recovery was painfully slow. In our case it was not recovery but a downward slope that was facing us. Many beautiful and useful buildings all over England were being destroyed and supplanted by monstrous ones, and no one believed that a house like Chatsworth would ever be wanted again, let alone lived in by the descendants of the family who built it. It was a period of limbo. No major decisions were being taken at Chatsworth but nevertheless a five-hundred-year legacy was beginning to come undone.

Hugo Read was the land agent during the time when the estate was in debt to the government. I was talking to Hugo one day about Pilsley, a village on the estate, and he said if he had the money he would pull down a row of semi-detached cottages called South View. 'Why?' I asked. 'Well, they're only Victorian,' was the answer. Luckily there was no money and the cottages with their remarkable gardens are still there.

The exuberantly Victorian Barbrook House, built by the Sixth Duke's head gardener Joseph Paxton for himself and his family, was not so lucky. It had been the home of the land agent till 1939 but was left unoccupied at the outbreak of the war. By the late 1940s it was used for storage; potatoes and wheat were shovelled into the dining and drawing rooms and it was riddled with dry rot. As Victoriana was looked on with derision, no one thought Barbrook worth keeping. With so many out-standing repairs on the estate cottages hanging over us – few had indoor lavatories let alone bathrooms – there was no question of restoring such a white elephant and the house became a victim of the time. It was succeeded by an ugly and useful warehouse, designed by Hugo Read. Only the pretty lodge is left to remind us of the former grandeur of Paxton's days, which had included a nine-acre kitchen garden with innovative hot houses, melon pits and pineapples.

It was not just visible signs of the past that were disappearing, mo-rale was also low as no one could envisage a day when the place would be free of debt. The one bright spot in an otherwise dismal period was that the house and garden at Chatsworth were open to the public and, in spite of petrol rationing, visitors came. Hugo Read was infinitely more wise and far-sighted in his views on the future of Chatsworth it-self than of Victorian cottages. He was adamant that in spite of all the difficulties, the family – Andrew, me and our (then) two children – should move into the house because we were a necessary part of the whole. It was nearly twenty years since Eddy and Moucher had taken their belongings – which they had barely unpacked – back to Churchdale. On the face of it, Hugo's idea seemed wild, a complete reversal of all our efforts at scrimping and saving to pay off death duties. But Hugo, like Francis Thompson, who had emphasized the necessity of a family presence in his letter to my father-in-law in 1947, believed that Chats-worth and its family were inseparable. Both men warned that without a welcoming host the house would become a museum, as arid and life-less as so many others.

Andrew's initial reluctance to live at Chatsworth may have stemmed from unhappy memories of his grandfather's last years there, and per-haps from his parents' attitude towards the house after Billy's death. Eddy and Moucher lost heart and did not feel inclined to do much to the house. Even if they had wanted to, a limit of £150 a year was allowed by law to be spent on decorating, and for that a permit was needed. For a while we considered moving to Hardwick Hall when Granny Evie had had enough. Its astonishing beauty was a strong pull, but the disadvantages of extreme cold (tits pecked at the lead round the little window panes till they fell out and made cruel draughts) and the lack of bathrooms with nowhere obvious to put them always brought us back to the homelier Chatsworth. By 1957 Andrew was convinced that moving was the right thing to do. I had been longing to live there and was thrilled. When we had walked through the park in the past, I had often teased him by saying, 'Oh, look at that lovely house. I wonder who lives there.' And he would say, 'Oh, do shut up.' But now he threw himself wholeheartedly into the plans.

The house was begun in 1552 by Bess Hardwick, the most powerful woman in England after the Queen, and some of the Elizabethan walls have survived, embedded in the classicised house of today. Bess was married four times, but the only man with whom she had children was her third husband, Sir William Cavendish. Their son was created Baron Cavendish of Hardwick in 1605, and First Earl of Devonshire in 1618. (The reason for his choice of name is not known. The family have never owned an acre of land in that far-away county.) It is Chatsworth's great good fortune that the rebuilding of the old house was done between 1686 and 1707, a time when it was impossible to invent anything ugly. The design of each side of the square block, and the style and proportions inside and out, reflect all that was best in the golden age of English architecture. The result made Daniel Defoe describe it as 'the most pleasant garden and most beautiful palace in the world.'

The house looks permanent, as permanent as if it had been there not for a few hundred years, but for ever. It fits its landscape exactly. The stone from which the house is built comes out of the ground nearby, and so it is the proper colour, on the bird's-nest theory of using building materials that are at hand and therefore right for the surroundings. From inside the house the pleasure of looking out is intense. There is not an ugly thing to be seen. The rim of the park is planted in wedge-shaped blocks of trees, so that when one block is mature and ready to be cut down there is another growing up to take its place.

Perhaps the charm or character of Chatsworth is that it has grown over the years in a haphazard sort of way. It is a conglomeration of styles and periods and nothing fits exactly. Each room is a jumble of old and new, English and foreign, thrown together by generations of acquisitive inhabitants. You find a hideous thing next to something beautiful. The result is a collection of extraordinary breadth: Egyptian steles of 1340 B.C. through Greek and Roman sculpture to the exquisite Canovas to modern pieces by Epstein and Frink, Old Master drawings and prints, paintings from Rembrandt to Van Dyck to Freud. Each generation of Cavendishes had an unerring talent for employing the best people to build, to decorate, to garden and to buy: the architect and designer William Kent did not work at Chatsworth, but the Kent furniture from Chiswick Villa came to us when the house was sold in 1929; Lancelot 'Capability' Brown's carriage miles must have exceeded any other professional's in his ceaseless travels laying out parks in the mid-eighteenth century (though I regret the wreckage of the existing formal gardens when he planted trees to satisfy his new idea of 'natural' landscape). James Paine planned the perfectly proportioned bridge and stables in 1760; Jeffry Wyatville's reputation as an architect was sealed by his work at Chatsworth in the 1820s and 1830s, and he went on to remodel Windsor Castle for the King. Sometimes instinct played its part. When the Sixth Duke engaged the twenty-three-year-old Joseph Paxton as head gardener in 1826, none could have guessed what this man would go on to do.

Once the major decision to move into Chatsworth was made, life changed gear and there were daily decisions to be taken. First we debated which rooms to use. When it came to choosing bedrooms, we always came back to the west-facing rooms that the dukes and duchesses had traditionally inhabited. After that it was a question of which should be the drawing room, dining room and kitchen. We looked carefully at the north-facing rooms on the first floor but the lack of sun was a major drawback and we gravitated naturally to the three large, cheerful, south-facing rooms on the same floor. Our blue drawing room had been Andrew's aunts' schoolroom and then the billiard room; the yellow drawing room remained unchanged and what used to be the gold drawing room became our dining room.

Immediately below the new dining room was a light, airy room that had been used by Granny Evie's secretary, and we decided to make it the pantry. It had a painted ceiling of quality, which seemed unwise to leave exposed, so we put in a false one. Our chosen space for the kitchen was next to the pantry, but that left us with the problem of how to get the food upstairs. We decided to put a lift in the old stairwell that sticks out on the east side of the house, but a portrait by Lely of General Monk (founder of the Coldstream Guards), which was fitted into one of the Bachelor (the Sixth) Duke's ornate frames on the walls of the dining room, was in the way of the entrance to the new lift, just where the jib door had to go. There was nothing to do but cut the picture in half, so when the door was opened the old soldier's legs swung round, startling the diners, but when it was shut General Monk appeared complete, legs and all. Our guest bedrooms and nurseries were scattered over two floors. Sophy was two when we moved in. There was no lift in our part of the house, so Diddy humped this toddler along the passages and up the stairs. Arriving in the nursery, poor Diddy sighed, 'Oh dear', and these were Sophy's first words.

We turned the garden path along the west side of the house into a private drive and made our entrance through the west front hall, where it had been before the long north wing was built in the 1820s. This left the grander north front door and hall for people who come to see the public part of the house. Andrew, who insisted that as much of the house as possible should be open, was keen that visitors should arrive at the front door and not be shovelled in through a side entrance, as we had seen in other houses newly opened to paying visitors. The public route was sacrosanct, even though it altered in direction from time to time. For fifty years this scheme served us well and allowed tourists to circulate easily, visit the state rooms and descend the west stairs to the chapel.

Once we had decided which rooms we would use and for what, Andrew left the rest entirely to me. He did not want to hear about domestic details and never questioned my decisions. So now I had a job – big enough to occupy every waking moment. My budget was small and most of it had to be spent on plumbing and wiring. (Later, when I worked on the Cavendish and Devonshire Arms hotels, I had become used to this squeeze on what I was allowed to spend, but it made me wary of builders' budgets.) Repainting nearly all the rooms and rearranging the furniture was a fascinating job which made me familiar with the house from attics to cellars as nothing else could have done. It forced me to look at the rooms and their contents as if for the first time and to pay proper attention to detail, because if I did not decide what was to be done no one else was going to.

I am thankful that I was thirty-eight when I found myself making these decisions. The house had had time to impress its powerful character on me and prevented the wholesale use of white paint, which was my only idea of decoration when I first grew up.

I used to think that you could arrange one of the big rooms upstairs, and that it could be frozen like a photograph, and that nothing need be changed as long as it was kept clean. I was wrong. Curtains, bed hangings, upholstery and silk on walls fade and perish with alarming speed; furniture and leather bindings (like the beasts from which they are made) must be fed, paintings on walls and ceilings restored, carpets mended if old and beautiful, replaced if newer and much walked on. Nothing is permanent. Lead on the roof wears thin, and a hole the size of a pinhead lets in rain which can soon cause dry rot. Our local stone flakes when bedded against its grain; the weather finds the weak places and scoops them out as if with a giant spoon. Every householder is aware of these nuisances, but they are multiplied at Chatsworth because of its size.

People ask me how I did it. The answer is partly that when you are in your thirties you think you can do anything, but also – just look at the help I had. There can never have been a better group than the staff I worked with, for whom nothing was too much trouble. The team was led by Dennis Fisher, the comptroller – an old-fashioned job description meaning being in charge of the domestic staff and the fabric of the house, stables and garden buildings. Dennis was succeeded by Eric Oliver, who had been head carpenter. He was the son of Arthur Oliver, long-time chauffeur, and a grandson of the head gardener at Churchdale. Eric was succeeded by his brother John, who had also been head carpenter; both knew every inch of the place.

We made six flats for staff, which included a night watchman, a telephone switchboard operator and the head of the sewing room. They kept the house alive with their comings and goings, and their eyes and ears were extra security. Telephones were installed in rooms that had never seen such a thing, replacing the bells that had called the maids and valets who no longer existed. The trickiest and one of the longest operations was putting in central heating and the plumbing for seventeen new bathrooms where there had never before been running water ('Who is my sister going to wash in all those baths?' asked Nancy).

There were unexpected complications with the new bathroom that served the red velvet bedroom on the first floor. I wanted the ceiling lowered. Until this was done the proportion of the room was unhappy – being long, narrow and too high, a former cupboard. This was beautifully done, as were all such alterations, but the coved wall above the window had been painted white and was visible from across the park. So it was repainted a dirty grey like the Derbyshire sky and does not show at all. The painting was done by a Chesterfield firm; their foreman, Eddie Greenwood, and I worked closely together, choosing colours. He was always smiling, even when he swallowed a mouthful of tintacks that he had rashly parked between his lips while using both hands to hang some lining paper. We all waited anxiously for news of the tintacks and were relieved when a message came the next morning to say that there was no longer any need to worry.

As work progressed, I spent more and more time at Chatsworth. I put a chair on the corner of the busiest passage where furniture movers, painters, decorators and sewing room people were bound to pass, and where we could talk about what and where and why. The dogs got to know this and gave up following me round the house for the hundredth time; they knew the walk would not lead out of doors but that sooner or later I would pass this spot, pick them up and at last we would go out. As well as woollen stockings, jerseys, gloves and a master key, an essential piece of equipment was a carpenter's measure. These precious objects disappeared like summer snow, especially when there were carpenters about who slipped them into their pockets without thinking.

The joys and the difficulties of living in such a huge house are all magnified. 'Can I have a list of the chimney stacks and the rooms to which they belong?' This undated wail from Grannie Evie to the clerk of works typifies the unusual problems. Everything is bigger than life-size, and a bag put down in a rare bit of house can be lost for months.

The total living space, I learned, was 1,704,233 cubic feet. There were 1.3 acres of roof. Of the 297 rooms, 48 were very big indeed and some were no more than glorified cupboards. I did not employ a decorator; I was too mean to pay for something I could do myself and cannot imagine living surrounded by someone else's taste; and besides, I loved every minute of it. Best of all was seeing plans I had agonized over take shape; sometimes almost nothing seemed to be happening and then suddenly, like a conjuring trick, it was all there. I was pleased when

Nancy Lancaster, who was one of our first guests and whose decoration of Ditchley had been such an influence when I was growing up, said to Andrew, 'My God, you're lucky. If I had done this house for you, you would have had to sell it to pay me.'

Part of the fun was opening drawers and finding things that had been hastily put away when my parents-in-law left. I once looked in a chest of drawers and discovered a miniature of Georgiana Duchess, a Women's Institute programme of 1932, a bracelet given by Pauline Borghese to the Bachelor Duke to hide a crack in the marble arm of a statue of Venus, and a crystal wireless set. It was like finding Christmas presents wherever we went.

Excitement grew as the rooms began to look cheerful and became fit backgrounds for the furniture, pictures and carpets. Much of these came from other Devonshire houses: Chiswick Villa, Churchdale Hall, Hardwick Hall, Devonshire House and a few beauties saved from Compton Place. It was a motley collection but an extraordinary one from which to be able to choose. W. K. Shimwell, by then the clerk of works and head of the building yard, had an intimate knowledge of the house (where he had served since the age of eleven when he was errand boy and ran to Edensor post office with telegrams). He and Mr Maltby, who had been a house carpenter at Devonshire House and at Chatsworth since 1910, remembered where various pieces had been previously, which was invaluable. On one occasion Mr Maltby came to me bearing carved wooden draperies which he said Granny Evie had thrown out because they were Victorian, a period she could not abide. Regilded, they were mounted above the blue drawing room windows, for which they had been made.

The actual work, including redecorating the grubbiest and dingiest leftovers from Penrhos School's occupation, took just under two years (and rewiring the rest of the house a further three winters). We eventually moved across the park in November 1959. After all the anticipation, the move seemed quite natural. As soon as I arrived, I felt Chatsworth was home and a perfectly ordinary home at that. I realize now that it was anything but, yet that is how it felt – the obvious place for Andrew and his family to be. Waking the first morning in the bed I was to sleep in for the next forty-six years was a joy and I never tired of the incomparable view west across the park. In all those years, I never took the place for granted, but marvelled at it and the fact that we were surrounded by beauty at every turn, both in and out of doors.

•

At the time we moved in, Chatsworth had belonged to ten generations of Andrew's family. The Fifth was known more for his marriage to the fascinating Lady Georgiana Spencer, famous for her gambling debts, enormous hats and electioneering prowess, than for anything he achieved himself. The Sixth Duke, known as the Bachelor Duke, was their only son, and he became the scribe of Chatsworth, setting down its history and evolution in his vivid (and to me, indispensable) *Handbook to Chatsworth and Hardwick*, written in 1844 in the form of a letter to his sister. He was funny and sad, the irresistible combination that is one of the secrets of charm. He built and restored with great passion inside and out, including extravagances of orchid and camellia houses, peach houses and vineries, and the crowning glory of the Conservatory, created by Paxton in 1836–41, a glasshouse tall enough to house a tropical forest.

The pictures, tapestries and furniture were taken for granted by the Eighth Duke, who inherited none of the passion for collecting so marked in his forebears. When visiting the English section of the Paris Exhibition with a friend, he stopped in front of a superb porphyry table. 'This is splendid,' he said. 'I envy the man who owns this.' His friend glanced at the catalogue to see that it was lent from Chatsworth.

The dreaded death duties arrived after the Eighth Duke inherited. The great sum that had to be raised on his death to pay them forced the first of the major sales that have been such a distressing aspect of the management of the estate ever since. After the First World War the decision was made to demolish the Great Conservatory. The tropical garden needed ten men to look after it and immense quantities of coal to heat it through a Derbyshire winter. The structure proved so sound that it had to be blown up. One explosion was not enough and just shattered the glass, splinters of which still litter the garden.

As happened with most English families who have great collections, there was a long pause after the 1850s where nothing except the more or less obligatory portraits of the reigning owners and their wives were commissioned. Where are the Pre-Raphaelites, the Impressionists, the Surrealists and the Abstracts? Why are there no Lalique vases, no Art Deco jewellery or Charles Rennie Mackintosh furniture? Were they not admired? Would they have been considered unwarranted extravagances, or did the Eighth, Ninth and Tenth Dukes just think there was enough of everything?

Andrew and I used to talk about having portraits painted to join the parade of family likenesses at Chatsworth, but knew that that would have to wait until things looked brighter financially. Then Andrew decided that he wanted to make an exception and asked the Florentine portrait painter Pietro Annigoni, who came to London from time to time and worked in a studio in Edwardes Square, to paint me. In 1954 I spent a month sitting for him, sometimes twice a day. He admired the dark-haired Italian girls by whom he was surrounded and usually painted them or their beautiful northern counterparts. I felt a bit of an imposter and said, 'Sorry about my face, I know it's not what you like.' 'Oh, it's not your fault,' he answered (all this through an interpreter as neither of us could speak the other's language). After hours of staring, he decided to paint me in a high white collar and red velvet coat. 'You see,' he said, 'your clothes aren't *à la mode* so it doesn't matter.' The telephone often rang during the sittings. He wanted me to answer it. I was to say he was busy, but the girls soon rang back, hoping to plan a meeting. In spite of not being able to talk, I got fond of Annigoni's presence and his portrait is considered a success.

In the late 1950s I started sitting for Lucian Freud in his Paddington studio. He was a friend and only painted people at his own suggestion. I do not know how many sessions the portrait took, but time had no meaning for him and on it went. Whenever I was in London I used to arrive at the studio at 10 a.m. and sit as still as I could till lunchtime. During the sittings we sometimes talked and sometimes remained silent. Lucian made it obvious that I was not supposed to look at the canvas in the early stages (the case, I imagine, with all his sitters) but every now and again, walking round the room during a short break, I caught a glimpse of it. He started painting one eye, and slowly, very slowly, the rest of my face and hair appeared.

At last *Woman in a White Shirt* was ready for Andrew to see. Lucian was out when he called. Andrew hurried up the stairs and made his way between the rickety bedstead and rusty iron bath, almost the only furniture in the studio, to find he was not alone: two men were sitting there. Andrew went to the easel and gazed at 'me', all greenish khaki and with the resigned expression of one who had sat still for hour after hour. After a while one of the men said, 'Who is that woman?' 'It's my wife,' said

Andrew. 'Well, thank God it's not mine,' was the bailiff's answer, for that was the profession of the two strangers.

Andrew was an admirer of Lucian's work and was pleased to possess the portrait, which is liked or disliked according to taste. (When Diana Cooper came to stay, she stuck envelopes all over the glass so she could not see it.) For myself, I am glad it was done by an artist who is still a friend and who is acclaimed by critics as 'the greatest living painter' whenever his work is shown. And I believe that as I have got older, so my likeness to the portrait grows.

Lucian was our first guest at Chatsworth; he came to paint a tiny bathroom next to the Sabine bedroom. The idea was to cover the whole of the bathroom walls with cyclamen like the walls in the bedroom next door, which are covered with paintings by Thornhill of Sabine women being grabbed by Roman soldiers. But Lucian is a slow worker and greeted me most mornings with, 'I've had a wonderful night taking out everything I did yesterday.' After five days, the pull of London became too strong and off he went, so the bathroom was never finished.

Being driven in London by Lucian was hazardous; Marble Arch was terrifying, Hyde Park Corner even worse. He was Mr Toad, scarf and all, in his old but powerful car. He weaved its long body in and out of the swirling traffic, avoiding buses, bicycles and angry taxi drivers by inches. When I shouted, 'Slower. STOP. PLEASE,' he said, 'It's all right. They've all got brakes.' I had a black Mini which I kept in London and Lucian borrowed it several times. One day he arrived at Chesterfield Street, where we had our London house, swinging the key on his finger. 'This is all that's left of your car,' he said. It had been stolen and that was that.

Twenty years after painting me, Lucian made a portrait of Andrew. The lengthiness of the sittings shows. Andrew, who was not well at the time, is slumped in a chair and has either nodded off or is staring at the floor – it is impossible to tell which as eyelids take the place of eyes. Lucian also painted Moucher, Stoker and my sisters-in-law, Elizabeth and Anne. When hung together these portraits span several decades of his work and reflect the changes in his style.

In 1974, Andrew was painted by Theodore Ramos, dressed in the robes of Chancellor of the University of Manchester. It is a good likeness but the clothes are a far cry from his usual frayed silk shirt, pale trousers and tweed coat. Eighteen years later when he was painted by the Glasgow artist Stephen Conroy, in a portrait commissioned by Stoker, he was wearing his everyday clothes, and there stands Andrew to the life.

It was a daily pleasure to live among the pictures at Chatsworth. Gazing at Velázquez' *Lady with a Mantilla* in my sitting room, for example, was a real help when I was trying to do something difficult. There seemed no obvious place to hang Rembrandt's *Portrait of an Old Man* – it has to be studied close to and it is no good muddling it up with other pictures – so Andrew put it on an easel to be examined at leisure. Reynolds' portrait of Georgiana, Duchess of Devonshire, and her baby daughter, and Batoni's portraits of the Fifth Duke (looking supercilious) and his younger brother Richard Cavendish (looking drab as befits a second son), suited the blue drawing room. Liotard's pastels of the great actor Garrick and his wife seemed to demand to be hung against the deep colour of the red velvet room, which at the same time protected them from too much light as this visitor's room was not often used. It was the same with the furniture: certain pieces slotted into certain rooms, mixed up without a thought of dates or nationalities. I loved this mongrel arrangement. Even though it looks so big, the house and all its different rooms were surprisingly easy to get to know.

Domestic trials were few, but they existed. One was brought about by Nobby, a delightful, selfish and knowing whippet, who wanted to go out in the night; he insisted and there was no escape. So it was on with a thick dressing gown, down thirty-four steps to open the heavy front door and wait in the hall. Sometimes this coincided with the night watchman's thrice-nightly tour of the house. His heavy tread and powerful torch picked me out on my innocent mission. 'It's all right, only me and Nobby,' I would say. We passed the time of day – no, night – and on he went on his round. Nobby whined at the door and thirty-four steps later I got thankfully back into bed. The Collie dog was not so demanding, but he made his own trouble. At a coffee morning for a local charity where people had paid a stiff price for a ticket, a Chatsworth man said to me in a low voice, 'There's been an incident. Collie has bitten a lady.' The said lady had refused to be rounded up, which Collie thought was his duty, and she had paid for it with a bitten ankle. She was a good sport and did not sue, but such 'incidents' happened from time to time.

Owning a large house and land brings with it the feeling of being part of a whole, of being in it together with the many people who work there, living cheek by jowl and respecting each other's expertise. At Chatsworth, these people formed an organization unmatched in the country, including cooks, cleaners, archivists, art historians, education-alists, needlewomen, accountants, plumbers, joiners, electricians, lodge porters, security guards, retailers, lecturers, night watchmen, firemen, a computer expert, a photographer and a silver steward. This human kalei-doscope produced the philanderer, the drunk, the saint, the beauty, the troublemaker, the pourer of oil, the flirt, the bore (and Bore Emeritus), the talker and the doer, the observer and the instigator. Some had to be begged to take a holiday; others, like the unnamed artists of the fifteenth century who were known from the subjects of their work as the Master of the Legend of St Ursula or the Master of the Holy Kinship, could be aptly described as the Master of the Unfinished Job. The mixture was fascinating and the people in the different departments made me won-der at their knowledge and interest in the place. Something about Chats-worth makes people want to do their best for it – just as visitors return again and again to discover more.

My role, which was never defined in the way a job would be now, was a woolly Human Resource Last Resort. The knock at my sitting-room door came often enough to make me aware of what I was there for. What people wanted, as we all do, was to talk to someone about their worries, real or imaginary. I only had to listen and out it all came. Some-times I could 'do something', sometimes I could not, but the fact that the bottled-up trouble was given a hearing was often enough. In the days when the domestic staff lived in, they were at the mercy of their head of department and when things got too much they came to the fount. I did my best, thinking of poor Solomon, but I am sure I often made ter-rible mistakes. Like my father, I have a weakness in that I have always found it difficult to work with people I do not like. Inevitably in such a large company there were one or two of these, and I am sure I was often unfair when so confronted.

When asked if I found my role difficult, I could always answer no, not really, because I had seen it all my life. From Swinbrook days I was used to farms and to the field sports that go hand in hand with an es-tate, whether big or small. Farve did not farm himself but I was friendly with the farm tenants and familiar with their stock, crops and calendar. At Chatsworth everything, inside and out, was magnified a hundred times, but the underlying feel was the same. It all depended on the people who worked there. There were few demarcation lines between the staff, roles sometimes blurred and melted into the next profession and if one person needed help, the next person lent a hand. It may have been an amorphous organization, run entirely on trust and instinct, but it worked. In all the years Andrew and I lived at Chatsworth, we were let down seriously by only two employees. Our common aim was to leave things better than we had found them. That, I can honestly say, I think we did. And for us, to be surrounded with such beauty and such excellent people was a reward in itself, and the excitement of living at Chatsworth remained with me until I left.

15

BOLTON HALL

B olton Hall in Yorkshire was a holiday house, imbued with a holiday atmosphere, where, following family tradition, we spent August for the grouse shooting. The Hall is about seventy-five miles from Chatsworth, along a torturous route via the huge towns of Sheffield and Leeds. There was no formality and only one telephone in a cold cupboard under the stairs. It was a contrast to Chatsworth. The same six or seven guests came every year for the inside of a week and were replaced by another lot the following week; an annual reunion much looked forward to by all. English sporting events are often marred by bad (another word for 'appalling') weather, which produces camaraderie like nothing else, and because the same people came to shoot year after year at Bolton, this feeling was magnified. When we were bold enough to invite someone new, he must have felt as though he was starting at a new school or, worse still, joining a new regiment. Englishmen never seem to grow up and, like schoolboys, are wary of a new face. 'Who on earth is that and why have you asked him?' enquires an old boy of the new.

The Bolton Abbey estate had come to the Dukes of Devonshire in 1753, on the death of Lord Burlington, whose only surviving daughter married the future Fourth Duke. Some of the most varied and beautiful landscapes in Yorkshire make up the 30,000 acres of farms, woods and heather moors, well known for the sport they provide. The tall archway topped by a tower in the middle of the Hall was once the gatehouse to the priory opposite, founded by Augustinian canons in about 1150. The holy men chose a place of spectacular beauty, set in the fertile valley of the River Wharfe. After the Dissolution in 1539, the gatehouse survived when most of the other monastic buildings were knocked down and their stones pillaged. In 1720 the archway was blocked at either end and converted into a house. Extensions were added over the years and in 1843 Paxton enlarged the south wing to make a drawing room with a bedroom and dressing room above for the Duke. Pugin was brought in to decorate the drawing room in fanciful Gothic style. The lofty archway, once the entrance for all traffic to the priory, is now the dining room.

I first went to Bolton in 1946 with my father-in-law and his friends. The only other women in the party were my mother-in-law and Andrew's sisters (no women other than family were ever invited to Bolton – a tradition that Andrew followed). When Andrew was young, he and the other Cavendish grandchildren were boarded out, some in the Bolton Abbey post office, some in the farm across the road and others with tenant farmers. Until rationing came to an end, we stayed in the Devonshire Arms Hotel, half a mile from the Hall. We took it over, filling the bedrooms and queuing for the bath and lavatory. Moucher, Elizabeth, Anne and I rode hill ponies to join the 'guns' at the various heather-thatched lunch huts. This was all very well when the weather was fine, but getting on to a cold, wet saddle in driving rain when you knew there was no chance of being dry till evening was not so good. There was only one motorized vehicle to get the guns up the hill: an ex-army jeep that was usually occupied by the agent, Mr Hay, and his dog – so host and guest walked. A tractor and trailer took the lunch up from the Hall. Now some twenty vehicles trek along the rough tracks – an unheard-of luxury sixty years ago.

Until the early 1950s, when we put it in, there was no electricity at the Hall. The oil lamps often smoked and Pugin's drawing-room ceiling was blackened in places. A row of candlesticks was left out to enable guests to hunt for their bedrooms, up a narrow, winding staircase with ropes for banisters. The house was shabby and lacked the number of baths and lavatories now thought necessary for human habitation. Some of the mattresses were made of hard lumps, some sagged almost to the floor. No one minded. (The grand-looking bed in the King's Room was finally too much and we bought a new mattress.) Two of the bedrooms were pitch dark all day because of the tall yew trees planted a few feet from the house. The others had ancient curtains made of white dimity with long fringes, so there was no hope of keeping out the light.

No one complained. And no one noticed the hole in the drawing-room carpet that got a little bigger each year. Beautiful bits of furniture from Londesborough Hall (where the Earls of Burlington are buried) rubbed shoulders with hard settees covered in hideous cretonne and schoolroom writing tables, their drawers full of silver-framed photographs of King George V and Queen Mary. The King often shot at Bolton in the 1920s and 30s and the house was full to bursting when he came to stay. He brought his own staff, his own post office and a hill pony to carry him to the butts. Queen Mary stayed with her daughter, the Princess Royal, at nearby Harewood House. On 19 August 1921, at 2 a.m., a Privy Council was held at the Hall. It was an unusual hour for a meeting, and rare for it to take place in a private house. But the case was an emergency, and the King's formal consent was required before Parliament could be adjourned later that day.

Mrs Canning, our cook in earlier years, came with us to Bolton. A formidable woman of uncertain temper and curious views on life, she had a theory that you could not buy sugar in Yorkshire, so a sack was thrown on to the lorry with all the other comestibles sent from Chatsworth. Mrs White, who had worked under Mrs Canning at her previous job, helped out at Bolton and cooked at Chatsworth when Mrs Canning was on holiday. She was a far better cook than Mrs Canning and unwisely I once said to the latter, 'What a wonderful cook Mrs White is!' 'Huh, well,' said Mrs Canning, 'she could have been, but she only did seven years in the scullery.' There were not enough cooking utensils or linen at the Hall and the lorry from Chatsworth came laden with immense hampers, including 'the Bolton silver' which spent the rest of the year in the safe at Chatsworth. The lorry also brought a set of Derby dessert plates commissioned by the Sixth Duke in about 1815 and decorated with paintings of his houses. For some reason it was thought too risky to use this china at home, but it bumped along the road to Bolton where it formed a traditional part of the dinner table.

The days on the moor were long. The guns often did not get home till 7 p.m., when they would tuck into tea followed immediately by dinner. The reason for providing tea, however late the hour, was told me by Granny Evie: she thought that if the guns were awash with tea they would drink less whisky later. I cannot say I saw any evidence of this, but we stuck to her rule. When Lord Carnarvon came to shoot, I kept a loaded water pistol by my place at dinner and if the talk got altogether too much,

I threatened his velvet jacket with a short sharp shower. The energy of the younger guns inspired the older ones and late into the night everyone played desperate games of Billiard Fives, an often dangerous game round the billiard table when the ball can fly off the table in any direction or speed. You would think they would have been too tired, but not a bit of it (though no doubt their shooting suffered the next morning).

There was a large staff at Bolton and the guns often brought their own loaders, usually keepers from their own shoots. This added to the holiday atmosphere and the endless laughter from the low-ceilinged, smoke-filled room where the staff ate (and drank) set the scene for the week. One rare hot August evening after a good supper, a troop of them stripped off and jumped naked into the river. I was terrified that in their high spirits there might be an accident, but mercifully the same number came back as went in.

In Swinbrook days, I had loved going out with Farve and the guns, and had always longed to take part, but knew it was a vain hope. Eddy Devonshire would never have allowed a woman gun at Bolton or Chatsworth, but Andrew had no such prejudice. So at the age of thirty I bought a gun and enlisted the help of Mr Lord, the head keeper at Chatsworth (the famous Mr Maclauchlan had just retired after nearly fifty years' service). Mr Lord and I spent many hours walking the hedgerows, with dogs as beaters to begin with, while I slowly gained enough confidence to take the last butt at Bolton or stand last in the line at a pheasant shoot at Chatsworth. Women guns were rare sixty years ago and initially I was regarded with suspicion all round. Nancy, in her usual way, said that shooting turned me into Farve. 'Better give it up,' she teased, 'it'll ruin your looks.'

It was one of Andrew's many acts of generosity to have kept the shoots going for Stoker and me. He himself had never enjoyed shooting and colour blindness prevented him seeing grouse flying low over the heather. He gave it up soon after his father's death but still enjoyed the organization, having been part of it since childhood. He loved walking and Bolton Abbey gave him the opportunity. Scorning the Land Rovers and ritzy Range Rovers that have replaced legs in the last twenty-five years, he often arrived at a distant line of butts before they did. He sat in their butt with each guest in turn, a folded *Times* in his pocket and Portly, his big, almost white Labrador, by his side. The newspaper was a proper size in those days and when opened its broad white sheets acted as a warning to the grouse, the wildest of birds: STOP, GO AWAY. The presence of their host was inhibiting enough to the guns without the white and off-white deterrents that went with him. (As soon as the drive began Andrew did put the sodden, peaty newspaper back in his pocket.)

The beaters were mostly boys from Skipton Grammar School and they walked for miles through heather and – worse – wet, waist-high bracken. They soon got to know who the guns were and when Uncle Harold was shooting I heard, 'Watch out, lads. There's Uncle Mac up front.' The boys thought that like many old people he might be over-confident and shoot a bit close to the oncoming line of beaters, but there was no need to watch out, he was a good shot. At Bolton Uncle Harold took on the role of the elder statesman, not just of politics but of grouse shooting. Photographs in the local paper of him arriving spawned his 'grouse moor image', which then stuck. He was indulgent to Stoker and his friends, even when, aged sixteen and stumped for something to say to his august neighbour at dinner, Stoker announced, 'Uncle Harold, Old Moore's Almanac says you'll fall in October.' After a suitable pause for thought, the Prime Minister replied, 'Yes, I should think that's about right.'

Our old friend John Wyndham became Uncle Harold's private secretary in 1957. He dreaded the outing to Bolton, especially the rickety ride on the tractor that brought him out to the moor with lunch and any telephone messages that had arrived for his boss that morning. The guns were often late and while they waited John and the farmer who drove the tractor played a game. It was invented by the farmer and involved tossing coins into the heather and retrieving them within a certain time limit. As John was nearly blind and unaccustomed to heather, his opponent always ended with a triumphant, 'I've won.' John was wonderful company and used to make fun of everything to do with the government. At Bolton, we watched him throwing top secret Cabinet papers all over the room assigned to Uncle Harold as an office. The typists from Downing Street had never seen such a performance and were half-shocked, half-delighted. Uncle Harold loved John, as did we all. Under the chaos was the sharpest brain in the business.

When Jack Kennedy was President, I often wondered about the messages that went from the Prime Minister at Bolton to the White House.

In August 1963, Uncle Harold was staying with us at the same time as David Ormsby Gore, our Ambassador to Washington. Some international crisis was brewing as usual. Uncle Harold summoned David and read him the message he was proposing to send to Jack. It began with a long, flowery account of the day's shooting (something the President had never done) and was larded with such phrases as 'sunlit heather', 'birds plentiful', 'strong north-west wind'. The point of the cable came right at the end of this poetic description. David caught my eye and we started laughing at the idea of the poor puzzled President trying to guess what Uncle Harold was on about. I do not know what found its way to Washington, but I imagine David pruned it somewhat.

Out of the shooting season, Bolton was made thoroughly enjoyable for me by the visits of the architect Philip Jebb, whose company I loved and who worked with me at Chatsworth and at Bolton on the estate buildings. I looked forward to our winter picnics, sitting on crates by an enormous boiler in the beautiful sixteenth-century tithe barn (the only warm place available), surrounded by all the familiar paraphernalia of an estate building-yard. Noël Coward's notion that 'working is so much more fun than fun' was certainly the case with Philip. He was always ready to laugh and we often shared critical views about some of the people we worked with. Philip was in charge of adding the Wharfedale Wing to the Devonshire Arms Hotel, with the help of Harry Moon, a Yorkshire architect, who also became a friend. The building was originally a coaching inn dating back to the eighteenth century. In 1982 the family took over running the hotel, which had previously been tenanted. Working with Philip and Harry was a privilege and it was exciting to see the hotel expand from nine to forty-two bedrooms.

Philip died, aged sixty-eight, in 1995. The loss of his influence and good taste was unlucky for this country; he kept the flag flying during the disastrous 1950s and 60s, when the worst architectural horrors were springing up. Professionally he was second to none and he was incapable of designing anything ugly. He ensured that the site and scale of a building fitted the landscape instead of imposing a design that had been dreamt up in an office miles away (which seems to be the easy way out for architects today), and the builders who interpreted his work all agreed his drawings were the most exact they had ever worked from. If only more of his work survived.

16

A MINISTER'S WIFE

In 1960 Andrew was made Parliamentary Under Secretary of State for Commonwealth Relations, a job he described as 'not being responsible for making the tea, but for doing the washing up'. In 1962 he was promoted to Minister of State in the Commonwealth Office, liaising with countries that belonged to the ex–British Empire, a post he held for two years. He enjoyed his four years in government and must have known, by the reactions of all whose paths he crossed, how well he carried out his task. He had a flair for getting on with anyone, no matter who they were or where they came from – the more unlikely the individual the better. His work was not confined to office hours and there was many a diplomatic cocktail party given by the High Commissioner of this or that independent country, and often a dinner as well. Andrew's stamina was tested and he came out with flying colors. The only fly in the ointment was his boss, Duncan Sandys, whom he found abrasive and not easy to work with. More than once, Andrew saw him make senior civil servants cry with his sarcastic, tyrannical ways. He was also very slow in drafting speeches and memos, and Andrew missed train after train for Chesterfield on Friday nights as Duncan agonized over 'and' and 'the'. It is a pity that Andrew only ever had Sandys as his boss; had he had the chance to work for someone else, a friendlier atmosphere would have lightened his load.

I went with Andrew on several official trips to Africa and the Caribbean. Some of it was familiar territory because we had already been to Kenya, Uganda and Rhodesia in 1947, when my father-in-law wanted to invest in land and had asked Andrew to look into the possibilities. In

1947 the flight to Nairobi in a Douglas Dakota took five days, with over-
night stops in Brussels, Tripoli, Cairo and Khartoum. From Egypt onwards it was only possible to fly in the mornings, as later in the day the
heat had built up too dangerously for the low altitude at which those reliable old planes flew. Over the next three weeks we stayed with nineteen kind hosts, none of whom had we met before – a sure cure for
shyness and an experience that I have been grateful for ever since. We
enjoyed the free and easy way of life, the beauty of the country and
gardens, the richness of the land, and the unfamiliar birds and animals.
But I was shocked by the way some of the white women treated their
African servants, by their rudeness and the way they talked about their
shortcomings in front of them. Independence was a long way off, but
resentment was building.

One of our stops was with Lord Francis Scott, a dear fellow and long-
time Kenyan farmer. His daughter Pam was the very opposite of the rude
women and had started a school and hospital for workers on the family
estate. The scandal and mystery of Lord Erroll's unsolved murder, which
had taken place among the philandering, hard-drinking Happy Valley
set six years previously, was still fresh in everyone's minds. I realized that
Lord Francis must have known Erroll, Sir Delves Broughton (the suspected murderer) and the other characters involved. I asked him if he
had been in it. 'In it?' he said. 'Of course I was in it up to the neck.' But
he was too discreet to enlarge on what he thought about that extraordinary episode.

From Kenya we went to Zanzibar, the island of cloves and giant tur-
tles that moon about on the seashore looking as old and gnarled as Elizabethan oaks. There was no glass in the windows at the Residency and
the warm sea breeze came in, as did birds of all kinds. The hospitable
Sultana herself made scones for us. Later we went to Uganda in a tiny
plane and were met on a grassy airstrip by a young couple from Government House. 'We're only acting,' they told us. 'So are we,' I said, 'we don't
usually go on like this.' (Not being versed in diplomatic language I did
not know that 'acting' meant playing the role of a superior.) Andrew and
I loved the glorious greenness of Uganda and when we returned fifteen
years later for Independence we were delighted to see it all again.

My chief recollection of Southern Rhodesia (now Zimbabwe), where
we stayed with the Governor General, Sir John Kennedy, and his wife,

Bungs, is of Andrew's fury at being made to go to a children's party. The old-fashioned colonial code of conduct still applied to a ridiculous degree: at a reception one night, a woman guest, who had driven miles through the bush, was turned away because she had forgotten her white gloves. On the way home we had a long wait at Benghazi airport while we changed planes. In those days the little airport was not exactly luxurious and we tried to get out of the dust and into the VIP lounge, where we had spotted two deckchairs. We were soon turned out quite roughly and cut down to size by being made to sit on the sand floor till the trusty Dakota was ready to take us to our next stop.

Andrew's time in the Commonwealth Office coincided with the independence of eleven British colonies. In 1961 we went to Nigeria to attend the celebration of that country's first anniversary of Independence. Dr Nnamdi Azikiwe (known as Zik) was Governor General and Commander-in-Chief of the Federation, but Britain retained a High Commissioner in the shape of Antony Head. We stayed with him and his wife, Dorothea, and it was a breath of fresh air to find these old Wiltshire friends (their home was near Salisbury) in Lagos.

The High Commissioner's residence was bang on a lagoon and had been built at vast expense by the architect Lionel Brett. He had had an unequalled opportunity to create a beautiful building – modern architecture is well suited to the tropics – but the result resembled an oversized chicken house. Downstairs was one huge open-plan room for dining and sitting, dangerously like an airport lounge. A staircase sprang from there to what can only be described as nesting boxes, bedrooms with sloping wooden ceilings which gave the feeling they might be lifted at any moment to see if you had laid an egg. They had no balcony – surely the first necessity in a hot climate – and you could only open the windows by climbing on to the high window sills and dragging them down with all your might, like you do in Continental trains.

There was no escape from official duties. Andrew did his stuff marvellously at the schools, hospitals, universities, maternity homes, slum clearances, housing estates, sports grounds and government offices that we went round till we almost dropped. Antony Head's ADC was Pips Royston, a new face to us and excellent company. Pips banged on the door of our room soon after lunch one day when we were trying to snatch some sleep. 'Hats and gloves at six,' he announced. This was in order to meet Oba Adele II and other local rulers. These exotic gentlemen were not in their first youth and they danced for us half-bare, their extra flesh wobbling in time to the steps. They reminded me of heavy horses displaying at an agricultural show and I immediately liked the look of them.

My crowning moment in Lagos was to have been at a football match when Zik, then at the height of his popularity, invited me to accompany him in his official car for several circuits of the football pitch and present the cup to the winning team. Alas, my moment of glory never came as the match was a draw, but I had an unexpected instant in the spotlight. A huge crowd received Zik with acclaim as we drove round the pitch but by the second circuit they had started to laugh loudly. When we got back to where Antony and Dot were sitting, I asked one of the officials why they were laughing. 'Oh,' he said, 'they thought you were Zik's new wife.' From Lagos, we went to Kano in northern Nigeria, where the landscape was quite different, no longer lush and green with daily afternoon rain, but a desert, and the climate was hot and dry. We saw extraordinarily beautiful houses built of mud and an Emir sitting under a tree in full white robes, quietly pronouncing judgements.

In August 1962 Princess Margaret represented the Queen at the celebrations to mark the Independence of Jamaica. The British delegation was led by our old friend Hugh Fraser, Secretary of State for Air, who was accompanied by his wife, Antonia. We travelled with the royal party in a Britannia Bristol, a flying drawing-room, for twenty-two hours. When we arrived it was all very formal with the usual programme of official events, which meant hats, gloves and best evening dresses for Antonia and me. Our friend Drue Heinz, generous patron of the arts and the literary world, had kindly offered to lend us hats. By early August the events of the Season when Drue would have needed hers were over, and we took our pick. Trying them on in London turned out to be more fun than wearing them in Jamaica, where it rained enormous drops of warm water that created a sticky, frizzy mess of hair and straw. The American delegation to the celebrations was headed by Vice-President Lyndon Johnson, who was disappointed that Princess Margaret was the centre of everyone's attention and did his best to steal her thunder. At the celebratory ball Andrew offered £10 to the first of our delegation to dance with the Vice-President. I am sorry to say that Antonia won hands down and that I never even managed to be introduced.

The Jamaican Prime Minister, Sir Alexander Bustamante, was the living double of Obbie St Albans and whenever I saw one of them, I always thought it was the other. Like Obbie, Bustamante had a teasing nature, which in his case took the form of leading a bloody revolution against colonial rule. In their inimitable way, the British government imprisoned him and then installed him as leader of his country. Bustamante was a great figure in his native land and I found him no less impressive when he came to England for a Commonwealth prime ministers' meeting. I saw him again at a dinner at Buckingham Palace, mischievous as ever.

In October 1962, Uganda was next on the list and we flew there for an unforgettable week of festivities. It was like a fancy-dress party with people wearing national costumes not just from Africa but from all over the world. Jomo Kenyatta, who was staying in our hotel, minced about whisking his fly-whisk, and was followed by two tall, sinister-looking bodyguards. He pinched the room that had been given to Lord Carrington, who was leading the British delegation. We gave a dinner party one night when the Princess Royal (theirs not ours), an old lady with a crew cut, came in her slip; we kept thinking she must put on her dress soon, but the slip was the dress.

The Kabaka (Major General Sir Edward Frederick William David Walugembe Mutebi Luwangula Mutesa II KBE), King of Buganda, was a most attractive man, with that indefinable quality that drew all eyes towards him. He lived on top of a hill in a palace made of bamboo. Two of the big parties were held there and on both occasions the Ugandan electricity (never very reliable) failed, the lights went out and the Kabaka minded – a diplomatic party in the dark is hard to manage. The Kabaka's son and heir, Prince Ronnie, was seven years old at the time and we were delighted to find that his tutor was Mark Amory, an Oxford friend of our daughter Emma. Never knowing who you were going to meet next was what made these outings such fun, and Mark was a big help in explaining the locals and their way of life.

In December 1963 we were in Kenya to see the British flag being lowered. It was another case of poacher turned gamekeeper: Kenyatta was made leader of the country after being imprisoned for seven years by the British. The Duke of Edinburgh represented the Queen at the celebrations and there was the usual confusion along narrow mud roads; we were following Prince Philip's car and it looked for a moment as though we would be late for the flag ceremony. At the ball afterwards Andrew danced with Kenyatta's wives, two black and one white. As we left, the new President presented him with a fly whisk, a traditional honour to an official visitor, which Andrew always kept on his desk. The name Devonshire was well remembered by the new Kenyan government because in 1923, Andrew's grandfather Victor Duke, in his capacity as Secretary of State for the Colonies, had issued a White Paper declaring that, 'Primarily Kenya is an African territory . . . the interests of the African natives must be paramount.'

All the independence ceremonies followed roughly the same pattern: celebratory lunches, dinners, garden parties, cocktail parties, a grand ball, and then the lowering of the British flag and the hoisting of the 'new' country's own. Inevitably, there was an element of tragicomedy about these events, and emotions were mixed; the initial surge of elation and optimism that followed the lowering of the flag was often the signal for an outburst of violence and corruption. It reminded me forcibly of the triumphant British coal miners who, after the 1945 General Election, basked for a moment in the feeling 'we are the masters now', only to find themselves back underground with nothing changed. On our way home to England from one of these ceremonies, we were waiting at Kano airport with some newly ex–District Officers when one of their wives, horrified by her omission, suddenly gasped, 'Oh! I forgot to take down the portrait of the Queen.' I thought it a sad and telling remark; it was indeed the end. What was the future for these excellent people, who had worked so hard to build something that was so soon to be undone?

Let no one get the impression that these trips abroad were anything but work all the way. Andrew had to stick to a government brief in his speeches, which he did not find easy because he preferred speaking off the cuff. There was endless talking to strangers and having to change clothes several times a day, according to what was on the programme. 'You try a few protracted dinners between the Canadian Minister of Labour and the Jamaican Minister of Education,' I wrote to a friend. But in spite of these drawbacks there was always, without exception, some amusing incident; we met outstandingly interesting individuals who eased the way, added to which was the excitement of seeing new countries. Although it was always a relief to get home, I would not have missed it for the world.

Andrew's job involved not only travelling but also looking after the new Commonwealth heads of state when they came to England. In 1964 it was the turn of Sir Ahmadu Bello, the Sardauna of Sokoto, for an official visit. As often happened, the Commonwealth Office was at a loss as to what to do with him over the weekend. Answer: send him to Chatsworth. We invited Bobbety and Betty Salisbury and other friends to meet the Sardauna, and expected him and his entourage for lunch at 1 p.m. We waited and waited and waited. At 3.30 p.m. the cars finally appeared. Out piled not six people, as we had been told to expect, but thirteen. The only extra food I knew we had in the house was ham. Goodness knows what Mrs Canning found for our Muslim guests, but it could not have been the 'accursed' pig.

The Sardauna was friendly and his robes smelled deliciously of herbs. The 3.30 p.m. lunch passed off well, we thought, and the party went round the house afterwards. They stopped by the portrait of Henry VIII and the guide told them about his six wives. This was met with indulgent laughter – the Sardauna had quite a crowd himself. To our surprise, after a late tea the party began to say goodbye – we had been expecting them to stay the night. We later discovered that they preferred the floor to the comfortable four-posters that had been made up for them and, thinking we might be insulted, had decided to leave rather than risk offending us.

Another visitor was the Shah of Persia. He was inspecting factories round about and it was thought by his hosts that a visit to Chatsworth might end the day satisfactorily. This quiet, handsome, serious man arrived for tea in a helicopter. My mother-in-law, who was staying, said to me, 'He'll be tired, you must offer him a bed so he can have a rest.' The Shah was in the prime of life and would, I think, have been astonished if I had done as she advised, so I quietly forgot about it and we got on with tea. I had always admired the Shah's beautiful wives. Farah Diba, a vision in Dior and a worthy queen of the Peacock Throne, was voted one of the world's best-dressed women several times. I was disappointed that she was not with him on this visit.

The President of India, Dr Radhakrishnan, came to stay at Chatsworth in 1963. He was a silent academic whose religion did not allow him to eat meat, fish, chicken, eggs, milk or cheese. That left little but peas, pulses and fruit. It was not easy to devise two dinners and a lunch for him, but we managed somehow. Andrew and I took Dr Radhakrishnan round the house, pointing out objects that might interest him. He never uttered a word – neither a comment, nor a question – until we reached the Orangery at the end of the tour, at which point he turned to Andrew and asked, 'Has the Queen been here?'

After the 1964 General Election when Harold Wilson's Labour government came to power, Andrew was offered the job of Shadow Minister of Transport in the House of Lords. As he could not drive a car, he thought this was not a good idea and retired from active politics in the Conservative cause. He continued to attend the House of Lords but never again held a senior job.

17

THE KENNEDYS

When Joseph P. Kennedy arrived in England on 1 March 1938 to take up the post of United States Ambassador to the Court of St James's, it was not Joe who grabbed the headlines but his wife, Rose, mother of nine, whose youthful appearance and figure were the subject of much attention from the press and the envy of her English contemporaries. Mrs Kennedy, her eldest daughter Rosemary, and second daughter, Kick, were presented at Court on 11 May, heralding the start of their London season, which was also mine. Rosemary was mentally retarded and not able to join in the round of dances and other entertainments, but she did manage the curtsey at Buckingham Palace.

The Kennedys were masters of entertainment and the dinner-dance they gave on 2 June was one of the very best. Joe Jr and Jack Kennedy were not there as they did not arrive in England until the Fourth of July, just in time for a dinner given at the embassy on that important date in the American calendar. The two brothers were thrown in at the deep end but they soon mastered the routine, making friends as easily as Kick had. Twenty-three-year-old Joe Jr was as attractive and full of vitality as the rest of the family and made an immediate impact. He was his father's chosen one to go into politics and make a name for himself. I was always aware of his presence but hardly knew him as he preferred the company of more sophisticated women to eighteen-year-old debutantes. Jack was two years younger and a shadow of his brother. He suffered from poor health and it showed.

Towards the end of July 1938, Andrew and I went to the races with Kick, Jack, Jean and Margaret Ogilvy, Hugh Fraser and David Ormsby

Gore. There was no particular significance to this outing except that it was the start of the friendship between Jack and David, which was to play such an important part when, twenty-three years later, Jack became President and David was appointed Ambassador to the US.

David was a first cousin of Andrew and a lifelong friend. When he was up at Oxford, all he liked was jazz, racing and his future wife, the beautiful Sylvia (Sissie) Lloyd Thomas. Learning and lectures were not on his list and he spent his university days lying on the sofa in his St Aldate's lodgings, tapping a foot in time to Nat Gonella on a wind-up gramophone. He did no work and to his father's dismay managed a dismal Third. It was run-of-the-mill to all of us, who were used to our friends just scraping through or failing altogether when the crunch came with exams. David, who with Andrew and the Astor boys was the best company going, was quick to prick any balloon of pomposity, a trait that never deserted him, even in the important Foreign Office roles he played so well in later life. Like his elder brother, Gerard, and Sissie before him, he was killed in a car accident and I mourn them to this day. Years later Jack reminded me of that outing to the races – I had quite forgotten about it. Perhaps he remembered it better than so many other enjoyable days that summer because it was when he first met David.

From their arrival in England, Ambassador Kennedy kept his sons busy with the serious side of life and made sure they learned something of British politics and politicians, industry and the City. As well as sampling the delights of the Côte d'Azur, they also did a whistle-stop tour of European capital cities, gaining a greater knowledge of Europe than most American politicians, storing away these experiences for future use. Jack's time in England at an impressionable age must have influenced the 'special relationship' that he fostered during his years in office. He told me that when he was in hospital as a teenager he read widely and that after reading John Buchan's biography of the seventeenth-century Scottish general, his hero became the great Montrose.

Joe Kennedy Sr was pessimistic about England and France's chances of defeating Hitler and was viscerally opposed to America entering the war. His isolationism cost him his English friends. Joe Jr adopted his father's attitude while Jack remained more detached, but both brothers enlisted before Pearl Harbor. In spite of back pain and generally ailing, Jack somehow passed fit into the US Navy. In March 1943 he was in the

Pacific when the boat he was in was rammed and cut in half by an enemy destroyer. After clinging to the wreckage for many hours, the survivors, commanded by Jack, reached a small island. It was not until five
days later that they were rescued, and for his heroism Jack was awarded
the Navy and Marine Corps Medal.

Joe Jr was an officer in the US Navy Air Corps. He volunteered for
a perilous mission to attack a flying-bomb launch site near Calais and
was killed on 12 August 1944 when his plane blew up before reaching its
target. He was posthumously awarded the Navy Cross, the highest decoration. His death added to the list of catastrophes that took so many of
our friends and family during July and August that year. On receiving
the news, Kick, who had been married to Billy for just three months, left
for America to attend his memorial service. Wartime journeys across the
Atlantic were difficult to arrange, but as the daughter of the US Ambassador she managed it. Three weeks later, Billy was killed and Kick immediately returned to England.

In his letter of condolence to Moucher, Jack wrote that the news of
Billy's death was:

> about the saddest I have ever had. I have always been so fond of
> Kick that I couldn't help but feel some of her great sorrow. Her
> great happiness when she came home which even shone through
> her sadness over Joe's death was so manifest and so infectious
> that it did much to ease the grief of our mother and father. It
> was so obvious what he meant to Kick and what a really won-
> derful fellow he must have been that we all became devoted to
> him, and now know what a really great loss his is. When I read
> Captain Waterhouse's letter about the cool and gallant way Billy
> died, I couldn't help but think of what John Buchan had written
> about Raymond Asquith: 'Our roll of honour is long, but it holds
> no nobler figure. He will stand to those of us who are left as an
> incarnation of the spirit of the land he loved . . . He loved his
> youth, and his youth has become eternal. Debonair and bril-
> liant and brave, he is now part of that immortal England which
> knows not age or weariness or defeat.' I think that those words
> could be so well applied to Billy. I feel extremely proud that he
> was my sister's husband.

After Billy's death Kick, who was devoted to Eddy and Moucher and to her sisters-in-law, Anne and Elizabeth, wanted to be among the friends in England that she had known since she was eighteen. She bought a house in London, No. 2 Smith Square, Westminster, and for the next four years divided her time between England and America. Her old suitors returned: William Douglas Home was still enamoured of her, Anthony Eden was a friend, as were Richard Wood and Hugh Fraser (who had also been particularly fond of her sister Eunice), but as soon as Kick met Peter, Eighth Earl Fitzwilliam, he became the only contender. But there was a serious obstacle: Peter was married.

Kick had already made a major concession when marrying Billy and agreeing that any sons of theirs would be brought up as Protestants. She knew that her parents would never condone marriage to a divorcee and, indeed, Kick's mother warned her that she would be banished from the family if she went ahead. Hoping to talk her father round, Kick made a plan to meet Ambassador Kennedy in Paris on her way back from a few days with Peter on the Côte d'Azur. The pair set off for Cannes in a chartered plane on 13 May 1948. They hit a violent thunderstorm over the Rhône Valley and after being buffeted in the air for thirty minutes, the plane crashed into a mountainside, killing all on board.

Kick's body was brought to England and she was buried in the Cavendish plot at St Peter's Church in Edensor. I had never been to a funeral before and the solemn words affected me profoundly. She and I were both twenty-eight, not the time of life when you think about death, yet that most vital of human beings had been taken from us. Bert Link, the head gardener, lined her grave with pale mauve wisteria – the sweet-smelling, short-lived flowers so fitting for a life cut short so tragically. Ambassador Kennedy was the only member of her family able to get to the funeral. He wore a bright-blue crumpled suit, which was all he had with him, and this surprising colour accentuated the anguished misery of his face, an image engraved for ever on my mind.

We kept in touch with the Kennedys. When they came to England they always telephoned and we sometimes met in London, but we did not see much of them until 1961 when, to our surprise, Andrew and I were invited to Jack's presidential inauguration. Andrew was intrigued by the

invitation and realized what an honour it was to be asked. I did not want
to go. There were engagements I was looking forward to at home, including the last shoot of the season. But it was so good of them to think
of us that we accepted.

We stayed with the British Ambassador, Sir Harold Caccia, and his
wife, Nancy, and those three days we spent in Washington were among
the most extraordinary of our lives. The warmth of the welcome from
the Kennedy family, now happy and glorious, was something Andrew
and I never forgot. We were given the best seats at all the events, far
above anything we expected, and the bitter cold and unrelenting snow
made it all the more dramatic. I realized these were events of historic
importance and jotted down some notes at the time, which cover the
sublime and the ridiculous about equally. These appeared in my book
Home to Roost, and are reprinted here as an appendix.

Back at Chatsworth, before the week was out, Andrew got a hand-
written letter from Jack thanking us both for being present at 'the changing of the guard'. 'I was grateful for the kind letter from the Prime
Minister,' he continued. 'I wish you success in your service with him and
I hope very much that you and Debo can both come here soon again.
Best, Jack.' When you think of the number of letters he had to write
thanking his political supporters, to include us seemed incredible. Two
weeks later Jack wrote to me suggesting that I accompany the Prime
Minister (Uncle Harold) when he went to Washington in the spring to
'cement Anglo-American relations'. I was immensely flattered, but had
things planned that I could not change and proposed a date later in the
year, which seemed to suit him.

It was at their first meeting in March 1961 that Uncle Harold and
Jack decided on David Ormsby Gore for the post of British Ambassador
to Washington. David's sister, Katherine, was married to the Macmil-
lans' only son, Maurice, and Uncle Harold had known David for years.
David was duly appointed on 26 October 1961. The relationship between
ambassador and president was a much closer one than usual and Jack
and David met often informally. David was the link between Jack and
Uncle Harold, who also struck up a close friendship, and Jack was soon
referring to the Prime Minister as Uncle Harold like the rest of us. The
friendship surprised some of their aides, but it seemed obvious that the
much older, more experienced man, with his classical education and great

intellect (who nevertheless always saw the joke), would make a good ally for the young President.

I went to Washington in December 1961 and stayed with David and Sissie in the embassy. The evening after my arrival I dined at the White House for the first time. There were Jack, two men friends of his and me. We sat in the gallery for drinks and when dinner was announced, being the only woman and a foreigner, I went without thinking to the open door. On the threshold Jack threw out his arm and said, 'No, not you. I go first, I'm Head of State.' 'Good heavens,' I said, 'so you are,' and we sat down to dinner.

The Washington round was hectic: lunches and dinners here and there, including enjoyable ones at our embassy. I dined one night with Joe and Susan Mary Alsop before a gala reception at the National Gallery of Art. Joe, a distinguished political journalist, was friends with all at the White House. Twenty people had sat down to dinner when the door opened and in walked the President, unexpected. Joe Alsop got a chair, sat him down and we went on as if nothing had happened. To please its director, Johnny Walker, who was a friend of mine, Jack agreed to make a quick visit to the National Gallery; he had never been there before. I went with him in his car and it was raining when we arrived. As Jack got out to shake hands with the welcoming party, he turned to me and whispered, 'They think I like art. I hate it.' One of our delegates to the United Nations was Lady Tweedsmuir. She found an unexpected opportunity to buttonhole the President on some (to her) pressing matter. 'Not now,' he replied, 'it's your turn tomorrow.' He had got rid of her, but in such a good-natured way that she could not take offence.

From Washington I flew to New York on the same day as Jack ('I go presidential, you go commercial,' he said, putting me in my place). He gathered up various friends and relations in New York to see that I was not left alone for long and they did his bidding, however inconvenient it must have been for them.

Jack added enormously to any entertainment. He was such good company, so funny and straightforward – a mixture of schoolboy and statesman, and you never knew which was coming next. He was the only politician I have ever known who could laugh at himself and did. He never spoke of the posts he had held – as in my experience English politicians always do, starting conversations with, 'When I was

Home Secretary . . .' or 'When I was Parliamentary Under Secretary for Health . . .' so that your attention immediately wanders. Jack could say 'I don't know' (which our politicians never do) and in answer to questions he was direct, instead of beating round the bush. The atmosphere was refreshing after London officialdom. When the Shah of Persia was on a state visit to Washington, the press asked those present at Jack's welcoming speech what they thought of the visiting sovereign. One man, who was not a politician but a friend of Jack's, thought for a bit and said, 'Well, he's my kind of Shah.' It was this sort of remark that made Jack's White House so enjoyable and surprising. All the Kennedys had a trait of irreverence and fun. Some years ago when Eunice was in London, she fancied a ride in Rotten Row. Not caring that she had no riding clothes, she hired a horse and off she went in a full-length mink coat and sandals with two-inch heels over her nylon tights – an apparition – without a nod to convention.

In October 1962 Andrew and I went to America for the opening of an exhibition of Old Master drawings from Chatsworth at the Washington National Gallery. Again, we stayed at the embassy. Johnny Walker saw to it that we were fêted in the hospitable way of American museums. Francis Thompson, keeper of the collection at Chatsworth, was not well enough to travel so Tom Wragg, his deputy, oversaw the hanging of the drawings. The Cuban missile crisis was at its height and the world on the brink of nuclear war, but this did not deter the art lovers of Washington and its neighbourhood from flocking to the Gallery. Jackie Kennedy was not able to attend the official opening reception but came during the first day of the exhibition.

We dined at the White House on 21 October, the night before Jack's address to the nation when he told Americans about the situation in Cuba and called on Russia to remove the missiles or face retaliation. He was his usual self, showing no outward signs of the strain he must have felt. In the room where we met for drinks before dinner, photographs of the now infamous missiles (rhymed with 'thistles') were lying on a table and were being picked up and put down by the dinner guests as though they were holiday snaps. I suppose some of us did not realize how near to a world disaster we were; certainly the atmosphere in the White House was unchanged from the previous year – a tribute to steady nerves.

At one point Jack suggested, 'Why don't you call your sister in California?' He asked his switchboard to put me through and wandered off to do something more important. Decca and I talked for a bit but, brought up as we were not to use the telephone for long chats, Decca suddenly became aware of the cost of this long-distance call and said, 'Hen, are you on your own phone?' I had to admit I was not and we went on chatting. Over dinner Jack and I talked about his family's years in London before the war and about old friends. I described how Vice-President Johnson had tried to upstage Princess Margaret at the independence ceremonies in Jamaica and told Jack that Hugh Fraser had been at the head of our delegation. 'Not *our* Hugh Fraser?' he said. 'Yes, of course it was our Hugh Fraser,' I replied. He roared with laughter at the idea, just as Hugh would have laughed at Jack's elevated position.

On another evening in Crisis Week, Jack and I were sitting talking and laughing about the old days, about his sisters Kick and Eunice, and the girls he had met twenty-four years before. He asked about the home life of various politicians, Bobbety Salisbury, for instance. We moved on to war heroes and he wanted to know about Paddy Leigh Fermor and his capture of the German General on Crete in 1944. Suddenly he said, 'Tell me about Perceval.' 'Perceval?' I said. 'I don't know anything about him except that he was the only British Prime Minister to be assassinated.' Jack stayed quiet for a while and then we went back to chit-chat. I knew what he was thinking, and our conversation came back to me when I heard the news on 22 November 1963.

Towards the end of our stay, knowing that he would be interested, Jack found time to show Andrew the White House garden. The only event cancelled during the whole week was a dance that was to have been held at the White House on 22 October, the night of Jack's address to the nation. Uncle Harold and the President were in constant touch by telephone about the situation. It was evident that Jack was seeking advice from the old boy and the fact that they were by now such friends made a difference. As the crisis deepened so the night-time calls became more frequent. In the past, references to SEATO and NATO had often been followed by, 'How's DEBO?' then back to the serious stuff. This time there were no jokes.

At the end of that week of knife-edge diplomacy, Andrew went home on the Sunday night. On the Monday morning the President asked me to go for a last swim at the White House pool, where he swam every day to help his back. Again we talked of old times and especially of Kick. Afterwards I lunched with Eunice, Jean and Ethel before leaving for

New York, where there was a festive atmosphere and everyone was breathing a sigh of relief.

When I got home, Jack sometimes telephoned with a question about Uncle Harold or another member of the government or just for a chat, usually in the early hours of the morning. It was a convenient time for him but I was dead asleep when the telephone rang at 3 a.m. 'Do you know it's the Fourth of July?' he began one of these calls. 'Is it?' I said, barely conscious. 'Have you got all your loved ones with you?' he asked. 'No,' I said. 'Why?' and so on. On another occasion he sounded exasperated. 'I was put through to a tavern called The Devonshire Arms. It was closed.' He was always full of Uncle Harold and ready for any stories I could tell about him.

On an official visit to Europe in June 1963, Jack was to have talks with Uncle Harold at Birch Grove in Sussex, and came to visit Kick's grave on his way. Kick was generally agreed to have been his favourite sister and the two had been very close. Edensor was full of Secret Service men during the days before the President's arrival and one of them asked me what sort of people lived in the village. At that moment, Francis Thompson emerged from his house on two sticks, looking as old as the hills. 'That's the sort of person,' I was able to say. The visit was kept secret and our local police on duty had no idea why they had been summoned to this backwater.

Air Force One took Jack to Waddington RAF base in Lincolnshire and a helicopter brought him on to Chatsworth, landing as near as possible to the churchyard. Andrew and I were there to meet him. He came down the steps, obviously suffering from the back pain that plagued him but was never mentioned. A temporary wooden bridge had been built over the ha-ha that divides the park from the churchyard; we went across it together and then left him on his own by Kick's grave.

When Jack joined us at the car, he said he would come to Chatsworth, which he had never seen. This was against the wishes of the Secret Service who said they could not ensure his security because it was open to the public. On the short drive to the house, Jack described the helicopter that had brought him. 'It's even got a bathroom,' he said proudly. 'A bathroom? What on earth for?' I said. 'You couldn't possibly need a bath on that short trip.' What he meant was that it had a lavatory. When we arrived at the house, we joined the public who were making their way up the stairs. They looked at Jack, looked back at each other and looked at him again in a classic double-take, astonished to see the President of the United States sharing their staircase.

Jim and Alvilde Lees-Milne were staying with us, as was Yehudi Menuhin (the latter surprised me by practising scales for four hours at a time, which I could hear coming from his bedroom. I thought he knew all that and would not have to bother). There was time for a quick cup of tea then back to the helicopter and its bathroom. Jack was late for his appointment with the Prime Minister and a headline in the newspapers read, 'MAC MADE TO WAIT'. The next day I was talking to an Edensor resident. 'Wasn't it exciting to see the President?' I said. 'I didn't think so,' came the reply, 'that helicopter blew my hens away and I haven't seen them since.'

Andrew and I were in London on 22 November 1963. I heard the news of Jack's assassination on the wireless and, like the rest of the world, could not believe it. Andrew had to make an after-dinner speech that night; he kept the engagement but wrote in his memoirs, 'Whatever I was saying was of no consequence since all our minds were elsewhere.' We went to the funeral, which was arranged in three days and was, not surprisingly, rather chaotic. We were offered a lift to Washington in the plane chartered for Prince Philip, who was representing the Queen. Also on board were the Prime Minister, Alec Douglas-Home, and the Leader of the Opposition, Harold Wilson. Just as at the Inauguration, Andrew and I were included as part of the Kennedy family. We were closer to the tragic events, therefore, than almost anyone else present – certainly closer than heads of state who had come from all over the world to attend. We were both aware, once again, of our privileged position among the late President's friends. I made notes immediately after the funeral and these, too, appear in an appendix to this book.

Over the years, various members of the Kennedy family came to visit Kick's grave. Bobby stayed with us at Edensor in 1948, shortly after her death. It was summer and he wore shorts and ankle socks; I had never seen the combination and thought Bobby Socks must have been named after him. I loved Bobby, his directness, his blue eyes fastening on the person he was talking to, his quick questions, fired as though from a gun, about old times in England or anything else that came into his head. Like Jack, he was a mixture of childlike lack of sophistication and tough political acumen and, like Jack, he was a schoolboy until you hit the steel.

When visiting Ireland in 1966, I saw the dire state of the finances of the Queen's Institute of District Nurses of Eire. It occurred to me that Bobby might consider a donation to a charity that gave such important service to the people of Ireland. I boldly wrote to him and got a series of comical letters back. 'Dear Debo,' he replied, 'I am at last working on your project . . . I am sorry I have delayed but I love you and I hope it is ~~still~~ mutual. Bobby.' There was a note in the margin pointing to the crossed-out 'still', which said, 'I thought this might be a rather unfair assumption.' He then more or less instructed the regional director of the United States Post Office, Sean Keating, who was about to retire, to hand over the proceeds of the retirement luncheon being given in his honour.

Sean Keating kindly agreed but wrote to Bobby that he had spent many sleepless nights since receiving a copy of my letter, and that if his patriotic ancestors knew that he was having anything to do with a project called the QUEEN'S Institute of District Nursing, they would turn into the 'whirling dervishes of their respective cemeteries'. He ended, 'With the devout prayer that God and my sainted ancestors will forgive me.'

I got another letter from Bobby. 'Good news!' it began:

Sean Keating who is going to raise all the money for your ~~damn~~ nurses is going to Ireland. He would like to go fishing at our family estate which is presently in your name. Could he? Would you let him? He will raise even more money.

You would love him although I don't know if you will even be in Ireland at the time of his visit. Obviously that would not be necessary. He just wants to fish + he says all the fish in Ireland are kept by the British + especially by the Devonshires.

Lots of Love,
Bobby

The correspondence went to and fro between Bobby, his secretary, Miss Novello, Sean Keating and me. The retirement luncheon raised over $10,000 and Bobby duly sent me a cheque, with a covering letter:

'Why the hell do you write Miss Novello & Sean Keating and not me? I like to receive letters from you. Love Bobby.'

When Bobby was assassinated in 1968, I could not go to the funeral but Andrew felt he should represent the family. Moucher thought it important for the Kennedys to know he was there, so on the train that carried the coffin to Washington after the Mass in New York, Andrew made his way down the carriages to take his place among other mourners waiting to have a few words with Rose Kennedy. He found her composure extraordinary. 'We talked of Bobby and Jack and of other members of the family,' he wrote in his memoirs.

> She did not mention the actual assassination, but rather talked around it. When I felt my time was up I made my farewells and found Mrs Martin Luther King waiting to make her courtesy call. I have often thought about that afternoon, and I believe her amazing resilience in the face of the family tragedies was entirely a matter of her religious faith. No matter how shocking the events of this world that had overtaken her family, they were secondary to the expectations of the next.

Rose stayed at Chatsworth in July 1969. Andrew found her interesting to talk to and the time passed quickly, but not without a minor incident. At lunch she waved away the dish I had planned, saying, 'I'll have roast chicken.' There was nothing to be said but, 'I'm awfully sorry, Mrs Kennedy, but there isn't any.' For some reason, people often thought Chatsworth was like a hotel and could produce anything on demand. She wanted to go for a walk, but not in the way most of us would, to see something in the park or garden: for her it was a question of counting the steps the doctor had ordered and hardly looking up at what Chatsworth had to offer. Andrew took her to see Hardwick Hall and from there to catch a train from Chesterfield. They found themselves with half an hour to spare, so he walked her round the town which he knew well from his days as a parliamentary candidate. Rose's political antennae were sharpened and she became animated as he pointed out the various public buildings: town hall, school, hospital and the rest.

Teddy Kennedy came to Chatsworth more than once. The last time coincided with a visit from the Prince of Wales. They each planted a lime at the end of the avenue that borders the drive to the Golden Gates and marks the three hundredth anniversary of the creation of the Devonshire dukedom. Looking back, it is a strange quirk of fate that we should have had such a long connection with the Kennedys, who had such powerful political influence yet were visited and revisited by tragedy.

18

PUBLIC LIFE

The organizers of charities, both local and farther afield, often asked Andrew and me to open their money-raising events. As there were so many of these, we soon learned that it would be better to divide them between us. Where possible, I interested myself in charities close to home and was well aware that in the beginning I was invited because of whom I had married and not because of any merit of my own. People were used to female members of the Cavendish family being involved and I was simply following the tradition. Andrew had his own list, which stretched to Eastbourne and London. He was brilliant at public speaking: no matter what the subject or who the audience, he held them in the palm of his hand. Instead of finding a stuck-up fellow full of his own importance, they found themselves laughing at his self-deprecating words; the barriers came down and they sat back and enjoyed it.

One of the first charities I took on was the Children's Society and I soon found myself president of five different committees: Bakewell, Buxton, Chesterfield, Burton-on-Trent and Ashbourne, and a week was set aside for their Annual General Meetings. Then every church in the district seemed to be in trouble: the roof was leaking, the heating was broken, so was the organ (things do not change), or the Red Cross needed support. Events to raise money were ever in search of someone to open them and, as a result, Saturdays in summer and those leading up to Christmas were quickly booked up. The events were arranged months in advance, so you were pinned down if something thrilling turned up on the same day.

The local Women's Institute was a top priority. I inherited a love of the WI from Muv. She founded the Asthall and Swinbrook branch and gave talks on her three favourite subjects: Queen Victoria, Nelson and Bread. I was president of the Chatsworth WI for twenty-one years – a rule now stipulates that no one can be president for more than three, a much better plan. For those who do not know about the WI, it is to the country what the Townswomen's Guilds are to towns – somewhere that provides education and entertainment, and above all a meeting place for country dwellers who often live in isolated places with little or no transport. Ten years ago it hit the headlines when delegates from rural England gathered in the Royal Albert Hall in London for their Annual Meeting and slow handclapped the speaker, who was none other than Prime Minister Tony Blair. He had broken one of the WI's basic rules, which is No Politics. He was not accustomed to such treatment, especially from women, but was up against it that day and his discomfiture showed.

The WI is a great teacher. Once a year, every officer has to stand and sum up the year's activities, which is a marvellous lesson for anyone frightened of talking in front of a crowd, however small and familiar. It certainly helped me. Granny Evie, who was founder and president of the Derbyshire branch of the Red Cross, used to get in a terrible state of nerves before opening a fête or bazaar in one of the neighbouring villages. This was in spite of the fact that the Red Cross devotees were delighted to see her; it was not like electioneering where you could be heckled and hustled about or be the target of a bad egg. For two days beforehand Granny Evie was fidgety and unhappy, and sometimes took to her bed. Once the ordeal was over, she was a different person. There was no way of helping her overcome her nervousness and she never grew out of it. It seemed to me extraordinary that the daughter of a Viceroy of India, brought up to public life, married to a man who had been Governor General of Canada, mother of seven, the chatelaine of four enormous houses in England and a castle in Ireland, who was Mistress of the Robes to Queen Mary for forty-three years, should nevertheless have been terrified of the platform and a friendly audience.

I did not realize that I would be just as nervous myself, and I did not have Granny Evie's experience of public life to fall back on. I knew I had to do it but, like her, I dreaded even the smallest event when I had to talk to an audience. The worst moment came after the flattering introduction, so well meant but which made me squirm and go pink with embarrassment. There would be a silence and then the fatal sentence, 'Now I will ask Lady Hartington to say a few words.' All eyes on me, just what Nanny said would never happen ('It's all right, darling, no one's going to look at *you*'). My mouth went dry and my legs felt like giving way.

Clutching my bit of paper, I began: 'Mr Mayor, Madam Mayoress, Chairman of the County Council', or whatever organization was represented, 'Thank you so much for inviting me . . .' then heard myself trotting out, 'Best of good causes', 'obvious hard work of the organizers', 'please spend' and other tired expressions, before sitting down with relief to listen to a fulsome speech of thanks by someone else on the platform. My voice sounded all the more ridiculous in front of an audience of Derbyshire folk, who have their own, more harmonious way of talking. I was made acutely aware of this when speaking too loudly one day to a friend in the garden at Chatsworth. I was stopped by a stranger. 'I've read about a 30s voice,' he said, 'but I've never heard it before. Please go on talking.' So I did and we were doubled up with laughter at 'lawst' and 'gawn' and other old-fashioned pronunciations.

One day I was thrown in the deep end. I was staying in Sussex with Kitty Mersey, who was secretary of her local WI. On the day of their meeting, the speaker failed to appear. '*Please*,' said Kitty, 'you must talk to them. Tell them about Chatsworth.' No prep, no notes (something I had never before been without) and off I launched. I cannot say I enjoyed it and cannot believe the audience did either – in deepest Sussex they had never heard of Chatsworth – but it passed off all right and I realized for the first time that I could make people laugh. (It is easy when the audience laughs with you but it is out of your hands if they laugh at you.) When we got home, Kitty showed me the programme and the topic on which the real speaker was to have spoken: 'Ramblings of an Old Woman'. Exactly. The experience encouraged me and I dared to follow it up with after-dinner speeches to various agricultural organizations. The first, at the Oxford Farming Conference, was especially frightening as the guests were scientists, lecturers and heads of this and that.

I have given many talks since but always had to have the words in front of me and the nightmare of leaving my speech behind still haunts me. The nearest I ever got to disaster was to forget my specs; bad enough

for me and maddening for the audience. Other hazards lurk. One evening I was to give a talk for charity to an audience that had paid what
seemed to me vast sums to hear my twaddle. No sooner had I started
than I realized the projector was not working. My talk about Chatsworth
was useless without slides and while everyone excuses the odd upside-
down picture, when the whole apparatus seized up I felt I was drowning.
I sat and stared at the impatient rich people in the rows in front of me
kicking the floor and feeling for their car keys, while one or two amateurs
pushed and pulled at plugs – all to no avail. A few pictures eventually
came through but it was no pleasure to anyone; the thread had been
broken and could not be repaired. It was a miserable experience.

American audiences are indulgent. They are interested in Chatsworth, both the house and the garden, and one year I boldly accepted an
invitation to talk at the Metropolitan Museum of Art in New York. This
was thanks to Jayne Wrightsman who knows more about the contents
of museums worldwide than most professors and who, with her late
husband, is one of the Met's munificent benefactors. The event was
merciful in that I was not introduced; I just walked on to the stage
alone, like Elvis, and started.

It was on this occasion that I realized an odd thing: the larger the
audience, the less frightening it is. The lecture hall at the Met held some
seven hundred people and to my astonishment it was sold out. A huge
black space stuffed with faces is so anonymous that you can imagine
there is no one there, but a drawing room with, say, twenty-five friends
of the host, who have been told they must come whether they want to
or not, is terrifying. This happened to me in San Francisco and, in spite
of the audience's kindly good manners, I sensed at once that they were
neither interested nor amused. But I had to battle on. I have found talking in public easier as I have got older, perhaps because I no longer care
what I look like or whether my stockings are straight. But, oh, the apprenticeship is hard! I love the questions, some so deadly serious on a
light-hearted subject; but they keep the audience awake. Recently I gave
a talk about my childhood and someone asked me, 'Your sisters are buried at Swinbrook, are you going to join them there?' She did not add the
word 'soon' but that is what she meant.

It seems that people now prefer showbiz to open their events. It has
taken a long time but even the dimmest actor in the dimmest soap now

draws a crowd. I saw the first signs of this many years ago when the chairman of a bazaar in north-east Derbyshire said in his introductory speech,
'We asked Mrs Dale of *Mrs Dale's Diary*, but there was to be a charge. We
asked Dr Finlay of *Dr Finlay's Casebook* and he wanted a fee. So we had
to ask the Duke of Devonshire.' One organizer said to me about showbiz,
'It's great when they come, but "charge and chuck" is the risk you take.'
Apparently showbiz has no compunction in chucking (with the shining
exceptions of Alan Bennett and Tom Stoppard who do what they promise). Luckily the formality of the old days is fast fading and events now
open themselves: simpler for all concerned.

In 1972 the Royal Smithfield Club held its annual conference in Buxton
and Andrew was invited to be the guest speaker. He already had an engagement that day and, knowing of my interest in food and farming,
handed me their letter and suggested I go in his place. It was the beginning of my happy association with that triumvirate of farmers, butchers
and makers of agricultural machinery. I visited their Show and was hooked,
and for many years Earls Court was my destination for four days in late
November and early December. On my first visit I saw a tractor with a
price tag of £15,000, which made my jaw drop. Today my jaw would fall
off should I see the price tag on one of its vast successors.

The Carcase Hall was a carnivore's dream, with expert butchers on
hand to point out the excellence of the prizewinners. To the uninitiated
the names of some of the classes were puzzling: 'Carcase Cattle Alive'
(to which they could have added 'But Not for Long') and 'Combined
Live/Dead Butchers' Sheep'. The pig section showed the cream of the
porcine world. One pen had two lively prime baconers with a side of
bacon displayed overhead and a notice that read, 'Litter Mate on the
Hook'. (It was just as well those pigs could not read.) As for sheep, a girl
was spotted coming out of the nearby tube station wearing a shaggy
sheepskin coat with a red splodge on the lower back – a sure sign that
the original owner of the skin had received the close attentions of a ram
in his raddle harness. The townee wearer was oblivious of the reason
for the merriment of the group of farmers following her.

I was president of the Royal Smithfield Show from 1972 to 1974 and
president of the Royal Smithfield Club in 1975. The Queen Mother

honoured the Show with her presence and it was my good fortune to look after her during the more private moments of her day-long visits. The Show was just up her street and she was as at home with the butchers and stockmen as they were with her. I followed in her wake as she toured the stands, and I watched the amazing effect her charm had on all those to whom she talked or happened to meet on her path.

Afterwards, we were shepherded by the exhibition manager – Gerry Kunz, son of Charlie Kunz, the famous dance pianist of my youth – to a room called G9 (no relation of G8 or G20 and I never discovered where rooms G1–8 were). G9 had what are described as 'facilities' where we were meant to 'tidy'. It also had a cupboard with every alcoholic drink under the sun and we were able to settle down and chat, oblivious of Gerry and the other officials waiting outside to take us to lunch. During one of these chats, the Queen Mother told me of her pre-war visits to Chatsworth when Granny Evie was in charge, and how on her last visit, on the eve of the Abdication, she and the Duke of York had been acutely aware of the profound change about to take place in their lives. The association with this troubled time went so deep that, in spite of many invitations, she never came to stay at Chatsworth with us.

G9's drinks cupboard was on the floor, so it was hands and knees for me to find the necessary Dubonnet and gin. I soon learned the drill, kneeling again to pour a second helping – in the wrong proportions no doubt, but with no complaint from the consumer. I loved those moments and the memories. At lunch the Queen Mother asked the assembled company, 'What has happened to mutton? We always get lamb, but never mutton.' As a result, one of the farmers kept on some wether lambs for a second year, and twelve months later we fell on the mutton, caper sauce and all. The Queen Mother was president of the Royal Smithfield Show in 1983 and again in 1987–2001. Tradition has it that one who has held this office remains a vice-president for life and wears a large porcelain brooch to proclaim this. The Queen Mother, who had never been 'vice' of anything, was a little surprised at the wording on the brooch she was expected to wear. She looked at me quizzically, head on one side, and said, 'Shall I put it on?'

My eight-year association with Tarmac, the international building conglomerate, came about by chance. Eric Pountain, chief executive of

John McLean & Sons, a building firm based in Wolverhampton, had a friend who bred Haflingers, the small horses that I too bred. Eric gave a cup to be presented at the Haflinger Breed Show and delivered it to the Chatsworth home farm one day when I happened to be there. We had a chat and off he went to a more important engagement. Soon after this, he invited me to join the board of McLean. Perhaps he asked me because I was a woman (it was starting to be the thing to do to have a female on the board) or perhaps because my name was vaguely known in the Midlands. I did not know what to expect and went to the first meeting full of trepidation (Eric's people must have been equally surprised at my arrival). I kept quiet but soon learned the business language of the house builder: land bank, gearing, leverage, etc. McLean was doing well at the time and the company was looking forward with confidence to a great future.

In 1974 McLean was taken over by Tarmac; a shrewd acquisition as McLean was pounding ahead. Various things had gone wrong at the top of Tarmac and a new chief executive was required. Eric was the outstanding man and obvious choice. Again, a woman was required on the board and, as I had been a few years with McLean, I got a promotion and became a non-executive director of Tarmac plc in 1984. This led to journeys to South Africa and America, visiting the company's quarries and construction sites, with Eric and Nicholas Henderson, a fellow non-executive director. Nicko was a lucky appointment for many reasons, perhaps the chief one being that he could speak French, an accomplishment not shared by most of the top brass of the construction industry. The fact that he had been our Ambassador in the United States also helped and we were welcomed wherever we went.

Tarmac expanded into ten US States and our jaunts to America, including crossing the Atlantic on Concorde, were part of our education. One expedition stands out in my memory. Nicko and I were in Virginia and were sent in a helicopter to look at the quarries along the James River. We wanted to dip down to see the famous eighteenth-century plantation houses on this stretch of water; they have been so often written about and photographed and we were curious to see them in reality. The pilot, however, stuck to his instructions to show us the quarries and we managed only tantalizing glimpses of the houses. All the while the helicopter door kept flying open, which did not seem to matter and no one took any notice.

Nicko was chairman of the Channel Tunnel Group in 1985–6 and was instrumental in the run-up to, and making of, the tunnel. The work was done by a consortium of British construction companies, including Tarmac, in conjunction with their French counterparts – with whom Nicko was able to talk with the familiar ease of one who has lived in France. We went with the other directors on an exciting expedition under the sea when our side was about to meet the French tunnellers. The machines were like something out of a giant's toy box and I still have – given to me as a memento of the day – one of the claws that played its part in opening up this underground highway to the Continent.

In the late 1980s Tarmac gave a dinner in a private room at the Connaught Hotel where Andrew and I found ourselves in the company of princes of industry. Also present was Denis Thatcher and I sat next to him. When the Chairman tapped his glass and asked all present for their views on the political situation, two memorable things took place: Andrew predicted the future danger of escalating Muslim extremism, showing, once again, how he grasped the world situation before many others did. When it came to Denis Thatcher's turn to speak, I turned towards my neighbour to find that he had slid down in his chair and that his chin was almost on the table. Eric had the tact to pass quickly to another guest.

One day in 1988 I got a letter from the three directors of the auction house Bonhams, Nick Bonham, Christopher Elwes and Paul Whitfield, inviting me to go and see them. The Bonham salerooms in Montpelier Street were well known to me from Rutland Gate days when we passed them every time we walked through the Hole in the Wall to Brompton Road (often ending up at 'Wicked Old Harrod'). I had haunted their salerooms in the early 1980s looking for portraits of bulls to hang in the Devonshire Arms Hotel at Bolton Abbey and in the wild hope of finding a likeness of 'The Craven Heifer', a vast creature for whom the doors of her shed at Bolton had had to be widened.

Intrigued by Bonhams' invitation, I went to see them. After polite exchanges, I settled into my chair and they suggested I join the board. 'That is very nice of you,' I said, 'but do you realize I am very old?' 'Oh yes,' they said. 'We know you're very old, but we are very young and it will do quite well.' So I joined and looked forward with pleasure to the prospect of learning about another new world, based on an old family business in which the Bonham family was still represented. I stayed with the company till 1995 when, having done nothing for them, I thought I should make way for someone more spry.

In the same year that I joined Bonhams, I received a letter from Dr Steve Dowbiggin, principal of Capel Manor College in Enfield, inviting me to be patron. I was already too much occupied, but the idea of a College within the boundary of the M25, which taught all aspects of gardening, was too attractive to dismiss out of hand. Besides which Dr Dowbiggin's writing paper was decorated with a drawing of a fritillary growing up one side. So I accepted. It has been fascinating to watch the College develop over the years from 400 students based in an eighteenth-century manor house, to its present position in the world of horticulture with 2,600 students and five satellites in and around London.

The College owes its success to Steve (a man who talks you into doing just what he wants) and his brilliant heads of department who have been with him for many years. People who live in the city have an irrepressible need to get closer to the earth, to learn about it and dirty their hands in the process. The only Good Thing I did for Capel Manor was to introduce Steve to Andrew Parker Bowles. Andrew's family, which includes E. A. Bowles, the famous gardening writer, has many connections with Enfield. Forty Hall, where Capel Manor is planting London's first commercial vineyard, belonged to Andrew's family for many years. He has done more for the College than I ever did.

We had some memorable days with various distinguished visitors. Mrs Thatcher came when she was Prime Minister. Gardening is not her chief interest but she did the rounds of the show gardens and the classrooms, all in a day's work. What made her visit unforgettable was the Force 9 gale that was blowing. I soon looked like the Wild Woman of the West, hair all over the place, as did the other women in the party. But not a hair on the PM's head moved. I was so interested in this phenomenon I could not pay attention to anything else. When Mrs Thatcher left, as tidy as when she arrived, I gave her half a dozen of my best dark brown Welsummer eggs as a thank-you. She looked rather surprised and I wondered if she threw them out of the car window (before it was against the law to scatter unwanted eggs on the road).

In 1993 the Prince of Wales, who chairs the committee responsible for the Royal Collection, invited me to join it. A more fascinating 'job' cannot be imagined. The range of what Sybil Cholmondeley, chatelaine of Houghton Hall, called 'Things' that the committee look after is unequalled in the world, and the dedicated experts involved in the care of them are specialists in a class of their own. It was my good fortune to be a trustee for six years. One of the first projects the committee addressed was the extension to the Queen's Gallery at Buckingham Palace, and I was present at the meetings which decided what the building should look like and which architect should be appointed. It was no easy task to adapt an old building, already fully occupied, to one that could be used for temporary exhibitions of all kinds, but the difficulties were somehow resolved and the new Queen's Gallery feels as if it has always been there. (This was a criterion we tried to follow at Chatsworth when converting beautiful old buildings to a purpose different from that for which they were built.)

Another subject for discussion at meetings was the countless requests from all over the world for loans of works of art. At other times an object – a plate, a knife and fork, or even a chair from a set – that had escaped from one or other of the royal houses appeared in the saleroom. It was the committee's task to decide on their importance and whether to bid for them to gather them back into the Collection.

A complete inventory of everything not personally owned by the Monarch – and therefore belonging to the Royal Collection – was being undertaken and this apparently endless task was like Lewis Carroll's seven maids with seven mops sweeping sand from the seashore. The Collection does not stand still. Some departments, such as photography, were added to almost daily, as were presents from heads of state to the royal family. By the end of 2008, a total of 639,908 items had been inventoried and this database must have made the work of Sir Hugh Roberts, director of the Collection, and others in charge of the various departments more manageable.

Only on rare occasions did Andrew and I attend public events together. Most of these were in the early 1950s when Andrew was Mayor of Buxton, the spa town in the Peak District of Derbyshire. It was an office his father had held in 1920, the year Andrew was born, and 'Buxton' was added to his Christian names. In the early 1950s the popularity of the spa was declining, but Buxton was an up-and-coming conference town with many hotels from the days when an endless supply of warm water made it a popular destination. (Mary, Queen of Scots, benefited from the springs during her captivity at Chatsworth, probably the only time she was warm in the cruel climate of north Derbyshire.)

Food and petrol were still rationed in 1952 and a proper regard for the way public money was spent made the fare served at the mayor's welcoming dinners rather odd. We and our visitors all dressed in our best: white tie for Andrew, full evening dress with long white gloves for me. I grabbed anything that shone to pin on before I left home to drive the seventeen twisty miles to the Pavilion Gardens where many of the dinners were held. The first reception that Andrew gave as mayor was for three hundred commercial travellers. The main course at dinner was sausage rolls, followed by chocolate biscuits for pudding and coffee with the milk already in it – all handed round with appropriate formality. The three hundred commercial travellers, and the three hundred hairdressers we entertained the next night, had to eat this menu only once. We soon grew accustomed to it.

At these public events Andrew said that he often heard men say, 'That was before my little do.' He soon learned that this enigmatic statement referred either to a minor heart attack or to some charitable event that the fellow had organized (usually the former). It was this sort of remark that lightened what were sometimes dim occasions. On the whole we enjoyed our more than fifty years of public life. It was the people we met who made the job so intriguing and it gave us an insight into lives and organizations that we would otherwise never have known. Even when faced with a seemingly dull evening, there were always one or two people who made it enjoyable and reminded me of my luck at being present.

19

ORPHAN

After the war, when Farve went to live at Redesdale Cottage with Margaret Wright (now married to a Mr Dance), we had little contact with him. If we rang him, Margaret answered and we knew she would be standing over him while he talked, so we seldom telephoned. Failing eyesight had made it difficult for him to write. My letters to him do not survive but a reminder from the distant past turned up in the back of a drawer not long ago. It was one of Farve's stiff, top-quality blue envelopes, the sort that cuts your thumb when you rip it open. On it is written, 'Thorn removed from the foot of Stubby's dog.' He does not say which dog, but he understood the prime importance of such a thing to me.

Except for Decca, we all occasionally went to see him at Redesdale. Farve longed to see Decca, but she had said that she would only go on condition that he agreed to be nice to her family. This, of course, infuriated my father, as he would never have dreamt of being rude to them. Muv, who understood both sides, thought it wiser for them not to meet. On one of my last visits to Redesdale I took Kitty Mersey, who had been longing to meet him. We sat in his room, surrounded by metal filing cabinets ('mechanically sound, Stubby') and other purely functional furniture, the opposite of what Muv would have chosen. Unopened letters and magazines lay in piles around us. He was old and obviously ill, his one lung still battling with a continuous onslaught of gaspers. The classic features were still there but diminished, and 'my good dentures' were too big for the rest of his face. He was the ghost of what he had once been and had little interest left in life. Kitty said, 'You're not at all what

I expected – a fierce person who might not have let me in.' 'Lady Mersey,' he replied sadly, 'I've no savagery left in me.'

Muv, Diana and I went to see him for his eightieth birthday and stayed at the Redesdale Arms (the inn with a sign 'Last Pub in England' on one side and 'First Pub in England' on the other). Diana wrote in her memoirs: 'I shall never forget the expression on Farve's face when Muv appeared at his bedside, and his smile of pure delight.' It was a comfort to me that my parents' last sight of each other seemed to turn back the years to how I remembered them as a child. Farve died four days later, on 17 March 1958. He was cremated and his ashes buried in Swinbrook churchyard. I could hardly believe my eyes when a little box was produced with all that was left of him; his beauty, funniness, charm and fury all gone for good, and with it my childhood.

In contrast to Farve's, Muv's last years were spent surrounded by loving family and friends. She lived mostly in London and spent the summer months on Inch Kenneth, where the rigours of island life never seemed too much for her. The complications of transport were exemplified by the cows. Getting them to the bull to produce a calf (and hence some milk) is worth recording. There was a bull at Gribun, on Mull, and at the first sign of a cow being in season, a rope was put round her head and she was led to the jetty at high tide. The dinghy awaited her, oars at the ready, not as a passenger but to tow her. She was pushed into the deep water with an almighty shove and across the channel to Mull they went, the cow swimming behind with no difficulty. The sea had to be calm, of course, which added another factor to this tricky procedure. With luck, all went well at the first service but should she 'turn' at her next heat, the process had to be repeated or there would be no calf – and no milk.

Things got easier when Muv took goats to Inch Kenneth, pedigree British Saanens – quiet white creatures which produce a quantity of milk and are a delight to look after. A long-awaited kid was born. I telephoned Muv to ask whether it was a billy or a nanny. 'Well, darling,' she said, 'I'm afraid it's neither one thing nor another,' her way of saying that it was a hermaphrodite. The goats suited Muv and the island, being smaller, friendlier and easier to deal with than cows.

In old age Muv developed Parkinson's disease. She was stoical and saw the ridiculous side of her uncontrolled movements. When playing Scrabble, which she loved, her shaking hand made the placing of letters uncertain so with her right hand she used to seize her left, which was grasping the air and maddening her, and say, 'Stop it,' half laughing.

Although she was not a classical musician as Tom had been, the piano had always been important to her but now she could no longer control her fingers on the keyboard. Before the disease struck, she used to sing and play popular songs, and was amused by the liberties taken with some of the rhymes: 'I'm bidin' my time/That's the kinda guy I'm'. She loved jazzed-up versions of the classics such as Mendelssohn's 'Spring Song Swung' and Handel's 'Water Music' (renamed 'Mind the Handel's Hot'). *The Daily Express Community Song Book* provided old songs from the Boer War, and classics from the First World War such as 'Keep the Home Fires Burning'. The Irish revolutionary song, 'The Wearing of the Green', was a favourite, as were the inimitable 1930s songs 'Mean to Me', 'Miss Otis Regrets' and 'Goodnight Sweetheart' – so well remembered from Café de Paris days. After the war Muv sometimes used to sing Irving Berlin's sad song, 'Say It Isn't So', and I often wondered if she was thinking of herself when that one came along.

Muv and I were talking one day about old age with Tony Lambton. Knowing that she would not mind, Tony asked her how old she was. 'Nineteen,' she said. 'No, sorry, seventy-three.' I loved the idea of her being forever nineteen inside her ageing body. (She always said that the body is just an old sack – it does not matter what happens to it after death, and she could never understand why people made such a fuss about where and how they were buried.) 'So what's it like being old?' Tony pressed her. Muv thought for a minute and said, 'You aren't followed in the street any more and it's no fun trying on a hat.' Being followed in the street in her day was considered normal, though what outcome the poor followers hoped for I do not know. Perhaps they just appreciated beauty and wanted to see more of it.

The first months of 1963 were some of the coldest for years and frosts kept the ground iron-hard long after there should have been signs of spring. The park at Chatsworth was white with snow and the rabbits were dying of starvation. (Diddy said their corpses were like empty knitting bags.) The weather was bad, if not worse, in Scotland, but Muv travelled as usual to Inch Kenneth in early May. A few weeks beforehand,

Nancy had accompanied her to the wedding of our cousin Angus Ogilvy to Princess Alexandra and said how wonderful Muv had looked, 'Got up in black velvet, lace and diamonds . . . the most elegant person there by far.' Coming from Nancy this was extraordinary praise.

Muv was delighted to be back on the island but soon after arriving she collapsed and her daughters were sent for. Nancy, Pam, Diana and I got there as soon as we could but the journey to the Inner Hebrides was never straightforward and the various waits and loss of connections were even more frustrating than usual because of the urgency and the uncertainty of what we would find. Decca was in California. As always in a crisis, my good Old Hen wanted to come, but the journey from San Francisco would have taken at least two days and as the doctor thought Muv might die at any moment, it was likely she would arrive too late.

The cold was bitter, even for the hardy Black Face sheep. There was not a blade of grass for them to eat and dead ewes and their newborn lambs lay beside the road from Salen to Gribun – a pitiful sight. We found Muv in bed and weak. She could talk, but eating and drinking were painfully slow because the muscles in her throat had all but given up. She was pleased to see us and knew why we had come: 'Of course I know why you're here,' she said, 'I'm dying.'

The next two weeks were all alike; she slept most of the time but had some hours of wakefulness, sometimes in extreme discomfort when she was beset by what she called her 'horrors' and was unable to lie still. It was awful to watch and it brought home to me how it is often as difficult to die as it is to be born. There was little we could do to help but it was a comfort to her that we were there. We got a routine going. Pam did the cooking while Nancy, Diana and I sat with Muv. We took it in turns to be with her in the night when she wanted a hand to hold. Every now and again she made us laugh and kept saying how she would be loving it all if she were well. 'Somewhere you'll find my ridiculous will,' she said, 'do change it if you want.' We said we would like to but feared we would go to prison if we did. 'Oh, so you will,' she said and relapsed into sleep. The two young and cheerful nurses from the mainland made the whole difference; not only was their presence a comfort, they could explain to us what was happening.

For the fortnight, while Muv's life drew to an end, we had the intense pleasure of being all four sisters together for the first time since I was a child. It was an unexpected bonus of those sad days and it was never to happen again. Of course we laughed and went back to the old jokes and teases. Nancy complained that her clothes were dirty. 'I'm going to make Woman teach me to wash,' she said, 'and I'll stand and look on while she does.' It worked like a charm. We all knew what the other was thinking and (like my old Collie dog) knew what the other was going to say before she said it. I wondered how anyone could die without at least four daughters at their bedside.

It was only a month from the summer solstice and daylight came early. After one of my turns for sitting with Muv, I went upstairs to bed to hear the crash of the dawn chorus and wondered what on earth the birds were thinking of in this freezing weather. The song of the larks was dominant and when I hear a lark now it takes me straight back to the stairs at Inch Kenneth.

We kept a coal fire going in Muv's bedroom night and day, and finally the coal ran out. It was delivered every two years and it was months before the next load was due. (It used to arrive on a coal boat and was tipped on to the beach at high tide, shovelled into wheelbarrows as quickly as possible and pushed to the coal shed before it could be claimed by the sea.) We took it in turns to scour the beaches at low tide for driftwood. Our eyes soon grew accustomed to picking out the battered white wood from the rocks and stones, and we carried it home in triumph. Sometimes the white object turned out to be the bone of some unfortunate cow that had toppled over the cliff in search of something to eat, and we were disappointed as it was no good on the fire. Soon our food began to run out. At last Diana was able to cross to Mull and drive to Tobermory with a long list of groceries. She returned victoriously some hours later carrying a ham on her head.

No one knew how long our vigil would last. The outside world was so far away it did not exist; only frequent telegrams to and from Decca brought us down to earth. I felt for her being so far away. Over the years her attitude to Muv had changed, as her reactions in those final days of telegrams and letters showed. After Muv's death, she wrote to Nancy that having loathed Muv when she was growing up, she then became 'immensely fond of her, really rather adored her'. She also loved Inch Kenneth, which had been hers since 1959. (After Farve's death, she had bought out Pam's, Diana's and my shares in it, and Nancy had made her a gift of hers.) Decca's love for the island pleased Muv greatly and it was a bond between them.

Three times during those days we thought Muv had gone, but each time she rallied. On one occasion her voice strengthened and she appeared to have a vision: she spoke of bright lights and many people she had known, and said, 'Perhaps, who knows, Tom and Unity?' She slipped into unconsciousness and died on 25 May, aged eighty-three. It was a relief that her 'horrors' were over and that the end was peaceful, but hard to believe in the finality of her death. We held a service over her coffin and took her over the water to Mull, with a piper playing and the flag of the *Puffin* at half mast. The funeral was held at Swinbrook. The winter had relented in the south and the beauty of the churchyard, with its rush of cow parsley and buttercups and the song of thrushes and blackbirds, took me straight back to the mayfly hatching on the Windrush and the sound of Farve's reel in pursuit of a rising trout.

In a lucid moment a week before she died, Muv said to us, 'Now, children, you'll cry at my funeral and then you'll start laughing.' We did. Our sorrow came in waves but so did the laughter. There has to be relief after sorrow, no one can manage without it. Even the saddest, most painful moments do not last, however difficult it is to believe it at the time.

20

MIDWAY

T he years of middle age passed in a misty dream. Luxury was a day with nothing written in the diary and such days were rare. All householders know the problems, big and small, but magnify them by the size of Chatsworth and its environs, and you have the picture. The major problems went straight to Andrew, the day-to-day to me – a broken curtain rail, a fallen tree in the garden, a dead stag in the river. As soon as the house and garden staff had started work, some at 8 a.m. and some at 9 a.m., the telephone began to ring: something had arisen in a faraway place that required an immediate decision or at least on-the-spot consideration. I was needed by the head housemaid on the private side of the house, the housekeeper on the public side, by the sewing room, the head gardener, head house-carpenter, cook, butler's pantry, signwriter, farm manager, head keeper, farmyard, house shops, farm shop or restaurant. When Roger Wardle became land agent I was able to refer to him on all estate matters and, on the rare occasions when there was a fiery disagreement between two Chatsworth men, both certain they were right, he was able to settle the dispute to the satisfaction of both parties. I saw him in action on several occasions and came away impressed by his tact.

I loved all this activity, largely because of the pleasure of working with some of the most remarkable people I have ever met. One Chatsworth special was Mr Clegg, who seemed to spend all his days scrubbing the stone passage leading from the back door to the kitchen and elsewhere. The water he scrubbed and mopped with got browner and browner but it did not seem to matter. One Christmas, Mr Clegg volunteered to do lodge duty, which involved opening and shutting the gates to the private drive. I went to visit him in the narrow room of the lodge, where whoever was on duty sat keeping an eye out for the intruders who never came. Mr Clegg was not watching but was deep in a book. I asked him what he was reading. He turned to the title page: *Advanced Algebra* – a lesson to me that you cannot put people into categories.

Maud Barnes, who came from several generations of Cavendish family employees – her father had been the clerk of works at Hardwick – was another of the Chatsworth 'characters'. She did not marry, being one of the thousands of dutiful women who stay at home to look after an ailing parent, but when she was eventually free to do as she pleased, she came to Chatsworth. Her ill-defined job was to clean and tidy my rooms and wash and iron. The mezzanine above my little sitting room was where she carried out these tasks. She had a frightful fox terrier called Spot or Scott (I never discovered which) that ruled her life and made lots of washing – or sending to the cleaners, more likely – of the loose covers where he had, *pour encourager les autres*, lifted his leg.

Maud was neither clean nor tidy, but she was intelligent, well-read, excellent company and willing to join in any fun on offer. In the early 1960s the Chatsworth WI put on an entertainment at an open meeting (where non-members are welcome). I went as the Oldest Miss World in the World, decked out in the Devonshire Parure – seven prickly and monumental pieces of jewellery, including a tiara, necklace and stomacher – which, until you look closely, might have been pulled out of the dressing-up box. Diddy, the children's nanny, whose shape reminded me of the kind of bread you can no longer buy – a round dollop sitting atop a larger round dollop – and who always gave the best of her unselfish nature, went as the Sugar Plum Fairy in a white tulle tutu and tights. Waving a wand wrapped in tinsel, this beloved creature, then in late middle age, pirouetted, jumped, flumped and pointed her toe at the audience. Maud went as Ringo Starr under a black Beatle wig that suited her classical features; to see and hear her drumming was sublime. I do believe that she, Diddy and I were the stars that night.

During the holiday my mother-in-law stayed at Moor View (home to the Suicide Squad in our Edensor days) and I loved having her close by. She had a cross cook who shouted at her and everyone else, and talked loudly to herself in the little kitchen. There was a hole in the wall between the kitchen and dining room through which she used to push the food with a furious shove. Moucher's guests always included her brother, David Cecil, and sister, Mima Harlech. The three of them loved each other's company better than anyone's and made the most of their days together, talking, talking as only Cecils can. They did not understand stacking so when they had finished eating and the dirty plates were ready to go back through the hole in the wall, they passed them round and round the table. No one thought to stop and make a pile of them – they were too interested in what they were saying. This display of their unpractical ways was one of the comic entertainments of the year for me.

However enjoyable my job at Chatsworth, it was often like walking on eggshells, not only because I never knew exactly where my remit ended, but because Andrew was a victim of alcoholism and his reactions had become increasingly unpredictable. Had he not written so openly about it in his memoirs I would not have mentioned my side of the story, but it may be of interest to others to read a first-hand account of what it was like.

Andrew was addicted to alcohol for much of his adult life, a weakness that ran through the Cavendish family and had also descended to some of his first cousins. Drinking had contributed to his father's premature death at the age of fifty-five and to his uncle Charlie Cavendish's at thirty-eight. Perhaps in Andrew's case things were exacerbated by underlying guilt at having what his brother should have had, and by the pressures and enormous responsibilities that came with this inheritance. After Billy's death, although he enjoyed many things in life, he was driven by a sense of guilt and duty in equal parts.

Living with someone with an addiction of any sort, be it gambling, drugs, alcohol or even compulsive spending – anything done to excess – is wearing. If you have never had the experience it is hard, almost impossible, to understand what it is like. The character of the sufferer changes, in Andrew's case from Dr Jekyll to Mr Hyde and back again with little warning, and to pretend that life is normal is to deny reality. To me *in vino veritas* was the very opposite of what happened: *in vino* brought out the nasty side; it was without the vino that Andrew was himself.

Although he was never physically violent when drunk, some of his actions – now unbelievable and best forgotten – were directed at those

closest to him, which I believe is usual, and the effect on his relationship
with our three children was dire. When we had people to stay I often
found it difficult to concentrate on those next to me at dinner as I always
had half an eye on Andrew and his neighbours at the other end of the
table, knowing that a flare-up could come at any moment and that they
might suddenly be the recipients of his anger. On several occasions he
simply left the table and we went on as if nothing had happened.

Sixty years ago none of this would have been discussed; it would
have been swept under the carpet by the addict's family in the pretence
that it was not happening. I saw my mother-in-law do this and observed
her unhappiness. In an attempt to keep Eddy away from his club, where
drinking too much was usual among some of the members, she tried to
distract him by inviting people she thought would interest him. She did
not succeed. For an alcoholic, as with other addicts, the time of euphoria gets shorter and the hangover longer; depression lifts momentar-
ily only to return worse than ever. Today, at last, addicts are treated as
ill and are openly spoken of as such. It is understood that sufferers need
help in order to free themselves from the bonds of whatever addiction
allows them to escape, however fleetingly, from life and its troubles.

Andrew was surrounded by five loyal employees. Not knowing that
it was the worst thing they could do, they made a cocoon around him
of which I, unwittingly, was part. So successful were we at hiding Andrew's problem that even a senior member of the estate staff who joined
in 1981 was unaware of his trouble. Concealing it was a double-edged
sword: had it been exposed, Andrew might have sought help earlier, but
at the time none of us who thought we were protecting him knew any
better. I have now learnt that there is only one course of action, a
method developed in America that has been successful all over the
world. It comes at a price – the patient has to reach rock bottom, to go
so low as to cry for help, and this is painful to watch – but it is a price
well worth paying, as the success of Alcoholics Anonymous testifies.

I took advice from counsellors who told me that it was essential to
remove Andrew's props and bring his problem out into the open. So I
asked the heads of department at Chatsworth to come and see me; we
stood in the passage by my room and I was afraid of breaking down as I
told them that Andrew was ill and that the nature of his illness was alcoholism. I could see, as these old and trusted friends walked slowly
away, that they understood the necessarily harsh nature of the treat-

ment. Henry Coleman, our butler who had been with us since 1963, must have understood it better than most, having been so close to Andrew and me during those difficult times.

Time dims the unpleasant or sad events in life and dates run into each other in a muddled way. What I do know is that Andrew twice made the mighty effort to give up drinking. The first, in the 1970s, lasted for two years and then he started again. In the early 1980s, he went to some counsellors who had treated his cousins with success and this encouraged him to agree to try their method. The cure should have lasted six weeks but after two he rang his sister Anne, who lived near the clinic, and told her he could stand it no longer and would she please fetch him. 'If I had stayed the full six weeks,' he wrote in his memoirs, 'it would have destroyed me.'

> Having no wish to see my family and friends I went to a hotel in Eastbourne. My hair – what there was of it – seemed to be even more shocked than I was. It stopped growing for three months. My spell in Eastbourne coincided with Wimbledon fortnight and I have never been able to watch the tournament on television since.

He came back to Chatsworth, doubtful of the success of what he had endured, and started drinking again. Matters reached a head in September 1983. We had guests staying for four days racing at Doncaster and Andrew's behaviour was out of control and frightening to watch. After two days I telephoned the counsellor in despair and asked her what to do. Without hesitation she told me to tell the guests to leave. (Three close friends immediately understood the desperate situation; the others said they were Andrew's guests and were staying.) She instructed me to cover my bedroom and sitting room with dust sheets and leave the house. The idea was to give Andrew a shock, to make him think that I had left for good – and for all I knew I had.

Stoker and Sophy were indispensable to me during those knife-edge times. Emma and her husband Toby were stalwart supports and asked me to stay with them for an unlimited time, but in the event Stoker and Amanda took me to Bolton Hall. After a few days, the telephone rang with an agonized request from Andrew, 'Please will you come back?' I said I would if he would give up drinking once and for all. 'The miracle occurred,' he wrote. 'I realized that apart from all the suffering I had caused, I was not my own master. I decided this slavery must stop once and for all.' He went into a nursing home for four days to ensure that no alcohol remained in his blood and started to take Antabuse, the pill you cannot mix with alcohol without feeling extremely ill.

For all of us at Chatsworth it was indeed a miracle. Andrew slowly got better physically, which must have helped him resist the longed-for drink. Those of us who have been spared such craving cannot understand how hard it must be to give up a lifelong habit. But Andrew did it and for two decades, until the day he died, he never had another drink. My optimistic nature had faith in his resolve and I was proved right. A laden drinks tray was always in his study, to the astonishment of friends who knew his medical history, but he never went near it. The nightmare was over. People he had been unable to face came back as though nothing had happened and he began to take an interest in things he had avoided for years.

The turnaround was all the more remarkable as he was beginning to go blind. Eventually he could not see to read, a terrible deprivation, and radio and television could not take the place of books. As his eyes got worse, he could no longer recognize faces, so the endless engagements in Derbyshire and elsewhere, which he had started to honour again, must have been difficult, and people thought he was cutting them when he failed to speak to them. Yet in spite of the effort it cost him, he continued to play his part to the full until shortly before he died.

Despite the worry of Andrew, which was always in the background, I enjoyed entertaining at Chatsworth; not the official sort where hosts ask people off a list and guests accept because it is part of their job, but having friends to stay. Not long after we moved into the house Cecil Beaton came for a night or two. I was proud of a new border outside the Orangery which was planted with clashing bright-red plants and a few orange flowers – a startling antidote to the pastel colours then favoured by garden designers. I took Cecil to see it. 'It's *arful*,' he bleated. 'It's a *retina irritant*.' Cecil lived at Reddish House in Broadchalke, one of those Wiltshire houses that are so pretty and easy to live in that you feel nowhere could be as good. It was stuffed full of anything that had caught his eye, and because it had caught his eye it became fashionable. Baubles, china objects, ornaments, shawls, bronzes were scattered over every surface, including in the conservatory where watering the plants must have been a tricky job. I stayed at Reddish when Sophy was at nearby Hanford School, and when I fetched her back for lunch my heart was in my mouth as the ten-year-old swung her heavy winter coat, narrowly missing the piles of precious objects.

Cecil was a wonderful host, taking *petits soins* everywhere for the comfort of the guest. Perhaps it was a bit too theatrical, but theatre was part of his trade. During the war Rex Whistler, Lady Juliet Duff, Cecil and several other talented and sophisticated people who lived near the Pembrokes at Wilton House got up a pantomime. *Heil Cinderella* was made unforgettable by Cecil as an Ugly Sister. Wearing an unadorned black velvet dress – no brooch, no necklace, nothing but a thin, long-sleeved slinky creation described by dressmakers as a 'sheath' – he swayed about, tall and maiden-auntish, singing, 'Don't look now, there's Hitler close behind you.' It was one of the best things I have seen on stage.

In 1976, Lady Bird Johnson, widow of President Johnson, brought her daughter Lynda Bird to Chatsworth. We laid on a tour of neighbouring houses, gardens, villages and public buildings in an attempt to show our part of England at its best. Andrew and I were delighted to have the chance to get to know our guests: a more easy-going, charming pair you could not hope to find. Before they left, Lady Bird told me that she was going to Greece that summer and was reading up on its ancient history. 'I'm trying to figure out . . . who . . . slew . . . who,' she said, very slowly, in her lovely Southern accent. As their car was about to drive away, I said to Lynda Bird, 'Do stop at Sudbury on your way south, it is so well worth it.' 'We can't,' she said. 'Mother is just about Housed Out.'

In 1979 an exhibition, 'Treasures from Chatsworth', travelled to several American museums. I was asked to the opening at the Kimbell Art Museum in Fort Worth and Lady Bird invited me to visit the Johnson Ranch in Austin – all new worlds to me and exciting. The foreword to the exhibition catalogue was written by Professor Sir Anthony Blunt, keeper of the Queen's pictures. He had been to stay at Chatsworth to see the works of art and I had looked forward to his visit. Nancy and Diana had been to one of his lectures in Paris and had fallen for him, and I knew he was revered by his pupils.

In the event I was disappointed and found my guest difficult to talk to. Andrew was away, and dinner on the two nights Sir Anthony stayed

ABOVE: Hardwick Hall

RIGHT: Sitting for Pietro Annigoni, 1954

Lismore Castle

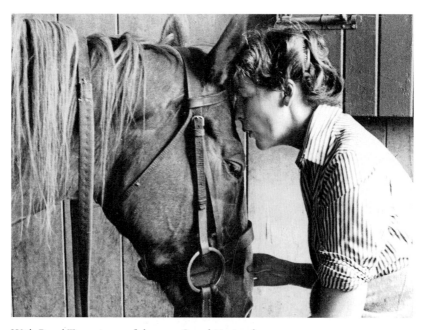

With Royal Tan, winner of the 1954 Grand National

Andrew and Violet Hammersley. Lismore, c. 1950

Lucian Freud, Andrew, Penny Cuthbertson. Careysville, 1972

Robert Kee and Patrick Leigh Fermor. Lismore, 1960

ABOVE: With Andrew in the garden at Chatsworth

LEFT: With Sophy in the yellow drawing room. Chatsworth, 1960

Emma's wedding to Toby Tennant: (*left to right*) Mary Devonshire, Stoker, DD, David Skailes, Sophy, Toby, Emma, Matthew Yorke, Andrew, Christopher Glenconner. Chatsworth, 1963

With Cecil Beaton, 1969

At Stoker's wedding, 1967: (*left to right*) DD, Nancy, Pamela, Diana, Emma

In the west garden with Sophy (*left*) and grandchildren Isabel and Eddie Tennant, 1968. (*By kind permission of Ron Duggins*)

My bedroom at Chatsworth. (*By kind permission of Simon Upton*)

My sitting room at Chatsworth. (*By kind permission of Simon Upton*)

With the 'guns' at Bolton Abbey. DD and Harold Macmillan mounted, early 1960s

Shooting at Chatsworth, 1960. (*By kind permission of Snowdon*)

With Stoker at the Game Fair. Chatsworth, 1966

Lagos, 1962: (*left to right*) the Olori of Lagos, Andrew, the Oba of Lagos, DD, Dorothea Head

With Dr Nnamdi Azikiwe (Zik) and my sister-in-law Elizabeth Cavendish. Chatsworth, 1961

Visit of the Shah of Persia to Chatsworth

LEFT: Invitation to the Inauguration of President John F. Kennedy

BELOW: Greeting Robert Kennedy on his visit to Chatsworth in 1964 (Eddy Sackville-West is immediately behind me). (*By kind permission of Ron Duggins*)

Pushing over a pile of pennies at a charity event in Whitwell, Derbyshire

Serving behind the counter at the Orangery Shop at Chatsworth

With Sophy at the Countryside March, 1997

Celebrating our Golden Wedding at Chatsworth with more than 1,000 couples from Derbyshire who also married in 1941. (*By kind permission of Ron Duggins*)

Tercentenary of the dukedom. Chatsworth, 1994

With the Prince of Wales, 2000

With Sybil Cholmondeley at Houghton

Diana, Pamela and DD at Chatsworth

With my granddaughter Stella Tennant

With Jean-Pierre Béraud, chef and entrepreneur, wearing his fortieth birthday
party wig, 10 August 1996. He was killed
in a car crash two months later

At Andrew's and my eightieth birthday party in the dress made by Worth for Duchess Louise for the Devonshire House Ball in 1897. Chatsworth, 2000. (*By kind permission of Simon Upton*)

Feeding the hens. (*By kind permission of Bridget Flemming*)

With my great-grandchildren in 2009: (*left to right*) Barney Dunne, Rosa Tennant, Jake Carter, Lily Hill, Victor Hill, Marcel Lasnet, Cecily Lasnet, Alfie Carter, Harry Tennant, Ned Carter, Georgia Tennant, Jasmine Lasnet, Iris Lasnet, Willa Carter, Cosmo Dunne, Isla Tennant, Maud Cavendish. (*By kind permission of Charlotte Bromley-Davenport*)

Aged ninety at the Old Vicarage, 2010, under the portrait of Muv painted by Philip de Laszlo in 1916 – four years before I was born. (*By kind permission of Bridget Flemming*)

seemed to drag on. Perhaps he had expected me to invite people to meet him; he was certainly bored. I was thankful when the time came for him to leave and take his cold eyes and unpleasant personality with him. What followed was unexpected. Waking in my hotel bedroom in Fort Worth on the morning of the opening at the Kimbell, I turned on the television and there, filling the screen, was Sir Anthony's thin, gloomy face and the scandal of his exposure as a traitor. The telephone started ringing. In view of this extraordinary development, should we withdraw the catalogue from sale? After much discussion, it was decided not to. The catalogue sold out and more attention was paid to it and its disgraced author than to the finest exhibits Chatsworth could provide.

Lady Bird Johnson gave a great deal of her time to me and took me to the Harry Ransom Center in Austin, where I saw letters by Evelyn Waugh in his neat little handwriting, and many works by my hero, Edward Lear. Anyone who can write a poem like 'The Akond of Swat' or paint such landscapes as *The City of Syracuse* at Madresfield Court is worthy of reverence. After poring over these treasures I happened to look up and see, on top of a display cupboard, three cardboard boxes marked 'Jessica Mitford' in large letters. I asked if I could look at them. The librarian told me apologetically that the contents were unsorted, but he brought one down and in it were random notes in my Old Hen's writing – dinner engagements, shopping lists and the like. When later I asked Decca how they had got there, she told me that the Center had paid a huge sum for what she was about to throw away. Wonders will never cease, but I was delighted to find a bit of home in that distant land.

Back at the Ranch after dark, Lady Bird took me to the garden to show me her Jacuzzi, the first I had ever seen. We got in and splashed about, lit by searchlights and surrounded by security guards. Neighbours came for dinner and arrived in their own planes. Late at night we stood and waved goodbye as the neat little jets took off into the starry Texan sky, as if it were nothing out of the ordinary. The next morning, Lady Bird asked me if I would like to go with the cowboys to round up some cattle. Of course I would. I was not disappointed by the handsome men, dressed as I had often seen them in films with Stetson hats, check shirts, leather chaps, cowboy boots and spurs, but I was surprised when they pointed to a helicopter instead of a horse, and up and off we went with a cowboy at the controls. The Hereford cattle were driven along by this noisy machine, which dipped and wove as it herded the beasts into the open gates of the corral. I enjoyed this new experience, but wondered why the cowboy pilot had bothered to put on his spurs.

When Uncle Harold was very old he came to stay for weeks on end. By then he was becoming infirm and walking was not easy. I met him one afternoon in a passage looking rather anxious and forlorn. 'The trouble with this house,' he said, 'is you have to throw double sixes to get out.' He slept in the red velvet bedroom, which opens on to a busy first-floor passage, and sometimes liked to go to bed early with tea and bread and butter for supper. One evening he heard us talking outside his bedroom and could not bear to miss the chat. A figure in pyjamas and dressing gown emerged, demanded champagne and spent a cheery evening with people generations younger than himself. He knew his lines and spouted them to his audience. Sophy often longed to be anywhere else as she had heard it all before, reminding me of Jeremy Tree at glorious Ditchley during the war. Winston Churchill used to stay there at full moon, when Chequers and Chartwell were easy targets for enemy bombers, and held forth at the dinner table. Most of the guests were spellbound, but not Jeremy, who longed to go to bed and whose wide yawns while the oracle spoke did not go unnoticed.

After lunch with us Uncle Harold retired to a chair in his bedroom, holding a cigar over a wicker wastepaper basket – can you imagine anything more dangerous? He was nearly blind and had taken to Talking Books, especially Trollope, which he must have known by heart. One day he told me in a very serious voice that something odd had happened to Trollope and he could not make it out. I looked at the packet and saw it was *Lucky Jim* by Kingsley Amis. When Andrew was in London, I was often alone with Uncle Harold. No good at politics, I was nevertheless fascinated to hear about the people he had known and worked with for years. Such were his good manners that he never hinted that he would have preferred a more intelligent dinner companion and treated me as if I were a fellow ageing ex-PM. He was easy to laugh at, but also easy to laugh with. When Mrs Thatcher became Prime Minister, she asked him to go and see her. 'That was a good idea,' I said. 'Did you talk?' 'No – she did.'

It was to have private talks with Uncle Harold that the Prince of Wales came to stay in June 1984. What Uncle Harold told him I do not know, but they made good friends and the Prince felt his time was well spent. He reminded me recently that he had asked for a reading list to fill the gaps in his knowledge, and that Andrew and Uncle Harold had scoured the bookshelves to produce one. He says it is invaluable to him still. Thereafter, the Prince stayed at Chatsworth whenever he had an official engagement near by and he was often able to stay on and fit in a day's hunting with the Meynell. In December he used to bring sack loads of Christmas cards to sign – a chore which meant putting an extra table in his room for the seemingly endless piles. The Prince liked the freedom of being able to walk in the woods and over the moor, exploring unknown country. If he did meet one or two walkers and they recognized him, they respected his privacy, greeted him and walked on. One winter weekend I drove him to see the beautiful late-eighteenth-century mill at Cressbrook. A 'Road Closed' sign stopped us just before we reached our destination. The Prince got out of the car and knocked at the door of a nearby cottage. After a while, a man answered and the Prince asked him if we could drive on. The man scratched his head, stared at the visitor and said, very slowly, 'Haven't I seen you somewhere before?'

There was usually a big party of friends when the Prince came to stay and we enjoyed it to the full, but there was no opportunity to get to know him well in a crowd of people who all wanted to talk to him. In March 1988, however, the Prince was in a party of skiers holidaying in Klosters when an avalanche overtook them. He narrowly escaped death but two of his close friends were buried, one of whom died. It was a shattering experience. When the mourning survivors got home, it occurred to me that the Prince, whose diary is crowded with hardly an hour to spare, now had a few days ahead of him with nothing planned. I talked to Andrew and we decided that I should ring up the Prince's private secretary and say how pleased we should be if the Prince would come to Chatsworth to do just what he liked – walk, talk, be with us or stay alone – and to our delight he accepted. It was during those days of slow recovery from shock and the death of his friend that I got to know him. Our friendship has lasted through good times and bad for both of us, and I value it more than I can say.

From the early 1990s my New York friend Jayne Wrightsman, the designer Oscar de la Renta and his wife, Annette, stayed with us every summer. As they always came at the same time of year, there was a limit to the variety of flowers that the Chatsworth head gardeners, Jim Link and later Ian Webster, could produce for the dining-room table. Good and spectacular though the rambler roses were, we soon got through Bobby James, Himalayan blush-pink and the like, so I tried chickens. A Buff Cochin cock was washed for the occasion and sat on some hay in one of the rectangular glass containers made many years ago for the batteries of the turbine house. He was a steady old fellow and made no objection to his new surroundings. A couple of hens of uncertain ancestry occupied another glass container and, as luck would have it, there had been a hatch of Welsummer and White Leghorn chicks that morning so just before dinner I put them in little china baskets lined with hay to keep them warm. The Paul Storr silver wine-coolers were filled with brown and white eggs, and our driver, Alan Shimwell, who was helping with the chicken side of things, slipped an egg into the so-called nest which held the two hens. Our efforts had the desired effect on our American guests, but the old Cochin cock remained unmoved by their loud reactions to his and his consorts' presence, and the chicks presumably thought it was all quite normal as they had only been alive for twelve hours.

The following year I had to think of something better. Piglets. The glass containers were pressed into service again and half a dozen piglets, replete from a long drink of milk from the sow, lay sound asleep on their straw beds in the middle of the dining-room table. The decoration did not last long. 'This really is too much,' said Andrew after the first course. 'Henry, take those pigs off the table.' So Margaret Norris, manager of the Chatsworth Farmyard, who had arranged the *mise-en-scène*, came back, packed up her beloved piglets and took them home to their mother. The following year there was no more livestock; I had done my best, but that was it. I resorted to Old Master drawings on miniature easels in front of each place, which I thought might appeal to our guests as both Jayne and Annette are the recognized backbone of the Metropolitan Museum, which goes in for that sort of thing. I do not believe the Raphaels, Rembrandts and Co. were splashed by gravy or ice cream, and after dinner they returned to their cold, unwelcoming, air-conditioned, thrice-locked shelves. I would rather be one of Margaret's piglets any day.

Entertaining is full of pitfalls. The Spanish Ambassador to London, Santiago de Tamarón, and his wife, Isabella, came to Chatsworth one summer weekend. Santiago is an admirer of Paddy Leigh Fermor – who he said was his reason for wanting to come to England – so we had a bond. He had given a memorable party for Paddy at the embassy where all Paddy's fans and would-be imitators recited, sang at the top of their voices and jostled for attention. Paddy himself was in Greece so we asked some other friends to meet the Tamaróns. I was about to introduce them to Isabella when my mind went blank. Her name had gone out of my head and, in a panic, I said, 'May I introduce you to . . . Mrs Thing?' Instead of leaving in a bait Isabella was amused. We have remained friends and she now signs herself 'Thing'.

I met the sculptress Elisabeth Frink when I was staying with Edward and Camilla Cazalet, old friends who live in Sussex. Army-bred, blue-eyed, beautiful and quick to laugh, Lis was not at all what I expected and had that larger-than-life personality that has to be felt rather than described. Some of it survives in her work and the pieces I love best are her animals – horses and dogs of such exceptional quality and character. The pick of the horses, I thought and still think, is *War Horse 1991*, which I fell for when I first saw it in plaster in her Dorset studio. I have always preferred heavy horses to thoroughbreds, Shires and Shetlands to racehorses, and here was the epitome of all I admire: tail plaited, ears back, head and eye giving warning that he is about to strike and bite. I wanted so much to see him at Chatsworth and knew where I would put him. After the usual hurdle of persuading the Trustees to buy him, *War Horse* arrived, as did his maker, keen to approve his situation and to supervise his installation. He had travelled in a horse box (what else) and was transferred to the bucket of a forklift truck that trundled through the garden, driven by Brian Gilbert, the precision expert. Brian could move a china war horse without damaging it and this bronze fellow presented no difficulty. Lis approved of the spot at the south end of the canal, facing out over the Old Park where his ancestors must have grazed. I was thrilled by the whole performance and by the fact that Chatsworth now possessed a monumental example of Lis's art. I too own a couple of her works, thanks to the sales of a book or two: dogs that are to the life.

Lis and I shared a love of poultry and she wrote to me one day telling me that her favourite cock, Reggie, had been unwell and that she had taken him to the vet. It conjured up such a picture: a distinguished Dame of the British Empire, Companion of Honour and Royal Academician, sitting, cock on lap, in the queue in the vet's waiting room. It was to no avail: Reggie died. Lis herself was already mortally ill when she came to see *War Horse* installed and, to my lasting regret, soon followed Reggie into the next world.

In all the years I lived in Derbyshire, Andrew and I went out to dinner in private houses only four times; in each case it was to a dinner given by the High Sheriff for the High Court judges when on Circuit in the county, one of the duties of the holder of that ancient office. Other dinners – civic, charitable, annual celebrations for clubs and associations, from Rotary and WI to golf – came thick and fast, but they were not held in private houses. We had what could be described as a 'full social life', both in London and with friends in the country, and when at home there was already too much to do without going out to dinner. Once in every fifteen years was enough.

One of these dinners stands out. It was at Calke Abbey, near Ticknall, in 1961 when Charles Harpur Crewe was High Sheriff of Derbyshire. Charles was a recluse who lived an intensely private life, in an intensely private house, in his own little kingdom hidden in a vast park in the south of Derbyshire. The dinner for the judges must have been a huge effort for him. Owing to an engagement in London, Andrew could not come, so I went alone. Full of curiosity as to what I should find, I put on my best evening dress and settled into the car to be driven to Ticknall on a damp November night with the prospect of fog.

After some forty miles, we reached the entrance to the park. There were no more white lines or cat's eyes; the secret road was the same colour as the dead grass, and the oaks, stricken with age, seemed to threaten my invading car. The fog swirled round us as we crawled along the seemingly endless drive, skirting uncomfortably close to ponds and avoiding ghostly fallow deer on the narrow twists and turns. I thought we were lost when, round a corner, a dim light appeared. The curtains were drawn back on the ground and first floors of Calke Abbey and the rooms were lit only by candles, something I had never seen in a house of that size before; not even oil lamps reinforced the flickering flames. The judges must have thought they had arrived in a fairy story. I certainly did.

I was led through the cold and stony hall, its walls decorated not with the usual antlers but with heads of Longhorn cattle, whose tapering horns nearly met over their muzzles and must have touched the ground when they had bent to graze, almost preventing their tongues from reaching the grass. How these cattle managed to eat I do not know. Our hosts consisted of Charles, his younger brother Henry and sister Airmyne. The dining-room table was set with more candles – the only light in that high-ceilinged room, which I imagine had not been used for years. The first course was melon; it was followed by cold beef; then melon for pudding.

After dinner Airmyne led the women guests back to the drawing room, leaving the men to their port. 'Would you like to see Nanny?' she whispered. I was flattered to be singled out for this honour and we set off up a magnificent flight of shallow, mahogany stairs, along a passage and through a bedroom door. I could just make out a tiny, ancient creature, curled up fast asleep in bed. Airmyne roused her. One eye opened and she just managed, 'Good evening.' We left her in peace and as we trekked back to the drawing room, Airmyne said, 'She was the Kaiser's Nanny' (presumably nanny to the Kaiser's son, Little Willie).

Airmyne had been kicked in the head by a re-mount at the Melton Mowbray cavalry depot at the beginning of the Second World War and Henry told me that she had a silver plate in her skull. The wretched accident had affected her personality and she was never quite the same again. She lived for the animals who were her friends: her horses, dogs and poultry, including a goose. 'Would you like to see the stables?' she said. Of course I would, with Airmyne for guide, but the judges were in court the next day and the fog was thickening. We returned to the drawing room, had a last talk with the other guests and set off home after the strangest evening I can remember.

Charles Harpur Crewe died suddenly in 1981. He was found in his beloved park, apparently setting mole traps. His brother Henry succeeded him and, in 1985, after complicated negotiations to raise the necessary capital endowment, he ceded Calke Abbey to the Treasury in settlement of death duties and it was handed on to the National Trust. The house is now open and the Trust has tried its best to preserve the spirit of the late owners. The clutter that filled the house from hall to attic, including a remarkable collection of natural history objects accumulated over centuries, is still there, and the four-poster state bed – a wedding present to the Fifth Baronet and Lady Caroline Manners from Princess Anne, daughter of George II – has been unpacked. (It had been in its packing cases since it arrived from London in 1734.)

Henry remained in a tiny part of the Abbey, which gave it a whiff of the past in the same way that Granny Evie did at Hardwick. Both ex-owners were treated as Exhibit A and visitors were thrilled to find them *in situ*. Henry gradually cast off his shyness and took to social life with enthusiasm. We met at all sorts of Derbyshire functions and his unexpected point of view on any subject was refreshing after what was often banal social chat. It was a joy to find him in Washington in 1985 when he accompanied the now-famous bed to the 'Treasure Houses of Great Britain' exhibition. I was with him when the art correspondents from serious American periodicals questioned him as to why the bed had never been unpacked. 'Oh, I don't know,' he said, 'I suppose they had something else to do.' A friend who was also present reminded me how worried the curator looked when I said, 'Do get into bed, Henry, just to show everyone that it is real.' The Harpur Crewe siblings were the only true eccentrics I have ever met. They have all gone now and with them the mystery; in spite of the Trust's best efforts, Calke Abbey is a lovely house containing an exhibition of curiosities but no Harpur Crewe among them.

21

LIVING ABOVE THE SHOP

It is a popular misconception that it was thanks to me that Chatsworth was 'saved'. It is not so. When my father-in-law died and the near-lethal blow of death duties had to be faced, it was Andrew who was determined to keep Chatsworth independent. He turned down overtures from the V&A and Manchester University, who wanted to buy the house and its contents, and he chaired all the meetings that were held to decide how best to pay the bill. He wanted it to stay as it had always been without adding a zoo or safari park. He was proved right and people come to walk, run, talk, shout, play games, bring their dogs and their children, picnic anywhere, and do what they like (the only private area is the Old Park to the south of the house, where the deer are allowed to calve undisturbed). I believe this freedom is one of the reasons that visitors love the place and I get letters from many people who tell me how peaceful and comforting they find Chatsworth. Even when there is a big crowd, you only have to walk a little way to be on your own, in tranquillity. The house itself has always drawn people, many of whom find it hard to believe that it could be anyone's home; a few come to see the works of art; all come in search of beauty, indoors and out, and most seem to find it.

I think that Andrew would have liked the public to see round the house for nothing, but he knew it was an impossible dream given the expense of its upkeep. In 1980, in order that Chatsworth could continue to be kept open to visitors, Andrew, Stoker and the family's legal advisers created a charitable foundation, the Chatsworth House Trust, whose object is 'the long-term preservation of Chatsworth for the benefit of the public'. An endowment fund was created from the sale of works of art from the private side of the house and from other family resources. The income from this trust fund goes towards the upkeep of the house, garden and park, which are the responsibility of the Council of Management of Chatsworth House Trust. (The first official position I had at Chatsworth was when I was invited to become a member of this council in 1981, thirty-one years after the death of my father-in-law.) In spite of the huge numbers of people coming to Chatsworth and latterly its satellites – the restaurant, farm shop and educational farmyard – it had to be bolstered by family money from other sources. The first year it ever paid for itself was in 2004, the year Andrew died, and he was rightly proud of his achievement.

Andrew had an instinct for what was right for the estates, and was always concerned for the people who worked at Chatsworth, as well as for its visitors. It was his idea, for example, to provide the much-used heated indoor swimming pool, tennis court and gymnasium for the staff. He insisted on a free car park at the south (Beeley) end of the park; he made access agreements with the local authorities for paths across the grouse moors, at Bolton Abbey as well as Chatsworth; and out of his own pocket, he provided electric buggies for the disabled to be able to drive on the paths through Chatsworth's 105-acre garden, and also up to the Strid, a narrow section of the River Wharfe two miles from Bolton Hall. He was always looking for ways to ensure the survival of Chatsworth. When it was realized that we had many regular visitors – not just numbers in a survey but people who had become well known to our staff – Andrew suggested the 'Friends of Chatsworth' scheme and it has been a success. In 2001, when the house had to delay opening for three weeks because of the threat of foot and mouth disease, it was his idea to try to make up some of the deficit by keeping the house open till 23 December with the public route decorated for Christmas. Most great houses in England are closed from November through March, and so I thought this would fail but I did as he asked. Thanks to the enthusiasm of the staff, it was – and is – a great draw, with people coming from all over the country to see it. It proved a great boon to the local hotels and guest houses. Andrew got many letters from the proprietors of these places, and even a bunch of flowers, in gratitude for providing them with customers at a dim time of year. It also pleased the Head of Retail at Chatsworth because it was pain and grief to her to see the place empty when other shops were having their best two months' trading of the year.

My own involvement started with Dorothy Dean, our housekeeper from 1968 to 1981, who was the first person to realize that people wanted to take something home from Chatsworth, a souvenir to remind them of their visit. We talked about it and she set out guidebooks, postcards, playing cards, matches and bonbons on a trestle table in the Orangery, a lofty glass-roofed room in the north wing of the house, and, after working all morning with the cleaners, she changed her clothes from housekeeper to shopkeeper and stood behind the table. Sales rose steadily and in 1978 she reported that the takings from the Orangery and a small kiosk in the garden selling plants and ice cream had enabled her to bank £75,000 that season. The Orangery Shop was on its way. Philip Jebb designed stalls in the shape of bookcases, which stood in a circle in the middle of the room around the enormous marble copy of the Medici vase. It all looked very pretty, but the space was almost immediately too small and the stalls were moved against the walls to make more room.

I loved the shop and often served behind the counter. I was so interested in what people wanted and why – shades of Muv's ambition to be the woman behind the till in a French restaurant. We printed better guidebooks, improved our range of postcards, laid in stocks of the ubiquitous tea towels, and out they all flew. We ordered various items with pictures of the house and its contents, an expensive outlay that took some persuading of the Management, of which I was not yet a part. The tinware, our most successful line, generated cash like nothing else. Why? Because the trays, bowls and tea-caddies were pretty, eye-catching, useful *and* were decorated with views of the house, painted by the artist Patricia Machin. The only drawback was the number we had to order at a time – the minimum quantity for trays, for example, was 20,000 – but each one we sold was a silent advertisement for Chatsworth, and worth far more to us than just its cash value. The trays became quite famous and sold through the General Trading Company and other London outlets; today they turn up in antique shops at many times their original price.

We introduced a line of knitted garments made from the wool of the Jacob Sheep that grazed in the park. People were intrigued by these four-horned creatures (even the ewes sport this decoration) and snapped up

the brown-and-cream coloured jerseys, hats, scarves and gloves until demand exceeded supply. One of the knitters became so obsessed with her
work, knitting all day and most of the night, that she lost track of the patterns. Garments of the strangest proportions appeared, either too long or
too short or with sleeves a mile long and little else. She was a 'case' and I
knew that if we stopped taking her work, it might tip her over the edge,
so we gave up the hand-knitted garments and turned to other wares.

We commissioned porcelain manufacturers to make a few items of
exceptional quality, also decorated with pictures of the house, and expensive reproductions of seventeenth-century delftware tulip vases at
Chatsworth. While these were still for sale they provided high-quality
decoration for the shop and even though they were the most expensive
items, they did eventually go (you have to sell many postcards to gener-
ate the same turnover). At the other end of the scale, for ten pence
children could buy colouring-in sheets showing scenes of Chatsworth
and the Duchess of Devonshire's Ball of 1897. In a quiet way the Orangery Shop became well known and in 1983 we engaged a professional
manageress. For some years I went to the Birmingham and Harrogate gift
fairs, but I soon discovered that our trusted buyers, sisters Sue and Jane
Brindley, liked the same things as I did, so I gave up, knowing their eyes
would work better than mine.

In the 1960s and early 70s, I received many letters from teachers asking
for information to give to their pupils about our farms and woods. The
teachers themselves were often ignorant about farming practices, knowing little about the use of common arable crops, for example, let alone
about the animals they saw out of the bus window. I was aware of the
growing division between town and country and wanted to do something about it. We thought long and hard and decided to convert the
disused building-yard near the house into a farmyard, so that children
could see cattle, sheep and free-range hens close up – just the opposite
of a safari park.

When the educational Farmyard became reality and not just a dream,
it grabbed my attention as a new baby would have done and I spent hours
there, trying to get it all right. I feel pleased that today about 200,000
people, mostly children, come to enjoy and, I hope, to learn from it every

year. It was not designed to be a collection of pets but to show the un-sentimental facts about the life cycle of commercial farm stock. Life-size diagrams of butchers' cuts are pinned up in the pigsties and cattle yard, in case there is any doubt as to the animals' fate.

The Farmyard opened in 1973 with pigs, goats and a Shire horse, as well as the unavoidable lavatories and tea shop. Before tractors, Shires were the only source of power on the land and (except for steam engines that did the threshing before combine harvesters took over) Andrew's grandfather's stud was famous. There is great excitement when our Shire mare is about to foal; she has obliged several times with a daytime birth and this is watched with fascination by all. The daily highlight, however, is the milking demonstration. The cows are milked, one at a time and sideways on – the better to show the operation – in front of an incredu-lous young audience. Watching the children watching the milking is bet-ter than any theatre; they remain riveted to the spot until a teacher or parent insists on moving them on. I asked one little boy from a school in the middle of Sheffield what he thought of this performance. 'It's the most disgustin' thing I've ever seen,' he said, vowing never to touch milk again.

We then began to hold Open Days in the park for children and teach-ers. The men from Elm Tree Farm, an arable farm seventeen miles from Chatsworth, brought bundles of half-grown wheat, barley, oilseed rape and potatoes. Few teachers and even fewer children could guess from the leaves which crop was which. The keepers from Chatsworth brought their dogs, guns and a batch of pheasant chicks with their surrogate mothers: broody hens. There were displays of clay-pigeon shooting; some of the teachers tried their hand at it (against the law now, no doubt) and I imagine some of the children would have liked to have a go too – at the teachers. Shepherds and their sheepdogs showed off their skills; it was before *One Man and His Dog* had become so popular on television, but our audience loved it. Foresters were there to explain that trees are a crop and, like other crops, have to be planted, weeded, thinned and eventually harvested – in other words cut down. 'What? *You cut down trees?*' said a furious teacher, who had been brought up to think it a crime. The children were interested in the giant saws and watched David Rob-inson, a born teacher himself, climbing a tree in the harness used by tree surgeons. Afterwards, teachers and children all piled into their buses and went back to their built-up surroundings, but we hoped that a little of what they had seen had rubbed off. I felt that if they understood that the very grass they walked on was a crop, then we had gone a little way towards explaining the use of the land.

If the aim of the Farmyard was educational, the aim of the Farm Shop was purely commercial. Agriculture was in the dumps and I feared for the future of the in-hand farm at Chatsworth and for the men who worked on it. Both were an integral part of the whole. The idea of a farm shop came to me during the Royal Smithfield Club's conference in Buxton in 1972; I was listening to the farmers and butchers and it occurred to me that selling our farm produce direct to the public might help change the farm accounts from red to black. This was long before the public at large had started taking an interest in local food, but instinct told me that the same people who came to Chatsworth to walk in the fresh air and enjoy the glorious landscape would also be attracted by the idea of buying beef and lamb straight from our farm. No doubt too in the back of my mind were memories of Muv's poultry farm of long ago, of her passion for fresh, wholesome fare, and Uncle Geoffrey's campaign for 'unmurdered food – nothing added and nothing taken away'. The Smithfield farmers and butchers, acknowledged experts in the livestock and meat for which these islands are renowned, not only became lasting friends but were also gen-erous with their advice. 'You'll sell all the fillet steak and be left with the forequarters,' they cautioned, and warned of other pitfalls of the trade that they had learned the hard way.

I presented my idea to the Trustees of the Chatsworth Settlement, who did not take me seriously. It was depressing to be met with a no. After years of death duties and debts, the estate office staff seemed to be suffering from inertia; 'anything for a quiet life' was their motto and new ideas were looked on with suspicion. 'We are an agricultural estate,' the land agent explained to me, 'with village property, minerals and woods, and that is what we understand. We have no experience in retailing food.' I was aware of all this but did not give up. I knew that nostalgia for the past was a big attraction for the visitors who came to the house and that the same 'feel' would entice people to a farm shop. Tears at home and arguments elsewhere eventually won the day and we set about getting planning permission.

Andrew wanted the winter months when the house was closed to be quiet, so the only suitable building was the Stud Farm at nearby Pils-ley, which was built in 1910 for Victor Duke's Shire horse stallions. Planning permission seemed to take for ever but finally, in 1976, we were granted permission to market produce from the Chatsworth farm and from our tenant farmers. We were allowed to sell freezer packs of meat only, the smallest quantity of beef being one-eighth of a beast, and half of a pig or lamb. We made sausages in a second-hand machine, sold game, including venison, in season, and the arable farm supplied potatoes and flour.

I wanted the shop to be the opposite of a shiny, American-style supermarket with wire shelving and to look like a rough and ready farm outbuilding, with shelves of thick wooden planks and as little metal as possible. Refrigerators do not make tempting showcases, but we had to have some (more is the pity) and I wanted the service to be human and friendly. All went well for a time, then demand dropped, the shop began to lose money and the Trustees said it would have to close unless it turned to profit within a few months. It was saved by Jean-Pierre Béraud, the whirlwind French chef who came to cook at Chatsworth in 1978 and who took over the Farm Shop in 1984.

Jean-Pierre was a born entrepreneur as well as a marvellous chef, but putting him in charge was something of a risk as he could speak little English, did not know the difference between a pound and a kilo and once told me that he had sacked a waitress because he could see from the way she walked that she was no good. He used to storm into my room without warning and sound off loud criticisms of the estate office and anyone who stood in his path. But Chatsworth, and I, never had a better friend. He rescued the dying Farm Shop by installing a kitchen and selling cooked (value-added) food and soon made his presence felt further afield. Cooking demonstrations have become popular and we recently had a visit from Claire Macdonald from the Isle of Skye. She has a glowing reputation as a cook and is a first-rate demonstrator. To the surprise of our audience, she was generous with the double cream and there were mutterings about health risks and cost. 'Well,' she said, 'they sell skimmed milk in my supermarket but I couldn't look a cow in the face if I bought that.' Excellent woman.

If I say the Chatsworth Farm Shop was the first of its kind, I shall get a hundred letters saying, 'No, we were', but it was certainly ahead of the game and is still a leading player. In 2004, the year of Andrew's death, it employed 48 full-time and 52 part-time staff, the turnover was just short of £5 million and it had won many awards. The Farm Shop, like the Orangery, slowly changed from a cottage industry to a serious business, thereby losing much of its charm for me. I prefer the WI way of people making jam, marmalade, bread and cakes in their own kitchens, supplying eggs from their own hens, and knitting garments from a herd of Jacob Sheep. I despair at the current regimentation, the wild rules over hygiene and the insidious and, to my mind, dishonest practice of 'Own Label', which gives the false impression that goods are made on the premises when in fact they come from a factory that supplies the same product to many other shops. There seems to be no way of going back to giving real food, made by real people, to the public on a large scale; it is thought to be too dangerous.

Until 1975, the catering at Chatsworth was a cold water tap by the lodge, now relabelled 'Water for Dogs'. I tentatively suggested to Dennis Fisher, the comptroller, that we should try to offer something more like tea to our visitors. He answered that it would be unpopular with the owners of the tea shops in nearby villages, who relied on the custom of our visitors. And, anyhow, where would we put it? I retreated, but demand was persistent and I eventually made an amateurish attempt to please visitors by persuading some of the local ladies to serve tea, coffee and cake in the stables, where the customers were squashed together in the old horse stalls, perched on iron-hard benches. It pleased nobody and we had to do better. Jean-Pierre came to the rescue again; we invested in some second-hand equipment and he and his staff set up their kitchen underneath the hayracks. Jean-Pierre never allowed anything to be fried, so we were spared the High Street smells, and I am happy to say his edict still holds.

The ever-higher expectations of our visitors began to make us look for a way to expand the restaurant and in 1986 Philip Jebb produced plans for a new building incorporating the old game larder, which was built in 1910 to hang up to four thousand pheasants and was a short distance from the entrance to the house. Chatsworth is a Grade 1 listed building, in a Grade 1 listed park, which itself is in a National Park. All plans had to be approved in advance and they were first submitted to the local planners, who, seeking support, referred our case to a higher authority, the Royal Fine Arts Commission. So Jean-Pierre, Bob Getty (the clerk of works), Derrick Penrose (the land agent) and I went to plead our case to the Commission, which was chaired by our old friend

Norman St John-Stevas. It was an odd experience. We were not asked to sit down, so we stood like children awaiting a beating from the headmaster. And we got it: permission was refused. 'Have another look at the stable block,' they said. Andrew and I were angry with all concerned, and I still have the formal typed letter from Lord St John refusing us permission. (At the bottom, out of sight of the typist, he has added 'With love from Norman' and three kisses.)

The stable block at Chatsworth was designed in about 1760 by the architect James Paine for the Fourth Duke of Devonshire. Philip, Jean-Pierre, Bob and I explored every nook and cranny of this magnificent building, from the blacksmith's shop and brew house to the horse stalls, loose boxes and harness room. The Victorian carriage house, added by the Sixth Duke in the 1830s, was a possibility but did not look inviting: it was being used as a garage and housed all sorts of cars and clutter, including the Yellow Peril, Victor Duke's 1914 Humber. There was a glass-roofed area where cars were washed, and the pools of oil on the floor in the main building reminded me of Rutland Gate Mews. It took a great deal of imagination to picture what it could become, but my colleagues had that ability in spades and when we were satisfied that we had solved all practical difficulties regarding the kitchens, cold rooms, prep rooms, washing up, heating, lighting, lavatories, delivery space and rubbish disposal, we put in for planning permission again. This time it was granted.

The arches of the covered ride, originally an exercise track for the horses in bad weather, were glazed in so people could sit and eat in comfort. Heavy chains were hung between the pillars to stop too many noses being broken on the new glass. Bobby Jones, far and away the most skilled in his profession, tiled the walls of the ladies' lavatories with camellias and the gents' with horses. It won a Loo of the Year award and Jean-Pierre and I went to London to receive it from a minister, which we found very pleasing. I had to admit the planners were right: the stables would never again be neglected, their new role was too important for the comfort of our visitors. The conversion of the Carriage House Restaurant was finished to our entire satisfaction in 1991, a year ahead of schedule and within budget. Swallowing what was left of our pride, we asked Lord St John to open it.

•

The Peacock Inn in Baslow – so called because it had once belonged to the Duke of Rutland whose family emblem is a peacock – came in-hand in 1972. It was run down and needed a complete overhaul. The Chatsworth Trustees decided to refurbish it to a high standard and Philip Jebb was invited to redesign the hotel so that the bedrooms should all face south over the home farm. I worked closely with him and, when the time came, it was my responsibility to decide on decoration and furnishing, which I did with pleasure, using furniture in store at Chatsworth. Perhaps I was given the job because I had done up Chatsworth itself when we went to live there and was thought capable, and perhaps also because I did not cost the Trustees a penny. Had I not done it, they would have had to employ a professional decorator, which would have been a shock to their system. (When we added ten new bedrooms to the inn in 1986, there was more budget trouble, and I had to go for the cheapest materials scoured from wholesale shops north of Oxford Street.) Eric Marsh took the lease when it opened in 1975 as the Cavendish Hotel and he still runs it thirty-five years later. Under his aegis the hotel has thrived, largely patronized by people who come to see Chatsworth.

The enlargement of the Devonshire Arms at Bolton Abbey in 1982 was a bigger project and produced an unexpected bonus for me, Chatsworth and, I hope, for John and Christine Thompson. Christine was one of three people who answered my advertisement for someone to make the curtains and loose covers for the furniture. The applicants brought samples of their work to the interviews and hers were the best. She carried out the job to everyone's satisfaction, on time and on budget, and a few months after the hotel was finished, I got a letter from Christine saying that if we needed four willing hands at Chatsworth – John Thompson was a French polisher and could turn his hand to anything – they would be interested. 'I'm thirty-five years old and I'll work for you for twenty-five years, then I'll retire,' said Christine. A woman of her word, that is what happened – except that she and John completed twenty-six years.

In 1980 Andrew got a letter from Tom Harvey, an old friend who lived in Norfolk, whose wife, Mary Coke, a daughter of Lord Leicester, had been brought up at Holkham Hall. Tom said that the Country Fair at Holkham was extremely successful and suggested that we should hold one along the same lines at Chatsworth. Andrew passed me Tom's letter, saying, 'This is more up your street than mine.' Tom introduced me to Andrew Cuthbert, who was in charge of the team of volunteers who ran the Fair, and my Andrew agreed to give it a try. When our first Country Fair opened the next year there was something for everyone. You could buy gumboots, gloves, garlic and guns, fishing tackle, ferrets, fudge and frocks from the best shops from all over the country. In successive years there were massed pipe and military bands from the Household Cavalry, the Gurkhas, and the Royal Horse Artillery with their horse-drawn gun carriages, as well as terrier and ferret racing, clay-pigeon shooting, archery and sheepdog trials.

The Fair was a success from the start and has become an increasingly popular annual event. Its appeal is twofold: it attracts people from the industrial conurbations surrounding Chatsworth, as well as country people who enjoy fishing, shooting and hunting; and it is a rendezvous for those whose livelihoods depend on country sports. Andrew Cuthbert, who retired in 2002, was indefatigable. I used to look out of my window at daybreak and see him, hours before anyone else turned up, marking out the positions of the various tents and tracks. Thanks to him and his team of Red Socks (worn for instant identification) the Country Fair not only makes a major financial contribution to the upkeep of Chatsworth but also creates an immeasurable dollop of goodwill between Chatsworth and its public.

In 1956 we had followed Badminton and Burghley in staging annual horse trials in the park. Horse trials had become so popular and their calendar so crowded that a date was difficult to find, but early October was eventually chosen. The competitors and spectators loved the course, with its steep hills and turf that had never been ploughed, and all went well till 1988 when, at the end of the first day, a mighty storm devastated the tents and the ground was flooded. Dragging out the heavy vehicles ruined the look of the park and, as it was so late in the year, it took many months for the ground to recover. Regretfully the trials were cancelled, but in 1999 Stoker's wife, Amanda, who is devoted to the sport, reinstated them, the same year she won the three-day event at Badminton with Jaybee, ridden by Ian Stark. With Amanda's experience and support to ensure its success, this event now takes place at Chatsworth in May and once again horse-trial followers come to enjoy this demanding test of horse and rider.

In the early 1980s my friend the designer David Mlinaric told me that several of his clients had been looking without success for classic garden furniture of the kind found in old established gardens. There were several highly skilled joiners at Chatsworth, as well as the enthusiastic Bob Getty, so we thought we would try our hand at making some. Many of the models sought after by the new generation of garden owners were to be found in J. P. White's early-twentieth-century *Catalogue of Garden Furniture*. We chose a selection of sturdy, unassuming benches, which would look good in gardens from Northumberland to Cornwall, and took a stand at the annual RHS Chelsea Flower Show.

I loved selling and for each of the twenty-one years that we went to Chelsea, I was on our stall Tuesday, Wednesday, Thursday and Friday, and got to know the showground, exhibitors and organizers well. Garden designers favoured our products and we exported them to the United States, France, Switzerland and Ireland. Our carpenters' workmanship was second to none and we soon had designs of our own, some copied from seats at Chatsworth and one from the popular wheelbarrow seat at Mount Congreve, reproduced with the permission of Ambrose Congreve, whose County Waterford garden has a grove of pink magnolias as tall as forest trees.

The largest seat of all was the 'Chiswick', a faithful copy of what must surely have been a William Kent design for Chiswick Villa. Copies by new manufacturers, light-heartedly named the 'Lutyens', are flimsy ghosts of the real thing. The Kent design was a much sturdier, long-lasting version of extreme beauty with rounded arms and slatted back. Our best sellers were classic plant tubs with fibreglass linings to hold large shrubs. We also did well meeting the revived fashion for wooden lavatory seats, whose middles we made into cheeseboards. We supplemented these products with items from the Orangery Shop. The Chatsworth tin trays flew off the stand – handing them over was like feeding the birds. The shop staff from Chatsworth came to help, as did Bob Getty and Wendy Coleman from the building-yard office. Alan Shimwell was invaluable, carrying boxes of trays from the car park till the string nearly cut off his fingers.

One year our stand was opposite a sandwich bar and a trail of old women, seeing somewhere to sit at last, plonked themselves down on our expensive benches, making it impossible for customers to look, measure and ponder. I had not the heart to move them on, but I was pleased that the sandwich bar had gone the following year. Nicko Henderson came to help on the stall, giving the Chatsworth staff a chance to go round the show. He put on the blue apron, tied at the neck and waist, which we all wore. Several people who had served under him in one or other of his embassies glanced at the tall figure in the apron, could not believe their eyes, walked on, came back to make sure and, still astonished, stayed for a chat. He was a brilliant salesman, but when we checked the pockets of his apron at the end of the day, his inexperience as a shop assistant was exposed and we found hundreds of pounds of forgotten tray money in notes and coins that he had thrown with his apron into the laundry pile as he left.

It is pleasing to look back at our successes, but there were failures as well. Chatsworth Food, a company selling jams, chutneys, biscuits and cakes, which were supposed to make Chatsworth's fortune, was a dismal flop. The management was useless and it quickly went out of business. One good thing came out of it for me, however: Helen Marchant. I did not have a secretary till 1986, when the secretary for Chatsworth Food worked part-time for me. By then the piles of paper on the floor of my little sitting room were toppling. When the business failed and she left, I moved my piles of paper to the ground-floor flower room, where it was easier for people to find me, and began to pester Helen, who was Andrew's secretary, for help with some typing. I was deeply appreciative of Helen's help – and still am.

The most expensive failure was the Chatsworth Farm Shop in Elizabeth Street, in London's Belgravia. It started with a bang. I took a cockerel on a lead to welcome the Prince of Wales, who had kindly agreed to open the shop, but in spite of this and a daily crowd of customers, the cost of twice-weekly vans taking the meat and other specialities 160 miles from Pilsley to London and back, as well as the difficulty of finding reliable staff, were too great. The shop lost money and sadly had to close.

Few people realize how a house like Chatsworth, the land and the people who live on it are interdependent. Families, some of whom had been with the Cavendishes for generations, were traditionally able to find jobs as disparate as butchers, housemaids, gamekeepers, seamstresses, accountants or librarians – all with the same employer. In the nineteenth century Joseph Paxton, who came to Chatsworth at the age of twenty-three as head gardener, developed skills under the generous patronage of the Sixth Duke that later allowed him to become an MP, director of the railways and the designer of the Crystal Palace. In the twentieth century, Tom Wragg, the Edensor school master's son, became keeper of the collection; Sean Feeney, the smiling butcher whose health prevented him standing for long hours, got a job as a river bailiff. Everyone knew that an effort would be made to accommodate people's needs – something that was seldom possible for other big employers. This created a 'family' atmosphere which I have never met elsewhere. To me it was spoiling, because starting with new people is something I find difficult. Luckily this seldom happened at Chatsworth; most of the old people remained till they retired and were usually replaced – sparing the bother of advertising – by the next-in-line from their department.

22

DISTRACTIONS

Life at Chatsworth seemed to leave hardly a moment unoccupied, but thanks chiefly to the wonderful staff, my role there was flexible, and hobbies could be fitted in as well as friends. There was often no defining line between work and other interests, and sometimes one of the organizations connected to a hobby would ask me to become involved in an official way. When this happened there was a danger that what had once been fun would become work and, however enjoyable, would pin me down and I would have to sit at a table listening to everyone mumbling their thoughts. The Bakewell Show was an example. My sisters-in-law and I looked forward keenly to the Thursday after August Bank Holiday. We entered our ponies without a thought of winning and loved every moment of the parade of cattle, sheep, goats, Shire horses, hunters and successful children's ponies. When I was asked to join the committee, it became work; I still enjoyed the Show but it was different.

I have nevertheless been lucky in my life to be able to pursue several interests purely for pleasure. In middle life, grouse shooting ruled the month of August, and pheasant shooting much of November, December and January. I loved all that went with a shoot: the reunion of friends, seeing a new bit of country or finding the same patch of dying leaves beneath my feet, well remembered from the year before. Drive fifty miles in this country and you find different crops, different stone and different voices. Even the BBC has not succeeded in levelling out the latter and listening to the beaters you know if you are in Derbyshire or Devon, Somerset or Sussex, Aberdeen or Anglesey. I liked the battle with the weather, the layers of clothes and the discovery of Derri boots, after which I never had cold feet again. I loved the company of the loader – as long as he made no comment on my shooting. Alan Shimwell, who has done nearly sixty years' service at Chatsworth, both on the farm and in the garden, as well as thirty-three years of chauffeuring, never said a word as chance after chance flew over our heads with nothing to show for it. He was the perfect companion on the long car drives and so popular with our hosts that my theory was that one day they would say to me, 'Don't you bother to come next year, let's just have Alan.'

A shoot is bait for persuading people to travel a long way for a winter weekend. When I had had enough practice for friends to realize I was not intent on murdering their other guests, they invited me to shoot. An annual treat was Keir, Bill Stirling's Perthshire home, where we some-times had five days' shooting on the trot, a sporting highlight that became known as The Festival. The same team of guns gathered every year, with Bill's sons, Archie and Johnny, representing the younger generation. The same old jokes were repeated – we would have resented any new ones. General Sir George Collingwood, Royal Artillery, was part of The Festi-val scene, as was Lord Sefton, the legendary Lancastrian owner of Crox-teth in Liverpool and Abbeystead in the Forest of Bowland. Collingwood was not a good shot and after a drive in which he had failed to distin-guish himself, Lord Sefton said with mock scorn, 'Call yourself a gun-ner?' One icy morning our convoy was driving along a main road with a nasty drop on the left. Archie's Land Rover skidded and landed upside down in the field below. His father saw it happen and drove on. 'The stupid boy will be late for the first drive,' is all he muttered. Of such were the Stirlings made. Bill's brother David has gone down in history for founding the Special Air Service, and when Bill led the 2nd Special Air Service Regiment, the SAS was known as 'Stirling and Stirling'.

After two or three days, Bill, who was the most restless man I have ever known, would disappear to Greece, Abu Dhabi or wherever his business interests took him, and we carried on without him. The head keeper at Keir was Jimmy Miller. He was as square as a wrestler (which he was in his spare time) and I would not have liked to meet him on a dark night if I were up to no good, but as a guest of Bill's I could do no wrong. When Archie was about ten and at a loose end in the holidays, he said to Jimmy, 'Shall we go to the cinema this afternoon?' 'Nature is the best cinema, Mr Archie,' came the reply.

Through Ann Fleming, I got to know Sybil Cholmondeley. The second time we met she said, 'I believe you are fond of shooting, would you like to come to Houghton in December?' I would. Sybil was already old, but brimful of energy, opinions and brilliance. She was born Sassoon and she and her brother Philip were of Middle Eastern origin, which gave them a touch of the exotic. A product of pre–First World War Paris and London, Sybil had acted as her father's hostess from the age of seventeen and her upbringing had given her the impeccable manners of her generation and kind. I have seen her sitting bolt upright, in apparently rapt attention, being talked at by a thumping bore. She was an example to us all.

After marriage in 1913 to the Marquess of Cholmondeley, Sybil took on Houghton Hall, the magnificent eighteenth-century Norfolk house built for Sir Robert Walpole. Rock Cholmondeley, who was beautiful looking – and aware of it – was a sportsman, soldier, landowner and hereditary Lord Great Chamberlain. He was not fond of social life and as Sybil was of a generation of women who arranged their lives around their husbands, they did not invite many people to stay. Sybil took to country life, learned about the farms, woods and the people who looked after them, and soon joined Rock in the excellent shooting the estate provided. It was unusual for a woman to shoot in the 1930s but Sybil quickly became proficient, as she did in everything that interested her.

I had never seen Houghton before and, like everyone else, was knocked sideways by its unique beauty and by the Cholmondeleys themselves. The approach to the house is past rows of white estate cottages, through a display of white iron gates by a white lodge and into the park; more white comes as ghostly fallow deer pass to and fro under the great oaks. William Kent's opulent rooms were the ideal background for Sybil. On an easel in the sitting room, which was hung with yellow silk, was Holbein's *Lady with a Squirrel*. In the room next door, Oudry's *White Duck* overlooked the French furniture that Sybil described in a throwaway line as 'My brother Philip's things, the best of their kind'. The portraits of her mother and herself by Sargent and one of her by William Orpen ('Old Orps' she called him) positively glowed. Whatever she said was made important by her precise enunciation and clipped tones, lips closing on the last word and often followed by a laugh. When talking one day of diminishing congregations in country churches, she said, 'The trouble is that they don't understand what "verily verily" means.' You soon got to know who 'our neighbours' were: the royal family at Sandringham. The Queen Mother told me that one evening after dining with the said neighbours, Sybil looked for her sable coat in the hall. 'Where's my weasel?' she said to a bemused footman.

I was the only guest on that first visit – the other guns were local Norfolk farming friends – and I felt honoured to be there. We set off in a white Land Rover to see country unknown to me but which was to become familiar over the years. An east wind straight from Russia can make waiting in a field of frozen plough uncomfortable, but at Houghton there were no long waits because the pheasants were wild and got up as soon as the beaters entered the woods – unlike reared birds that are apt to flush. Sybil was impervious to wind or rain and wore a miserable little pair of short gumboots. 'Naval issue,' she announced proudly (she had helped to found the WRNS during the First World War and rose to be a much respected Commander during the Second). She knew the army of beaters by name and fully appreciated their efforts, which involved tramping through wet kale up to their waists, to provide the sport she loved. Like all well-mannered hosts she was often the 'walking gun', dealing with the birds that fly back over the beaters. She shot with a pair of 16-bore 'over and unders' (instead of the gun barrels being parallel, or 'side-by-side', they were above and below), and she missed few. I was impressed and remained so every time I saw her in action.

Sybil came to Chatsworth to shoot, complete with loader, guns and heavy luggage. She went up to change for dinner but could not find her jewel box. There was a frantic search. Where could it be? It transpired that the box was so big and heavy that the pantry staff had mistaken it for her cartridge case and taken it to the gunroom. Andrew asked her what she would like for breakfast, always plentiful before a cold winter's day in the open air: 'I like lifting the lids,' was the answer.

I was visiting a friend in King Edward VII hospital one day and as I was leaving an ambulance drew up. I stepped aside for the stretcher to go in and realized its burden was Sybil. She had broken an ankle tripping up in her hurry to answer the telephone. 'Stay and talk,' she said, so I followed the stretcher into her room. A nurse with a clipboard came to take her details. 'Hello,' she said breezily. Not used to being addressed in the modern manner with such familiarity, Sybil gave a withering look and said, 'What is all this HELLO?' and dismissed the nurse with, 'I will ring when my friend has gone.'

•

Andrew's family had been connected to the Sport of Kings for centuries and racing was one of his great loves. I had been passionately interested when I was growing up but the reality of owning a racehorse was different from my dreams as a sixteen-year-old and I never saw the point of it. Had the stud been at Chatsworth, it would have been a different story and we would have known the horses since they were foals. As it was, they were bought, trained and sent to stud by A. N. Other. It was remote control and therefore not attractive to me, though of course I understood the thrill for Andrew whenever he had a winner, and I still keep a keen interest in the progeny of Bachelor Duke and Compton Place, two of his horses that were good enough to stand as stallions.

Race meetings were part of the social round which we both enjoyed. In 1948, and again in 1950 and 1953, we were invited to stay at Windsor Castle for the Royal Meeting at Ascot. During those bleak post-war years, these visits were the most cheering days I can remember. It is uplifting to see something arranged and carried out to perfection, down to the most minute detail. The invitation was for five nights (Monday to Saturday) and four days' racing. The weather is always a gamble and had to be taken into consideration, but somehow four daytime outfits for the races and five best evening dresses were gathered up.

Andrew and I were allocated a bedroom, dressing room and even a sitting room looking out over the Long Walk – the straight double avenue of trees that leads to the famous copper horse. The day's plans and the times when we had to be ready were typed out and left on our writing table each morning – all very helpful in an unfamiliar world. The welcome and 'putting at ease' by the ladies-in-waiting and equerries made everything immediately enjoyable. One year I had not been well and was allowed breakfast in bed. The tray was as big as a table and apparently made of cast iron – a knee-breaker – but the exquisite set of china and the delicious things on it reminded me that it was old-fashioned and therefore desirable. A band played under our window every morning and also in the room next to the drawing room where we sat (or rather stood) in the early evenings.

The drawing rooms were brilliantly decorated with lashings of gold leaf and the furniture, which was upholstered in bright green in one room and bright red in the next, was polished to such a degree that it nearly outshone the guests and their diamonds. The King and Queen and the Princesses Elizabeth and Margaret were the last to enter so there was plenty of time to gaze at the scarlet, six-foot-high standard fuchsias growing in Sèvres tubs. There were about twenty-four guests at dinner and the King and Queen sat opposite each other in the middle of the long table. If an owner or trainer had a winner whilst a guest at the castle, it was traditional for him or her to say a few words after dinner. Jeremy Tree, who was successful from the start of his career as a trainer, turned out a winner and was so worried about having to speak that he was unable to eat a morsel, most unusually for him – as his figure showed. The superb china plates followed by gold ones were whisked away from him as clean as they arrived. But his speech passed off well and I expect he had double helpings for breakfast the next morning.

On our second visit to Windsor, I found sitting next to the King at dinner a rather difficult and frightening experience. No doubt because of frustration at his increasing frailty, his mood was uncertain and at one point he banged his fist on the table so hard that the glasses trembled, and so did I, thinking I had said or done something wrong. The Queen, opposite, gave me reassuring glances. No doubt the King's anger was a symptom of his illness, the cancer about which we knew nothing. It must have been an ordeal for him to sit through all those dinners and if we had been told how unwell he was, we would have understood the outburst.

To be driven in a carriage as part of the procession down the race-course at Ascot was a fascinating experience. As well as the obvious fun of it – the jockey's-eye view of the course and the intoxicating smell of horse and harness – it had an unexpected side. We were taken by car through the park from Windsor Castle to join the carriages. Trotting down the narrow lanes to reach the racecourse, our route was lined with on-lookers who, I imagine, had no idea that whatever they said could be heard by the occupants of the carriages: 'Doesn't she look awful in that hat?' 'Who's *he*?' as well as admiring words for the Queen. When it was our turn to drive between the lines of critics, there was an audible 'Ohhh', a groan of disappointment when they realized that all the royals had passed and they were left with a few unknowns, not even a movie star.

Some forty years later Stoker was made Her Majesty's Representative at Ascot, the senior of three Trustees appointed by the Queen and directly responsible to her for the management of the racecourse. I stayed with Stoker and Amanda in the house that goes with the job, just behind the stands. It looks like nothing from the outside – it could well be offices – but inside it has an old-fashioned, charming air. You can see at once that it is the lodgings of people devoted to racing and to Ascot in particular: the hooks on the wall for hanging hats are widely spaced to allow for top hats, and it is furnished with excellent sporting pictures, comfortable sofas and a dining room where those in charge can entertain. There was an interesting hole in one of the carpets, which I noticed getting a little larger every year. I was always pleased to see it: replacing the carpet was not high in the Ascot authority's budget. Stoker took me round the private boxes used by the most prosperous owners. These were decorated in a way new to me, with walls covered in a loose backing on which hung rows of waterproof pockets. Once the florists had finished filling these, the walls were solid with lilies, roses and other midsummer blooms – the last word in sweet-smelling luxury – and they looked like extravagant chintz. It was as entertaining to see these preparations as to watch the racing itself – the best horses in the world competing for the glory of winning (as well as for prize money).

On Epsom Derby Day, racing affects the English public across the board – as the old saying goes, 'All men are equal on the turf and under it.' Four-in-hand coaches and gypsies with their coloured horses join open double-decker buses in the jostling crowds. When the Derby was run on a Wednesday, things seemed to come to a full stop in government and elsewhere, and anyone who could headed for Epsom. Andrew's cousin Betty Salisbury (married to Bobbety, who joined his House of Lords colleagues at Epsom) was not a regular racegoer. In 1968, when the American-owned horse Sir Ivor won, a friend asked her if she had seen Sir Ivor. 'Sir Ivor who?' she said. There was a long walk from the members' enclosure to the paddock, all of it in full view of what is called 'the general public'. I often thought that when the Queen and the royal family walked down to the paddock they were as close to their sporting subjects as they would ever be, drawn together by a shared enthusiasm for racing (today the paddock is immediately behind the stands). One year when Uncle Harold, the popular Minister of Housing at the time, and Aunt Dorothy were walking to the paddock, the crowd seemed extraordinarily vociferous in their welcome, clapping and cheering him all the way. He took off his top hat and smiled at these devoted supporters. What he did not know was that immediately behind him were the newly wed Aly Khan and Rita Hayworth.

In 1965 Andrew achieved his ambition of owning a top-class horse. Park Top had cost five hundred guineas as a yearling when she was bought by Andrew's friend and trainer, Bernard van Cutsem, for another of his owners. The owner thought the filly too cheap and decided he did not want her, so Bernard offered her to Andrew – a proof, if proof were needed, of the part played by luck in racing. Andrew had to be patient; Park Top did not run as a two-year-old, but Bernard saw a future for her and she went on to be a successful three-, four- and five-year-old, winning the Coronation Cup at Epsom, the Hardwicke Stakes, the Ribblesdale Stakes and the King George VI and Queen Elizabeth Stakes at Ascot, among other important races, as well as coming second in the Prix de l'Arc de Triomphe.

Andrew's book, *Park Top: A Romance of the Turf*, which was published in 1976, revealed as much about him as it did about the mare. The ease and speed with which he wrote it were amazing: he went to a hotel in the north of Scotland for a weekend and came back with the manuscript as good as finished. In 2003, when he began work on his memoirs – drawn from notes he had made over a period of twenty years – it was a different story. He was unwell and found it difficult to concentrate for more than an hour or so at a time. Had it not been for Helen Marchant, who persuaded him to produce a little more each day, and his publisher, Michael Russell, *Accidents of Fortune* would have fizzled out unfinished. As it was, his two helpers were in constant touch and wove his words into a highly readable, honest account of his life. It is too self-deprecating but people can read between the lines, especially when it comes to his account of war service in Italy.

In the 1960s, Shetland ponies became of paramount interest to me. Muv had bought two mares and a stallion to run on Inch Kenneth and their first foal, Easter Bonnet, was born a few days before Muv died. She bequeathed the ponies to Sophy and they came to Chatsworth, but Sophy was more interested in riding ponies than in showing them and so I took them on. Their numbers grew as foals were born and purchases made; at one point I had fifty-five Shetlands, both standard-height blacks and coloured miniatures.

The ponies were looked after by Tommy Jones, a Welshman who came to Chatsworth for a few weeks in the late 1930s to walk a Shire stallion and stayed for the rest of his days. After the advent of tractors, he had had the dismal task of taking the magnificent Shire stallions, pride and joy of Andrew's grandfather, to be shot and hauled away for dog meat. From Shires to Shetlands was a downgrade in Tommy's eyes, but our success in the show ring made up for it, and he and his wife, Emily, became part of the Shetland scene. I bought a big horsebox with a sleeping compartment, which became known as The Queen Mary by fellow exhibitors. Tommy and Emily stayed in it and gave tea and drinks all round. We showed the ponies all over the country and in 1973, our best year, three of my Shetlands took the championships: 'Chatsworth Darkie' at the Royal Welsh, 'Chatsworth Drogo' at the Royal, and 'Wells Erica' at the Royal Highland.

In 1969 Tommy drove The Queen Mary to Austria and came back with Maximillian, a Haflinger stallion, and two mares – some of the first of the breed to be imported into this country. To announce their arrival to the British horse-loving public I took a stand at the Royal Show where they created a tremendous amount of interest. My sister Pam and I hired a caravan, parked it behind the horses' stalls and spent the week there. Pam made lunch for crowds of friends, we sat on straw bales and were totally happy. Across the grass was the caravan of the renowned show jumper Harvey Smith and his early morning ablutions became of increasing interest as the days went by. The Haflingers soon grew in popularity and numbers, their quiet temperament and sturdy shape making them suitable for heavy riders and disabled adults. I like the heavier type of Haflinger, capable of hauling thinnings in woods too steep for tractors. These were set to work at Chatsworth but I soon realized that the handlers needed training as well as the horses. A young man on our forestry staff, who had never led a horse or pony, put his foot in the way and was trodden on. After this the head forester thought it wiser to withdraw the horses from service.

A regular in the sheep lines at the Royal Show was Araminta Aldington, founder of the Jacob Sheep Society. Araminta lives, breathes, dreams, sleeps, shears, feeds, doses and eats her sheep. Her clothes are made from their fleece and it is sometimes hard to tell the shepherdess from her flock. There she would be in her caravan, talking to visitors who had never heard of Jacobs. A flock have run in the park at Chatsworth since they were first documented in 1762 and when Araminta asked me to join the Society, I happily accepted. The breed had always been of interest to a few owners but until Araminta took charge of the Society they were just park ornaments. With her at the helm, I knew it would do well but I had no idea just how successful it would become and how the quality of sheep would improve; Jacobs have long since been erased from the Rare Breeds list. In 1971 I was invited to be the Society's first president. Our inaugural meeting was held in a room in the old Farmers' Union building in Knightsbridge. A group of 'fanciers' were shuffling around, uncertain quite where to sit and what to do, when the door opened, a man put his head in and said, 'Are you Watercress?'

Poultry has been important to me since childhood, when selling my hens' eggs to Muv brought me extra pocket money. I thought there should be something alive in the garden at Chatsworth and hens were the answer. Stately Buff Cochins waddled around the greenhouses and when threatened by visiting dogs and toddlers crept under the branches of the yew trees that trailed to the ground. The legs of Buff Cochins are feathered down to the feet and they do not like getting wet, so the flower beds were spared their scratching. They were free to go wherever they liked and must have been the most photographed poultry in the British Isles. Meanwhile more and more pens went up to house various rare breeds of chicken.

I realized that the game larder, rejected as the site for a restaurant, would be a handy place to keep a flock of commercial hens. The feeding of the game larder hens was a daily entertainment for the visitors. Sometimes some of their children helped me to collect the eggs, and it was a required expedition for my own grandchildren, who called it 'The Granny Show'. The new flock had 1,000 acres of park at their disposal but soon congregated around the visitors' cars, having discovered that the occupants were apt to bring picnics. They became increasingly tame with the car-borne humans, snatching sandwiches and hopping into the cars in the hopes of finding the source of the picnics. All was well until twenty of my dear ones got into a school bus, to the delight of the children. They were not noticed by the staff until they had reached the other side of the bridge, when a teacher shooed them out, expecting them to find their own way home. A fox came in daylight and murdered for fun, as these serial destroyers do. The corpses were photographed, mostly headless with feathers all over the place. I hung the photos in the Farmyard to show the children the nature of this random killer.

The eggs went to the Chatsworth Farm Shop and sold out as soon as they arrived. A television camera came. 'What do you feed them on?' the interviewer asked. 'Pellets, wheat, maize and kitchen scraps,' I said. The next day a fellow turned up, the double of Hodges, the ARP Warden in *Dad's Army*: 'Is it true you give your hens kitchen scraps?' he asked me. 'Yes,' I replied. 'Well, it's against the law and you must stop at once,' he said. 'Don't you think that the food we eat is good enough for them?' I ventured. He went off, muttering, 'Next time . . .' which I suppose meant prison.

I still have a varied flock: Welsummers and enigmatic Burford Browns for their dark brown eggs; pretty, shy, idiotic Light Sussex; even stupider White Leghorns who dash around on long yellow legs; and neat, clever, sociable little Warrens. My Warrens brains do not know their luck – they had been destined for an intensive poultry farm. The pecking order rules among the flock: there is a general, some colonels, captains galore, and private soldiers who get out of the way of their superiors at feeding time. The carry-on of this all-female cast is as good as a play and, like a play, is repeated, word for word, gesture for gesture, every day – with the odd matinee thrown in. (Alan Bennett and Tom Stoppard please note: you are welcome to come any day for copy.)

Border Collies are said to be the cleverest dogs in the world and mine was certainly the cleverest dog I ever had. His mother belonged to a Chatsworth shepherd and he was born in a shed at Dunsa, the farm buildings nearest to Edensor. The puppies in the litter were all spoken for except one and the shepherd agreed to let me have him. I soon understood that Collies are different from other breeds. They yearn to work but not all come up to the necessary standard to be of use to shepherds. I realized that I needed lessons before I could co-operate with Collie (his name as well as his breed). My tutor was Chris Furness, trainer of many winners at sheepdog trials. Chris came to give me one-to-one tutorials (or one-to-two in this case) but it was soon evident that I was more in need of teaching than my dog.

The first lesson showed the strength of instinct in a Collie, whose ancestors have been bred to work sheep for generations. We were in a paddock with thirty ewes. Collie was getting excited and was eyeing the sheep in a threatening way so I had him on a lead. 'Let him go,' said Chris. Heart in mouth, I did as I was told and off to my right went Collie. He knew to get behind the sheep and obeyed my shout of 'Lie Down' (which we had already practised in the sheep-free garden at Chatsworth). The ewes trotted past us and Collie stayed prone, watching their every move. His behaviour during that first lesson gave me confidence and we went on practising the orders, 'Come Bye' (for go to the right) and 'Away' (for go to the left). I never mastered the whistle with two fingers stuck in the mouth, so I cheated and bought a little metal one. I lived in terror of swallowing it but never dared say so. The rapport between handler and dog is uncanny and after a while Collie often anticipated the command I was about to give. The tone of voice is enough to tell the dog when he has overstepped the mark; I was not immediately forgiven when I ticked off the headstrong but touchy workman and Collie sulked.

When the International Sheepdog Trials were held in the park at Chatsworth, I took Collie to watch. The poor dog sat intently, paws on the chair in front, so longing to join in that I had to wind his lead round and round my hand to hold him. He hated the clapping (sheepdogs' ears are super-sensitive and can hear commands and whistles over long distances) and he did not appreciate the stands full of onlookers, friends and relations of the competitors, to whom the outcome meant so much. Collie and I never became proficient enough to enter a trial, but we had fun at home. I was sitting in my car in a stationary queue one day, waiting to cross the bridge in front of Chatsworth. Visitors are polite to the cattle and sheep that get in their way on the drive and I realized that there were some sheep standing in front of us. They could not go forwards because of the fence and cattle grid, and would not turn back because there were pedestrians on the bridge. I got out of the car and Collie was off in a flash, doing his job of bringing them back. The visitors were entertained by this unexpected cabaret turn that enabled them to reach the house. After Collie, I always wanted a sheepdog by my side, but Andrew thought the rounding up of children in the garden was not a good idea as the nipped ankle of a child (going in what Collie thought was the wrong direction) was a bit too much for the mothers of our young visitors. So I have never had another of these canine geniuses.

.

In 1995, to my joy and amazement, I was invited to be president of the Royal Agricultural Society of England. Had I been told in my caravan years that this honour would come my way, I would never have believed it. The distinguished members of the Council, who could teach good manners to all and sundry, allowed me hours in the Poultry Tent, the Sheep Pens, the Rare Breeds Survival Trust stand, the Shetland Pony lines and other treats. I had one small triumph as president: persuading those illustrious gentlemen to ride on the miniature railway around the showground. I have some photos of them, in bowler hats, of course, knees up to their chins, pretending to enjoy this new experience. A victim of the foot and mouth outbreak of 2001 and several years of bad weather, the last Royal Show took place in 2009. It came as a blow to the exhibitors and to all of us who had enjoyed it over the years, but the sad fact was that it could not afford to go on. I have no doubt, however, that good will arise from the ashes and that the Stoneleigh Park site will continue to be put to use for excellence in everything to do with the land, albeit in a different form.

Although I have not hunted since I was nineteen, I am still passionate about field sports. The march organized by the Countryside Alliance to demonstrate against the banning of fox-hunting and other field sports was the highlight of 1997. Chatsworth provided a bus to take gamekeepers, river bailiffs, foresters, gardeners, office staff, cleaners and other field-sports supporters who wished to join in this unique outing. Some had only ventured to London once or twice in their lives; one had never set foot so far south before or seen a motorway service station. Our land agent, Roger Wardle, who went with the Chatsworth group, told me that when they got on the tube at Wembley, the train was empty. It started to fill as they drew closer to Central London and a passenger, staring at this noisy, hairy, tweedy crowd, turned to Roger and said, 'Who are all these people? Gay Rights?' The Chatsworth party enjoyed the march and the company of men and women of like mind, but were thankful not to live in such a squashed-up place.

Sadly, Sophy and I, who had set off from Chesterfield Street, never found them. Perhaps this was not surprising as some three-quarters of a million people from rural England, Wales, Scotland and Northern Ireland had flocked to London to show the strength of their feelings. Talk about a cross-section: farriers and fishermen, dukes and drainers, all marching for the freedom to enjoy the sports of their forefathers. There were velvet-capped huntsmen and whippers-in from all over the country, from the Quorn to the Blencathra (John Peel's Lake District pack), from the Devon and Somerset Stag Hounds to the Banwen (the South Wales miners' pack) – picking up the Duke of Beaufort's on the way. All accents mixed: a merry crowd on a serious mission. Sophy and I crossed Park Lane into Hyde Park where there was a stand for the speakers. We were in time to hear Baroness Mallalieu, the Labour life peeress who adores hunting, give her impassioned speech: 'Hunting is our music. It is our poetry. It is our art. It is our pleasure. It is where many of our best friendships are made. It is our community. It is our whole way of life.' She understands.

Sophy carried a banner saying, 'I'M READY TO GO TO JAIL'. Another slogan spotted was, 'EAT BRITISH LAMB, 50,000 FOXES CAN'T BE WRONG'. We left Hyde Park for Piccadilly where we paused to collect a badge from David Hockney that said, 'END BOSSINESS SOON'. Sound advice indeed. With Piccadilly Circus and the Haymarket behind us, we turned right into Trafalgar Square and down Whitehall where for centuries groups of demonstrators from every conceivable minority have marched for justice or recognition. In spite of the passionate feelings of the marchers that day, there was no trouble with the police. When we reached Downing Street (which was well fortified against us) I pointed out the sign to the Welshmen who had become our companions. They stopped as if shot and started shouting insults at the Prime Minister to awaken the dead – but not Mr Blair, he had gone to ground.

Parliament Square, where the tall, handsome keepers from Keir suddenly appeared, was so full of people we could hardly move. Having, we hoped, made our point, Sophy and I walked home through St James's Park, past the Horseguards, up the Duke of York's Steps and into Pall Mall. The famous gentlemen's clubs had opened their doors, even to women, and were handing out sandwiches to anyone who asked for them. Then we had a stroke of luck. One of the Hambro family was walking with us up St James's Street and said, 'Where are you going to have lunch?' and we joined him at Wilton's, a haven after the excitement and the long walk.

One incident from the march remains in my mind. Emma (my grandson Eddie Tennant's wife) was born and brought up in Northumberland where she went out hunting from an early age. She was detailed by the organizers to stand at the top of the moving stairs of the tube station to meet the demonstrators from Northumbria. The first person to emerge was astonished to see 'Our Emma'. 'Oh,' he said, 'I thought London was a big place and the first person I see is you.' No doubt there were many such stories, but one that particularly pleased the organizers was that this vast crowd left no litter. Yet in spite of the huge crowds of enthusiasts who turned out that day, the government passed an Act that outlawed hunting with dogs. The new laws are strictly adhered to by the masters and huntsmen of what has become an ever-increasing number of packs of hounds.

Writing was an interest that came unexpectedly into my life. I wonder what my sister Nancy would have made of the efforts of the 'nine-year-old' (the mental age beyond which she said I never developed) whose fist, according to her, was incapable of holding a pen. There would no doubt have been a torrent of scorn, but I think she would have liked some of the jokes sprinkled in my books. I am often asked where my sisters' and my urge to write comes from. I cannot answer, unless it is from our grandfathers. Grandfather Redesdale wrote half a dozen books, including *Tales of Old Japan*, an anthology of short stories that is still in print a century or more after it was first published. Grandfather Bowles was not only the founder of *The Lady* and *Vanity Fair*, he was also a prolific author on many subjects.

I began writing at Uncle Harold's bidding. He was looking at the *Handbook of Chatsworth and Hardwick*, written in 1844 by the Bachelor Duke, and said, 'You ought to write down what has happened to the house and garden since.' So I did. I enjoyed the work, in spite of the fact that Andrew did not like the idea. He would have done it brilliantly himself and perhaps thought that Uncle Harold should have asked him and not me. As it was, he retreated from the scene, which made things tricky for me. My mentor and editor was Richard Garnett, whose patience and all-seeing eye meant everything to me. *The House: A Portrait of Chatsworth* was published in 1982 as a bumper guide to Chatsworth. I described how we lived in the house, which looks so grand and is so friendly, and included extracts from the *Handbook*, with a lot of family history and old jokes thrown in. Sales were extraordinary and for one heady week it topped the *Evening Standard* best-seller list.

I felt a bit more confident after this and realized that there was a captive market for books about Chatsworth and the family in 'my' shops. *The*

Estate: A View from Chatsworth came about because I was conscious that people thought Chatsworth – the house, park and garden – was the full extent of the Cavendish family's land ownership in Derbyshire. I wanted to give a larger view and wrote about the farms, woods and other properties that constitute the background to Chatsworth. I loved doing *Chatsworth: The House* (the sequel to *The House: A Portrait of Chatsworth*). It is a large book, profusely illustrated with Simon Upton's remarkable photographs, and because Chatsworth is so big and varied I found plenty of new ground to cover. The record of the interior of the house as it looked in the last decade of the twentieth century is already an historic document as the changes that are now being made to it are far-reaching. For the same reason, I am pleased that I wrote *The Garden at Chatsworth*, a record of Andrew's and my years in charge.

Pens and pads of ruled paper were in my basket during my last twenty years at Chatsworth. Often lost for days on end, the basket would eventually be discovered by a seat in the garden or camouflaged in a seldom-visited attic room filled with jettisoned furniture. These hazards made progress slow. Deadlines frightened me because something unexpected might turn up and the lined pages of the notebook remain blank.

Writing the weekly Diary and other articles for the *Spectator* was good fun, and for six months I did a regular piece for the *Telegraph*, mainly about life in the country. I was flattered to be asked. One magazine commissioned an article of 1,000 words – about what I forget – and I duly handed it in on time. The editor telephoned and, after beating about the bush a bit, said, 'Could you add a few more words please?' I said I could, but that I had produced the required number. 'Yes, I know,' he said, with embarrassment, 'but they are all so short we have got a lot of space left.'

I enjoyed doing these occasional articles; it did not seem to matter what was noted down and some pieces found a more permanent home in *Counting My Chickens* and *Home to Roost*. Readers often wrote to me, pulling me up for mistakes or saying that something I had written reminded them of their own experience. Do not believe it when people say that letter writing is finished (although having an address so easy to remember perhaps encouraged it in my case). Writing becomes a habit. Although my eyes are failing, I still go about with a pen in my hand. I wish I could type and use the Internet, but that is beyond me now.

•

I became an Elvis fan by chance. In 1977 I was looking for a television programme on a different subject when I pressed the wrong button and there was the phenomenon. I was riveted by what I saw and heard. I knew about him, of course, but thought he was just another American pop star. Now I understood why he was the most famous man in the world. It was too late to see and hear him in the flesh but some years later I went to a clever resurrection of him in an arena in Manchester, where members of his band, including some of his girl backing singers, the Sweet Inspirations, and the pianist who played such wonderful introductions to the songs, were performing. The girls in their black dresses, covered in sparkles of every description, had grown into ample reincarnations of their earlier selves. In the middle of the stage was a vast screen and there was Elvis singing his best-loved songs, his incredible voice ringing out into the huge arena. The audience went wild, among them many Elvis impersonators, beautifully turned out in the sequinned jumpsuits we all knew so well.

Thanks to the generosity of a friend who lent us a plane to go to Memphis for the day from New York, I was able to visit Graceland. Jayne Wrightsman, Blanche Blackwell and Ashton Hawkins of the Metropolitan Museum were three of the party. It was a cold, bright day in January and the Graceland summer crowds were absent. Excitement mounted as we went through the gates decorated with musical notes and into the house. We were accompanied by the audio-guide spoken by Priscilla, Elvis's wife, who gave an excellent picture of what it was like when they lived there together. The 1950s furniture and decoration must be some of the few examples left of those years of spindly tables and chairs, and shag carpets so deep you lost your shoes in them.

In some rooms, carpets covered the ceiling as well as the floor. White pianos and giant ancient television sets filled one room while next door in the Jungle Room the arms of the chairs were carved crocodile heads. Elvis saw this bizarre furniture out of the corner of his eye as he was driving past a shop window and was so intrigued that he went back and bought it. Gold discs lined a passage, evidence of his world-wide fame, and the people from the Met put on their specs and studied them closely as if they were seventeenth-century vermeil. His grave in the garden was obliterated by flowers and other tributes that arrived daily at the shrine from his fans. There can be nowhere like Graceland – students of the decorative arts should see it as part of their education, lovingly conserved as it is, whether they are Elvis fans or not.

Back in New York I had an engagement to talk at a lunch arranged for ten influential journalists who wrote about tourism. The idea was for me to tell them about Chatsworth and for them to entice their readers to Derbyshire. I told my journalist neighbours at lunch about the Graceland trip and how moved I had been by it. They looked at me in amazement. Then it was my turn to be amazed: *none of them had been there*, and they seemed almost embarrassed to think that I had – in their eyes – sunk so low. Graceland is the second most-visited house in the United States after the White House, and I was left pondering on what they and their readers had missed.

23

FESTIVITIES AND
CELEBRATIONS

Andrew's generous nature made him want people to enjoy themselves and he pushed out the boat whenever there was an excuse for a party. These extravagances, some unique in concept as well as execution, were entirely his idea, fired by his wish to give a good time to others.

The first big party we gave at Chatsworth was in 1965 for Stoker's coming-of-age and to celebrate the restoration of the house. A special train brought guests from London to Matlock; some stayed in local hotels, others put up with neighbours, and the house itself was full to bursting. We had wanted to use the state dining room to dance in but the floor would have collapsed, so we used the great dining room instead. Supper was in the sculpture gallery and guests could wander round the house, upstairs to the state rooms and in and out of the private drawing rooms. Many of the young men there that night have remained good friends with Stoker and come back to Chatsworth as hoary seventy-year-olds. Three memories stand out from that night forty-five years ago. Stoker and Amanda Heywood-Lonsdale dancing together; I thought then, perhaps . . . and indeed they were married two years later. I remember Uncle Harold taking Oswald Mosley, his old political adversary, by the arm and the two of them walking through the state rooms for all to see. They came of a generation that could lash each other with words in the House of Commons and dine together the following night as if it were perfectly ordinary, which it was. My third memory is of several uninvited guests being discovered fast asleep in two attic rooms the next afternoon.

Stoker and Amanda were married at St Martin-in-the-Fields on 28 June 1967 and were among the first married couples to have a party on the evening of their wedding instead of disappearing after the reception, or 'going away' as my generation called it. Hubert de Givenchy made Amanda's dress and she wore the Cavendish tiara, which lived in the vaults of a London bank. She went to try it on, accompanied by her mother and Hubert – ever the perfectionist. The three of them squeezed into an underground room where they could scarcely turn round and Hubert was much amused when the only available mirror was a small pocket one from Amanda's bag. In spite of this, the results of his efforts were lovely and the bride looked radiant.

At the dinner party after the wedding, my sister Pam sat next to Lord Mountbatten, a friend of Amanda's family. The last Viceroy of India and Commander-in-Chief of Allied Forces in South East Asia had been briefed about his dinner partner. He turned to her and said, 'I believe you are called Woman by your family?' 'Yes, I am,' she answered, looking at him with her bright blue eyes. 'And may I ask who you are?' Mountbatten was floored by this question and turned to his other dinner partner. When I heard of this comical exchange I said, 'Oh Woman, you MUST have known that face.' 'Well,' she said, 'if he had got all his medals on I might have recognized him.' One of the wonderful things about Pam was how unimpressed she remained by names, money, titles, reputation or any of the world's extras attached to some people.

Over the years, the usual family events – births, marriages and deaths – were duly celebrated. Andrew was one of twenty-one grandchildren on his father's side and in 1988 he invited all his surviving Cavendish cousins and their progeny to lunch at Chatsworth to mark fifty years since they had last been together under the same roof. We had never met many of the children before so had fun matching parents to their offspring. The latter were unruly in the extreme and the next day the housekeeper said to me in a solemn voice, 'Would you like to see the damage your guests did yesterday?' They had had free run of the house, including the state rooms, and some of the damage was indeed interesting.

On 6 July 1990 the coming-of-age of Stoker's son, William, was the incentive for another celebration. It was – I can say it myself because I had little to do with it – perhaps the best party we ever gave. The house remained open to the public throughout the preparations as Andrew was always delighted for visitors to see anything that was going on, private or public. The garden was floodlit for several days before and after the party, and visitors were able to enjoy the floral extravaganzas, including a giant copy of the family crest – a knotted serpent – made with green and yellow flowers.

The south side of the house was unrecognizable: a tent was stretched over the steps that lead down from the first-floor drawing room and went out to the Sea Horse pond, making room for 250 diners. The sides were painted with Derbyshire landscapes and banks of flowers lined the perimeter. The inner courtyard was tented over and became a dance floor with a live band; a tented disco went up on the south lawn and another tent held a flight simulator and bucking bronco machine. I saw Andrew Parker Bowles, Silver Stick-in-Waiting (a ceremonial position in the Royal Household), being neatly bucked off and I decided not to hang around for any more accidents. The Prince of Wales lent us his Arab tent for sitting out, which we covered with a weatherproof outer tent as its exotic contents would have been damaged had it rained. The Prince and Princess of Wales were to have come but he had broken his arm in a polo accident a few days before and they had to cancel.

As well as the beauty of the house, there was something wonderful to look at wherever you turned. Shortly before midnight we were summoned by figures on stilts dressed in costumes inspired by Inigo Jones designs for a royal masque. Their height lent them authority and we trooped after them, through the tent on the south lawn – where tables were now laid for breakfast – to the canal. A firework display began at midnight, synchronized with Beethoven's Fifth. It was the first time I had seen and heard fireworks set to music and the effect astonished the company. As the display came to an end, up rose Jimmy Goldsmith's helicopter into the night sky with another kind of firework on board. I was delighted with a gatecrasher in the elegant shape of Jerry Hall (brought by Christopher Sykes), so easily recognizable that she turned all heads.

On 19 April the following year we celebrated our golden wedding anniversary. Andrew decided to ask everyone in the county whose golden wedding fell in 1991 and we advertised in the *Derbyshire Times* to compile the guest list. A nun from the convent in Matlock wrote to say she had been a bride of Christ for fifty years and could she come. Of course Andrew said yes. (There was a great deal of speculation as to whether she would bring her bridegroom, but in the event she came with her brother.) Every couple was invited to bring a keeper, just in case, and our children and grandchildren came too. We thought we might get a few hundred people, but 3,700 sat down to tea in the biggest tent yet. The local newspaper produced a special celebration issue and Andrew commissioned a souvenir plate from Crown Derby to give to each couple.

The tercentenary of the dukedom fell in 1994 and Andrew went to town. A stage was built on the banks of the River Derwent, west of the house, and tiered seating for 3,000 was erected on the opposite bank. Richard Evans, a professional actor and son of our former doctor, wrote a pageant that spanned the years from Bess of Hardwick to the present day. The Pilsley school children and dozens of local amateur actors were roped in, while professional actors, some of whom also took leading roles, directed the pageant. 'Queen Victoria' drove through the Great Conservatory in a horse and carriage, just as she had done in real life in 1843, and Donald Sinden's voice rose out of the water as 'The Spirit of the Derwent'. The centuries came to life as other ingenious inventions unfolded. On the first night we invited employees, tenants and pensioners from Chatsworth, Bolton Abbey, Lismore, Eastbourne and London. The second night was held in aid of the Children's Society. The events took place in May and it was none too warm, so each guest was given a silver space blanket that folded to the size of a pocket handkerchief – a life-saver on such occasions.

Suddenly Andrew and I were eighty. It was also the year of the millennium: two reasons for a party. Up went another huge tent and a revolving stage on which John Hyatt, the husband of Tristram Holland who edited four of my books, performed a wonderful rendition of Elvis. The invitation said 'fancy dress', and there were plenty of other Elvises, men in gold lamé suits whom I never thought to see in anything so uninhibited and shiny. I wore the gown designed by Worth of Paris for Louise, Duchess of Devonshire, to wear at the Devonshire House Ball in 1897. It is made of green and gold shot-silk gauze, with a velvet train embroidered with jewels, metalwork and gold and silver thread, and weighs a ton. The original headdress has disappeared so I wore the largest of the three family tiaras, adorned with ostrich feathers for added impact.

A party the following night was held for what is loosely described as 'the great and the good' of Derbyshire. Some were neither great nor good but they all seemed to enjoy themselves, even though they were decidedly sticky compared to the rumbustious company of the previous night – black tie keeping inhibitions well in check. Tony Benn, MP for

Chesterfield, and Dennis Skinner, MP for Bolsover, neatly avoided being tainted by coming to a party at Chatsworth and did not answer the invitation. It all looked very pretty and music was provided by young local talent. Another incredible firework display was accompanied by a screen of water over the canal on to which photographs from our lives were projected.

Our diamond wedding was in 2001. The list of our golden wedding guests was unearthed, which produced the survivors of sixty years of marriage. The party should have taken place in April, to coincide with our anniversary, but had to be postponed until September because of foot and mouth disease; it was dangerously close and we feared for the park deer and farm animals. The theme of the party this time was 1941. We laid out a week's wartime food rations on a trestle table and our astonished younger guests could hardly believe what they saw. 'Two ounces of bacon for one week?' 'Two ounces of butter? Impossible!' But that is how it was. Utility clothing was not easy to find as it had been worn to death and thankfully thrown away when clothes rationing came to an end, so the staff dressed up in RAF, Royal Navy and Army uniforms of the period. Few knew how to fasten a Sam Browne or with which uniform it should go; Sergeant Major Brittain, who greeted us outside the church after our wedding, would have had apoplexy, and I think Andrew, with his military training, was close to putting the offenders on a charge.

The New Squadronaires Orchestra, inspired by the original RAF Dance Band, played songs made famous by Vera Lynn: 'We'll Meet Again', 'There'll be Blue Birds over the White Cliffs of Dover' and 'I'll be Seeing You'. Our ancient guests joined in the singing with gusto and 1941 seemed like yesterday. Andrew commissioned a porcelain loving cup for each celebrating couple and when they eventually tottered off home, a forest of sticks and an array of wheelchairs, with Chatsworth staff at the ready in case of falls, an old gentleman said to me, 'Goodbye and thank you. See you in ten years.' It would have been a small but extra-special tea party. Sadly it was not to be.

As well as giving parties, we went to some marvellous balls and celebrations given by other people. The first – and perhaps the best ever – grand ball after the war was given in September 1951 by Charles de Beistegui,

heir to a Mexican silver fortune, to celebrate the restoration of his magnificent Palazzo Labia in Venice. The extravaganza gave rise to green-
eyed jealousy over invitations and was the talk of London, Paris and New
York for months. Andrew and I were lucky enough to be invited. He
went in eighteenth-century costume and I wore a simple, white muslin
dress with a pale blue satin jacket, copied from a portrait of Georgiana,
Duchess of Devonshire, by John Downman.

The ball was an unforgettable theatrical performance with entrées
of men and women in exquisite costumes. M de Beistegui, in a vast
wig of cascading golden curls and a lavishly embroidered brocade coat,
stood on stilts so as to be easily recognized. Daisy Fellowes, regularly
voted the best-dressed woman in France and America, portrayed the
Queen of Africa from the Tiepolo frescoes in Würzburg. She wore a dress
trimmed with leopard print, the first time we had seen such a thing (still
fashionable today, sixty years on), and was attended by four young men
painted the colour of mahogany. So many women threatened to be
Cleopatra that the host decided to settle it himself and named Diana
Cooper for the role.

One memorable entrée was Jacques Fath, the Paris couturier, who
came as Louis XIV in a headdress of white ostrich feathers as tall as himself, and a shimmering white satin jacket and skirt – like a doublet and
hose – embroidered with gold. Cecil Beaton, dressed as a French curé
and dancing with Barbara Hutton, was worth watching. Wine, food and
entertainment were provided on the public square outside the palazzo
for the citizens of Venice. At least one Frenchman of noble birth, who
thought he should have been asked to the ball, enjoyed himself among
the crowd who were climbing greasy poles for chickens and hams and he
was visited every now and again by the glamorous figures from the palazzo. As this extraordinary night turned into dawn, we splashed our way
down the Grand Canal back to our hotel, having had the time of our
lives.

In 1953 Moucher was made Mistress of the Robes to the new young
Queen. One of her duties was to arrange the rota for the ladies-in-
waiting and I can see her, head clasped in hands, saying, 'I must get
through' – the expression for telephoning – 'about the Waitings.' Hers
is an important job, even in everyday life at Court; at a coronation the
role is vital. I was not planning to go to the ceremony as I was pregnant

with my fifth baby, due around the end of June. When the baby was born too soon and did not survive, I was not in the mood for celebration and stayed quietly at home trying to recover. As weeks went by someone suggested it might be cheering for me to go after all, especially since Stoker was to be page to Moucher and carry her coronet during the procession. To allow Stoker to take such a prominent role was a big concession on the part of the Earl Marshal, who was in charge: the minimum age for pages was twelve and Stoker was only just nine, but he was considered 'reliable'. Moucher and Andrew encouraged me to go and I am so glad that they did.

Then came the problem of what to wear, as obviously Moucher was to have the robes that had been carefully put away by Granny Evie in 1937 after King George VI's coronation. Chatsworth, as always, came to the rescue. There were a number of tin boxes containing old uniforms and other relics. In the vain hope of finding something for me, we started going through them and, lo and behold, from beneath a ton of tissue paper in the box that had held Moucher's, appeared a second crimson peeress's robe. The velvet is of exceptional quality, so soft your fingers hardly know they are touching it, and of such pure, brilliant crimson as to make you blink. Miraculously the robe fitted; we had found what we were searching for. But there was a hitch: unlike other peeresses' robes it was cut off the shoulder. Moucher or Andrew asked the Queen's permission for me to wear this irregular style and it was granted. Stoker wore the uniform last worn in 1911 at the coronation of George V, and it was not a bad fit.

In for a penny in for a pound: Andrew and I despatched the Chatsworth state coach to London so we could arrive at the Abbey in style. The coach was tested for roadworthiness, a pair of stout grey horses and a coachman were hired from the Red House Stables in Darley Dale and two burly Chatsworth farm men crammed into Devonshire livery to ride as attendants at the rear. The coach was taken by train to London and the horses stabled at Watney's Brewery. Although it looks large, the coach has surprisingly little room for passengers. On that cold, wet June morning Andrew and I could just squeeze Stoker on the seat between us as we trundled down Park Lane to Piccadilly. We waited for Gerry Wellington's coach to reach us from Apsley House then processed at a stately pace to St James's Street, where the crowd was treated to the sight of the handsome Henry Bath (on his own as he was between marriages) in a well-sprung yellow coach, a faster version than ours, drawn by a pair of Hackneys, smart as paint and stepping out. The people waiting in the empty, rainy streets, many of whom had been stationed there all night, were pleased to have something to look at.

Our route took us to Victoria Street and then we were lost. Neither the coachman nor our farm men knew London and our only communication with them was by a string attached to a button on the coachman's coat. Energetic jerking told the coachman something was wrong but not what. Poor Andrew was sweating with anxiety that we would be late and Stoker would not find Moucher. He lowered his window, a tricky business as it was made of thin real glass and the leather strap that held it was so highly polished it could have slipped from his hand. He put his head out, craning round so the coachman could hear his instructions, 'Turn right, turn left' – a scene that delighted the crowd – till at last we arrived at the entrance to the Abbey.

All was then plain sailing and the organization faultless. Stoker was whisked away to find his Granny, while I joined the female side of the congregation and Andrew the peers. I have never seen a photograph of the massed peeresses and it is a pity if there is none because, young and old, they made an extraordinarily beautiful sight. They had worked hard to look their best: the country ones had been to the bank to get out the family diamonds and the town ladies had spent early hours at the hairdresser with splendid results. Everyone was dressed alike (except for me with my bare shoulders) and the effect was like the chorus in a sumptuous film production.

All eyes were on the monarch, who was dedicating herself to the service of her people. When the Archbishop of Canterbury placed the crown on her head the peeresses put on their coronets and the sea of arms in white gloves rising in unison was unforgettable. The Abbey was lit for television cameras and the dimmest corners were visible for the first time. It was a spectacular and moving combination of splendour and solemnity, a bringing together of Church and State. (I wondered what the Californian communists, my companions of the previous year, would have made of it all.) Moucher carried out her part to perfection. I had never seen her stand so straight before and it enhanced her beauty. Stoker was indeed reliable, except for one enormous yawn which happened to be caught by a photographer. I have no recollection of what happened to us afterwards, how we got home or how we spent the rest of the day, but I was keenly aware of my good fortune at being in the Abbey with history being made in front of my eyes.

Twenty-eight years later Andrew and I were invited to the Prince of Wales's wedding to Lady Diana Spencer. Celebrations began two nights beforehand with an evening party for hundreds of people at Buckingham Palace. Emma, Andrew and I dined at Chesterfield Street, where we were joined by Father Harry Williams, who had been Dean of Chapel at Trinity College, Cambridge, when Prince Charles was an undergraduate. Harry was worried about his clothes: an old grey cotton overall worn over a short black cassock that stopped well above his ankles and gave him the droll appearance of an overgrown French schoolboy.

There are two entrances at Buckingham Palace when big parties are held and the invitation clearly stated our time of arrival, but the whole of London seemed to be making for the palace at the same time and there was a long queue to get in. We were fortunate in having an 'entrée' pass, given to diplomats, government officials and a few others, so we were able to go through a side door by the Queen's Gallery where we found a milling throng and an apparently stationary queue waiting to get up the stairs. We spotted the Archbishop of Canterbury, Alec Douglas-Home and Quintin Hailsham, the Lord Chancellor, who was wearing old-fashioned court dress with lace ruffles and knee breeches and looked like a mischievous boy with his hair scraped down. We were all staring sadly at the queue when some knowing person said, 'Let's take the lift.' So this strangely assorted company, including portly Father Williams, took the lift and when the door opened we found ourselves spat out just where the Queen and Prince Philip were receiving their guests.

The spectacle was better than any film. The women had all made an effort to look their smartest – rare today – and were wearing new, or anyway clean, dresses, and had got out anything that shone to put in their hair. The men, some in unfamiliar foreign uniforms, looked splendid, and there was the usual sprinkling of Africans in multi-coloured robes. The palace brings in outside staff for these occasions and some of the footmen's uniforms did not exactly fit. I often saw old friends among the retired butlers and looked out for Henry Bennett, who had been a footman at Chatsworth before going to be page to the Queen. (The Queen called him 'Bennett' and I called him 'Henry', which made me feel in the swim.) I did not see him that evening – he was probably in the rarefied atmosphere of the supper room where the Queen and the royal family were entertaining their foreign guests.

At 1.30 a.m. Andrew announced, 'We'll go home now.' His sight was beginning to fail and parties had become a strain. Once he had decided he wanted to go home, home it was with no waiting about. But that night it was not so easy. The crowd was still huge and I could not remember which stairs to make for to reach our waiting car. I was almost desperate when I spied Lord Maclean, the Lord Chamberlain, whom I had known when he was Chief Scout. I collared him and said, 'You're a Boy Scout, how about your good turn for the day? Show us the way out.' He looked surprised but, good Scout that he was, took us downstairs and shoved us into the passage that eventually led to the side door.

The next day I was sorry we had not stayed longer. Emma did, and at the very end of the party some high-ranking soldier cut down the balloons from the ceiling with his sword. There was a stampede of dowagers, fighting like mad for the blue and white souvenirs to take home for their grandchildren. Emma managed to get three, one for each of her children.

The following night we joined a vast expectant crowd for the firework display in Hyde Park. Part of the magic of those days and nights was the warm, still weather – the first fine days of a miserable summer – and going out at night was like going out in a southern country. It seemed to take for ever to get dark but when at last the fireworks began they were spectacular. Getting away, however, in a surging mass of half a million people was difficult. The crowd was not pushing deliberately but could not help doing so as they were being pushed from behind and several people were crushed against a barrier on Park Lane.

As we were being swept along in this human tide, I nearly fell over a small old woman. I asked her if she was all right and whether she had anyone with her. She was naturally very frightened and said she was alone. Andrew and I got her between us and waited behind a tree while the crowds surged by. She told us she lived in Brixton and I asked her how she was going to get home. 'I'm not going home,' she said, 'I'm going to spend the night on the pavement in the Strand to see the Prince go by tomorrow.' The last I saw of her was walking purposefully towards Piccadilly, determined not to miss any of the fun. She was typical of many of the people in the crowd that day: a Londoner and an ardent royalist, and nothing was going to prevent her from showing her colours on such an occasion.

Another memorable celebration of that decade was Sybil Chol-mondeley's ninetieth birthday, which was held in great style at Houghton in 1984. 'You simply can't imagine the beauty of it all,' I wrote to Paddy Leigh Fermor:

That staggering Stone Hall set up for such an entertainment made me think I should never see anything so beautiful again, gold plate dug from the cellar by D Rocksavage, orchids on every shelf because the present-givers mostly plumped for flowers & somehow Sybil IS orchids, daffs wouldn't do, Sèvres china and the room itself, decorated & yet hardly because of it all being one colour viz. stone. Oh heavens it was wonderful. All their old servants came out of cotton wool to do the job & do it they did most wonderfully.

Cake [Queen Mother] wore something shimmering as per, Pss Alexandra a terrific tartan thing in silk with huge sleeves, Dss of Kent came dressed as a clergyman – black silk with white col-lar & cuffs – we all made a monster effort, jewels galore &, a rare thing, there was exactly the right number of people. Surrounded by the Oudry *White Duck*, many a Gainsborough, Sybil's mater by Sargent, the Holbein of a squirrel & '*my brother Philip's Things*' positively gaudy among the indigenous Kent kit, French clocks surrounded by sort of diamonds, eastern this & that all one size too small but adding a lot, the royal people, seven minutes of block busting non-stop fireworks seen through the fat glazing bars & the old glass which is full of swirls & distortions, fires & flowers everywhere. Oh do try & picture the scene. SHE wore a pink cut-velvet & satin dress made for her mother in 1901. The Duke of Grafton said some good words after dinner, & she, swearing after that she had no inkling anyone was going to do that, answered most brilliantly. She quoted from Horace Walpole something about dowagers being as common as flounders. The fact that the Queen & all the rest of her push were there made the dreamlike feeling more so. Those rooms were made for all that & so was Sybil. I kept thinking how lucky I was to be there.

Five years later, on Boxing Day, Sybil was found propped up in bed, specs on nose, book in hands, dead. Oh how I loved her.

In 1996, the Queen honoured Andrew with the Order of the Garter, which dates to the fourteenth century and is the personal gift of the monarch. It is the highest accolade of all and I have never known Andrew so thrilled or so moved. We were at Lismore when the letter from Buckingham Palace arrived, and he waved it above his head in joy. I thought back to the thousand and one things he had done for every kind of organization in Derbyshire, to the years of public service he had given elsewhere and to the countless evenings he had spent at functions when he might have been in his book-lined sitting room, and I thought how well deserved this honour was.

The ceremony in the Queen's ballroom at Windsor Castle is witnessed only by those being admitted to the Order, its existing members and their spouses. Andrew and Timothy Colman, the two newly appointed knights, were presented one by one. I described what followed to my sister Diana:

> They get dangerously close to the Queen who does something with a 'collar' & something else with a sort of dressing gown cord. She is highly practical, quick & neat & of course the 'presenters' are not and fumble with the cord etc etc till she grabs it herself to get on with the job. The language is thrilling, ancient & frightening, nothing but battling with things & people. All v. moving, partly because it has happened since Edward 3rd & partly because of the slowness of each movement, like a slow-motion film.
>
> Then a long wait for disrobing. All of us round the walls while the Queen says how-d'you-do to everyone, followed by Prince Philip, Friend [Prince of Wales], Cake [Queen Mother] & Pss Anne. Another long wait & drinks & cigs for Denis [Thatcher] then lunch in the Waterloo Chamber. I drew husband & son, & Andrew 2 queens. I had exactly the same Nature Notes talk to Prince P that we had done 2 months ago when I last sat next to him. I wonder if he noted it, not I suppose or he'd have thought of something else. Friend sweet as always.

Then, after fairly ages, the wives & Denis went out into the brilliant sun to walk down to St George's Chapel between the crowds of people who had tickets to be on the walking route.

I greatly looked forward to the annual Garter ceremony and to lunch afterwards, with the long table, the flowers down the middle, the speed with which the delicious food came – no hanging about for a slow eater – and the lottery of whom I would sit next to. I used to pray that it would not be Ted Heath but, with luck, Field Marshal Lord Bramall, with his long and distinguished army career; a man in a million. But whoever my neighbour was, it all passed too quickly. The procession from the castle to St George's Chapel was like a scene from some ancient drama, the knights in their velvet robes and black hats with white feathers, and the heralds dressed as playing cards. The Order is limited to twenty-four non-royal knights. As the gift is for life, many of them are old and there are always a couple of wheelchairs. Andrew's driver told him that the other drivers ran a sweepstake, betting on which of these venerable ladies and gentlemen would be the next to create a vacancy. Lord Longford used to arrive in a London taxi, which looked funny squeezed between the Bentleys. He climbed in and out with difficulty and the danger of some important bit of his clothes coming off was ever-present.

As with so many English ceremonies, the men in their finery made even the smartest women look dim. We hen pheasants walked down the hill to the Galilee Porch and had a moment to glimpse the invited crowd on either side of the road – I seldom managed to pick out the Chatsworth contingent but knew they were there – before trooping into the Chapel and settling ourselves in the stalls of the Quire. Above us hung the Garter banners and you needed a doctorate in heraldry to know which coat of arms was whose. Back up the hill to Windsor Castle for tea and proper iced coffee, then off home to real life until the following year.

I go to far fewer parties today, but the one given in 2009 by Sister Teresa Keswick, someone I have loved since she first came to Chatsworth as a friend of Stoker's in the early 1960s, was a corker. Held at the Carmelite Monastery in Quidenham, Norfolk, it was to celebrate Teresa's twenty-five years in the Carmelite Order. As a girl, Teresa was immensely popular, throwing herself wholeheartedly into whatever was happening, and making it 'go' – the opposite of many of her contemporaries, most of whom were silent and hidden under a curtain of hair, their jerseys pulled up to their ears. They were no help to me, poor old hostess, and I had to carry the whole thing – except when Teresa came. Now, for a quarter of a century, she had led a monastic life of prayer, toil and fasting.

Sister Teresa has three brothers and countless cousins, many of whom stayed the night before the party at Hatfield House, as did I. The joy of that night with Robert and Hannah Salisbury was made all the more remarkable for me as I could remember the old days at Hatfield when Roman Catholics were frowned upon. The people who mounted the steps of the bus that took us to Teresa's celebratory Mass could not possibly have gathered together under that roof when I first knew the place in 1943.

The chapel was full when we arrived. Teresa was the only nun visible and the service was taken by priests. I do not remember much of what was said, my mind was full of thoughts of Teresa as a young woman. Even now, forty years later, I still feel her absence whenever there is a gathering of her contemporaries. After Mass, we left the chapel and stood outside on the gravel. The guests fell silent while Teresa's eldest brother, Henry, began to speak. Teresa stood next to him holding a large bell.

Henry's words were full of teases and memories of old days and suddenly the two of them were back in the nursery. Teresa was listening, laughing and crying in turn, and when she sensed that Henry was about to say something out of bounds, she rang the bell loudly to muffle his indiscretions. It was a sublime performance on both their parts. After these formalities, Teresa whirled around making sure her guests were fed and given champagne. When it was all over, she retreated into her silent life of prayer.

24

THE OTHERS

After Muv died, Nancy wrote to Gaston Palewski, 'I have a feeling nothing really *nice* will ever happen again in my life, things will just go from bad to worse, leading to old age and death.' Those words were a rare exception to her usual effervescent cheerfulness. She never had the happiness that most women seek; luck plays such a big part in meeting the right person at the right time and that luck eluded her. She made her own way through her own efforts and was rewarded with the enormous success of her books, but she never had the wholehearted love and support of a husband, lover or children.

Even her sisters were ignorant of her innermost thoughts, and her disappointments remained private. She never complained and gave an everlasting impression of light-heartedness and jokes. After *Don't Tell Alfred* she said she had run out of plots for novels and turned, with equal success, to history. *Voltaire in Love* demanded serious research and she worried about her eyes and the long hours of reading tiny print; *Madame de Pompadour* and *The Sun King*, both best-sellers, were acclaimed by historians and the reading public alike. Of her last book, *Frederick the Great*, she said to me, 'It's not only the best book I have written, it is the best book I have read,' which was greeted by 'Oh, shut up,' from me, as she knew it would.

Nancy's annual visits to Venice were as regular as clockwork. While writing her history books, she stayed in a small hotel on Torcello and spent the day in her room working. Day-trippers invaded the island but as soon as they had gone, Nancy went out to look for a discarded Continental *Daily Mail*. In latter years she stayed with Anna Maria

Cicogna in her house on the Grand Canal and went every day to the Lido where she lay baking in the sun, venturing from time to time into the tepid sea. Could that annual overdose of sun have led to the cancer that eventually killed her?

Nancy had a wide circle of friends including Field Marshal Montgomery. It was an unlikely friendship on the face of it, but you did not need much imagination to see that he had a great deal of Farve in him. Added to these familiar traits was a comic side that came to the fore during his television interviews when one could not help laughing at his certainty that he was always right. (It is high time the BBC gave us a repeat of his unique performance.) Nancy used to lunch with the Field Marshal at Fontainebleau when he was Deputy Supreme Commander of NATO forces in Europe, and she recounted these visits in some of her funniest letters to Evelyn Waugh:

> He is terribly like my Dad – watch in hand when I arrived (the first, luckily) only drinks water, has to have the 9 o'clock news and be in bed by 10, washes his own shirts, rice pudding his favourite food. All my books by his bed and when he gets to a daring passage he washes it down with Deuteronomy.

The world saw Nancy as a town person: she was always elegant and, even when alone and working, never looked sloppy. But underneath all this she loved the country, the seasons and the people who worked the land. In January 1967 she left Paris for her adored Versailles where she bought a house with a garden, something she longed for. Two years later she was diagnosed with cancer. The news coincided with the announcement of Gaston's marriage to his long-standing love, Violette de Talleyrand Périgord. None of us knew what this meant to Nancy. She made a joke, of course, of what must have been a shattering blow – her way of dealing with bad news. Gaston had always told her that his political career would be ruined if he married a divorced woman, thereby ruling Nancy out. And then he did just that.

Nancy's last illness has been described by her biographers and, most poignantly, by Nancy herself in her letters. Suffice it to say that for four and a half years, from March 1969, when a malignant lump was removed from her liver ('Of course, it's my white-bearded twin brother', she said), to when she died at the end of June 1973, she was rarely out of pain. She had several spells in hospitals in Paris and London, including ten weeks at the Nuffield in Bryanston Square where fashionable doctors brought her flowers but did nothing to improve her condition. She saw twenty-nine doctors in all, ranging from famed surgeons to quacks. After seeing a new one she would say, 'The doctor tells me I'll be much better in three weeks,' but she never was. During days free of pain she would say 'I'm cured', but the raging torment soon returned.

When her housekeeper Marie retired another prop went and Nancy missed her homely countenance. As the pain got worse we tried to visit her in turn. Diana never failed her and drove the fifteen miles from Orsay at all hours of the day and night. Decca made the long and expensive journey from California several times. I went to stay with her as often as I could, or I stayed at Orsay with Diana and we would spend the day with Nancy. But Pam was the sister Nancy most wanted when she was ill – just her presence was a comfort. All childhood teases were forgiven and forgotten as Pam recounted tales of her dogs, her household affairs and Derek's eccentricities during their married life.

It was not all gloom. The garden, an imitation of a hay meadow of her youth, gave Nancy pleasure. Such plots were all the fashion in England until their owners realized that Mother Nature needs a lot of help to keep the garden looking 'natural', and that, without it, the meadow readily turns into a beige tussocky desert in July. Nancy wrote hilarious descriptions of the mating tortoises in the garden and her dismay at the flowering of a plastic-pink cherry tree, which she longed to cut down but never dared as Marie and her neighbours admired it so.

When Decca came over from America to see Nancy, she and Diana met for the first time since 1936. I shall never forget the look of wonderment on Decca's face. After Unity, Diana had been Decca's most adored sister as a child and there she was, her beauty unchanged. They embraced and the past seemed to evaporate. They even exchanged a letter. But Decca told me that it was impossible to re-create her love of Diana; it had been too important to her in childhood and it was better not to try. They never saw each other again.

I visited Nancy a few days before she died. It was very hot and she was lying on her bed, covered by a sheet that did not conceal her pitifully thin body. The years of pain had crushed even her spirit and at last she was ready to go. I sat in silence near her and after a while she stirred and opened her eyes. 'Is there anything, *anything* I can do?' I asked her.

'No, nothing,' she said. 'I just wish I could have one more day's hunting.' She died on 30 June and was buried next to Unity in Swinbrook churchyard.

Pam came back to live in England in 1972. She had let Woodfield – the house in Gloucestershire that she had bought when Tullamaine, her Irish house, was sold – and while she waited for it to become available she came to stay at Chatsworth. She moved into a flat on the third floor with grand views across the park and soon made the rooms feel like home. Friends used to make their way up to the flat (christened 1A, Chatsworth Buildings by Nancy) to sit by the fire with her. She was the inspiration behind the making of the kitchen garden at Chatsworth. She had often talked about the possibilities of a neglected plot above the stables, known as the Paddocks, and a few years later it was transformed into the kitchen garden of my dreams. I got into trouble with the estate office because I forgot to tell the budgeting people about it, and it was not cheap. Never mind, there is a kitchen garden at Chatsworth now.

I loved staying with Pam at Caudle Green and often think it was her happiest home. Woodfield House stands close to the village green, and to the south it has a stupendous view over a deep valley with a stream, both sides lined with the old trees of the Miserden Woods. It had eight acres of land, pigsties, stables and a cowshed. It was the ideal house for anyone who loves the Cotswolds. Pam's presence there felt exactly right: the house, garden, paddocks and owner all suited each other.

When you walked through the back door of Woodfield (I never saw anyone use the front door) you were met with a delicious smell of herbs – Pam's trademark, to be found wherever she lived, and the stone passage behind the kitchen held it as a welcome. The single bedroom where I slept had a bedside table with *Lark Rise to Candleford* on it and this, admittedly excellent, reading matter remained there for the next twenty years. In the kitchen–dining room was a blue Rayburn stove where Pam produced the best soups, roasts and stews imaginable. (When Nancy heard of the Rayburn she pretended to think it was a room hung with portraits by the famed Scotch artist.) I often asked Pam, 'How *do* you make this soup?' 'Oh, out of my head,' was always the answer. She was a careful shopper and discussed his trade with her butcher. 'Mrs Jackson *selects*,' Diana's driver, Jerry Lehane, used to say.

The kitchen garden was Pam's heaven and the vegetables cherished far above orchids. Her guests sat down to eat to tales of where the seeds were from, how they had been planted and the rest of their life history. Gerald and Gladys Stewart were her next-door neighbours and became her dear friends. She was lucky to have the services of Gerald in the garden and I wish she had lived to see his autobiography, *Pipe Lids and Hedgehogs*, with its evocative descriptions of life in the Cotswolds seventy-five years ago.

In the nicest possible way, all Pam's geese were swans. 'Look, Stublow, my tree peony,' she once said to me, 'isn't it wonderful?' as if I were being introduced to the plant for the first time. She was not boasting, just celebrating excellence. In 1977 Caudle Green marked the Queen's Jubilee in its own way. Pam took charge of the celebrations and wrote to Diana that the village residents were thrilled with her plan and that most had accepted the invitation when they heard that it was to be in her cowshed. Even the few dissidents bold enough to refuse had 'caved in' eventually. The cowshed, where she kept her chickens, was described by Pam as the room with 'the great west window' – in fact a rusted iron contraption with ill-fitting panes. Pam forged ahead and ordered (spelling was not her strong point): 'Sausages from the Moncks and rolls from the Nudist Colony.' There was also to be 'a real Cheddar cheese in its own skin, a barrel of jolly beer' and some Appenzeller eggs pickled in vinegar. 'Oh Debo,' Diana wrote, '*why* weren't we there.'

Life for Pam at Caudle Green went steadily on, ruled by the seasons and her black Labrador, Beetle, who was an improvement on the yapping dachshunds and a popular guest wherever she went. On a spring weekend in April 1994 Pam drove to London to stay with her friend Margaret Budd. They did the shops, had dinner with another friend, Elizabeth Winn, and more shopping the next day. That evening while they were having drinks with a neighbour, Pam fell down some steep stairs and broke both bones in her right leg below the knee. I wrote to Decca:

Ambulance men perfect & very quick ('we've got an English *lady* here' they said – rare bird, true enough), hospital at once – wonderful in every way, new, off Fulham Road. Spent a dopy night & next A.M. was operated on to put plate in the usual way. All went well & on waking she asked what won the Grand

National. I spoke to her (asked for the nurse & got her) THAT EVENING, still a bit sleepy but quite OK. That was Sat. Sun & Mon never better, seen by E. Winn who said she looked v. pretty in bed & was in fine form & very funny. Tues A.M., Andrew & I went to London from Cork, punctual, drove to Margaret's where we found her outside her door saying quick, they've just telephoned to say come at once. So we dashed. Found curtains round the bed, I said I'm her sister I must see her & the Sister said talk to the Dr. He took us to a little room which I suppose ought to have been a sign of the seriousness, he said all the technical things which had happened in her poor body & I said so what's her future & he said she died 10 minutes ago. Hen. Please picture. After a bit we went to see her, so odd, just a bod with no one there.

The loss of Pam meant more to me than I ever thought it could. She seemed so permanent, so rock-steady. One who was impressed by her outward calm was the author Brian Masters, who wrote to me after her death, 'Your sister Pamela did not mind being laughed at. There was a rare kind of serenity, almost floating above life rather than fighting through it.' But, as with Nancy, there were rumblings of anxiety in Pam that she never allowed the outside world to see. She would sometimes say to one of us, 'I worry terribly about . . .' but not if we were in company. Margaret Budd, who had been a friend since her husband, George, and Derek were in RAF 604 Squadron together, told me that she had stayed with Pam at Tullamaine soon after Derek had left. Margaret told Pam how she admired her keeping cool at such a difficult time. 'If only you knew,' Pam said, 'I may seem calm but everything is churning underneath.'

After Muv's death, Decca's visits to England became longer and more frequent, and each time she seemed increasingly reluctant to leave. Her London friends, including the television presenter Jon Snow and human rights lawyer Helena Kennedy, saw a good deal of her when she was over. She and Bob stayed at Chatsworth but I got the feeling they were delighted when the time came to leave, taking with them a store of anecdotes so easily gathered from the Chatsworth way of life and relayed with much derisory laughter to their London friends. Decca could be spiky and took offence easily, not on her own account but when her politics were challenged. Andrew was as hospitable as he knew how, but the truth was that none of the brothers-in-law liked each other (except for Andrew and Sir O who both got on well with Derek), and it was a question of family duty when they did meet.

Decca's courage was never in doubt. She and Bob worked tirelessly for civil rights campaigns, often in the face of danger. In the spring of 1963 she published *The American Way of Death*, an exposé of the powerful funeral industry. It flew immediately to the top of the best-seller list and remained there until President Kennedy was assassinated, when it disappeared. It was a wonderful book, funny and shocking, a remorseless attack on the undertakers who took advantage of the recently bereaved, played on their emotions and persuaded them to fork out for the most expensive coffins and elaborate burials. Embalming was encouraged, even when the body was being buried without delay, and the poor corpse, dressed in his or her best clothes, was made to look ready to spring from the coffin.

Decca's descriptions of the technicalities involved were disgusting and she enjoyed keeping me informed:

Dearest Henny,

Glad you liked Practical Burial Footwear. Yes there are some other fascinators: such as New Bra-Form, Post Mortem Form Restoration, Accomplish So Much for So Little. They cost $11 for a package of 50, Hen you must say that's cheap, shall I send you a few? There's also The Final Touch That Means So Much, it's mood-setting casket hardware. Hen do you prefer a gentle Tissue-Tint in yr. arterial? It helps regain the Natural Undertones. It's made specially for those who prefer a fast Firming Action of medium-to-rigid degree.

Hen I bet you don't even know what is the best time to start embalming, so I'll tell you: Before life is quite extinct, according to the best text-book we've found on it. They have at you with a thing called a Trocar, it's a long pointed needle with a pump attached, it goes in thru the stomach and all liquids etc. are pumped out. Thence to the Arterial. I do wish the book was finished, it seemed to be going along well for a bit but now it's all being totally reorganized.

Decca's first volume of memoirs, *Hons and Rebels*, was, and still is, a huge success. At times imagination takes over from the truth – which is more amusing, of course, but unfair on the uncles, aunts and other figures of our youth who never did us any harm but stumped up at Christmas without fail. But that was Decca. These two books set her on the road to fame: universities asked her to be visiting professor, or some such title, her pupils adored her and invitations proliferated. She and I were talking one day about her second book of memoirs. 'What's the title?' I asked. 'The Final Conflict,' she replied. 'A Fine Old Conflict?' I said, having only half-listened to the answer, and that is what she called it.

Decca was the only sister who drank spirits and smoked, and in her seventies these two habits caught up with her. In 1994 she fell and broke an ankle. She realized the trouble that her drinking was causing her family and stopped that very day. She did it without any help, just steely determination. Two years later she was diagnosed with lung cancer and even she could not prevent the disease from spreading. Her daughter, Dinky, a trained nurse, was with her and the doctors gave her six to nine months to live. I was about to set off for America to see her when Dinky rang to say it was too late. She died on 23 July 1996, aged seventy-nine.

Decca had made arrangements for the simplest and cheapest possible funeral: a cremation, no ceremony and her ashes scattered at sea. Her friends in San Francisco arranged a joke funeral with six black, plumed horses drawing an antique hearse, which she had once laughingly said she had wanted, and her friends in London arranged a send-off in a theatre where they recited eulogies. I could not face it so stayed at home with my own thoughts about my remarkable dear old Hen.

Diana's memoirs, *A Life of Contrasts*, were published in 1977 and she was interviewed on television by Russell Harty. The camera stayed on him for a few seconds longer than usual at the end of the interview and he wiped his brow and said 'Phew', so unusually impressed was he by his subject's reactions to his questions. The trouble for him was Diana's honesty: she told him exactly what she thought and why, in intelligible English, without guile, hesitation or exaggeration. Her beauty and serenity coupled with honesty was a bit too much for Harty. The media, even then, were unaccustomed to such truthfulness. This was Diana's strength, but it was also what made her unpopular in many circles.

Diana loved the Temple and was completely happy there, able to go to Paris whenever she wanted in the knowledge that she had that beautiful place to return to. Her garden was the source of much satisfaction and never failed to produce flowers for the house. There was no greenhouse, so she grew annuals but was never quite sure what would come up. One year she forgot to order ahead and filled the flower beds with zinnia plants, much to the amusement of Les Amateurs de Jardin, who were regular visitors. In one corner of the garden was a long, narrow swimming pool designed for exercise and, like everything of Diana's, it fitted its place perfectly. The walls of the pool were painted a dark colour – so much nicer to look at than the usual bright blue – and a shed provided shade in the summer.

Sir O was a persuasive talker and as a politician had been not just a speaker but an orator of the first order. On the platform his words poured out of him with passion and he took his audience with him willy-nilly. I only once saw him addressing a meeting but the memory of his delivery and his electric personality when aroused for a cause stayed with me. He liked to hold forth at meals. Sometimes our chat got too silly for him. When Diana and I were describing something we had seen and could not quite remember, we would spin it out, to hold the other's attention, with a lot of 'If you see what I mean . . . kind of . . . well, sort of . . . you know', and Sir O took this up himself – very much in inverted commas. Diana's way of talking was unique. One day when she was driving with Sir O along the Riviera he had to turn the car round, which involved backing it dangerously close to the cliff. 'Vaguely whoa,' was all she said quietly as he got nearer and nearer to the edge.

Sir O was always kind to me and I was fond of him, but I realized that as he got older he was a full-time job for Diana. He demanded all her attention and anything that took her away from him was not well looked on. This made life difficult and a climax was reached when Nancy was ill and needed Diana's constant support. Diana told me that there were times when she drove over to Versailles early in the morning and rushed back to the Temple to be there when Sir O woke up. She had suffered from intermittent migraines since the 1950s and these got progressively worse, making it impossible for her to plan ahead with certainty. They became so serious at one point that she had to lie in a darkened room sometimes for a day or more at a time. The doctor prescribed Cafergot, a strong drug that alleviated the pain but did not make it disappear altogether.

Sir O died suddenly at the age of eighty-four on 3 December 1980. Diana was devastated and felt that life without him was not worthwhile, a state of mind she never really shook off. She slowly came back to what seemed normality but she was, in fact, inconsolable and, every year, the first week of December brought what she described as her 'dark days'. In 1981 she had what was thought to be a stroke which left her semi-paralysed. The doctors in France said that nothing could be done and simply suggested suitable nursing. Diana's son Max asked Professor Sidney Watkins, head of the Formula One on-track medical team, if he would see her. Max hired an ambulance plane to take Diana to England and on arrival at the London Hospital the Prof diagnosed a brain tumour. It was removed and mercifully proved to be benign.

I went to see Diana in intensive care; she was conscious and shivering and begging for a blanket. It was awful not being able to get her one, but the orders were to keep her temperature low. She came to Chatsworth to convalesce and I put her in the centre dressing room with a bed near the window so she could see the view across the river to the end of the park, which she found comforting. No one appreciated beauty more than Diana and I believe her time at Chatsworth helped her to recover. It was wonderful for me to have her pinned there so I could go in and out for a chat. She had been my confidante since the end of the war (our correspondence would fill a library of its own), and at difficult times I do not know what I would have done without her.

Diana never burdened people with her sorrows or disappointments. In her late eighties the upkeep of the Temple became too much and she decided to sell the house she had loved for fifty years and move to Paris. She left without a murmur, never turning to look back, but what a terrible wrench it was. Her daughter-in-law Charlotte was her prop and stay and found her a flat. She also found Elo, the Filipino housekeeper of whom Diana became very fond, and in return Elo gave Diana her complete devotion. The flat became the centre for Diana's friends and family; it was easier to get to than the Temple and the welcome was just the same.

Diana seemed ageless, as beautiful as ever and generally in good health. Her flat was near the offices of *Vogue* magazine and she was oblivious of the fact that the girls inside pressed their faces to the windows to watch this elegant, upright great-great-granny walk by. As she grew older she had become cruelly deaf, an affliction that was doubly hard on her as there was nothing in the world she liked better than to chat; she also missed music, which had always meant a great deal to her. She was plagued by hymn tunes, dredged up from her youth, which went round and round her head. We laughed about it, of course, but they went on troubling her.

The heatwave that hit France in August 2003 was too much for Diana, now aged ninety-three. I made a dash to see her in the suffocating heat; we pulled the blinds, shut the windows and opened the inner doors in the wild hope that the air would move and bring some relief. The air may have moved but it was hot air to hot air. I have never experienced anything similar – it was like Africa. On 11 August, when a loved granddaughter was in the room with her, Diana slipped away. Never was there such a loss to me, perhaps the closest of her relations, and to everyone who was lucky enough to know her. For months afterwards I picked up a pen to write to her only to throw it down again when I remembered there was no point.

Muv, Farve, Nancy, Pam, Unity and Diana are all buried in the churchyard at Swinbrook, lately joined by Diana's grandson, Alexander Mosley, after his tragic death in 2009. The graves seem to be a magnet for people who have enjoyed Nancy's and Diana's books and every time I go there I find flowers on one or other of them; sometimes a single stalk, sometimes a bunch with a note attached. The other day I saw people gazing at the gravestones and being addressed by a lecturer. I hurried away but could not help wondering what she was saying.

25

THE OLD VICARAGE

Andrew's decline in health was long. For some years he had been nearly blind and was finding getting about increasingly difficult, but I never once heard him complain about his lot. Towards the end he did not want to go out of doors or even leave his room. He stayed in bed, eating nothing, sometimes for days on end. When he did get up to walk to the dining room, and later when he was pushed there in a wheelchair, he sat at the table shaking his head at everything that was offered him. All he wanted was to go back to bed, where he literally turned his face to the wall. No radio, no television – just silence. The only people he wished to see, other than me, were Helen Marchant and Henry Coleman, our butler. Nothing sparked his interest; politics, racing, it was all over. He had lost the will to live.

Seeing him so deeply depressed and unhappy about the various indignities of his physical condition, no one could have wished him to go on living. During the last two days, Henry seldom left him and stood at the end of his bed, watching in case he wanted some little thing. When Andrew slipped into unconsciousness and quietly left this world it was almost a relief. He died late on the evening of 3 May 2004, aged eighty-four. The finality of death hits only long after the event, but everyone at Chatsworth realized immediately that the old order had gone.

Andrew's funeral took place seven days later at St Peter's Church, Edensor. Because there were to be three memorial services I thought that it would be a quiet country funeral attended by the family, a few friends and the people who lived round about. In his wisdom, John Oliver, the comptroller, knew otherwise. Thousands came. It was the first beautiful day of spring and the park was at its best, the pale green of the trees half-transparent against the richer green of the grass. John Oliver led the procession from Chatsworth to the church and walked the whole mile without once raising his head. The route was lined on either side by members of staff, pensioners, friends and strangers, who stood, heads bowed, in silence. The newspaper chose to publish photographs of the waitresses from the Carriage House Restaurant, in their black dresses, white aprons and caps, and described them as our 'parlourmaids' – another reason for not believing everything you read in the papers. Guardsmen from the Coldstream Guards, Andrew's old regiment, soldiers from the Royal British Legion, with which he had had long connections, and Worcestershire and Sherwood Foresters, with their ram mascot, lined the churchyard path.

I went in Andrew's car, driven by his long-time driver Joe Oliver (of that indispensable family), accompanied by my sisters-in-law, Elizabeth and Anne. Stoker and Amanda walked behind the hearse, leading the enormous crowd of mourners. Paddy Leigh Fermor, aged nearly ninety, walked with the family – to which he almost belongs. We were too many to be seated in the church and there were tents for the overflow, but the beauty of the day meant they were not necessary. At the exact moment the coffin was lowered into the grave a group of Derbyshire Microlights, of which Andrew was patron, passed overhead making wispy, whining noises. For me, the whole event was like something being enacted, not real. However much you realize that death is inevitable, when it happens to someone you have known so well for so long, it does not seem possible.

John Oliver and Helen Marchant arranged the wake, which was held in our last big tent to go up on the south lawn. When they saw the procession walking back to the house for tea, the regular Chatsworth visitors, who come to the park in search of freedom and beauty, joined in. Ramblers with backpacks, women with babies, men in shorts and little else mingled with bishops and members of the House of Lords. No one was turned away and it became a party after Andrew's own heart. Again I had a dreamlike sensation as I watched the people arrive, wondering what it was all for, then suddenly remembering.

I was astonished by the number of condolence letters I received – over three thousand. When answering the kind things people said, I learned more of Andrew's many acts of generosity over the years. The three memorial services held later that summer at Bolton Priory in York-shire, the Guards Chapel in London and St Carthage's Cathedral, Lis-more, each reflected different aspects and events in his life and brought back many memories for those of us who were there.

A year after Andrew's death, I went with my daughter Emma to visit friends in the south of England. I probably overdid it and shortly after getting home I suffered a 'transient ischaemic attack', lost conscious-ness and was hurried off to the Hallamshire Hospital in Sheffield in an ambulance with the siren ringing and lights flashing (or so they told me afterwards). I woke up a few hours later to find my bed surrounded by doctors from all corners of the earth and wondered why these busy fel-lows were staring at me as I felt perfectly all right. They ordered a brain scan, then went about their business. The nice black porter who pushed me in a wheelchair along the endless passages called me 'Darling' and that encouraged me. The scanner made a noise like a rattling London tube train, only much louder. I was shown the photos immediately afterwards: one looked like an inaccurate map of Europe, another was an exact replica of a hotel carpet. I would have preferred a landscape by Atkinson Grimshaw but the camera could not lie. The friendly porter wheeled me back to my room with its view of all Sheffield, and I soon went home (fetched by my grandson Eddie Tennant), humbled by the kindness and skill of all concerned at the Hallamshire.

I stayed on at Chatsworth for eighteen months after Andrew died, but the passages began to seem long and the stairs steep. It was time to move, to make way for the next generation. Stoker and Amanda had made their home at Beamsley Hall, near Bolton Abbey, but in the knowl-edge that they would come to Chatsworth in due course. They have settled with enthusiasm into the house – the heart of the Chatsworth 'business', which is what country estates now are.

In December 2005 I moved to the Old Vicarage in Edensor, the village a mile from Chatsworth where Andrew and I had lived sixty years ear-lier. The house, the older parts of which are eighteenth-century, has no architectural merit, but its atmosphere makes it a happy place – the in-fluence, I believe, of the devout men who occupied it for two hundred years. Parts of it had been built on and knocked down in a haphazard sort of manner, and it was in poor condition. After the builders had done their work of rewiring, plumbing and heating, of moving walls, stripping paint and putting in new windows and floors, it was ready for decorating. David Mlinaric, a friend in need if ever there was one, was an indispensable help with the placing of electric points, light switches, baths and so on; these are easy to take for granted but you rue the day if you get them wrong, and he gets them right.

David made another important contribution: I wanted to reinstate the fireplace in my bedroom that had been blocked up in the 1950s on the orders of the Chatsworth land agent, so David went to the building-yard with Malcolm Hulland, the clerk of works, to have a look at the old grates and other bits and pieces stored there. With his infallible eye, he spotted some small white tiles like the ones on my bedroom floor. He brought them back and, to our satisfaction, they were the ones that had been removed fifty years earlier.

I chose the colours and arranged the furniture – as I had done many times before in houses big and small. My essential tools were an Old Vicarage–sized tape measure (rather than the builders' ones I had used and lost by the dozen at Chatsworth) and a picture in my mind's eye of what I wanted. A bonus from my short stay at the Hallamshire was the plastic bracelet they put on every patient's wrist. It was a thrilling cerulean blue and I held on to it for the colour of a guest bathroom at the Old Vic. This bathroom, which is bristling with FACILITIES (including a bed covered in towelling – muddling for guests), seems to be a success, thanks to my unexpected spell of unconsciousness.

Amanda and Stoker were generosity itself and allowed me to take whatever pieces of furniture I liked from Chatsworth. I have never regretted my choice, and being able to bring these old friends with me made the move easier. I am especially happy to have the pair of Wellingtons (not boots) that used to be in my sitting room at Chatsworth. These tall, narrow, red-leather-fronted drawers, replicas of those that the Iron Duke took with him on his campaigns, are a godsend for storing papers and add the necessary *coup de rouge* to my new drawing room. (Paddy Leigh Fermor says this means a glass of red wine, but to me it is the essential bit of colour that gives something extra to a room.)

The house has several guest bedrooms, which seem to be elastic, and it is a joy to be able to have my children, grandchildren and great-grandchildren to stay. From the first night that I slept in my bedroom, where I now write, I felt as if I had been here for years. A new window to the east lets me see the unwilling winter dawn through the trees in my neighbour's garden and it is a daily treat. The other window looks south. Before I moved in, a bank came right up to the front door of the house and, spoilt as I was by the views at Chatsworth, I found it too close for my liking. A bulldozer scooped out a semicircle, giving more light and a feeling of space.

Much of the garden was a building site for the first winter (the ground takes a season to settle) but the flower beds had to be planted with light-ning speed in spring, a method described by Jim Link, the retired head gardener at Chatsworth, as 'cheque-book gardening'. Jim, Alan Shimwell and Ian Webster (the present head gardener) are walking, talking, living garden encyclopaedias. I call these three founts of knowledge 'the appren-tices', to the amusement of Adam Harkness (a generation or two younger), who now looks after the garden at the Old Vic. My favourite part is the kitchen garden. How I wish my sister Pam were here to see my sorrel and herbs. She would be full of criticism, of course: 'Stublow, you're doing that *all wrong*.' Nancy would think my chosen marigolds perfectly fright-ful, adding, perhaps, 'For a nine-year-old the garden looks quite nice.' Decca would not look but would head straight indoors to the fire, clasp-ing her dress – too thin for the Derbyshire summer – tightly around her. As for Diana, if only she were still here to spend weeks with me.

In extreme old age you suddenly find you are unable to run uphill, two buckets full of hen food are heavier than they were and the cheer-ful scream of hearing aids, proving that they are working, is a welcome sound. Other things go wrong. Paddy Leigh Fermor, aged ninety-four, came to stay, got into the bath, looked down at the tap end and to his dismay saw that both feet had turned black. 'Oh God,' he thought, 'teeth, ears and eyes are wonky and now my feet.' He need not have worried. He had got into the bath with his socks on.

Twenty years after the Bible's allotted span of three score years and ten, faces also change and nature warns you that more than a little pow-der is necessary. A photographer was coming to take snaps for publicity for a book. I thought some make-up might mask the stalactites and other horrors that appear from nowhere on old faces, so I called on the ser-vices of Victoria Noakes, a trained beautician and the daughter of my old friend John Webber, hairdresser. John has driven over the moor from Chesterfield every week for forty-five years to do my hair ('Go on, get up and shake,' he says when he has cut it) and has never once cancelled because of bad weather. Helen Marchant telephoned him: 'How much sand and cement does she want?' he asked. I do not know what Helen answered, but Victoria arrived armed with 'Industrial Strength Concealer'. All this was good for the character, and my head, swollen by fan letters about *Home to Roost*, shrank to normal size. Victoria made me look positively decent, the 'Industrial Strength' did a great job – many untoward bits were concealed – and I faced the photographer with confidence.

I love being back in the village of Edensor. 'Sleepy' it is not: it is as animated as the cross-section of people who live in it. Some are very old like me, some are still hard at work, and there is a troop of children who keep it all alive. My sister-in-law Elizabeth lives at the top of the village; we telephone each other daily and, as in *Mapp and Lucia*, often meet for lunch. I open the Old Vic for people to visit on 'Edensor Day', which is held as close as possible to 29 June, St Peter's patronal festival. We hold a village fête in the garden with stalls, teas and races for the children, and the look round my house is popular. Every nook and cranny is on show: the bathrooms, my shoe cupboard, the kitchen with scones fresh from the oven, the downstairs lavatory lined with silver paper and portraits of Elvis, the incubator in the old laundry where chicks are hatched – the lot. One or two customers are disappointed: 'I came to see the chandeliers and all I found was Habitat.' What is wrong with Habitat? Anyway, the disappointing lantern was from Conran and is just what I wanted.

Now that I am ninety, I suppose things ought to slow down but it does not seem to happen. There is life in the Old Vic yet and, far from feeling 'a lilac relic of bygone days' (which is how I was described recently by a journalist I have never met), there is rarely a blessed day with nothing written in the diary. I do not feel cut off from the past, the present or the future, and there are innumerable occasions that take me to London or elsewhere for a night or two. Old friends and their children come to stay, as do all my descendants. On Boxing Day 2009 a photograph was taken of me with my then seventeen great-grandchildren. They lined up beside me like so many carriages attached to an engine, in similar formation to Victor Duke and sixteen of his twenty-one grandchildren in a photograph taken in 1931. The differences are interesting: the straight partings, buttoned gaiters and shine on the shoes of the obedient, pre-war children are in contrast to the stockinged feet and tousled hair of my lot. Both Victor Duke and I are holding a baby, but the Duke has a cigarette in his mouth with the ash about to drop on his youngest grandchild.

Great age is a question of luck not skill and yet you are congratulated or rewarded as if you had done something clever. During the last month of being eighty-nine I had the sort of treats that anyone of any age would dream of. I received a lifetime achievement award from the Derbyshire tourist board, which delighted me. Stoker and Amanda gave a dinner-dance for 910 guests: pensioners and estate employees with their spouses, from Chatsworth, Bolton Abbey and Lismore. This coincided with the Chatsworth long-service awards when my old associates Alan Shimwell and Henry Coleman and I were given enviable presents (our combined years at Chatsworth added up to nearly 170). The stable yard was tented over for the event, and the Carriage House Restaurant, Jean-Pierre's Bar and every table in the old covered ride were full of people enjoying themselves. Andrew would have loved it.

A birthday treat of a different kind was an invitation from the Prince of Wales and the Duchess of Cornwall to see *La Fille Mal Gardée* at Covent Garden. I was allowed to bring four guests and took two grandchildren, a great-nephew and his girlfriend. We sat in the Royal Box with our host and hostess, drinking in the atmosphere of the place that I had first visited with Adrian Stokes, and Nanny Blor as chaperone, in 1936. I hope it was the start of a love of the ballet for my grandchildren. The next day was a book launch at Claridges with the best mix of people I have ever seen at such an event. It was given by *Tatler* and Dior for Penguin's relaunch of Nancy's novel *Wigs on the Green*, first (and last) published in 1935. Such parties did not take place when Nancy was writing and she would have been surprised at the outpouring of admiration for her work. As her literary executor, it gives me pleasure to see how she still makes people laugh in this strange new world we live in.

These galas coincided with the unveiling of the changes, both structural and decorative, made by Stoker and Amanda over the last two or three years to the house and garden at Chatsworth. Although I no longer have a role there, I am still interested in all that happens. The reviews in the press and on television were without a dissenting voice: there was nothing but praise, summed up by the *Sun* as 'See Chatsworth before you die'.

This brought home to me the astonishing change of heart that has taken place over the last sixty years towards places like Chatsworth. The attitude in the old days was: 'Pull it down, it's dirty, damp and of no interest. Tax the owners (19/6 in the pound – 97.5 per cent) till the pips squeak and till neither house nor garden survive.' Neglect and decay of large houses was the order of the day and nature made sure that lack of maintenance resulted in snow and rain finding their way through weak places in roofs and broken windows. Dry rot and deathwatch beetle invaded the interiors, while self-sown sycamores and rampant brambles made sure the garden walls fell to bits. Chatsworth, Hardwick Hall, Compton Place, Bolton Hall and Lismore Castle were what is now described as 'at risk', along with hundreds of other houses, gardens and estate villages all over the country. It was not until 1974 (twenty-four years after Andrew inherited his father's possessions along with the eighty per cent death duties they carried) that an exhibition at the V&A, 'The Destruction of the Country House', drew attention to the numbers of such places that are lost and gone for ever. It may have been the turning point in public opinion.

Slowly, slowly, hostility towards owners who had been struggling to maintain their old homes turned, first to grudging admiration of their efforts and then to adulation if they had managed to keep their roofs on. I have watched with incredulity this turn of events, from the days when coal was dug from opencast mines within a few yards of the front of Wentworth Woodhouse in Yorkshire (the largest private house in England), when no English women would do domestic work at a place like Chatsworth and when it was rumoured that Derbyshire County Council intended to run the A6 road along the river in front of the house, to the present, when pride and delight is taken in what is now called our 'heritage' – the word itself reflecting the sense of proprietorship felt by many people.

These developments are near the heart to me and mean a great deal to the people who live round about. The fact that so much survives at Chatsworth is in large measure due to Andrew, and I believe that his liberal attitude towards our visitors may have played a part in turning the general view upside down. I have also enjoyed watching some of my own ideas come to fruition: the Farm Shop (which opened against all professional advice), the house shops and catering (in 2005, my last year at Chatsworth, the latter had 114 employees, the largest number of people in any one department) and the Farmyard (which plays its part in linking country and town). The reputation of these ventures spread and many owners of other houses open to visitors came to Chatsworth 'to see how to do it', and then went home to put something similar into practice – the highest form of flattery.

In spite of Andrew's assertion that I did not know the difference between turnover and profit, the businesses have prospered in a most satisfactory way, and make a significant contribution to the Chatsworth House Trust and the Chatsworth Settlement Trustees. When I left Chatsworth in 2005 they had a combined turnover of £7.6 million and employed 269 people – 51 per cent of the estate payroll. It goes without saying that without the support of the staff none of this would have been possible.

My new house and garden are a continual delight and I find twenty roses just as interesting as two hundred, and so on down the line. I am sure that, with the affection and encouragement of my children, my grandchildren and my great-grandchildren, together with that of my most valued friends, there is lots more to come.

For now, I look back on a wonderful life watching other people work.

APPENDIX I
President Kennedy's Inauguration, 1961

Appendix I describes a joyous celebration; Appendix II is stark tragedy. After half a century these events are part of history. Andrew and I were lucky to see them close to, in a way that only the Kennedy family did.

The jumble of impressions of the last three days is so thick with oddness and general amazement it's very difficult to put them in any sort of order. The utter sweetness of our Ambassador, Andrew hopping about being humble and saying that his job as parliamentary under-secretary makes him a very junior minister, the deliciousness of the brekker, the warmth of the embassy, the dread coolth of outdoors, the friendliness of the Kennedys and the extraordinary informality of the most solemn moments. My word, it is an odd country.

Thursday 19 January
The first day was mercifully quiet after the journey, which was very long (we came down at Shannon for some strange reason, also the plane from New York was late so we arrived at the embassy at what was 4.30 a.m. for us, having left London at 2 p.m. the day before – fourteen and a half hours).

They raked in some embassy people for lunch, so that was easy. Then it started to snow and it snowed and snowed, and although Snow Plans A, B, C *and* D were put into operation, the capital city of the USA pretty well seized up, as they are not prepared for such an eventuality. Cars were abandoned in the middle of streets; engines chuck it very easily it seems and snow gets packed under the mudguards so that the wheels won't go round.

We were given tickets for the gala performance which was to raise money for the Democrats, who are $4 million in debt after the election (seats $1,000). So we buggered off to the place called the Armory, which is about twice the size of Olympia and the same idea. The embassy gave us a car while we were there, a very old-fashioned English thing called an Austin Princess. It took two and a half hours to get to the blooming Armory. It should have taken twenty minutes but the traffic was solid and so many cars broke down in the queue to get there. Our heater broke and I had only a fur cape, my word it was bitter. Andrew panicked all the way as the tickets said we had to be there at 8.30 and the President Elect was due at 9.00. At about 10.00 he said we'd better give it up and go home but luckily we couldn't as we were hemmed in on all sides by dread cars. The cold was extreme, about twenty degrees of frost, snowing hard and a bitter wind.

We finally loomed and by a miracle arrived at a very good time, viz. about ten minutes before the Kennedys. We needn't have worried as people were coming and going all the time, which we weren't to know. I thought it would be like a royal do in England but it was far from it.

We had marvellous seats, next to the Kennedys' box and between two very grand senators and their wives, who looked slightly down their noses at two complete strangers having such good places, till various Kennedys came and were fearfully nice, especially Bobby (who turns out to be attorney general with a staff of 35,000) who hugged us. Old Joe Kennedy, that well-known hater of England and the English, was very welcoming, and to crown all Jack came and said hello, to the astonishment of our senatorial neighbours.

The performance included all my favourites: Frank Sinatra, Jimmy Durante, Nat King Cole, Ethel Merman, Tony Curtis, Ella Fitzgerald, to mention a few, also Laurence Olivier and the chief American opera singer called Helen Traubel, who sang in a huge voice some ridiculous verses about the Kennedys' baby. It was WONDERFUL, especially at the finale when they had all done their turns and they ended up doing skits on popular songs with topical words. So unrehearsed were they that they had to read their lines and somehow it *was* so funny, just like Women's Institute theatricals at home, but when one looked again, there were all those famous faces. I adored all that.

We got home at 3 a.m. The heat in the house was fantastic. I opened all windows and slept with one blanket but it was still BOILING.

Friday 20 January
Next day was the actual inauguration. Left the embassy about 10 a.m. in order to be in our places at 11. Long queues of cars as we neared the Capitol. Anyone of note – ambassadors, senators, governors of States – had their name or country on the side of the car. We were next to some ratty-looking souls from Bulgaria in one traffic block, it made one think.

Eventually arrived at the Capitol. Horrid getting out as it was so cold with a cruel wind. The ambassadress had given me some long nylon stockings and knickers combined, also some rubber boots to put over my shoes. It was fearfully cold *with* these things – without them, heaven knows, I think I would have frozen to death. They gave Andrew a flask of whiskey but he still shivered throughout and put his scarf round his head (like the Queen). We were told to wear top hats and smart things – both absolutely unnecessary as people were dressed for the Arctic. Some women had come in ridiculous flowered hats, which they soon covered up with scarves, rugs and anything to hand.

It was difficult to find our seats, no one knew where anything was, not even the few policemen who were about. When we eventually found our places they were very good for seeing – we were on street level, immediately in front of the Capitol where the ceremony was to take place, on a large balcony, high up but all plainly visible. Our seats were wooden strips, no backs, no floor and snow everywhere. No numbers or reserved places, one just sat where one liked on forms like at a school treat. Next to us were two Pakistanis with cameras. Just in front of me was old Mrs Roosevelt who had arrived an hour before we did and must have been terribly cold. The organization seemed so vague I was afraid it would all be very late and we would be pillars of ice but in fact it started only a quarter of an hour after the appointed time.

The balcony of the Capitol was full of senators and congressmen sitting either side of the roofed pavilion from where Jack was to speak. The Capitol is faced with gleaming white marble and looked fine against the blue sky and snow, though the dome is painted just off-white, which slightly spoils the brilliant effect. Various members of the Kennedy family arrived. The girls – Eunice, Pat and Jean – were without hats, which seemed surprising for such a formal event. One could pick out the Eisenhowers, Trumans – Margaret and hubby – old Joe and Mrs Kennedy, but they were about the only people I knew by sight. Nixon and Mrs soon joined them.

Tension was mounting for Jack's arrival but it was badly arranged from a dramatic point of view – so different from things in England. No proper path was made for him through the crowd – people started shouting and suddenly there he was. Jackie looked very smart indeed in plain clothes of pale beige; the only woman who looked dressed at all.

There was a long pause after his arrival. People were cold and were stamping their feet. The star was there but nothing was happening. Eventually, the master of ceremonies announced some tune by the band and a famous gospel singer, Mahalia Jackson, whom I'd never heard of, sang 'The Star-Spangled Banner'. Then the swearing-in and four prayers – Roman Catholic cardinal, Jewish rabbi, Greek Orthodox priest and a Protestant – all much too long and not at all moving or impressive. Nobody paid the slightest attention and even the senators took photographs throughout, moving about to get in better positions. Some people in our row didn't stand up for the prayers. My Pakistani neighbour, at the third one, gave me a wink and said, 'Let's sit this one out', which I was going to do anyway as the rug fell in the snow every time we stood up.

Jack's speech was wonderful, the *words* were so good, almost biblical. Everyone was thankful to get up and move when it was over as we could only think of getting out of the cold and wind. We were told there was a bus reserved for the Kennedy family which we were to get on, but it seemed impossible to find. No one knew anything and there was no official-looking person to ask. After pushing and shoving and, in desperation, even stopping to ask a police car, we found it at last and the relief of getting into an overheated bus was wonderful.

In the bus we found Eunice and her husband (whose Christian name is Sargent, if you please, *fearfully* nice though). We were driven to a hotel for lunch with the family and close friends. Lots of grandchildren milling about, lots of delicious buffet food. Jack and Jackie, and Bobby and Ethel had lunch in the Capitol with the Cabinet, so weren't there. Back into the bus (which had a label on it 'Kennedy Family' like 'Chatsworth Tours') and through the guarded gates into the garden of the White House, whereupon all the people in the bus gave a loud cheer, led by Eunice, and shouted 'Here we are'.

As I got into the hall of the White House, a Marine stepped forward, gave me his arm and armed me all the way through the house to the President's stand, from where we watched the parade. Andrew and I had seats several rows back. (All the seats were marked with people's names. The Marine asked me mine, I said, 'Devonshire', so he said, 'Mrs Devon*shyer*, you are heeere.') Next to us were Mr and Mrs Charles Wrightsman, who never turned up because they thought it too cold. The box had a roof and was enclosed at the sides with perspex but it was still extremely draughty and bitterly cold, even though there were army rugs on each seat.

The stands were gimcrack and the decorations practically nil, just a few small flags. Queer for such a rich country. The diplomats were next to us, sitting on raised forms, completely in the open. The Eastern ones looked so cold I felt terribly sorry for them as there was no escape and they couldn't leave till the parade was over.

The parade itself was an extraordinary mixture of Army, Navy and Air Force with girls' bands, majorettes in fantastic uniforms with long legs in pink tights, crinolined ladies on silver-paper floats, horses from the horsy states all looking a bit moth-eaten, army tanks, dread missiles (rhymes with 'epistles') on carriers, bands everywhere. One man marching by in an air-force contingent broke ranks, whipped out a camera, took a photograph of the President and joined in again. Imagine a Coldstream guardsman doing the same at the Trooping of the Colour.

The television cameras and a host of other photographers were immediately opposite the President's stand. The cameras were on him the whole afternoon. The informality was so queer – the President drinking coffee and eating a biscuit as the parade marched by. But he stood there for over three hours.

After about an hour and a half a message came, Would I go and sit beside him. It was the oddest feeling I've ever had, finding myself a sort of consort, standing by this man, talking to him during lapses in the parade. The telly people were stumped by the advent of a strange English lady; they knew the politicians and the film stars but not ordinary foreigners. We told Sir Harold Caccia when we got back and he said no English woman had ever done that before, so I *did* feel pleased.

Jack Kennedy has got an aura all right and he was obviously enjoying it all so much. After about three-quarters of an hour he said would we like to go with his father to the White House for tea, which I took to mean I'd been there long enough. The White House is very good inside, big rooms covered in silk, one dark red, one dark green, a huge creamish-coloured ballroom and a rather awful round room covered in a horrid blue Adam-design silk, which everyone seemed to like best. The diner is green, I'm sorry to say, painted solid gloomy green, pillars and all. Pictures of presidents all over the shop, all ghoulish.

We didn't see the President again as he was still at the parade when we left after tea. Got back to the embassy about 6.15 to be told dinner at 7.15, so I rushed to dress for the ball. Luckily I didn't take a tiara, which various people said I ought to have done, as no one wore one and I would have looked like a daft opera singer dressed up for Wagner. Mercifully only the Caccias for dinner. Afterwards we were taken by them to a party given by some cinema people. Lots of ambassadors and grandees there, a sort of after-dinner cocktail party. They don't mind the press like we do, and no wonder as they write in a very different way from ours, perfectly friendly and no sting in it.

Then back to the Armory for the Inaugural Ball. This time no traffic jam and we arrived without difficulty. All the seating at floor level had been removed and a vast dancing floor put in its place. Shown to the President's box again, where we sat until someone said there was drink and a telly in a room at the back. So we made off there and saw Mrs David Bruce, a friend of Nancy [Mitford]'s, rather beautiful and probably coming to London with her husband as ambassador. Without any warning, the President suddenly walked into the room and was taken off to a television interview next door. Meanwhile we watched his inaugural speech again on the telly.

Back to the Presidential box to watch the dancing, which didn't happen because everyone stood looking up at the box, waiting for Jack to appear. When he did he got terrific applause. He didn't go down to the dance floor but talked to various people along his row. Wherever he goes he is like a queen bee, surrounded by photographers, detectives, nexts of kin and worshippers. By this time, we were sitting in the topmost tier just below the roof. As Jack came back along the first row, fenced in as usual by humans, he saw us, broke away and climbed over seven rows of seats to say goodbye, to the utter astonishment of the people sitting either side of us. A photographer who had got, as he thought, a very bad place and who had been grumbling, was now able to take the closest close-up of all.

I told Jack about Unity [Mitford]'s letter of twenty-one years ago saying how he was going to have a terrific future. I also asked him if he knew Harold Macmillan and he said he was going to see him soon. We said how we were loving everything that had been arranged for us, to which he replied that we'd stuck it well. He and Jackie then left. We waited till some of the crush had dispersed and thought we'd leave too. Andrew went out into the bitter night to look for the chauffeur – no sign of him. Eventually he was found, the car had broken and there we were with no hope of getting home. After an hour and a half the chauffeur suggested we take Labour leader Mr Gaitskell's car and send it back for him. By a miracle we saw Gaitskell among the 10,000 people there and thankfully squashed into his car, me sitting on a drunken lady who answered 'balls' to everything I said.

Saturday 21 January
We went to the Senate the next day, taken by a new senator's wife who had lunched at the embassy. Hideous place; they each have a desk and chair, like in school. Andrew went into the Chamber (they have a reciprocal agreement with members of certain foreign governments) and two senators immediately launched into speeches of welcome. I was sweating in case he would make one back but he only bowed. Good old Andrew.

The upshot of the whole outing is two new bodies to worship – Sir Harold Caccia and Jack Kennedy. I've written him a letter beginning 'My dear Jack'. I do hope I won't have my head cut off for impertinence. One of the comical things was that Andrew had some secrets from Harold Macmillan to tell the ambassador and nothing was said until we all went to bed on the last night, when I heard them talking in the passage outside my room for hours. I can see that's the way things are done in high life, very odd.

APPENDIX II
President Kennedy's Funeral, 1963

Sunday 24 November
Left Chatsworth with Andrew at 12.40 to drive to London airport. Found Mr Wilson in the VIP lounge. Talked to Marie-Louise de Zulueta, who had come to see her husband off. The PM and his wife arrived soon afterwards. Prince Philip arrived exactly on time. We got into the plane at 4.50 and took off at 5.10. There were headwinds of 140 mph that slowed us up and the flight took nine hours.

It was a huge Boeing 707. There were 150 empty seats behind us – something I have never seen before. Prince Philip called us up to his seats in front and asked Mr Wilson to join him for dinner. I sat next to Wilson with the Prince opposite, and Andrew sat with the Douglas-Homes on the other side of the aisle.

My lot started talking about aeroplanes (a safe subject, I suppose) in such an incredible, almost technical, way that it was quite impossible to listen to them and I found my mind wandering. Wilson had such dirty fingernails it put me off dinner. I wished I was with Andrew and the Homes but kept thinking how extremely odd the company and that I ought to be interested, but it was impossible to be so. Wilson has a level, grating voice and podgy face with a too small nose. After dinner tried to sleep a bit.

When below was all lights on the east coast of America, the sad reason for the journey hit me again and I dreaded arriving. We were met by a 'mobile lounge', a vast bus-like thing with room for many more people than we were. Our Ambassador, David Ormsby Gore, and his wife, Sissie, looking red-eyed and worn out, the Secretary of State, Dean Rusk, whose face was puffed up, and some others welcomed us on the tarmac and joined us on the bus.

At the terminal were the Commonwealth ambassadors, including nice George Laking from New Zealand with whom I'd had tea on my last visit. Television cameras and lights, then a procession of about six cars with police sirens at front and rear. Twenty-two miles into Washington and no stopping at red lights. It was a strange feeling arriving at the embassy. We had a drink and short talk in the drawing room before, thankfully, going to bed.

David said that Bobby Kennedy was taking the brunt; not only was he bitterly sad himself and having to deal with arrangements that were chaotic because of everything being at such short notice, but also he was the one person who could comfort Jackie. He said that General de Gaulle was the only Head of State who had demanded to see

Jackie, so she said she would see them all. Jack's belongings have already been removed from his office and bedroom and the White House has taken on a deserted look.

Sissie said that Mass at the White House for friends and the Catholics who worked there was the most tragic thing she ever saw – everyone crumpled with grief.

Monday 25 November
Prince Philip, the Prime Minister and David left for St Matthew's Cathedral before we did, as they were to walk in the procession from the White House. Andrew and I, Sissie, and Prince Philip's ADC left at about 11 a.m. Brilliant sunshine, frosty day with bright blue sky. We arrived at the Cathedral without a hitch. It is not very big and has only about 2,000 seats. We were all seated separately as the pews reserved for friends were already full. I was on an aisle, having arrived late, and the people already in the pew moved up for me. Prince Philip seemed very far towards the back of the church. Apparently he had no seat and the Douglas-Homes had moved to make room for him.

When I could bring myself to look round, I saw Jayne Wrightsman and behind her Fifi Fell, as beautiful as ever. There was no music for a long time. I never saw so many sad faces and when Jack's great friends came in – Bill Walton, Chuck Spalding, Evelyn Lincoln, Charles Bartlett, Arthur Schlesinger, MacGeorge Bundy – it was too much. Then the family arrived with Jack's two little children. Rose Kennedy looking small and hunched and Bobby too. Eunice, Jean and Pat with no veils but wearing black-lace mantillas, their faces set and staring and so so sad.

The coffin was carried by eight soldiers. It was impossible to believe that the vital, fascinating and clever person was shut up in that box. Quite impossible.

The service, luckily, was incomprehensible and the cardinal faced the altar most of the time. No agonizing hymns, so it seemed far away and impersonal. There was Communion in the middle and quite a lot of people besides the family went up to the altar. On our way into the church, the Scotch pipers had played very fidgety music, as had the military band. We heard afterwards that it was because they do not do a slow march here, so it does not sound nearly as solemn as in England.

On the way out of the church, the overseas visitors stopped several times and for a full minute General de Gaulle stood next to me. He has the strangest appearance I ever saw – very tall, yet collapsed somehow and a long ugly nose. Haile Selassie looked fine – small and beautiful. The rest looked as they do in their photographs.

Our car arrived wonderfully quickly and we followed the procession to the cemetery. When it began to go at a slow pace, the secret service men – who were guarding Prince Philip, Alec Douglas-Home, De Gaulle and the Canadian Prime Minister, Lester Pearson – all got out and walked three-a-side of each car. There were crowds all the way for the three miles to the cemetery, which is on the side of a hill and beautiful. We arrived just as the last part of the service had begun. Aeroplanes flew overhead, including the President's plane that we'd seen at Lincolnshire airport in June when Jack came to Chatsworth. Prince Philip was jostled to the back again, behind a lot of soldiers, so he was not among the foreign visitors when they came away from the grave. The Russians were completely enclosed by secret service people. I saw Colonel Glenn and that ghastly Queen of Greece with her dangling earrings, and many famous faces mixed up with police and hangers-on, who were all ambling about in the bright sun waiting for cars. Jackie looked tragic, with tears glistening on her veil, and Rose so very pathetic. The Kennedys are so good when things are going well but they are not equipped for tragedy.

We drove back to the embassy through thinning crowds. There was a great sense of sorrow and emptiness everywhere. We drank a lot of tea. I was very tired, as were all – we had left at 11.00 and got back about 4.00. Andrew went up to change and pack. Prince Philip went to Lyndon Johnson's reception at the White House. We watched it on television and, as usual, De Gaulle hogged the limelight. He arrived late so there was much speculation as to where he was and, when he did arrive, all was focused on him. The TV commentator was not too nice about Prince Philip or Sir Alec. Andrew and the Prince left for New York in an air-force jet and then on to London on a scheduled flight, Mr Wilson in tow.

The Canadians came for dinner – Ambassador Charles Ritchie with his talkative wife, Lester Pearson and his wife and their foreign secretary, Paul Martin, who had to go to the lav in the middle of dinner. David and Sissie looked slightly better, I thought. The very fact of having to have people in the house is probably a good thing; having to go on with ordinary life, though the outlook here is very bleak for them. They came and talked for ages in my room. Very, very sad, but we talked about other things. I wonder so much what David will do. No doubt he will have to stick out another year as ambassador here, which must be an awful prospect. It will be very difficult working with the new administration – no intimacy, no shared memories and no jokes.

Tuesday 26 November
The Prime Minister went to see Lyndon Johnson and came back saying he was friendly, tried to make a good impression and said that he would carry out Jack's foreign policy, etc. David said the White House was completely changed. Jackie had wanted to move by today but has put it off till Friday.

I went over to Eunice and found her perfectly extraordinary, laughing almost as if the thing had never happened, yet talking about everything in the past tense. We walked round her house about twelve times. How awful to live in a place where you can't go for a proper walk. Horses and dogs everywhere and one little boy aged about three. Bill Walton came for lunch, so nice, and both were wonderfully cheerful and talking about a memorial for Jack and what it should be. They suggested a long street from the White House to the Capitol, paved in different colours and with graded heights so people could see processions etc.

It seems Jackie has been extraordinary, planning everything with Bobby to do with the funeral. She was even laughing about going to see Johnson as the widder woman with lowered eyes and asking him to carry on various things Jack had been interested in. She is going to live in Georgetown it seems.

I left with Bill, having telephoned Bobby who said I could go and see him. His house is near the road and had a few sloppy policemen outside it. A man opened the door in his shirtsleeves. Jack's special assistant, Kenny O'Donnell, was there. Bobby and Ethel have built on a big drawing room, a lovely room, where there was a cot for the new baby. Ethel came in looking about seventeen – it's impossible to believe she has eight children. She's so terribly nice and good. I love her. Then Bobby arrived in a dressing gown which did not reach his knees and all hairy like an animal from top to bottom, but a v. lovable face and stout legs. I did not stay long. The house was in turmoil, telephones going everywhere.

Back to the embassy. Much chatting with Elizabeth Home, who is cast in the same mould as Dorothy Macmillan – a large reassuring body and great niceness pervading all. Johnny Walker, director of the Washington National Gallery, and his Scottish wife came for drinks. Then the Russian Ambassador, Anastas Mikoyan, suddenly turned up with interpreters. An odd roomful.

For dinner came Joe and Susan Mary Alsop, Ted Sorensen – Jack's special counsellor – and his girlfriend and Bill Walton. Sorensen scarcely spoke all evening. Sissie says he is one of the worst affected of all. I sat next to the Prime Minister. He says his brother, William Douglas-Home, has written a play about a peer who gives up his title to become PM. What a surprise. Had a talk with Joe Alsop after dinner about Mollie Salisbury and Pamela Egremont and their different roles in life. Everyone left quite early and we went to bed because of the early start. Somehow the atmosphere has lifted a bit but I would not stay here for *anything* and long to get out of it.

Wednesday 27 November
Called at 6.45. Quick breakfast downstairs with everyone. Sissie and David came to the airport in an overheated mobile lounge and suddenly the atmosphere was like that at our arrival. Did not say much. Felt David so overwhelmed again with pent-up emotion. He kissed me goodbye – something he has never done before. I feel a strong bond with him. He loved Jack so much and saw the funniness better than anyone.

I do not know what I remember most about these strange two days, which is all it was though it seemed like three months. Perhaps it was three-year-old John Kennedy leaving the church, touching the flag on the coffin and being led away by some huge man, followed by a sobbing nanny; or General de Gaulle standing just by me as he waited for the heads of state to leave the church; or Prince Philip's stern blue look as he stood in the same place while tears poured down my face; or Dean Rusk all crumpled when he came to meet our PM; or Chuck Spalding and Bill Walton as they arrived at church; or Fifi Fell's beautiful face in a trance at the end; or David and Sissie, blotchy and thin – I came away feeling so terribly sorry for them that words were impossible. The light has gone out for so many people and for David and Sissie it has been a hammer blow.

Besides the secretaries, there were only the Douglas-Homes, Liberal leader Jo Grimond and me in the PM's vast chartered plane on the way home. Went across the aisle to talk to Mr Grimond, who is charming and woolly and hopeless but sees the point, very quick. The four of us had lunch together. It was dark outside because of the time change. Any strain there may have been soon wore off. We had a friendly talk as politicians do with people of opposing convictions, yet there sat the man, Grimond, who is probably going to do-in any chance Home has of getting back at the next election. Sir Alec's sweet string vest showed through his shirt. He has a strange, saintly streak, so quiet and calm and good. When Elizabeth Home and Jo Grimond were talking, the PM said he had wanted to make David OG foreign secretary but Rab Butler had said he wouldn't serve unless he was given the job. Home evidently has a tremendous regard for David. His patience is extraordinary.

About half an hour before we were due into London, a message came to say there was fog and that we would have to land at Prestwick or Manchester. I said do let's go to Manchester and all come to Chatsworth for the night. They politely said they must get back to London whatever happened. In the end we made for Manchester. I repeated my invitation and sent messages for cars to meet us.

We arrived at Chatsworth at about 11 p.m., after what seemed an endless journey. House floodlit. Dennis, Bryson and Henry standing at the door. It all looked warm and welcoming. The only sad thing was no flowers in the rooms. Jo Grimond, Harold Evans – the PM's public relations adviser – Timothy Bligh and Philip de Zulueta all turned up. Sir Alec said if he crept into bed and lay very still we would not have to change the sheets for Princess Margaret who was coming the next day.

I so wished they could have stayed the weekend but they were called at 6.30 and to catch the 7.24 train. They arrived and left in the dark.

ACKNOWLEDGEMENTS

My grateful thanks are due to my children Sto, Emma and Sophy; and to Mark Amory, Sally Ball, Stuart Band, Claire Barlow, Patrick Beresford, Mrs P. Blackett, Henry Coleman Sr, William Cumber, Julie Davison, Peter Day, Gerard Dempsey, Caroline Dick, Ian Else, Richard Evans, Bridget Flemming, the Venerable David Garnett, Breda Geoghegan, Fortune Grafton, Linda Gustard, Ben Heyes, Tristram Holland, Derek Latham, the late Peter Maitland, Mary Marsden, Edward Marshall, Patricia E. Martin, Denis Nevin, Phonsie O'Brien, Dr Margaret O'Sullivan, Jane Ormsby Gore, Jaime Parladé, Andrew Peppitt, the Reverend Richard Pyke, Hugh and Janie Roberts, Christine Robinson, Douglas and Sue Seel, Claudia Severn, Iola Symonds, Mark Terry, Roger Wardle and Marie-Lou de Zulueta.

As for Charlotte Mosley and Helen Marchant, I am not sure if they are aware that without them there would be no book. Thank you to both.

Unless otherwise credited, the illustrations are privately owned. Most are securely fixed into family albums and are the property of the Mitford Archive. I am extremely grateful to the following for giving permission to use their work: Charlotte Bromley-Davenport, the Cecil Beaton Studio Archive at Sotheby's, Marina Cicogna, Ron Duggins, Bridget Flemming, Tony Snowdon and Simon Upton.

INDEX

A NOTE ABOUT THE AUTHOR

Deborah Mitford, Duchess of Devonshire, is the sister of Nancy, Pamela, Tom, Diana, Unity, and Jessica Mitford. She is past president of the Royal Agricultural Society of England and of The Royal Smithfield Club. She is the author of several books, including *Counting My Chickens . . . and Other Home Thoughts* (FSG, 2002).